The Union

*England, Scotland and the
Treaty of 1707*

Michael Fry

BIRLINN

First published in 2006 by
Birlinn Limited
West Newington House
10 Newington Road
Edinburgh
EH9 1QS

www.birlinn.co.uk

ISBN 10: 1 84158 516 5
ISBN 13: 978 1 84158 516 1

British Library Cataloguing-in-Publication Data
A catalogue record for this book is available from the British Library

Typeset by Iolaire Typesetting, Newtonmore
Printed and bound by Creative Print and Design, Wales

The Union

Contents

 ℮

List of Illustrations

❧

Illustrations on chapter opening pages are from John Slezer's *Theatrum Scotiae* (1693)

Introduction

❦

I should first record with deep gratitude my debt to the libraries where I have worked on this book: especially, and as ever, the National Library of Scotland, always so welcoming; then others I was new to, or almost, the special collections of Glasgow University Library, housing the papers of Principal John Stirling; the Huntington Library at San Marino, California, final destination of papers of the Earls of Loudoun; and the William A. Clark Memorial Library of the University of California at Los Angeles, where the cross-referencing of a huge collection of print from the eighteenth century, a good deal of it not available in Scotland, is a wonder to behold – and where the technophobia of the scholar will be instantly dispelled by the courteous care of the staff. During the months of research and writing I have discussed problems and ideas with many colleagues, but faults and errors in the final text are my own.

The book is written to mark the 300th anniversary of the Union between Scotland and England which falls on May 1, 2007. In England it is not a date likely to loom large even in the minds of most people interested in history; in standard works on the period, it generally takes up no more space than other domestic developments in Britain, the Act of Settlement, for example, and less space than the War of the Spanish Succession, one of the great stepping stones to global power for the United Kingdom about to be born.

A historian may despair of bringing the English to any deeper appreciation of the Union's importance, as one of the acts of foundation of the state we all live in. Among Scots there is no such problem, since the Union stands as a central event, perhaps the central event for good or ill, in the two millennia of their recorded history. At any rate it must rank along with Wars of Independence, Reformation, Enlightenment and Empire as one of the keys to understanding what Scotland is

I

and what Scotland means, or how her always uncertain history may yet run.

Yet the historiography of the Union is by no means in a settled or even a satisfactory condition. Till the mid-twentieth century, at least, it was marked by the same complacent unionism as pervaded many other spheres of Scottish discourse, scarcely questioning that the nation had for 250 years lived on in the best of all possible worlds, otherwise known as the United Kingdom. While some of the transactions in 1707 did look a bit murky, we could be confident they had been inspired at heart by far-sighted statesmanship which, if never expressed in anyone's actual words at the time, could still be inferred from its beneficent results.

But in the late twentieth century, and for a range of reasons needing no rehearsal here, the United Kingdom slid into crisis, external and internal, in its relations to the outside world and in the relations of its component parts. One result came in the emergence or re-emergence of Scottish nationalism, which among scholars sympathetic to it demanded a rewriting of history so as to point towards a conclusion hardly even dreamed of before, the restoration of national independence. Oddly, the most striking reflection of this in the historiography of the Union came not in Scotland at all but in the work of the late Dr P.W.J. Riley at the University of Manchester, who for all I know had no personal opinion whether the United Kingdom should endure or not. In a fecund series of books and articles he set out an unsparing interpretation of the Union as a gross political job, typical of its time yet egregious in the way it betrayed the independence of a nation so long vindicated by a proud people against the odds. Riley struck the tone which colours one side of the ensuing debate down to the present, amid which his own views have been amplified in various aspects by the work of William Ferguson and Paul Scott, among others.

Yet it was not as if the Union would die quietly, either in real life or within the covers of books. Just as the United Kingdom was able to reassert its claims on the loyalties of Scots, and not without success after suitable political accommodation, so unionist historians have refused to swallow the claims of nationalist scholarship and have answered back. In books by Christopher Smout, Thomas Devine and Christopher Whatley, the smugness of earlier unionism vanished and some tougher thinking went into the task of parrying the undoubtedly cogent contentions of nationalism. It yet seems to me a shame that this revived unionist school has been unable to find a more robust base for its counterattack than a sort of Marxist determinism without the Marxism, in other words, a reiteration of the idea that Scotland's economic woes made Union inevitable.

That is to say, we still have a problem with this central enterprise of Scottish historiography. Detachment is hard to attain. Had I not read a word of what all the scholars mentioned above found to write, I still think I could have made a good guess at which views they would espouse. There remains a tendency, if not here then elsewhere, for people to start off from their own attitude towards the Union and then seek justification for it in whatever historical evidence comes to hand. I would, however, certainly exempt Riley from my stricture. It seems to me that his fault, if any, was the more innocent one of excessive academic shock at the seamy side of politics, in particular of Scottish politics. Having myself dabbled in both the political and the academic life of Scotland, I hope I am free of illusions on either score.

Readers acquainted with my previous works may be surprised by the conclusion I reach at the end of this one (look now). I decided the way to approach the Union was to take nothing for granted but give a close reading to the evidence, as free of prejudice as I could render myself, and let it lead me where it might: hence the conclusion. I am especially pleased at one product of my labours, the at least partial reconstruction of certain crucial debates in the last Scots Parliament. Its sessions between 1702 and 1707 were often dramatic, as worthy of attention as any other parliamentary occasions in British history. But their flavour has been lost in the existing literature. Records of proceedings are infuriating in that they quote the speeches, often at length, yet omit, except in a few instances, to say who the speaker was; some convention of propriety appears to have dictated this bizarre reticence. Words disembodied from their speakers lose interest, but there are enough private memoirs of proceedings to have allowed me, by diligent attention to and collation of sources, to name the sequence of speakers in some debates with reasonable certainty, though the word 'probably' will be found hovering nearby if I am much less than certain.

My conclusion does not wholly concur with either side in the debate on the Union as described above. In particular, for example, I am unable to accept that the struggle over the terms of the treaty in the final session of the Scots Parliament was nothing more than a thin disguise for the brutal process of ramming a done deal through – the view put forward by Paul Scott or if anything yet more strongly by the late David Daiches.

3

And persuasive as Riley's particular arguments often are, still I find it hard to agree with his general view that contemporary politicians were never moved by anything higher than the basest personal motives; politicians in all times and places have been moved by the basest personal motives, yet may manage to find at least a little room in their hearts and minds for a few higher considerations. If I would force myself to concede that even in the Scotland of 2006, I cannot in reason be harsher on the Scotland of 1707.

Edinburgh,
January 2006.

CHAPTER I

❧

1702

*Edinburgh from the north-west, the Scottish capital with its
new industrial suburb in the Dean Village*

'Strange people'

ひ

During the morning of February 21, 1702, William of Orange, King of England, Scotland and Ireland, Stadholder of the Dutch Republic, felt like a little relaxation from the cares without number which weighed on him.[1] He had a new horse, Sorrel, and he wanted to try her out in the park of Hampton Court. This was his favourite English residence, up the River Thames about 15 miles from London. He had found it a crumbling old Tudor pile and remodelled it in the magnificent style of his own age to resemble nothing so much as the Versailles of his arch-enemy, King Louis XIV of France. Round it stretched formal gardens, water-meadows and tree-lined avenues. Into these, on a chilly morning, William rode his untried steed at a walk, then a canter. Next he wanted to gallop, so he spurred Sorrel on. She had scarcely started forward when she fell to her knees and pitched the king off, hard on to his right shoulder. She had stumbled on a molehill. For years afterwards William's enemies would toast the 'little gentleman in black velvet' who laid him low as his human adversaries, in the mêlée of battle or in the broils of politics, had never been able to do.

Though this proved at length to be a fatal fall, William had only broken his collar-bone. His frame was just too frail to stand the shock. His life had been one of ceaseless struggle, first to reassert the influence of his princely house in the Dutch Republic, next to vindicate its independence against the French, then to do as much for the three kingdoms of his uncle and father-in-law, King James VII and II, whom William had to depose and exile. Nor did he merely direct policy from his cabinet. In his native country's struggle for survival he took the field in person, displaying reckless courage. It was by force, if without an actual clash of arms, that he won control of England in 1688 and seized the British Crowns for himself and his wife, Mary II. To defend them he then had to go to Ireland in 1690 where, once again, he fought at the Battle of the Boyne, leading a

7

victorious charge across the river at a decisive moment. All this exacted a cost even while it ended in triumph for him. By the winter of his death he was sick and tired, his heart failing and making his limbs swell. It would take no more than a fall from Sorrel to finish him off.

Yet at first, and as ever, this austere, untiring man took a setback in his stride. He got the fracture set at Hampton Court, then insisted on returning by coach to Kensington Palace over roads so bumpy that the bone had to be set again after he arrived. Though he could not write and was obliged to spend all day in a dressing-gown rather than in any close-fitting coat, he worked on as usual at affairs of state, rising every morning at eight o'clock and going to bed every night at eleven, regular as clockwork. At the end of a week he was again wearing normal clothes and appearing in public. But when his doctors had taken the bandages off they found the fracture unknit and his shoulder still somewhat swollen, along with his right arm and hand. In fact inflammation was about to spread to the lining of his lungs and give him pleurisy, then to the lungs themselves and bring on the pneumonia which would kill him.

Doctors of the time could never have diagnosed this, but William took no notice of them or his condition anyway. He did not for a moment cease from his labours. He now prepared to go and give in person, as was then the practice, royal assent to measures just passed by Parliament. They included the Abjuration Act excluding by name from the throne his cousin James, the thirteen-year-old son and heir of James VII and II, who had died in exile at St Germain near Paris not long before, in September 1701. William also wanted to commend to the House of Commons a project of Union between England and Scotland. He sent members a message ahead of his intended visitation: 'His Majesty would esteem it a peculiar felicity if during his reign some happy expedient for making both kingdoms one might take place, and is therefore extremely desirous that a treaty for that purpose might be set on foot, and does in the most earnest manner recommend this to the consideration of the House.'

Then on March 4, while William was walking up and down the corridors at Kensington Palace for some gentle exercise, soothing his eyes on his Dutch paintings, weariness overcame him. He flopped down in a chair and fell asleep. When he awoke he was cold, feverish and coughing. From that point on he grew weaker. His pulse was feeble. He could not eat. His doctors took alarm. On March 7 he developed a high fever and they gave him quinine, which did not work. He was in great pain, worse because his senses remained clear. All at once he stood at death's door.

In those times kings died, as they did most things, in public. When William took to his bed, courtiers constantly pressed round it. From The Hague arrived his closest confidant, Arnout van Keppel, a handsome young Dutchman whom he had made Earl of Albemarle in the English peerage. Albemarle, though distressed, tried to cheer the king up. He returned the bleak reply: 'Je tire vers ma fin.' He hardly slept that night. The Archbishop of Canterbury, Thomas Tenison, came at dawn with the Bishop of Salisbury, Gilbert Burnet, a fat and garrulous Scotsman. They gave the king communion and waited. His agony grew so acute that he asked his physician, Prof. Gorvaert Bidloo, how long it would last. The answer was 'not long'.

Without fear William composed himself to die. His final visitor turned up, Hans Willem Bentinck, Earl of Portland, the friend of his youth who had once nursed him through a near fatal bout of smallpox, fought by his side at the Boyne and been the faithful, indefatigable servant whose diplomacy secured his new Crowns against foreign machination. But the English hated Portland for the Dutch avarice he displayed, and he flounced off once William took a fancy to Albemarle. Now, after two years' absence from court, Portland reappeared. The king, by this time no longer able to speak, grasped his old comrade's hand and laid it on his heart. Burnet recorded: 'Between seven and eight o'clock the rattle began, the commendatory prayer was said for him, and as it ended he died, on Sunday, the 8th of March 1702, in the fifty-second year of his life.'[2] He would be buried privately in Westminster Abbey four nights later.

William's sister-in-law, Anne, younger daughter of James VII and II, was proclaimed. As Queen of Scots she summoned those of her northern kingdom's noblemen who happened to be in London and took the coronation oath before them. A military officer had already set off to bring first word of her accession to Edinburgh. It was received there with little emotion.[3] Orders went out to delay transport of a Lowland regiment to the Netherlands and raise the level of vigilance round the main Highland garrison at Fort William. When the official notice of the king's death reached Edinburgh on the night he was interred, the royal councillors decided it had got too late to do anything: they could wait till morning to proclaim Anne from the Cross and make sure of some sleep before all the fuss that would follow.

William of Orange had been loved by the Scots even less than by the other nations of the British Isles; only Protestant Ulstermen cherish his memory. As for the English, recent historians have written that he

9

deserved better of them than they were ready to concede, though they could never display much affection for such a cold, hard, humourless man.[4] They showed no relish for rule by a foreigner in any case. It did not even help that he quelled France, their arch-enemy, and set the Britain of the future on the road to becoming a great power. At home he saved England's parliamentary constitution, indeed accorded the legislature a stronger position than it had ever enjoyed before. With that he brought a return to political stability at the end of a century of revolutions. Yet all this counted for little in making the English like him, then or now.

In Scotland no such paradox appears. William of Orange was the worst of all Kings of Scots. Since the nation had been in chaos through much of the seventeenth century, his Revolution of 1688 made little difference. And to call it in English fashion the Glorious, let alone Bloodless, Revolution is risible.

&

William left his indelible mark on the history of Scotland by bringing down the legitimate line of the House of Stewart. Of course, he counted through his mother as a member of that house himself, and a fuller member of it, Anne, would reign on after him till her death in 1714; the Hanoverians who followed her descended through another female from Scotland's native dynasty. Yet these were all monarchs *de facto*, not *de jure*. The royal succession – which, according to Scots, had followed without a break from Fergus mac Erc in 330 BC to their own day – sundered in 1688. And the royal succession was their proudest boast, not least because it put them one up over the English. A lawyer of high culture, Sir George Mackenzie of Rosehaugh, Lord Advocate under James VII, looked back to Scottish antiquity and found that 'we are still the same people and nation, but the English are not the old Britons, but are a mixture descending from Danes, Saxons and French'. This was the root and stock of the Scots' independence: 'No historian can pretend that we obeyed any race, save that which now reigns: whereas we can condescend, where the English and French were conquered by strangers, and had their royal line dethroned and inverted.'[5]

All nations cherish their myths but without that one the Scottish nation might have been unable to preserve itself. For such a small country it had always shown an extraordinary, though perilous, diversity. It still bore marks of its origins at the turn of the millennium as a union of Gaels in the west, Picts in the north, Britons in the south-west and Angles in the south-east, to which in course of time Vikings of the Northern and Western Isles were superadded. Names of petty kingdoms where these different peoples had dwelt – Moray, Fife, Lothian, Galloway and more – survived up to and beyond the seventeenth century; another, Strathclyde, was to be resurrected in the late twentieth century as a monstrous local authority. The patchwork could have dissolved and almost did about 1300. It was then that the heroism of King Robert Bruce refounded nation and monarchy which, burgeoning by triumph over English aggression, became entwined round the sprig, a rather distant one, of the ancient royal stem he represented. Scotland maintained herself as an independent nation into the dawn of the modern era, though always more untidy, precarious and provisional than other nations, than its southern neighbour especially, and never able to efface its variegations through any durable centralising force: all the better for that, Scots would say.

Like other nations of Europe, Scotland meanwhile saw struggles between king and nobility, if here somewhat less severe because the king was often a child, his father having usually suffered a gruesome and premature death. Constant external threats to national existence made for greater internal stability than England or France enjoyed till their kings could impose royal absolutism on aristocratic aggrandisement. At any rate the unique result in Scotland was to place king and people on an easier footing than could ever be possible in England or France, where the monarch had to overawe his subjects.

For example, during James VI's journey south in 1603 to claim the throne of his late cousin, Elizabeth of England, the people swarmed to welcome him in almost intolerable numbers. English courtiers who went to meet the king halfway noted how the throng seemed to upset or even alarm him. Scots in his entourage explained that at home a crowd was a sign of trouble. Rather than smile and wave as Elizabeth had always done, James cursed. He asked what all these people wanted, and smooth-talking Englishmen replied they came of love to see him. He cried in Scots: 'I'll pull doon ma breeks and they shall see ma erse.' When he had spoken like that at home, his people answered in kind. That was how Scots treated their kings, worthy of loyalty but on a level with themselves. True, this bonhomie could turn into insolence from Scotland's thuggish lords. They would try to bully James. When the Master of Glamis had trapped him at Ruthven Castle in 1582, and made the fifteen-year-old lad burst into tears, he said with contempt: 'Better that bairns should greet than bearded men.' But James learned to surmount this sort of intimidation. Early one morning in the summer of 1593 he was in bed at the Palace of Holyroodhouse when a group of armed nobles burst in on him. The king defied them, then got them to parley. Meanwhile the people of Edinburgh, hearing he was in trouble, gathered in the courtyard outside. The last thing he wanted was a fight round his person. He leant out of a window, shouted down that he was fine: they should all go home. They bawled happily back in answer, and the danger vanished.

From scenes like these we get some inkling of how much Scotland lost after her kings departed in 1603. James VI returned just once. His son Charles I, though born at Dunfermline, grew up to all intents and purposes an Englishman, coming back only to treat Scots with disdain where it hurt most, in their Calvinist religion. That was why they got hold of Charles II young and drummed into him that he was a covenanted king, bound by oath to God and his people. The result turned out the opposite to what they intended: a sovereign resolved to sit never again through three hours of a ranting Presbyterian sermon but rather to terminate the rule of the saints in the Church of Scotland. The episode in which he all but exterminated their remnant was grimly known as the Killing Time. James VII and II tried his absolutist but blundering best with the Scots. Before he succeeded he came and resided in Edinburgh for a time so as to take the heat out of efforts in England to exclude him, as a Catholic, from the throne. His sojourn in Scotland as a sort of viceroy offered him a chance to show his monarchical potential. He did not too badly. But his religion still set up a bar between him and this most Protestant people – especially as he was said to enjoy watching captive Covenanters tortured.

The final crisis between dynasty and nation rose towards its climax on the afternoon of Sunday, December 9, 1688. It was then that the House of Stewart, which over three centuries had done more than anything else to ensure Scotland's survival, commenced its fall. Edinburgh was in the hands of a mob. They knew that 500 miles away William of Orange had landed at Torbay in Devon and with his army was advancing on London to save Protestantism. There, that same afternoon, James VII and II prepared to send his family to France as a prelude to his own flight. The king's cause in Scotland seemed just as dire. Rather than try to restore order in his name, the Duke of Gordon, governor of Edinburgh Castle, shut himself up behind the ramparts. At Holyrood the Scottish government under the Chancellor, the Earl of Perth, was running out of time. It would not have lasted the night but for the presence of mind of the Lord Provost, Magnus Prince, who at the waning of a gloomy winter's day ordered the gates of the city locked and posted guards to stop trouble-makers getting out over the walls to the palace beyond.

On the Monday morning Gordon ventured a sortie, clattering down the High Street with an armed escort. He wanted to urge the Chancellor to come and take refuge with him. But Perth said he was about to leave for his own Castle Drummond, 40 miles away beyond Stirling, in case he had to escape abroad; he would be taken prisoner as he embarked for France. All he would do was sign an order authorising the duke to draw on the revenue for any military needs. When Gordon tried, officials of the Exchequer refused to pay him. Once Perth was gone that afternoon, the rabble moved in on the palace and the Abbey of Holyrood next to it, housing the Chapel Royal.

James VII had made the chapel a symbol of his reign. While resident in Edinburgh, he ordered mass to be celebrated there for the first time in more than a century. Later he invited the parishioners of the Canongate, who used the abbey as their kirk, to shift to an elegant new building nearby, which still stands today. Then he paid for the chapel to be fitted out for the order of chivalry he founded, the Knights of the Thistle, with a throne for himself and a dozen stalls for them. It was a high-class job: Grinling Gibbons did the carvings. The king sent up more lavish fittings for it in his own royal yacht – an altar, an organ, vestments and images.

Just before the popular reaction to all this now burst out, the abbey had been on royal orders sprinkled with holy water and reconsecrated for St Andrew's Day. Nothing was more likely to provoke the Calvinist citizens of the capital. Students started the trouble. After they left their classes at the university on the Monday of the crisis, they gathered on the Meadows nearby so that the Lord Provost could not again trap them within the walls of the city. They marched round towards Holyrood. As they approached, the commander of the guard, Captain John Wallace, drew up his 100 men in the forecourt. Outnumbered, these had to retain the initiative – and contemporary methods of keeping order were rough. They opened fire, then for good measure lobbed hand grenades into the crowd. Twelve students were killed and many wounded. The rest fled in panic back up the hill. Blood had been shed and Gordon sent word that he was ready to deploy his troops, but the Lord Provost did not want general carnage in the streets. Prince disposed of the town guard and trained bands of militia, about 700 men in all. With these he sought to defuse the situation. He sent a messenger to Holyrood, offering to escort Wallace and the guards to safety in the castle. The messenger arrived too late.

This was because what remained of the government of Scotland had blundered in. While the Lord Provost stayed cool and collected, those privy councillors still lurking in the capital were trying to calm their nerves in a drinking den but instead worked themselves into a panic. They too gave orders to the town guard, that it should go down and take over security at Holyrood – in other words, they signalled royalist surrender. The students followed cheering. Wallace, yet more outnumbered than before, told his men to run but they were all chased and caught.

Militia and mob were now in merry mood, ready to carry on in the common cause. They decided to break into the abbey and destroy its splendours. They tore down throne, stalls and organ, and paraded with the debris up the High Street. Some paused at the Nethergate and reverently took down for burial the skulls of Covenanting martyrs stuck up there on spikes. They proceeded to the Cross, where they lit a bonfire and danced round it while they burned the blasphemous baubles. They made an effigy of the pope and burned him too. Others, finished with the abbey, turned on the palace. They aimed first at a college of Jesuits installed by the king, but these had fled. So the rioters, shoulder to shoulder with the forces of order, hammered down the doors of Perth's suite and rifled whatever he had left behind. Next they penetrated the royal apartments, smashing what they did not want, destroying what they could not bear away. It was this jape that brought on such an act of sacrilege as would have appalled any previous generation of Scots. Under Holyrood lay the Stewarts' burial vault, though none had been interred there since James V in 1542. Hallowed though the place was, the rabble did not spare it. They burst in, hacked at the tombs and scattered the royal dust. This was the sorry end of the direct line of Scotland's native dynasty which, except in futile rebellion, would never set foot in the country again.

❧

These events led on to civil war as Jacobitism emerged, so-called after the Latin form of the name James. The aim of the movement, which had a century's life ahead of it, was to restore the legitimate line of Stewarts. It relied first on loyalists to James VII who refused to accept the Revolution, yet in time found means to draw in wider groups suffering the consequences. Jacobitism at one or other of its peaks would be for many Scots above all an expression of their patriotism, crystallised in fidelity to a dynasty supposed to be 2,000 years old, older than the nation itself. If the dynasty went, then so might the nation. There were rival interpretations of Scotland's history, but this proved a powerful one.

To settle the affairs of post-revolutionary Scotland, a national Convention gathered in Edinburgh over the winter of 1688–9. One leading Jacobite, James Graham of Claverhouse, Viscount Dundee, soon abandoned it and rode for the North. He had been a brave, but stupid, and no doubt for that reason ultra-loyal servant of James VII, as of Charles II before him, especially in brutal suppression of the Covenanters. Claverhouse went to the Convention in hope it might reverse the Revolution. Once it dawned on him that this was not going to happen he walked out. In the North he would find many other Jacobites among aristocracy, gentry and clergy, while in the Lowlands, too, there were Jacobite lairds. Claverhouse managed during the summer of 1689 to raise more than 2,000 men – quite enough, given the modest scale of Scottish warfare, to launch a rising. Having ranged up to the Highlands and along the Great Glen, he was by the end of July moving south. He crossed into upper Strathspey towards the Pass of Killiecrankie, leading into the Lowlands.

Marching in the opposite direction came a force loyal to King William under General Hugh Mackay of Scourie. He was a Gael from a far northern clan – its lands included Cape Wrath – the only one to have switched sides during the Revolution. He brought about the change of heart himself, coming home after a long mercenary's career in Europe. Mackay did not know or did not believe that Jacobite forces had mustered so fast. So when, on July 27, he was advancing through the pass, he remained unaware of their approach from the other side. Claverhouse could and did read the situation. Leading his troops at a run in the heat of summer, he mounted a hill above the pass. An astonished Mackay turned his regiments to face them, suddenly aware of his great peril. For a couple of hours the two sides skirmished, each meanwhile trying to extend its lines and outflank the enemy. Claverhouse resolved matters at seven o'clock in the evening, when the sun was no longer in his men's faces. He ordered a Highland charge down the braes of Killiecrankie. It smashed Mackay's thin, stretched lines. His troops fled back along the pass, being cut down as they ran. In this moment of supreme triumph Claverhouse, rising in the stirrups to rally his irresolute cavalry, was shot under the left arm and fell dying. The first Jacobite rising had won a great victory, but its leader was no more. The scale of the loss could be gauged days later when the clansmen tried to debouch into the Lowlands. At Dunkeld, guarding the southern end of the pass, they were stopped dead by the Cameronians, a regiment raised from the most extreme Covenanters to defend the Revolution. These, outnumbered three to one in fighting round the cathedral, would not yield even when their commander, Colonel William Cleland, lost his life.[6]

With an about equal disposition to heroism and sacrifice on either side, stalemate followed. It was this that at length brought the most infamous episode of William's reign, the Massacre of Glencoe. In February 1692 his troops killed thirty-eight MacDonalds during a snowy dawn in their fastness among the mountains. The cull was modest by Highland standards.[7] In earlier bloodbaths, prisoners or innocents had been slaughtered in hundreds by their conquerors; to clansmen in arms it was routine. Yet somehow the carnage in Glencoe seemed more horrible. The Mac-Donalds had, despite a notorious reputation as marauders and thieves, been at peace on that winter's morning, had indeed for days beforehand been offering Highland hospitality to the soldiers about to murder them. The affair went down in legend as the treachery of the Campbells, their hereditary enemies. Yet it was much more the treachery of their nation's rulers, servants of King William.

The king had been brandishing both carrot and stick at Highlanders. He offered Jacobite chiefs inducements to abandon their cause, but threatened if these were spurned to come in person and exact submission by force – the nearest he ever got to visiting Scotland. The chiefs took a little while to weigh up his subtlety before they concluded that William meant what he said. They were required to take an oath of allegiance to him by December 31, 1691. As the deadline approached most all at once fell into line. MacDonald of Glencoe arrived on that last day of the year at Fort William. He presented himself to the governor, General John Hill, only to find he had come to the wrong place. The oath was to be administered by a civil, not military, officer: in this case by the sheriff-depute of Argyll, Sir Colin Campbell of Ardkinglass, 50 miles away at Inveraray. In fear and trembling MacDonald set off through snowdrifts and got there on January 3. But Ardkinglas had gone home after the deadline, and storms hindered his return for three more days. Even then, MacDonald found himself reduced to pleading in tears before his oath was accepted. When Ardkinglas went to Edinburgh with the certificate of all oaths from his county, he was obliged by the clerks of the privy council to erase the name of MacDonald of Glencoe, as one who had sworn too late.

Behind this lay the wiles of the Scottish Secretary, Sir John Dalrymple of Stair. He had drawn up orders against chiefs still holding out, for MacDonald of Glencoe was far from alone. 'I hope the soldiers will not trouble the Government with prisoners,' Stair concluded.[8] But it was fantasy to think of a punitive campaign against diehards in a Highland winter. Talks with them continued behind the scenes well after the deadline. Dalrymple thought he might best prove the king meant business by making an example of somebody: 'if MacIain of Glencoe, and that tribe, can be well separated from the rest, it will be a proper vindication of the public justice to extirpate that den of thieves.'[9] By January 23 the message got through to Sir Thomas Livingston, commander-in-chief in Scotland. Taking his cue from a political superior, he wrote to an officer at Fort William:

I understand that the Laird of Glencoe, coming after the prefixed time, was not admitted to take the oath, which is very good news here, being that at Court it's wished he had not taken it . . . So Sir, here is a fair occasion for you to show that your garrison serves for some use . . . begin with Glencoe, and spare nothing which belongs to him, but do not trouble the Government with prisoners.

This echo of Stair was in effect the formal order for the massacre which followed and which was never punished.[10]

❦

It was through acts not just of man but also of God that Scotland suffered affliction. Lying at the climatic limits of primitive agriculture, she had often gone hungry. But the famine of the 1690s went beyond anything known or remembered. The whole nation seemed to fall back to a lower stage of development. The economy ground to a halt as merchants exported coin to buy grain from abroad. The people reverted to barter. The state struggled to function without the taxes it could not collect. Highland bands debouched in quest of sustenance on the Lowlands. The Jacobites spoke of 'King William's seven ill years'. That term drew an analogy between him and the wicked Pharaoh of the Bible to suggest a divine judgment on the Scots for the sin of dethroning James VII and II.

The memory long outlasted the crisis. A century later when the *Old Statistical Account* was being written – itself the expression of a new, scientific approach to national prosperity – the authors still cited stories from 100 years before of corpses in the fields and by the roads or on the seashore, with survivors swarming to beg in the burghs after failed harvests on their farms. Even in the twentieth century oral tradition had not forgotten: when human bones were uncovered by workmen near the foreshore at a village on the Moray Firth, local people at once identified them as victims of the famine who had died after trying to survive on shellfish and been buried above the high watermark.

At least among forward-thinking Scots a new spirit sought to put the terrible experience to some good use. They were starting to come to terms with their physical and social reality in a methodical way that would make the nation a cradle of new sciences in the Enlightenment of the following century. Andrew Fletcher of Saltoun, a choleric laird from East Lothian, dwelt on the miseries of the poor and indifference of the rich. He thought that at the height of famine 200,000 beggars were on the move in Scotland. Never a man to shirk drastic solutions, he proposed reducing these wretches to a sort of benign slavery, regulated by law to secure their basic human rights, rather than leaving them to their fate. The scientist Sir Robert Sibbald wrote how 'everyone may see death in the face of the poor that abound everywhere; the thinness of their visage, their ghostly looks, their feebleness, their agues and their fluxes threaten them with sudden death'. He often came across unburied corpses: 'Some die in the wayside, some drop down in the street, the poor sucking babs are starving for want of milk which the empty breasts of their mothers cannot furnish.' Patrick Walker, a clerical biographer, found women in the markets crying, 'How shall we go home and see our children die in hunger? They have had no meat these two days, and we have nothing to give them.' Martin Martin, author of a survey of the Western Isles, said 'many of the poor people have died by famine' after failed crops caused by 'the great change of the seasons, which of late years is become more piercing and cold'. He got closest to the real explanation. This decade saw widespread agrarian crisis in Europe and America. Its cause seems to have lain in the solar system, in a cyclical fall in output of energy from the Sun, rather than – as Scots assumed – in their own sins.[11]

King William's seven ill years probably thinned the national population by between 5 and 15 per cent, with drops of 20 per cent in the worst areas. Perhaps half of this was due to a higher death-rate, half to a fall in births and increased emigration, notably to Ireland. Once the horror of the physical suffering passed it left mental scars in a feeling that Scotland was a nation which had failed, which was trailing far behind its neighbours in the British Isles and in Europe.

The feeling ought to have been belied by the start of some promising development: a shift from communal to individual agriculture, greater security for tenants in longer leases, growing payment of rents in cash rather than in kind, foundation of a banking system, a quest for methods of fostering industry, all to be taken as evidence of improvement in the next century. Scotland's first, halting economic discourse had begun in an intellectual advance after the Restoration with a technical literature dwelling on such changes – *Of Husbandrie* (before 1666) by John Skene of Hallyards, *Husbandrie Anatomiz'd* (1697) by James Donaldson and *The Countrey-Man's Rudiments* (1699), possibly by Lord Belhaven, a later enemy of Union. But this literature was not yet vigorous enough to offer aid or comfort to Scots brought face to face with their backwardness.[12]

❧

The disposition to gloom was finally reinforced by one of the most spectacular of all national failures, of the attempt in 1699–1701 to establish a trading colony at Darien on the Isthmus of Panama. This, too, drew its impulse from the feeling among Scots that they had fallen behind their neighbours, a condition which might find at least partial remedy from rational planning and patriotic exertion in colonial trade. Since it was enriching Dutchmen and Englishmen, Scots thought they could follow. This was in embryo a modern thought, that a society intent on economic growth could discover means to achieve it.

The expedition to Central America set out in the summer of 1699 in blithe indifference to the dim view of it taken by King William, though ominous signs of his displeasure could have been read. The colony was organised by a Company of Scotland Trading to Africa and the Indies, or Darien Company. It had at first tried to float itself in London as well as in Edinburgh, with English as well as Scottish directors, to the tune of £600,000. The attempt provoked uproar among powerful metropolitan interests which saw here a threat to the English East India Company's monopoly on oriental traffic. William himself said, pandering to the brouhaha: 'I have been ill-served in Scotland but I hope some remedy may yet be found to meet the inconvenience that may arise from this Act.' The Parliament at Westminster needed no better authority to vote prosecution of the Darien Company's directors living under its jurisdiction. That was the last seen of them or of the £300,000 they had engaged to stump up.

The basic problem was that William cherished strategic aims beyond the ken of Scots, from which he would stand no domestic distraction. In Spain, the ruling Habsburgs were reaching their degenerate end and he had to stop Louis XIV of France seizing the succession for the Bourbons, so overturning the balance of power in Europe. As a solution William meant to arrange partition of the Spanish realms. For this he conducted the diplomacy in secret. He could not make clear in Scotland what he was up to, even if he had wanted. He was obliged to keep Spain sweet, and she would not tolerate a colony on the Isthmus of Panama over which she carried her transfusions of economic lifeblood, the precious metals from Peru. He afterwards claimed to have been deceived about the aims of the Scottish expedition, otherwise he would have at once understood that it breached treaties with Spain, a friendly power, and done something about it. Darien lay in territory he recognised as Spanish. In his eyes it therefore counted as an unlawful colony. In the summer of 1699 he issued a proclamation forbidding all his English subjects to sell arms, ammunition and provisions to it, or to deal with it in any way. The king's will was communicated to every colonial governor along 2,000 miles of American seaboard from Boston to Barbados.

The Scots at Darien, already aghast at the vile tropical conditions and daunting death-toll these exacted, remained in the dark about two further problems: why nobody would come to trade with them and why they had heard nothing from home. Their first query was hardly to the point for they had carried with them little that could well be traded, since Scotland did not manufacture much desired by other nations. A colonist wrote: 'We cannot conceive for what end so much thin grey paper and so many little blue bonnets were sent here, being entirely useless and not worth their room on the ship.' The answer to the second query was a matter less of royal hostility than of their own countrymen's incompetence. But when the colonists found out by chance about the king's proclamation from a passing ship, everything seemed to fall into place. One of their leaders was William Paterson, a typical 'projector' of the age, full of ingenious schemes, some good, some bad: a good one had been the Bank of England, which he helped to found in 1694, while a bad one was Darien. 'The long silence,' he now concluded as he recalled the joyful crowds waving them off from

Leith, 'proceeded from no other cause but that they were brow-beat and durst not so much send word to us to shift for ourselves.'

For the colonists, then, the future could hold no relief, but only deeper despair. Suddenly they felt they had to go. Paterson alone opposed immediate evacuation. Even if he had been able to think or speak clearly in the bout of fever he was suffering, another event brought all argument to a halt. A French ship appeared, which would have been cause of jubilation a week before. Now it confirmed the Scots' worst fears. The captain said he had come from Cartagena, a city further along the Caribbean coast, and learned there of a new governor appointed from Spain who meant to prove himself by gathering a force to destroy Darien. The Scots' fortitude dissolved into panic. They rushed about packing their possessions and, with nobody taking charge or keeping order, fought each other to get into boats ferrying them from shore to ship. In four days most were aboard with servants and baggage. A rearguard remained in the fort with Paterson and the commander, William Drummond. Just six would stay behind when the rest sailed away, too ill or mad or stubborn to move. They would be there to greet a second Scottish fleet which arrived to re-establish the colony on the same site in November. It lasted a still shorter time, and would surrender to a Spanish force in April 1700. Of all those brave Scots just a handful ever got home.

Thus ended the last, greatest but most calamitous colonial undertaking of Scotland as an independent nation. The loss of life among so many enterprising Scots was grievous enough. They also wasted the £200,000 they took with them to their doom, one-quarter of the country's capital. All this taught not only an economic but a political lesson too. Apart from contingent misfortunes, the Union of Crowns was one obvious root of the disaster. Fletcher assessed that it came about 'partly through our own fault, and partly through the removal of our kings into another country'. Scotland was thus reduced to unique impotence:

> This nation, of all those that possess good ports and lie conveniently for trade and fishing, has been the only part of Europe which did not apply itself to commerce; and possessing a barren country, in less than an age we are sunk to so low a condition as to be despised by all our neighbours and made uncapable to repel an injury, if any should be offered.[13]

To cap everything, a King of Scots resident in England had subjected the interests of his smaller to those of his larger realm. So the English possessed colonies and oceanic trade while the Scots possessed neither. Failure at Darien did not kill Scottish aspirations to a better future, only made clear it was not going to emerge from the existing political order. This might mean that the future would have in some sense to be a more independent one. Or it might mean that if the Scots could not beat the English, at this as at other endeavours, then perhaps they had to join them.

ఴ

Yet Union was never a practical proposition while it just meant English takeover of Scotland, by conquest or otherwise. New prospects had opened in 1603 once James VI ascended the English throne. He himself sought to turn the Union of Crowns into a Union of Parliaments. But neither side yet felt ready for it, the English even less than the Scots. In the course of time various further schemes were put forward. The sole actual attempt at closer Union, the Cromwellian one, served to underline that it could not last without some degree of Scottish consent. By the end of the seventeenth century, at any rate, the Union of Crowns was in disarray. So far from converging, the two nations now seemed to be drifting apart as Scottish aversion to English domination grew. Relations between them turned cold and sour. Change of whatever sort appeared imperative.

Release of Scotland's pent-up energies by the Revolution of 1688 complicated the connection still further. Her Parliament saw a period of development which showed a promise to be snuffed out in 1707. Before the Revolution the Parliament had done little more than ratify the king's commands. In this it was much like the Estates General of continental nations, which also tended to vanish in the early modern era. Like them again, it suffered a structural defect in consisting of a single chamber where lords and commons and sometimes clergy sat together: in other words, the Commons had not been set apart, as in England, to deliberate on their own and formulate a general will for the nation. Here was the unique evolution of the English Parliament towards its classical form, of a legislature checking the executive, from which it set a universal example.

Yet for a while after the Revolution the Scots Parliament almost seemed to be progressing faster than the English Parliament. At Westminster members resorted to fictions to explain why they were overthrowing their king. They asserted he had abdicated; the truth was anything but. The verdict in Scotland, opposed by just five members at the Convention's final vote on the matter, stated rather that he had by misrule forfeited the Crown. This implied obligation to something higher than both king and people – what a later, enlightened age would call a contract. The Claim of Right then voted by the Convention would confirm as much. It listed James VII's offences and resolved that he had violated 'the fundamental constitution of this kingdom and altered it from a legal limited monarchy to an arbitrary despotic power'.[14] That was why he had to go.

In the light of Scottish history it was a bold claim, to say the least. Perhaps it can be better read as a statement that in future the monarchy ought to be limited. William and Mary, when offered the Crown in 1689, were obliged to accept it on those terms. The terms were spelled out: the monarchy had to be Protestant; its prerogatives would be subject to the rule of law; its supply of finance should depend on the consent of Parliament; this must meet often and enjoy freedom of debate. The last point was a hit at a peculiarity of the Scottish constitution, the Lords of the Articles, a committee appointed by the king to control the agenda of Parliament, underlining its impotence and subordination to him. The Lords of the Articles vanished a year later, against William's will. In Scotland the Revolution seemed to have brought a big shift in the balance of power as between Crown and Parliament, more dramatic even than in England.

But the practical results disappointed. The emergence of Jacobitism, the Massacre of Glencoe, the affair of Darien when William acted as anything other than a King of Scots – all went to demonstrate the distance, mental as well as physical, between the monarch and his northern kingdom. A new equilibrium might have brought them closer together and given them through an interplay of interests some deeper appreciation of each other's needs. Yet William lacked the time or the incentive to master Scottish affairs. The wary rapprochement between him and the political nation in England, often fraught but finally to the good, never occurred in Scotland.

Instead, the liberated Scots Parliament took off in the opposite direction. At last able to function in its own right, the first thing it learned was to impede royal government. This was, of course, how English constitutionalism had started too, and during a fraught post-revolutionary period the Parliament at Westminster hardly settled into serene stewardship of the common good. But it could look back on a long evolution, just as it could look forward to a long evolution through times when men might better judge from experience what among current developments ought to be of durable value. In the 1690s the English legislature was laying down a matrix for the deployment of executive power in an elective majority. As yet, this seldom represented any exercise of will on the voters' part. Rather, a Minister chosen by the monarch, often reliant at the outset only on a parliamentary minority, would gather strength as he went through his own measures and the aspirations of those wishing to connect themselves with power in the state. It did not yet bring out the best in English statesmanship.

In Scotland the normal pattern was the reverse: once a new Ministry formed, parliamentary groups would move into opposition so as to make its life impossible and in that way to extract concessions from it. The scene was no prettier than the English one though the system had a different purpose, being concerned less with the convenience of the executive than with a balance among all the interests that had to be balanced. The composition not only of the Scottish Ministry but also, for example, of the Bench in the Court of Session reflected this: every faction felt entitled to its representative. The penalty was that principle and policy counted for less than patronage, place, pensions and privileges. The English Parliament had by no means left that stage behind. But the monarch's presence in London, the consequent immediate interest of the court and the more pressing propinquity of national and international problems did make a difference. By contrast, in Edinburgh everything was at arm's length: the first thing the king had to do was choose among the great noblemen one to stand in for him as Lord High Commissioner to Parliament and leader of the Court party. There were always candidates, none seeing why another should be preferred. So royal authority easily degenerated into aristocratic faction.

The short remaining life of the Scots Parliament never allowed all these difficulties to be ironed out, and in fact they carried over into the nation's representation at Westminster after 1707. It was ironic that then the management of Scotland would come to be well, indeed superbly, organised for themselves by Scots; the repute of their own old Parliament would again suffer in comparison. Perhaps it could have undergone a more productive evolution over time – but time, in the event, was what it did not have. Or else there lay deep in the nature of either nation something that made for the crucial disparity.

☙

William, knowing little and caring less about Scotland, was obliged to depend on others' advice – above all on his Dutch confidant, Portland, of whom Burnet said 'he had that nation . . . wholly in his hands'.[15] He chose the Scottish Ministers. He had to ride out the storms of Glencoe and Darien. Even after he retired in 1699 he still gave support to contending Scots politicians, to William Douglas, Duke of Queensberry, and to Archibald Campbell, Earl of Argyll. Yet Portland never once set foot in Scotland and his grasp of her politics remained tenuous.

It was through the prism of Portland that the king perceived the basic problem to be religious, a matter of struggle between rival parties in the Church of Scotland, Presbyterian and Episcopalian, as rekindled by the Revolution and reflected in subsequent political divisions. The two Dutchmen tended to the view that they did not amount to much, and thought this confirmed by what was known to them of the recent background.

The religious persecution between the Restoration of 1660 and the Revolution of 1688 indeed belied the fact that in this period a compromise of a kind had come to prevail, not much loved but attaining a rough-and-ready equilibrium. Presbyteries and bishops co-existed once Charles II grafted episcopacy back on to the Kirk, after the examples of his father and grandfather. The compromise saw to authority and order, with bishops choosing moderators at the different levels of the Presbyterian structure. Otherwise – notably in forms of public worship – little changed from the days of John Knox. Eucharist was still offered to communicants sitting rather than kneeling. Presbyterians prided themselves on preaching to the people in the language of the people but not every Episcopalian stood gorgeous in the vestments of a priestly caste to recite a sonorous liturgy. A Dutch eye might dwell on similarities, yet Scotland was a kingdom of the mind. In her mind's eye she saw the crucial fact that Episcopalians erected hierarchy while Presbyterians held fast to the priesthood of all believers.

In large part the two Dutchmen owed their blind spot to reliance on the Revd William Carstares, the leading Presbyterian of the time, nicknamed the Cardinal by his compatriots. He had probably started working for the Dutch secret service while a student at the University of Leiden, *alma mater* of many Scots, whence he graduated in 1672. Some irrepressible impulse to skulduggery sent him back and forth across the North Sea, suffering torture and imprisonment from time to time. By means not altogether clear he at length penetrated William of Orange's inner circle.

There Carstares would remain, not just as chaplain but also as confidant – like his master a secretive Calvinist. His judgment of events was often borne out by the sequel and he knew about subjects, not least Scotland, obscure to his princely master. He tells us he admired William for his determination and courage. In return Carstares offered his own brand of bravery, the bravery of resolute moderation in an immoderate age and the willingness to endure the opprobrium of more impassioned figures. He was 'a fat, sanguine complexioned fair man', one said of him, 'always smiling, where he designs most mischief'.[16]

William was a practising member of the Dutch Reformed Church, which enjoyed its own Presbyterian form of government. He preferred plain worship and he attended it daily. In private he followed regimes of spiritual self-examination. In public he sought to make his court more godly, though like most Calvinists he did not think much of Anglicanism. Burnet, who had abandoned the Church of Scotland for the Church of England, was habitually in the right place at the right time and he turned up at Torbay in 1688: after the safe landing William ragged him, asking him how he could doubt predestination now he had seen God's blessing on the expedition to depose King James VII and II.[17] A man at whom William could throw an earnest jest was a man he might have trusted in greater matters, but Burnet, beside not standing at quite the right point on the religious spectrum, was also too indiscreet. King William preferred to trust Carstares. It was he, not Burnet, who led the service of thanksgiving on the beach at Torbay and who, for the future, offered better acquaintance with events and personalities in Scotland. At least William sought to make up for his ignorance with vision. One way he set himself apart from his fellow monarch Louis XIV was that he did not accept religion should be imposed by persecution. He urged toleration everywhere he could exert any influence. He employed men of all faiths, Catholics and Jews too, in civil and military service. How could such a king deal with bigoted Scotland?

A bad sign came from the start, when William found his coronation oath required him to root out heresy. He objected. Red-faced Scots hastened to persuade him the oath did not mean what it said. With the Crown he also accepted the Claim of Right, which denounced bishops and said their office 'ought to be abolished'. This might imply acceptance of a Presbyterian settlement. Yet, as Burnet pointed out, 'the king would not consent to a plain and simple condemnation' of Episcopalians.[18] What he wanted above all was a Kirk that would cause him no political problems, so for preference one open to all shades of Protestant. Then it might come to resemble the Church of England, and in course of time the two establishments would be able to identify a community of interest, perhaps so far as to merge.[19] The existing college of Scots bishops, while Jacobite, advocated passive obedience, that is to say, non-resistance to civil authority. In that case, there was a chance of wooing a complaisant minority of their clergy. William wished such men to remain within the Kirk, and hoped to keep them there by letting them swear an oath of allegiance to him as king *de facto*, if not *de jure*. So in the post-revolutionary mirk lurked a point towards which the views of King William and Carstares could converge: on a moderate Presbyterian settlement of the Kirk avoiding punctilio over prickly problems.

Their deliberate vagueness began to dissolve as soon as a hair-splitting Scots Parliament got to work. The Act of Supremacy was repealed, by which Charles II had asserted his authority in religion. William gave royal assent to an Act Abolishing Prelacy yet swithered over Presbyterianism. He wanted it defined as 'the government of the Church in this kingdom established by law'. But his formula was turned into 'the only government of Christ's Church in this kingdom'. Having indulged English dissenters who promised to live peaceably, he wished to deal with the Scottish Episcopal clergy in the same way. Yet the Kirk would soon take sweeping powers to purge them. The king, or rather Carstares, would have retained lay patronage of livings, another device by which clerical wildness might be calmed. It did not seem wholly at odds with presbytery, yet it went. The power to choose ministers passed from the landed gentry to local heritors and elders of congregations.

Not only in the Convention, but also in the country beyond, Presbyterians often dwelt, in preference to present needs, on a sense of grievance over what they had suffered before. In the West they rabbled Episcopalians out of their manses. Such deprivations, legal and illegal, outnumbered those suffered at the Restoration of 1660 by Presbyterians. Once reinstated they wanted to get their own back, with no bishops and with presbytery everywhere set up over a new order in religion and politics. Each minister would have to show his loyalty to William and Mary in saying public prayers for them by name. Presbyterians expected their policy to commend them to the new king.

The General Assembly of the Church of Scotland reconvened in 1690 for the first time since 1654. It drew up a Presbyterian settlement for the nation which remains in force to this day. It did so in more rather than less exclusive form. This was a Presbyterian institution and Presbyterians made all the running there. The government could counter only in the civil sphere, for example, by refusing to back excommunication with civil penalties. It could not avert vengeance wrought on Episcopalian ministers. The assembly set up a commission to test their credentials and within the year had them complaining of its harshness. In 1691 the king ordered a halt to the excesses. In 1692 the Presbyterians retorted with more obstruction of his schemes for accepting Episcopalians into the Kirk. This prompted the dissolution of the assembly. In the tit-for-tat it was not till 1696 that the aim of indulgence approached realisation, when Parliament passed an Act allowing Episcopalians who took an oath of allegiance to remain in their parishes. Nothing was done for those deprived meanwhile. They, together with others whose Jacobite loyalties stopped them taking the oath anyway, would remain outside the Church of Scotland.

As the General Assembly tested and affirmed its power in the Kirk it set out to lead Scots at large through a strait gate. In 1694 it recited their sins: 'God is dishonoured by the impiety and profaneness that aboundeth . . . in profane and idle swearing, cursing, sabbath-breaking, neglect and contempt of gospel ordinances, mocking of piety and religious exercises, fornication, adultery, drunkenness, blasphemy, and other gross and abominable sins and vices.' In parishes the ministers should 'denounce the threatened judgments of God against such evil-doers, to bring them to a conviction of their sin and danger', while the kirk-sessions must 'faithfully exercise church discipline against all such scandalous offenders'. Clergy and elders ought to visit every household to see domestic worship performed and children instructed. Servants might only change jobs or residence with testimonials of 'their honest and Christian behaviour'. The untiring assembly kept up its high moral dudgeon for a generation, reinforced by fasts to avert the 'heavy displeasure and just indignation of the Holy One'.[20]

Again, there was a human cost. Neither Presbyterians nor Episcopalians had ever shown much interest in toleration, and did not now through another change of regime in the Kirk. In 1697 the 20-year-old Thomas Aikenhead, a medical student at the University of Edinburgh, was hanged for blasphemy. The privy council had just ordered a search in the city's bookshops for volumes deemed 'atheistical, erroneous or profane or vicious', such as those by René Descartes, Thomas Hobbes and Baruch Spinoza. For voicing opinions alleged to be found in them Aikenhead was tried under two Blasphemy Acts then in force, one of

1661 prescribing capital punishment, a second of 1695 graduating penalties from prison and sackcloth for a first offence, to an additional fine for a second offence and to death only for a third offence. Though a first offender, Aikenhead received a sentence of death. He sought reprieve on grounds of his 'deplorable circumstances [as an orphan] and tender years'. The privy council refused it unless the Kirk interceded for him. The General Assembly happened to be sitting. It urged 'vigorous execution' to curb 'the abounding of impiety and profanity in this land'. The pathetically friendless Aikenhead was strung up, the last person to die for blasphemy in the British Isles.

It was a mark of how religion in Scotland had run away from King William and Carstares. A Revolution begun as a revolt against James VII's Catholicism – with equal support from Episcopalians and Presbyterians – ended in the triumph of presbytery over episcopacy and the construction of a monolithic religious establishment. Presbyterians preferred rivals for control of the Kirk not to be indulged but kept out of it.[21]

Yet Scotland at large still had to be wholly won over to the new order. In all regions but the West many of the nobility and gentry remained hostile to presbytery, and in the North the people followed their chiefs or lairds. With as yet too few Presbyterian ministers to replace incumbent Episcopalians a good many of these carried on serving their parishes, sometimes for half-a-century ahead.[22] An example was the Revd Michael Fraser of Daviot and Dunlichity in eastern Inverness-shire. He held his charge for 54 years, spanning the Revolution, though he was a Jacobite of the first water. The Kirk declared his parish vacant in 1694 yet he contrived to cling on till his death in 1726, despite an active role in the rising of 1715. He was sustained by local landowners, Farquhar MacGillivray of Dunmaglass and the Mackintosh of Mackintosh. Attempts to ease him out came to nothing: his parishioners threw stones at visiting presbyters till they went away. The heritors appealed for him to be left in peace – he could not, after all, live for ever – and this was what in effect happened. Yet as a minister he was useless. When he had had a bishop, that bishop told him off for neglect of his parish, in particular for going on long artistic holidays with easel, brushes and paints. He survived because he proved to be not a faithful pastor but a cultured, complaisant companion to the lairds – which, over most of Scotland, was what counted.[23]

William misunderstood the men who ran Scotland in this and much else. While religion may in part have motivated their public conduct, religion was not a solution to the problems they posed. When the king's advisers induced him to act on religion, they just pushed self-seekers from one religious position to another. Often these, in religion as in politics, aimed to make a solution impossible so as to extract advantages for themselves.

☙

With collapse of the royal authority of the Stewarts' legitimate line in Scotland, the personal ambition of ruthless noblemen became the driving force in national politics. This William and his advisers were equally unable to handle, or perhaps even to understand. The period witnessed the dominance of four great noble houses in particular. They had competed before the Revolution, continued in William's reign and carried on into Anne's. The four houses were Argyll, Atholl, Hamilton and Queensberry; each wanted not just power but monopoly of power, and showed an utter lack of scruple in pursuit of it.

It may be piquant to note where the head of each house had stood in 1688. The Earls of Argyll, chiefs of Clan Campbell, known to clansmen by the heroic epithet of MacChailein Mòr (Great Son of Colin, after a medieval warrior) were the most potent lords of the Gàidhealtachd. The ninth earl had been executed in 1685 for rebellion against James VII, but in defence of their patrimony – their sole consistent aim – Highland chiefs often took opposite sides in succeeding generations, and the tenth earl declared loyalty to the king. Campbells had given leaders to or martyrs for Scottish Protestantism since its beginnings yet this earl found it in himself to turn briefly Catholic, though without apparent damage to his iconic standing in clan and nation. He managed also to get aboard the ship carrying William to Torbay, an essential qualification for Scots on the make; Argyll it was who offered him the Crown and administered the coronation oath. As for Atholl, his grasping family would in its turn take both sides or neither up to the last Jacobite rising in 1745. When Claverhouse had passed through its territory on the Highland line, marching to Killiecrankie, it made no move. By contrast, Hamilton, premier peer of the Lowlands, 'the person of the first quality and most interest in the nation', was a gentleman of the bedchamber to James VII and refused to desert him: 'I cannot violate my duty to my master. I must distinguish between his Popery and his Person.' The young Queensberry, then Lord Drumlanrig, had left his mark on his native heath in the south of Scotland by going out to hunt Covenanters with Claverhouse. Also initially loyal to James VII, he soon reversed his position. According to the memoir of the Jacobite, George Lockhart of Carnwath, Queensberry was 'the first Scotsman that deserted over to the Prince of Orange, and from thence acquired the epithet (among honest men) of Proto-rebel'. Indeed, he 'has ever since been so faithful to the revolution party . . . that he laid hold on all occasions to oppress the royal party and interest'.[24]

A dozen years later and they had all moved on. A new Duke of Hamilton, James, succeeded in 1698 and found himself, for such a great lord, rather a poor man. His mother, strong-willed Dowager Duchess Anne, lived on and grudged him his allowance from their lands in Lanarkshire. Still, her son would soon make his name in parliamentary opposition to the Court, as leader of the Country party, to use the contemporary term. Of his rivals Tullibardine, heir of Atholl, had by the unexacting standards of the time kept his nose cleanest and advanced furthest in royal favour. That antagonised his rivals Argyll and Queensberry. By 1698 they had overborne him and touchy Tullibardine was to be driven by dismay over Darien still deeper into patriotic disaffection. Then Argyll, just after he had been raised to a dukedom in 1701, broke with Queensberry and at the king's death was rallying his own faction in Parliament, at least in the time he could spare from his women and his horses.

From these broils Queensberry came out for now on top. His father had been James VII's trusty taxman, extracting cash from every conceivable source and, by the way, siphoning off enough to build himself a splendid baroque palace at Drumlanrig in Dumfriesshire as well as a townhouse in Edinburgh in the elegant style of a Parisian *hôtel particulier*, today a portal to the new Scottish Parliament. The son, in a reversal typical of the man and the age, chose the Presbyterian side, if without neglecting to profess toleration for Episcopalians – at least he persuaded Carstares that this was his position and so won the ear of King William. To husbanding his inheritance the younger Queensberry preferred spending it, for example on anyone by his own name of Douglas. But his costly subversion of rivals paid off. In the parliamentary session of 1699 he became Lord High Commissioner, or king's representative, chairing proceedings and signifying royal assent to the laws. The tragedy of Darien was just unfolding yet he managed to damp down the outcry, if only within the walls of Parliament House.

With no less skill and guile, Queensberry would eventually carry the Union. He ought to count as one of the great figures of Scottish history but he was not easy to get close to, then or now. On good days he showed the irrepressible spirit of the parvenu, on bad days lapsed into unctuous coldness. Ruthless and covetous, yet friendly and funny, a deep streak of dishonesty helped him to plot devious paths to distant goals because he could see through his fellows' lesser concerns. 'To outward appearance he was of a gentle and good disposition,' wrote Lockhart, 'but inwardly a very devil, standing at nothing to advance his own interest and designs.' Still, it is precisely this identification of the public good with a private advantage that often, however objectionable, changes history.

For now, at any rate, Queensberry was the best manager of the Scots Parliament to be found, though even his pliancy would be baffled from time to time. King William had long been seeking such a man and during the following years kept him on as Lord High Commissioner. Just from doing a job for his monarch he acquired skills as a political operator. But the eventual effect was to pull together various factions of the opposition, arisen on different grounds, into a more formidable force. He faced a mounting wave of hostility and obstruction in the parliamentary sessions of 1700 and 1701.

Casual provocation from Westminster hardly helped. There in 1701 the Act of Settlement was passed to cover the prospect if the heir-apparent to the throne, Anne, herself should die without an heir, as now seemed probable. The succession would then devolve on the next Protestant in line, Sophia, Electress of Hanover, an elderly granddaughter of James VI and I. Like any English Act this one was without force in Scotland and Scots had never been consulted about it. Yet it roped them into the limitations it imposed on the Hanoverian successor. It stated, for example, that 'no person who shall hereafter come to the possession of the crown shall go out of the Dominions of England, Scotland and Ireland without the consent of Parliament'. One among the indignant retorts of the Scots was to refrain from defining the succession, now and for as long as possible afterwards. That annoyed and alarmed English politicians who feared Scotland might one day spurn the Electress of Hanover to recall the Old Pretender, together with the foreign forces he was bound to bring with him. So every effort had to be made to secure the same succession in both nations. There appeared to be an easy way and a hard way. The easy way was to bring such pressure to bear on the Scottish

Parliament that it would see for itself the high cost of any alternative to Hanover. The hard way was Union.

During that session of 1701 the Scots Parliament also heard rumours of war. There had been wars enough between Scotland and England in the previous century but none between Scotland and any continental power, or at least none of Scotland's declaring. England often fought European wars, however. Scotland was then dragged willy-nilly into them, to suffer from embargoes enforced by the English navy and from depredations of fierce French privateers let loose on what Scottish shipping still ventured to sail. The result was ruinous for trade and in general for the economy: Scots paid the high price of decisions taken in London.

The Revolution had improved nothing here. William of Orange spent the first years of his reign preoccupied with more war, till exhaustion on all sides brought a respite in the Treaty of Ryswick of 1697. Up to then Louis XIV had refused to recognise William's title to his British Crowns. Now he agreed to, though without repudiating the claims of James VII and II. The compromise was that Louis would not help anyone to overthrow William. James felt betrayed and Louis ashamed at being driven to this by his need of peace. He sought to atone for it, with a final gesture after James's death in immediate recognition of his son, the Old Pretender, as successor to the thrones of England, Scotland and Ireland. War then threatened again. It would break out in the spring of 1702 and be known as the War of the Spanish Succession. It was also in effect the War of the English Succession, not to speak of the Scottish Succession. In Scotland, with all this trouble brewing, Queensberry would be bound to find the next legislative session tough. William understood that, yet knew of nobody else to trust as his Lord High Commissioner. It was a reason why the king, in the days just before his death, had turned to advocating Union.

∽

Such were the circumstances in which Anne became Queen of Scots. She succeeded without fuss, as in England. She knew Scotland a little. In her younger days she had spent ten months in Edinburgh while her father did his viceregal stint there. She found the city dull and the Scots 'strange people'. No wonder she would never come north during her reign, doubtless fearing the land of her fathers might present to her blank gaze far too many of 'these unreasonable Scotsmen'.[25] A Stewart she may have been but she was to all intents and purposes wholly English.[26] Scots loyal to the legitimate line of her house yet accepted her as a temporary expedient to keep the throne warm for the boy James while she advanced Tory causes, as she meant to do anyway out of personal predilection. According to her the Church of England was 'the only true Church'.[27] Through go-betweens she kept up some contact with the exiles at St Germain. Her aims were not necessarily what Jacobites assumed them to be. Her character as a Tory could be in no doubt, all the same.

At the time of her accession Anne was thiry-seven years old, fat, plain, not too bright, with lesbian tendencies; she no longer got much pleasure out of life and consoled herself with brandy from a tea-cup. Set against these handicaps she showed a strong sense of duty and a deep piety. They made up for much, because it is in general to the good that British monarchs should not be too brilliant or dashing. They have, after all, to work with humdrum politicians disliking to be outwitted or outshone. For listless Anne, not least in the matter of Union, it was a matter of dogged does it, though in her life to date her stolid persistence had brought her little but frustration, indeed only pain in her role of mother or, more to the point, provider of an heir to the throne. Her husband, the drunken, genial, feckless Prince George of Denmark, impregnated her eighteen times but just five of the babies survived birth and of these the longest-lived, Prince William of Gloucester, had already died at the age of ten in 1700. Now her childbearing days were over. She turned in effect into a chronic invalid, not just physically afflicted but also mentally haunted by her desertion of her father in 1688, by quarrels with her sister unhealed at the time of Mary's death in 1694 and by her inability to effect any sort of reconciliation with her half-brother, the Old Pretender. Clear in any event was that she could not in her own body resolve the question of succession to the British Crowns, any more than the childless William and Mary had done.

Anne had so far played next to no part in politics and remained almost unknown outside a circle of intimates. But she set off resolutely enough and dismissed the Whig Ministers she inherited. She replaced them with Tories or men sympathetic to Tories, notably John Churchill, Duke of Marlborough, and Sidney Godolphin, the one the greatest soldier, the other among the greatest fiscal experts of the day. A rank of Captain-general was created for Marlborough in view of the imminent European conflict. He soon usurped control of foreign policy as well from the Secretaries of State, while his brother George took charge of the navy. The range of qualities in Godolphin made him in essence the queen's most senior civil servant, brilliant if testy, with the experience and capacity to run the government's finances, patronage, domestic policy and relations with Scotland (the rest of his time was his own; he liked nothing so much as a flutter on the horses). He had as little knowledge as most Englishmen of the Scots, though he knew what he wanted: a stable Scotland. But stability was not something Scotland offered.

As Queen of Scots, Anne's first action was to send, with official notice of her accession from London, a letter to her councillors in Edinburgh. It continued all existing royal commissions, civil and military, gave an assurance of her care for the Protestant religion and for the government of the Kirk established by law. It also sought advice on what to do about one ticklish matter, the sitting Scottish Parliament.

In England the rule was that death of a monarch dissolved the last Parliament called in the reign, and a fresh election took place on writs issued in the name of the new monarch. This rule overrode the Triennial Act (1694) which for the first time laid down a maximum term for Parliaments of three years. In 1701 there had actually been two General Elections. Even so, England went to the polls once again after Anne's accession. In the Commons the Whig majority of the Glorious Revolution had been melting away. Now voters responded to Anne's known preference and gave a thumping victory to the Tories.[28]

Things were nowhere near so easy in Scotland. In the summer of 1689 the Scottish Convention which ratified the Revolution had been without further ado turned into a Parliament and continued to sit for the rest of William's reign. Nor was it dissolved by the mere fact of his death. It stood at that moment adjourned, and an Act of 1696 provided for it in such a case to meet within twenty days and to remain in existence for up to six months longer if a new election did not follow at once; meanwhile its powers were limited to securing the succession without altering the constitution.[29] Yet neither early meeting nor quick election held much charm for Anne or, more to the point, for Queensberry the Lord High Commissioner, one of the Scots before whom she had just sworn the coronation oath in London. He knew what he was in for during the next parliamentary session. He did not want to defend to it the Hanoverian succession or an imminent war. An election, on the other hand, seemed likely just to return a yet bigger opposition waxing in ferocity towards him. The twenty days must have seemed to him far too short a time to assess, let alone solve the problem. The first thing was to get Anne to prolong the old Parliament.

In her message to Edinburgh, the queen therefore invited the privy council to think of some way out of the quandary. It obliged. It returned the ingenious but unfounded opinion that she could keep to the letter of the law if within twenty days she should command an adjournment of the Parliament rather than a summons to it; then it need not meet at the precise time appointed in the Act. She followed the advice, and the Parliament did not reconvene till June 9.

It was regrettable, to say the least, that foreign affairs meanwhile overtook these little local difficulties in Scotland. Even before William's death Europe had been drifting towards war. Louis XIV was weighing up whether he should really try to grab the entire inheritance on three continents bequeathed to his own grandson in 1700 by the last degenerate Habsburg reigning in Madrid, Charles II; this would defy the international understanding that the Spanish empire should be partitioned on the extinction of the old dynasty. Now, under Anne, the expected hostilities broke out. In fact, with Louis proving stubborn, she declared war on him. The Dutch Republic and the Holy Roman Emperor allied with her. The struggle over the decade it was to last would weaken France just as it contributed to Britain's rise as a European power. In England it proved from the start a popular war, fought in defence of the Protestant succession, a matter of concern to the people as William's wars in Europe, using British troops, never had been. Yet the queen consulted the English Parliament beforehand.

In Scotland, with the token delay of a fortnight, the privy council merely proclaimed on May 30 that Scotland was at war with France. It did so just ten days ahead of the date set for the Parliament to meet again, and it surely could have waited for that. Scotland was being dragged into hostilities once more for the recruits she could supply, to Dutch as well as to British armies, and because of the absolute necessity of keeping her out of the French camp, into which she might be propelled by Louis XIV's material and moral aid to Jacobites.

This Scottish declaration of war by royal prerogative, legal in itself, yet relied on the illegality of adjourning the old Parliament to a date further into the new reign than allowed for by statute. The legerdemain and the inequality with England put members journeying for the session to Edinburgh in yet fouler mood as they wound themselves up for another confrontation with Queensberry. He had a list of instructions from Anne modest enough to seem to him perhaps attainable. Proceedings would be kept short and business confined to essentials. It would ratify Anne's right and title to the throne. It would grant her supply, since as ever her Scottish government had no money. It would pass Acts securing Kirk and Protestant succession. And it would pass an Act for negotiating a Union. Then the members could go home. All these measures might be presented as pieties towards the glorious memory of King William. The dispatch of business left unfinished at his death was, it could be suggested, the least the Scots Parliament ought to do by way of tribute to him.

Queensberry's enemies were not so easily bid, however. The man among them who stepped forward to challenge the Court was Hamilton, already a sharp critic of the Lord High Commissioner's soft line on Darien, where the Dowager Duchess of Hamilton had sunk and lost £3,000. The duke was besides flirting with the Jacobites, how seriously we shall see in due course. He had in fact been playing up to every disaffected faction in Scotland. That now paid off for him in spectacular fashion. Straight after prayers at the opening of the Parliament he stood up to speak and 'though desired by the Lord Chancellor to sit till Her Majesty's commission was read and the house constitute yet persisted and said that for eviting of contests he had a paper to read'. The premier duke could not be shut up. He protested that the proceedings were illegal 'for as much as by the fundamental laws and constitution of this kingdom, all Parliaments do dissolve by the death of the king or queen'. Then he walked out, followed by seventy-four other members.[30]

Here was the Country party in action. We may pause to note its nature as an often shifting and variable coalition of those who happened to be disgruntled for one reason and another. In this case it consisted of the more thoroughgoing Presbyterians, men who thought Queensberry too indulgent to Episcopalians, and of Jacobites, with a rag-taggle of other malcontents. They added up to a third of the membership, though. They left the Parliament looking depleted and meagre. Two days later, this rump passed an Act defining as treason any attempt to call in question its own dignity and authority. By then it was too late. Hamilton had made his point, that Queensberry represented not the nation but a faction.

Of course, there were risks in Hamilton's conduct. It meant Queensberry could now do what he liked, so far as speeches and motions affected anything in the real world. He did try to carry on regardless, though this served to underline his embarrassment. But he could scarcely suspend a session he had just called, and his scant business was hard to curtail without abandoning it. The 120 members remaining, mostly Whig Presbyterians, ratified helter-skelter the queen's right and title, granted her supply, secured the Church of Scotland and Protestant succession, asked the Crown to nominate commissioners to treat for Union. There was at least a little pause for thought. To some members it appeared that Union and security of the Kirk might not be in all circumstances compatible. The Parliament agreed to send a letter to the queen stressing concern that, whatever the commissioners might at length recommend about Union, there should be no danger to the Presbyterian settlement of 1690.[31]

One further item caused more trouble. Queensberry had up his sleeve an Act imposing abjuration of the Pretender, similar to the one passed for England in King William's last days. Like some other business it was coded: what it meant was acceptance of the Hanoverian succession. Its passage might please powerful people in London but it would run counter to the preference among Scots for keeping the succession open, and was bound to reveal differences of opinion within the Court. Beyond that it would throw away a useful card in negotiations for Union; during the next few years Union and Hanoverian succession to an independent Scotland were viewed as viable alternatives, so there could be no point in confounding them now. An ally of Queensberry's, Sir James Murray of Philiphaugh, warned 'that such a step would carry us so far into measures of England about the succession, that they would become careless and indifferent about the Union'.[32] The Lord High Commissioner hesitated, wondering whether an Abjuration Act was such a good idea after all.

The hesitations were forestalled by Patrick Hume, Earl of Marchmont, Chancellor of Scotland and so, at least nominally, the senior officer of state. A stubborn, sanctimonious figure, he had won grim notoriety when his casting vote in the privy council sent the boy Aikenhead to the scaffold for blasphemy. Among the Ministers inherited by Anne, Marchmont was the staunchest Presbyterian and suspicious that Queensberry might subvert the settlement of 1690. Now he took it on himself to move the abjuration. Queensberry got wind of this beforehand and tackled the old sourpuss. He thought he had won a private agreement that, if the Chancellor were to receive a direct order from the Lord High Commissioner not to raise the matter, he would, out of loyalty to the Crown, obey – yet still be able to claim he had upheld his principles. He received the direct order, and at the next sitting moved the abjuration after all. It carried by four votes, 58 to 54. In this rump of the Parliament that was a huge defeat for the horrified Queensberry.

The truant opposition under Hamilton woke up to what was happening and threatened to come back into the chamber. Feelings ran so high that, to forestall a collapse of the Court party, Queensberry adjourned the sitting in haste on June 30, after just three weeks.[33] Hamilton, if unable to deliver a *coup de grâce*, could still feel pleased. Queensberry had tried to bluff his way through without concession to the Country party. Hamilton, aided by Marchmont's gaffe, called his bluff. The government of Scotland was humiliated and the nation at large found yet another grievance to nurse. Better still, a question mark remained hanging over the entire legality of the session.

Ministerial reshuffle was inevitable. Doddery Marchmont had to go. Trying to damage Queensberry, he dealt a bigger blow to his own faction of Presbyterians who would exert little further influence in the coming turmoil. In his place James Ogilvy, Lord Seafield, Secretary of State since 1696, won promotion to Chancellor. Lockhart said 'he was believed to be of loyal enough [that is, Jacobite] principles, but had so mean and selfish a soul, that he wanted both resolution and honesty enough to adhere to them, which evidently appeared from his changing sides so often, and cleaving to that party which he found rising'. In short, 'he was a blank sheet of paper, which the Court might fill up with what they pleased'.[34] Seafield was indeed committed to the Crown rather than to any faction, as a type of public servant which so far had had its finest hour in ruling Scotland for the absent James VI after 1603, *noblesse de robe* rather than *noblesse d'épée*; it had found no further scope, in such a furious nation, till now. The younger son of a minor peer, the Earl of Findlater, Seafield had received his own noble title for work well done as William of Orange's Solicitor-General. It was an official career in a proto-modern sense, as a sort of permanent secretary acting in the Scottish department with what composure could be mustered in the face of aristocratic mayhem.[35]

A contrast may be drawn with the figure who took over the vacated Secretaryship, George Mackenzie, Viscount Tarbat. According to Lockhart he was 'extremely maggoty and unsettled . . . never much to be relied on or valued', and to Burnet 'full of ambition . . . recommending himself to all sides and parties by turns'. Tarbat had once been a strong Tory, but profited from William's wish to employ experienced politicians of whatever hue; he served as Lord Clerk Register till 1696 and his dismissal for various rogueries. Now he made a comeback, a brief one in the event, at Anne's invitation and to Queensberry's displeasure.[36] The same constellation lit Tullibardine, soon to succeed to the dukedom of Atholl, into the vacant post of Lord Privy Seal. He had not got over his huff so far as even to attend the session of Parliament in June. Now, whatever Queensberry might say, Anne wished to show her eagerness to coax lost sheep back into the fold, especially if they enjoyed some standing among Presbyterian wolves, as both Tarbat and Tullibardine did. The whole amounted to an admission that if the government of Scotland was to be carried on at all there had to be at least a little understanding with people outside the Court. This was their intention, of course. It still could not add up to effective royal government.

೫

That grew clear as soon as the Court, its ranks thus strengthened somewhat, set off with the queen's blessing in quest of Union. When negotiations opened in London on November 18, she sent a message recommending 'an indissoluble union between the two nations which Her Majesty thinks the most likely means under heaven to establish the monarchy, secure the peace and increase the trade, wealth and happiness of both nations'. Queensberry, for the Scottish side, replied that Union would be 'highly advantageous for the peace and wealth of both kingdoms and a great security for the Protestant religion everywhere'. He stressed the 'sincere intentions' of his own delegation to 'advance this great design'.[37] He could speak of that with assurance because he had named them all, though indeed Seafield would have worked without prompting for a successful outcome.

But no matching response came from the English side, except from Robert Harley, well in with the new regime as for a third term he occupied the Speaker's chair of the House of Commons – a house which, however, he must have seen was less disposed to Union than the last. While the Tories owed their English victory that summer to Anne's manifest preference for them, it did not follow they would gratify her every wish. She expected them to act as a Court party, but by no means all wanted to. For her, Union meant the Scots' acquiescence in the Act of Settlement and the elimination of a potential foreign threat. Yet Tories had other priorities: they disliked the Scots as a Presbyterian and so a seditious nation. Typical of them was Sir Edward Seymour, MP for Exeter and a great figure in the West Country, said by Burnet to be 'the ablest man of his party'.[38] In 1700, hearing Union bruited abroad, he dismissed it with a brutal scoff that Scotland 'was a beggar, and whoever married a beggar could only expect a louse for a portion'. Neither he nor his fellows changed their minds now. Little more was to be expected of the Whigs. William's calls for Union they had backed but, having been sacked by Anne, they saw no reason to help her.

In fact the whole English membership of the commission appointed to negotiate between the two nations proved to be slack and indifferent. The Scots sometimes found they were the only ones to turn up to meetings. 'The Act for the Union', wrote a defensive official, Sir David Hume of Crossrigg, about the relevant Scottish legislation, 'is only a power enabling the queen to name commissioners to meet, treat and consult with the commissioners for England, and to set down their articles in duplicates, one for the queen, one for the Parliament of Scotland and two for the Parliament of England.'[39] But they never even got as far as setting down any articles.

After the opening speeches the two sides sank into a morass of argument about trade. At least they at once identified a central issue. Right through the coming negotiations – in both this first, abortive round and in the later, successful one – the English evinced not the slightest interest in any of the Scots' alternatives to an incorporating Union (or Union of Parliaments): limitations on the Crown, a federal system and so on. None could from England's point of view answer the purpose of the exercise, which was to dismantle any rival political authority in Scotland or indeed any possibility of it. So all attempts at compromise over the absolute supremacy of the Parliament at Westminster were to the English wholly immaterial, mere quibbling irritants.

Still, a sop to the Scots there had to be, otherwise Union would never happen. The one concession that might be dangled before them was free trade. It did not undermine the purpose of the exercise. It would simply admit Scots to the existing closed English system of trade which the commissioners from Westminster meant for their part to maintain (they could not know that a child of Union, Adam Smith of Kirkcaldy, would eventually argue it out of existence). Such a system could only be centrally regulated. That required a single Parliament.

This logic did not escape the serpentine Queensberry, who had at all events to get any deal past the Scots Parliament. There the Country party wanted free trade with England or at least freedom of trade from English interference, while the Jacobites, though having quite different ends in view, at least recognised the value of economic grievance as something to exploit. At a minimum, both parties wished to make sure Darien could never happen again, in the doubtless unlikely event that Scots should try to set up a second emporium where trade took precedence over the flag (Singapore and Hong Kong lay far in the future). Yet a good number of the English, in their wonderful way, could not grasp the Scots' logic. Certain commissioners seemed bemused at the idea of freedom of trade with Scotland. It might be allowed across the border, they conceded, but there could be no question of extending it across the ocean: 'The plantations are the property of Englishmen and . . . this trade is of so great a consequence and so beneficial as not to be communicated as it is proposed till all other particulars which shall be thought necessary to this union be adjusted.'[40] What the Scots wanted to put first the English preferred to leave to last, presumably till they had pared away at the principle of it in the small print of any deal.

℘

To this day historians debate the heated, because big, question how far economics drove the Union of 1707 in some deterministic fashion. By the turn of the eighteenth century the question already had 100 years of background behind it. After 1603 Scots, or strictly the *post-nati* born later than that date, were put on the same terms as Englishmen in living, working, owning property, buying and selling in all dominions of James VI and I, on both sides of the border and ocean. Evidence that the freedom worked for trade comes in reports of Scottish ships in America not long after the English settlements had been founded there; the first known cargo of tobacco entered the Firth of Clyde in 1640, to be seized as prize (and no doubt smoked) by Scots in arms against Charles I. Later the Navigation Acts, passed during the Cromwellian Union of Scotland with England, in effect invited Scots into the transatlantic traffic by restricting colonial commerce to British shipping, with a particular view to shutting out the Dutch who so far had engrossed much of the world's carrying trade. Though the advantages could scarcely be exploited in a Scotland ravaged by war and occupation, she still felt sorry to lose them after she regained her independence with the Restoration of 1660.

In England the restrictive economic policy known as mercantilism was then adopted. It set up a closed trading system between mother country and colonies, in imitation of other imperial powers, Spain in particular. In 1661 the Parliament at Westminster passed a new Act which treated Scots as foreigners and banned their ships from this system. They and their commercial partners in the plantations protested but the government in London would not be moved. It even tried to twist a strict construction out of its Act by which Scots, not being English subjects, would on English territory be debarred from business as merchants and factors as well, since such people only attracted Scottish ships. The line of attack suggests Scots were already engaged in transatlantic traffic.[41] In various forms that dispute between the two nations grumbled on, to be revived by Darien. The Scots claimed free trade, not without legal precedent; the English in their spite denied it.

What was the state of Scottish trade under these varying but usually unfavourable conditions? Nobody, least of all Scots, could be impressed with it. Other northern peoples, Dutch, English and French, had risen to challenge the command of intercontinental traffic established by Spaniards and Portuguese in the age of discoveries. Scots lagged far behind. Of the successful rivals they most liked and admired the Dutch, both being sworn nations of the Lord with a Calvinist faith and Protestant ethic. The affinity rested on old links across the sea. Ties of interest had become bonds of blood in Scots-Dutch families: the chiefs of Clan Mackay in the military service of the Prince of Orange, the banking dynasty of Hope migrant from Edinburgh to Amsterdam, the de Groots settled (at John o' Groats) on the northernmost coast of Great Britain, the burgesses of Dysart and Flushing who called themselves Black in the one and Zwart in the other. The Dutch, if a small nation too, had made themselves the leading economic power in Europe. Scots often wondered why God in his inscrutable purposes did not show the same favour to their own, if anything more deserving case. Only slowly did they come to see in the worldly wealth of the Dutch the operation not so much of divine favour as of economic choices. William Alexander, founder of Scotland's first and unsuccessful colony of Nova Scotia in the 1620s, had praised their spirit of enterprise. William Paterson, trying to woo them to Darien at the end of the century, put their good fortune down to 'generous principles of ease, freedom and security, which they have prudently opposed to the heavy restrictions, restraints and impositions of others'.[42]

There was indeed a lot for the Scots to learn from the Dutch. Both nations faced the challenges of nature in a hostile environment. The Dutch reclaimed land from the sea and exploited it with a high degree of social commitment and organisation. By contrast, the Scots felt little apparent desire to win from their bogs even quite accessible land, and their farming remained backward. As for manufactures, the Dutch

43

specialised and adopted a division of labour. The Scots saw no great need to follow suit: most of what they produced was produced by other countries too, usually in better quality, while their working practices had scarcely moved on from individual craft towards industrial production. Their resources of raw materials, later of huge importance, remained largely irrelevant for the time being. A special reason for Dutch success was prowess in navigation, which in turn arose out of skill in fishing, but most Scots were land-lubbers, even in a country lapped by the briny along every bourne but the 50 miles of English frontier. The North Sea formed a crossroads leading from and to the cities of London, Amsterdam or Hamburg, a channel of exchange for capital, enterprise and prosperity; Edinburgh lay in a backwater.

One caveat needing to be entered is that wealth gave no guarantee of political independence amid the onset of imperialism in this era. However rich, ancient and ingenious a city or the city-state it formed or the kingdom it belonged to, each could be eclipsed by more potent and aggressive political power, as in the Spanish Netherlands (modern Belgium), in Catalonia, in the petty principalities of Italy and Germany. The Dutch proved the exception, defying their circumstances. Their fortitude was above praise and won its just deserts, yet did not in the long run save them from the real limitations in the size and resources of their state. By the end of their heroic age they were, in political terms, back where they had started, prosperous but able to vindicate their independence only by ceaseless struggle – for which in the event they cared less and less. All this, *a fortiori*, throws light on the Scots' political inability to promote their economic interests in the conditions of the age.

Yet the Scottish economy does seem to have been advancing a bit, so as at least to rise above a level of bare subsistence. While traditional agriculture still prevailed, a few landowners improved their husbandry. Merchants began to export not only products of the soil but also simple manufactures such as linen. Contacts abroad widened, with a certain development of old trades to the Low Countries, to the Baltic region and to France, and through the numbers of Scots going to complete a European education in law, medicine or theology, sometimes picking up new commercial ideas from countries they got to know. Even so, progress had been slow, shaky and confined to a small class of merchants in the burghs.

In the overwhelming majority Scots still lived on the land by simple pastoral farming and payment of rents in kind. In good years they could produce a surplus for export but in bad years food had to be imported or else, from time to time, they starved. While grain was the main commodity, wool also figured along with animal hides and cured fish. Other products of nature might allow the bonds of subsistence to be loosened a little. An expansion of coal-mining after 1660 prompted construction of new harbours for colliers at Methil in Fife, Port Seton in East Lothian and Saltcoats in Ayrshire. As for manufactures, Scots in both countryside and burgh made for themselves what they needed by way of textiles. In some goods, such as metalwork, craftsmen reached higher standards but otherwise imports remained necessary. A deficit on the balance of payments was often a problem. Money minted in Scotland tended to leave. Most coinage circulating in the country was foreign.

At least an inkling of advance came in the mentality of Scots, no longer content to leave their livelihoods to divine favour but seeking means to better themselves by their own efforts. When the future James VII arrived in 1681 to rule Scotland, one of his initiatives was to call a conference of merchants at Holyrood and with them deliberate for the first time on an economic policy. They considered, but rejected, free trade. Instead they opted for giving Scotland a mercantilist system of her own. It was meant to force domestic industrial development by banning imports of foreign manufactured goods. This proved to be a far-fetched notion. On the one hand joint-stock companies set up with official backing, such as that at Newmills near Haddington to make cloth, never prospered because they relied on government for orders and faded away once these flagged. On the other hand, Scots suffered much more by retaliation from foreign countries than they gained from protection of their own infant industries.

Yet motion, even in as sluggish an economy as this, did not have to come from the state. There were different forces eating away at the antiquated privilege of royal burghs, for example. Their charters supposedly granted a monopoly of foreign trade to their burgesses, but this became ever harder to maintain against other Scots shut out but wanting a cut of it. In or about 1700 the Parliament heard petitions for the rules to be relaxed from, among others, the Earl of Melville who had sail-cloth made on his estate in Fife; from William Morrison of Prestongrange who went in for manufacture of glass; from John Udny in Aberdeenshire who asked to be granted free trade to and from his estate with its convenient haven at the mouth of the River Ythan; and so on.[43] Historians blinkered by modern assumptions tend to overlook that in its early stages industry did not have to be urban. Even the few remains of those early stages

45

extant in Scotland – none, unfortunately, from the period of the Union – all the same show at Bonawe amid the mountains of Argyll or at New Lanark on the bucolic upper reaches of the River Clyde that industry could on the contrary be rural. Progressive landowners carried on promoting industry on their estates right up to the time when great cities overbore it in the nineteenth century.

To royal burghs, too, the trade between hinterland and outside world might be more important than any manufacture within their regalities, that is to say, within their chartered bounds. In the corporations of most the merchants dominated the craftsmen, as in Edinburgh where the grand Merchant Company lorded it over the guilds, deigning to show respect only for the goldsmiths. In later times the company grew more charitable and took under its wing several schools, one of which is still today named after George Watson, its founder and benefactor. Born into an enterprising family, he received a professional education, partly in the Dutch Republic. It covered the learned and the practical alike, from mathematics and languages to bookkeeping, trading practice and the law of commerce. All this, together with the personal contacts Watson forged early on, stood him in good stead later as a successful businessman eager at the last to pass the fruits of his experience on to posterity. Trade, then, was not merely a matter of filthy lucre but fertilised Scottish life in general. On both grounds landed families took it up too. Some bought Dutch paintings or similar luxuries for their castles and houses, yet others ran commercial outfits, such as the family of Wemyss in Fife, who exported coal in industrial quantities to Scandinavia and to the Netherlands.

International traffic thus expanded also from lesser ports such as Aberdeen, Dundee, Montrose and Perth, even from small burghs in the West with little more than a harbour and a few warehouses for the trade to Ireland. In Aberdeen, more than thirty merchants were handling foreign shipments in the 1690s, as were about ten apiece from Montrose and Dundee. Lerwick on Shetland offers an example of a port lacking the privilege of a royal burgh which yet, with its sheltered anchorage, developed out of an original Cromwellian fortification by supplying their wants to the Dutch boats which fished the nearby waters.

Glasgow was the fastest growing port in Scotland and by the end of the seventeenth century her second city. Here, rather exceptionally, manufactures did link straight into trade after an oceanic haven with deep water, deeper anyway than the shallow moorings at the Broomielaw next to the medieval burgh, was built at Port Glasgow down the Clyde in

1670. Exports of fish or coal went to British destinations, but imports of tobacco already came from America and something had to be sent back in exchange. Glaswegians started to make soap, refine sugar and distil rum, then weave anything from woollens to ships' ropes: the foundation of their first industrial revolution in the next century. Edinburgh boasted more varied resources but followed in the start of manufacturing. This first arose in suburbs, with a paper-factory at Dalry and glassworks at Leith: in others words, outside the regality in the county of Midlothian and so, strictly speaking, in a rural rather than urban setting. At the same time, while bigger burghs had the diversity to adapt to economic crisis, some smaller ones – as in Fife – went into a decline in the event terminal. On no single example should too much weight be laid, for Scotland did not constitute a single national economy but comprised discrete regional units of diverse character rather impervious to muddled attempts at central policy.[44]

All the same, the Parliament responded to the nation's creeping economic evolution by 1672 when, against bitter opposition from the royal burghs, it slashed away slices of their trading monopoly. Further legislative fiddling after 1688, restoring some privileges but making more exceptions to them, did not much alter the balance: the Revolution cannot be presented in Marxist terms as a victory for one economic interest over another. By now the export of all native commodities, mainly agricultural but including minerals such as coal and salt as well, was free to everyone. Non-royal burghs, usually no more than villages with a licence to hold a market, could both export their own products and import raw materials or implements needed to make them. Royal burghs held on to not much beyond a right to import luxuries: notably claret, traditional drink of the lairds, along with fine textiles and metalwork, weapons and machines, glass, paper, toys, paint, soap, sugar and spices. These superior goods were often blamed for the deficits on the balance of payments – another source of pressure against the privilege of royal burghs.

❧

For economic determinists the oddest fact about Scotland at the turn of the eighteenth century must be that the strongest growth probably came in the poorest region, the Highlands. About half the population of Scotland lived there but it contained no burghs except Inverness at one extremity and Campbeltown at the other (and this a creation of the Earl of Argyll only in 1700). The people carried on with their ancestral way of life, organised in lawless clans. But the social structure was just starting to change. Chiefs knew something of the wider world: they had to go and vouch for their good behaviour in Edinburgh every year, while some got an education abroad. Nor were all clansmen bound to hill and glen, as the region generated a surplus of fighting men for mercenary service in Europe. If they survived they could bear their booty back, with tales of how they won it to while away long winter's evenings in the crofts.

The one non-human product that might be traded from the Highlands was cattle, traditionally raided rather than traded. The earliest Gaelic literature, the Ulster Cycle, celebrated cattle-raiding, and it was celebrated yet in song and story as worthy of a Highland warrior. The first MacDonald on Skye to take up droving of cattle to the Lowlands in the late sixteenth century had been Donald MacIain MacDonald of Castle Camus, his clan's fiercest warrior, famous for his great sword Cuig Mharg. His kin despised his commercial ventures.

A century on and the gentlemen of the clan were directing movements of vast droves of beasts which swam, nose tied to tail, from island to mainland in a new southward traffic which had become the motor of the Highland economy. The market extended at the trysts where cattle went to be bought and sold, spreading down from Muir of Ord to Brechin to Crieff and finally, in the eighteenth century, to Falkirk. They introduced money into the Highland economy for the first time on any scale. The proceeds became vital for purchases of grain and meal in a region barely able to feed itself. Once cash arrived, it might be used in other exchanges among Gaels, for dowries or rents. Money follows money, and to chiefs who had some, or could lay claim to some, Lowlanders might extend credit. So it was possible to enjoy from cattle a stream of income, a rare and precious thing to a chief. He might indulge in the intrigues or pleasures of Edinburgh, even of London, and pursue profit or treason in Europe.

Scottish resources were everywhere scarce but the north began to make better use of them by simple dint of putting to work the hands often idle in a system of bare subsistence: there were seasons when nobody worked in the Highlands because there was nothing to do.[45] Two chiefs offer examples of the trend, the Marquis of Breadalbane, head of the big sept of Clan Campbell in western Perthshire, and Cameron of Lochiel, on his lands round Fort William. Breadalbane was embroiled in the politics of the Revolution and later in the Jacobite rising of 1715. He financed his plots out of sawmills, worked by his clansmen's forced labour, to which he floated timber down river and loch, then sent the finished product on to Lowland towns or even to shipyards of the English navy. When Cameron of Lochiel marched off to join Claverhouse in 1689 he left behind at his estate of Achnacarry on Loch Arkaig a blast-furnace which made and sold good iron; it was destroyed in the subsequent warfare. Breadalbane proved often an equivocal, Lochiel always a steadfast Jacobite, but their loyalties put up no bar to a keen part in improvement. Though in the older Scottish historiography an equation of Whigs with progress and of Jacobites with reaction is found, this does not hold true for the Highland economy.

෴

Nor indeed does it hold true for the Lowland economy. Lockhart of Carnwath not only made acute observations of events but also challenged assumptions about what it meant to be a Jacobite. Legends picture those most loyal to the House of Stewart as poor but pugnacious lairds laden with debt, suspicious of businessmen and townsmen in general, hostile to all novelty, agricultural, technological or religious, unwilling even to talk to, let alone mix genes with, families of other commitments or connections. Lockhart, however, was an improving landlord who also exploited coal beneath his estate, built himself a new seat in modern style and married into the English Whig aristocracy. The economic and social determinism beloved of Scottish historians falls down in the face of Lockhart.[46]

Again, John Erskine of Alva, while disliking the English, admired much of what he saw them doing across the border. He was struck by the good husbandry that had turned theirs into a green and pleasant land, so different from a Caledonia still stern and wild. For his own estate Erskine drew up 'a handsome plan of policy'. His peasants thought it bad, but more especially mad, to do such odd things to the ground from which they had to wrest, in year after year of racking toil, a livelihood for themselves and their families. Erskine set out by imitating the practice of enclosure, of turning peasants' strips and common grazings into fields. He planted trees and grass, growth of which they had always left to nature. Beneath saplings, over green shoots, he scattered millions of tiny seeds of red clover, humble herbage never seen before in Scotland. Peasants scoffed at his eccentricity and at his English weeds, which produced hay so strange-looking that they refused to believe any beast would eat it. What they never knew was that red clover drew nitrogen into the soil and made it much more fertile. Erskine did not stop at agriculture. He knew there was coal in the Ochil Hills and started to mine it. In an era when commodities in bulk had to be carried by water, he built a canal, among the earliest in Scotland, between his workings and the River Devon, which leads into the Firth of Forth and so to the North Sea. He also found silver on his estate. He used it to buy his way out of the trouble he got into with the government for his Jacobitism.

By such individual initiatives there began a process of improvement, first agricultural, then industrial, which would turn much of Scotland into a green and pleasant land too, and much of the rest into a black and smoky one. For pioneers it was expensive, and in Erskine's case not profitable. It would in the end yield higher rents from his estate, yet only his creditors benefited because he had meanwhile gone bankrupt. An admirer of his courage later wrote that 'this gentleman may be regarded as the prototype of those men of speculation who of late years have done some good and much mischief to their country, without benefiting themselves or their families'.

Many Scots were moved by the urge for improvement, yet at the turn of the eighteenth century most felt frustrated. Their economy had shown some small developments and the capacity to recover from war, famine, plague and oppression. The consensus among them was that trade, the tide bearing along the economies of England and the Netherlands, would carry Scotland onwards and upwards too. But her flow of trade, if not quite stagnating, ran in torpid channels which did not look like flushing in the short term. Actually the trade floated on a sensible exchange of native agricultural and mining products for those of different climates or more advanced manufacture. In that, Scotland was a typical country of north-western Europe, at once self-contained and part of an international economy. Yet the very peaks of this modest prosperity were submerged by the flood of misfortunes in King William's seven ill years. To rise above the level of another such deluge Scots needed more strenuous aspirations and more solid achievements.

એ

Many Scots came forward with ideas, but two stand out. William Paterson, survivor of Darien, had no system of economics yet the weight of his views seems to come down on the side of free trade: that, at any rate, is how he has been represented in later literature.[47] In his prospectus for the ill-fated colony in Central America, he called for the breaking of mercantilism when he argued that:

> Trade will increase trade, and money will beget money, and the trading world shall need no more to want work for their hands, but will rather want hands for their work. Thus, this door of the seas and the key of the universe, with anything of a sort of reasonable management, will of course enable the proprietors to give laws to both oceans and to become arbitrators of the commercial world without being liable to the fatigues, expenses and dangers, or contracting the guilt and blood of Alexander and Caesar.

All the same, it is hard to say quite what Scots of the time meant by free trade. The same man might demand free trade with one breath and monopoly or privilege with the next. The fact was that economic ideas had not yet been systematised. But the kernel of liberal concepts can be discerned in Scotland in this period about the turn of the eighteenth century.

A different mode of thinking is represented in John Law. While Paterson lost influence by the failure of Darien, Law would gain it – though in 1702 he was still lurking in France, where he had fled after killing a man in a duel. He supported himself from gambling and in his spare time originated modern ideas about credit, in its distinction from capital. He did not, by today's theories, get the distinction quite right but he saw it was there. According to the general assumption of mercantilists, money equated to precious metal. So they recommended hoarding gold and silver. Law, reversing the alchemist's role, proposed to transmute solid matter into liquid assets at the service of new economic purposes, to enlarge exchanges, prompt division of labour, foster production, create demand not only for goods but also for itself. Precious metal was always in short supply. Law thought it better to turn into capital the other main asset held by men of property, their estates. In practical terms, this meant a land-bank. Then, with secured finance available for trade, Scotland could start to catch up with others, not least through lower costs: 'By a greater quantity of money and oeconomy, the Dutch monopolise the trades of carriage even from the English. Scotland has a very inconsiderable trade, because she has but a very small part of the money.'[48] The point was that she need not be condemned to poverty just because she had no gold or silver.

Scotland as yet seemed an unlikely candidate for economic progress. Its internal engines had been stoked, all the same. Scots began to exploit their resources better, stimulated by easy access to oceanic routes, but also by privation, to name just two of many forces at work. And trade was becoming vital to them. They wanted it to become more vital still. They opened their country to foreign products, techniques and ideas, essential elements in their agricultural, then commercial, then industrial revolutions. If often hampered by discord, famine and war, they reached the point of being able to aim to develop their economy.

All this ought to have gratified Queen Anne. On December 14, hearing that the negotiations for Union between the Scots and the English were getting bogged down, she waddled along to Parliament to find out from the commissioners what was holding things up:

> I am so fully persuaded that the Union of my two kingdoms will prove the happiness of both and render the island more formidable than it has been in ages past that I wish their treaty may be brought to a good and speedy conclusion. I am come to know what progress you have made in it, and I do assure you that nothing shall be wanting on my part to bring it to perfection.

Officials cleared their throats, shuffled their papers and admitted that the progress had been slow, though if she wished they could read out to her the proposals lying on the table. 'And the same were read accordingly,' says the record of the meeting, 'after reading whereof Her Majesty went away.'[49]

CHAPTER 2

∾

1703

*Glasgow from the south, Scotland's transatlantic port and
Calvinist stronghold*

'Much stumbled'

∾

On the evening probably of September 24, 1703,[1] William Douglas, Duke of Queensberry, Her Majesty's Lord High Commissioner in Scotland, sat waiting at his *hôtel particulier* in the Canongate, the most elegant residence on that street running down from the Nethergate of Edinburgh to the Palace of Holyroodhouse. He had a month earlier received an intriguing letter from two supporters, Archibald Campbell, Duke of Argyll, and George Melville, Earl of Leven, telling him how a Scotsman just arrived in London from Paris was offering information of use to the Crown and would hand it to Queensberry in person if provided with a safe-conduct for the journey north. He little trusted Argyll or Leven but they sat all three in the same boat, trying to run the royal government of Scotland against the odds. One of their methods was to play dirty tricks on their numberless foes. The letter reeked of opportunities for that.

The Lord High Commissioner had already informed his sovereign of the letter and how he received it, without mentioning any names. Queen Anne told him to go ahead and meet the mysterious stranger who, however, set prior conditions. He asked for his identity to be kept secret and for a pardon to be guaranteed to him for offences he had already committed or might in future commit, together with the grant of an estate large enough to maintain him. Queensberry replied that he could issue a pass to Scotland and pay for valuable intelligence, but not promise anything else. The furtive supplicant was apparently satisfied. He turned up at Queensberry House on the appointed day. His name was Simon Fraser, an ugly young man aged twenty-seven. The Lord High Commissioner lost no time to report back on their conversation. He began: 'I presumed lately to acquaint your Majesty that I had seen some letters from a gentleman come from France, in which he speaks with some assurance of overturning the government here . . .'.[2]

The business seemed serious, then, though overturning the government of Scotland was not the sole purpose of Fraser's visit to its head. Whether he did during his talk with Queensberry mention the matter actually uppermost in his mind can never be known. This was his claim to the title of Lord Lovat, which carried with it the chieftaincy of his clan, a big one with territory strategically disposed round the northern end of Loch Ness and the shores of the Beauly Firth near Inverness. For a decade Clan Fraser had been in crisis, with weak leadership and uncertain succession to the chieftaincy, which could go only through the male line. Hugh Fraser, ninth Lord Lovat, was a feckless fellow who on his death in 1696 left no sons, but a daughter Amelia. Simon's father, Thomas Fraser of Beaufort, then Simon himself, were the next legitimate heirs. Simon sought Amelia for a bride yet she eluded his clutches only to fall into the hands of the Mackenzies, an expansionist rival clan with territory to the north and west. She was married off to a nephew of their chief, George, Earl of Cromartie. By open violence and legal chicanery the Mackenzies steadily purloined the Frasers' property and power.

Nothing daunted, and with the support of many gentlemen of his clan, Simon Fraser kidnapped Amelia's mother and forcibly married her instead, since she as the relict of the last undoubted chief equally suited his purpose. The Dowager Lady Lovat had been born, however, into the House of Atholl. She was the sister of the present Lord Privy Seal in the government of Scotland, John Murray, Duke of Atholl, who assumed his title in 1703. His house maintained on its lands a private regiment, still in existence today, where Fraser had earlier served as an officer. At that time he stood on cordial terms with Atholl: the pair of them sought together to settle the affairs of Clan Fraser in advance of the crisis bound to break on the death of the ninth Lord Lovat.

Now, by any standards, Simon Fraser abused that old acquaintance and trust. Since he could not be sure of the dowager's consent to a proposal of marriage, he raped her. At his later trial *in absentia* there appeared Lady Lovat's servant, sixteen-year-old Amelie Rioch. She gave evidence how she had been summoned at two o'clock in the morning to assist as her swooning mistress, with hair and clothes already disordered, was stripped naked. A gentleman of the clan held her up while Fraser tore at her petticoats. They turned her face down on the bed and pulled her arms above her head so that another henchman could slit her buckram stays with his dirk, while a piper played to drown her screams. Then Simon had his evil way with her. All this went on in a chamber full of lairds and servants. True, some of them offered a different interpretation of the scene. It was supposed to represent authentic Highland tradition, including the custom that after a wedding the guests should accompany the happy couple to the bedroom amid much suggestive horseplay. Simon might have overdone it, but he was just that kind of guy. Now, at any rate, he and Lady Lovat lived together as man and wife, she spurning appeals to return to her ancestral home.

That did not assuage the wrath of the House of Atholl. Craftier than most clans, it seldom resorted to violence but it did now mount a relentless legal offensive against Fraser. This finished with his being convicted in the Court of Justiciary, the highest criminal instance, and sentenced to death. He went into hiding on Skye where, just by the by, he assumed for himself the title of Lord Lovat when his father passed away in 1699. After a year of skulking he managed to obtain a pardon from King William through the good offices of the royal chaplain, the Revd William Carstares, and the Duke of Argyll, an enemy of Atholl. When the king died, Fraser all the same crossed to France to be on the safe side; like many Scots he had out of prudence kept in touch with the Jacobite court at St Germain.

 confidence confidence confidence

Since the death of James VII in 1701 that down-at-heel court had been dominated by the widowed Queen Mary of Modena and a ladies' circle of fervent but gloomy piety soon seeking, for example, to get the late king canonised for his Christian resignation in exile. Already, by his intercession, a tumour on the face of a tailor's wife had vanished, a nun had been cured of cancer of the uterus and cripples had stood up straight when they thought of him at the elevation of the host.[3] But somehow the miracles were never to be of sufficient quantity or quality to clinch the king's sainthood.

All this devotion sat uneasily with the activities of the numerous rogues who prowled round St Germain, their desperate hopes set on restoring the legitimate line of Stewarts. Fraser joined them. He sniffed the wind and converted to Catholicism. Through the pious ladies he came into contact with Madame de Maintenon, once the mistress, now the morganatic wife of Louis XIV. She assessed Fraser, too truly, as *un homme ravissant*. He was putting himself into a position to reach still higher and, with his inborn effrontery, never hesitated to do so. He accosted not only the ladies of the Court but also the Protector of the English Nation at Rome and pensioner of France, Cardinal Filippo Antonio Gualterio, the Archbishop of Paris, Cardinal Louis-Antoine de Noailles, and the French Foreign Minister, Jean-Baptiste Colbert, Marquis de Torcy. Fraser broached the further acquaintance, through shared military interests, of James Stewart, Duke of Berwick, the illegitimate son of James VII and Arabella Churchill (thus a nephew of her brother John, Duke of Marlborough) who had grown up into one of the Bourbons' best generals. Fraser also flattered with a *faux-naïf* fervour for fortification the world's greatest expert on it, Sébastien de Prestre, Marquis de Vauban, who in person demonstrated to him how the walls of Fort William could be scaled by means of folding ladders. Fraser might have been an ill-favoured scoundrel, but he could turn on the charm like a tap.

What Fraser sought above all was an audience of Louis XIV – a ticklish matter, because the king did not usually deign to receive foreigners. The bait dangled before him was Fraser's claim to have come over as unofficial ambassador for compatriots eager to restore the Stewarts by waging war against England with French help. The bait was bitten and the crafty Scots blade appeared before the haughty Sun King. At his most irrepressible, Fraser began by recalling the Auld Alliance and 'observing that the Scotch, assisted by the French, had frequently beaten the English, and that, if they were now honoured with the protection of the greatest king that had ever filled the throne of France, they would not certainly be less successful than they had been in former instances'. Fraser proposed a novel Jacobite strategy of Highland revolt in tandem with French invasion. The resources he had to offer – 1,200 clansmen – might have looked a trifle meagre but they could readily link up with any army the king should care to send.

At Versailles nobody had so far spared a thought for faraway Scotland. Yet with the first phase of the War of the Spanish Succession being fought out in Flanders, where the grand alliance against Louis XIV could most easily concentrate its forces, the king saw the advantage of diversionary attacks. Scotland then appeared to him an obvious target with her long list of anti-English grievances and her potential welcome for foreign intervention to redress them. The French interest in Scotland thus awakened would persist right through the first half of the eighteenth century. So Louis XIV's reply to Fraser was a gracious one, to the effect that he and the whole French nation 'had their hearts unfeignedly Scottish and that, since Lord Lovat had been chosen to represent the whole body of loyal Scots, he desired to be understood as from that moment renewing with him all ancient alliances between the two nations'. He promised to supply Highland rebels with the reinforcements of troops and the supplies of money or of anything else they would need to beat the Englsh. Later he sent to let Mary of Modena know he was pleased with the audience, yet 'entreating her at the same time never again to demand of him a private audience with any of her subjects, since he had at no other time exposed his person in that manner to any foreigner'.[4]

Of course Louis had Fraser checked out, though not so far as to reveal much to his disfavour. At the Foreign Ministry, Torcy employed agents from the British Isles including Colonel Nathaniel Hooke, an Irishman who knew the Scots well. He had been educated for the Protestant ministry at the University of Glasgow and there imbibed the Covenanting fervour of the West of Scotland so far as to rush off with fellow students in 1685 to join the first rebellion against James VII. He soon repented of this youthful folly, begged and won pardon, but then went further and became a Roman Catholic – just in time for the Revolution, which put him back in clink at the Tower of London with other loyalists, including the current Duke of Hamilton. Hooke again appeared in Scotland with Bluidy Clavers before returning to Ireland to fight on the losing side at the Battle of the Boyne. He was one of the 'wild geese' of 1691, the 12,000 Jacobites exiled by the Treaty of Limerick.[5] Having meanwhile married and settled in France, except for the foreign tours of duty Torcy sent him on, he came before the king's *conseil d'en haut* in February 1703 to read a paper commissioned from him concerning the place of Scotland in a Europe again at war.

❧

The European powers had been continually fighting one another throughout the seventeenth century. Even after the most horrible and devastating of these conflicts, the Thirty Years' War, ended in exhaustion with the Peace of Westphalia in 1648, the outbreaks recurred. There were twenty-two more up to the Treaty of Utrecht which concluded the War of the Spanish Succession in 1713. The main source of the belligerence lay in the ambitions of France: she took part in seven of the wars and started five of them.[6] They made her the dominant power in Europe, remoulding the political configuration of the Continent in her own interests with whatever aggression it took. Through military and naval expansion, organised by Vauban and financed by Torcy's father, Jean-Baptiste Colbert, the fair face of France herself was remoulded.[7] She stood now protected by a chain of 160 forts along her frontiers, with arsenals and barracks in every big town. She developed into a power as much at sea as on land, with a navy of 230 ships (more than England could boast in the late seventeenth century), a new base at Rochefort, fortified ports at Brest, Le Havre, Calais and Dunkirk, all supplied with means and men by naval dockyards and schools. Military service was becoming part of French life, not in the rough-and-ready way of the old feudal levies but in a highly disciplined fashion which drilled and trained men into regimental automatons so that technical innovations such as the flintlock and the bayonet could at their hands attain a maximum of deadly effect. France had both a professional army and a militia, 500,000 soldiers altogether: the first force on a modern scale.

It cost a great deal of money, not only in France but also in other European states wanting or needing to follow her example. In those which supported absolutism with standing armies (France, Prussia, Sweden, Denmark and Russia) military spending absorbed the vast bulk of revenue. Yet parliamentary England hardly presented a contrast. Her expenditure brought about the creation of an elaborate fiscal apparatus. It demanded efficient collection of taxes, prompting financial reform and the formation of a professional bureaucracy, hallmark of modern government. Current revenue was even so never enough, and huge debts had to be run up. They more than doubled from 1697 to 1713, in their turn requiring new instruments and markets for raising or servicing the debts, so laying the foundation of London's financial future. Perhaps as a commercial nation England would have followed this development anyway, but war drove it pell-mell.

The manpower of the English armed forces reached 117,000 during the Nine Years' War of 1688–97, divided between the army and the navy in the proportion of nearly two to one. During the War of the Spanish Succession after 1702 the number of men under arms rose to 136,000, with most of the expansion in the army. Naval spending went not so much to recruitment as to construction of a more versatile fleet, which grew from 173 ships in 1688 to 247 in 1714. In essence the royal navy was equipping itself for that broader range of tasks it would assume with its coming role in expansion and defence of the British Empire. But for now England's focus lay in Europe. She took part in continental politics as if the Channel did not exist. She had changed her role from being, under Charles II, a rather unreliable ally of France to setting, under William of Orange, the absolute priority of defeating French attempts at continental hegemony.

This realignment continued into the reign of Queen Anne. The diplomacy of Marlborough had already built the grand alliance with Austria and the Dutch Republic against the Bourbons' prospective unification of France and Spain when in 1702, returning to his higher vocation as a general, he set off on campaign as soon as war broke out again. Before long it spread: Bavaria joined the French side, Portugal and Savoy the allies. For a while the strategic situation looked awkward. The Austrian armies were deployed in the Rhineland and in Italy. Bavarian entry into the conflict threatened their lines of supply. Yet it was difficult for Marlborough to come to their aid when his Dutch allies feared to move away from the Low Countries in case their own territory should be exposed to sorties from the French fortresses on its frontier. He showed these were not so awesome as they seemed. He stormed Liège and besieged others. Then he planned to strike at the French from the rear as they faced the Austrians on the River Rhine.

Scotland's role in the high politics and military strategies of Europe was trifling. Her army had an establishment of 3,000 with actual manpower closer to 2,000, as we know from Hooke's efficient spying.[8] Her navy boasted three frigates. A state so weak could do nothing better. It had no debt because it had no means of raising debt, let alone of redeeming it. It was indeed almost incapable of collecting revenue, thanks to the antics of the Scots Parliament. What revenue came in soon vanished: the Scottish state, with many mouths to feed, and those that were fed only greedy for more than a fair share, found nothing to spare for any greater public purpose, even one so fundamental as defence of the realm. The Chancellor, the Earl of Seafield, wrote that 'nothing is more disobliging to the generality of an unmonied nation than to see new men become rich by sucking in the public money, as they have done since the Revolution; most of those employed since having doubled or tripled their estates'.[9] He wanted official salaries cut, but nothing seems to have come of this.

Scottish civil society suffered twice over because in the eighteenth – as in the twenty-first century – it was often military expenditure that drove civilian investment too, with transfers of technology from warlike to peaceful purposes. Ships, guns and explosives all stood in the scientific vanguard in 1700. Yet no ocean-going ships were built in Scotland, only small fishing smacks and rowing boats; the three frigates of the navy had been constructed on the River Thames. Like Peter the Great of Russia, some Scots thought to import expertise by attracting craftsmen from the Dutch and English shipyards. But whereas the Czar just commanded this to happen, a Scottish state hardly able to afford any ships was not in a position to see that industrial skills would be rewarded. When the Company of Scotland needed vessels for its expeditions, it went to Hamburg and Rotterdam. Nor could the company find any Scots able to make cannon, small arms or ammunition of an acceptable quality. Even its gunpowder came from Holland.

It was not as if Scots had turned pacifist, or shown reluctance to fight for their country. Their latest, bitter civil war had ended only a decade before. Their young men served as mercenary recruits to the English, French, Dutch and other armies. But the Scottish state remained impotent to harness the martial spirit of the nation. Its mere size could not have been the reason – the Dutch Republic achieved the highest military spending per head in Europe. It was rather a matter of failure in the functioning of the state. The Scots ought not to be blamed for this: their state under James VI, only a century before, was if anything an advanced one in its small way. But meanwhile it had collapsed on one occasion and on others become the object of misrule, not to say studied malice, from its monarchs. No wonder the Scottish state was now a ruin, or at best a throwback to an earlier epoch, trailing far behind the advances induced by military revolution elsewhere.

Worse still, the turn of the eighteenth century was a testing time for all European states, the overture to an era of intense competition among them, of a classic war of all against all, when old states went under and new states arose. An outcome in favour of the large ones was not in every case a foregone conclusion. Prussia sprang fully armed from bits of the broad but sometimes barren stretches of the North German Plain. Yet Sweden, a great power in the mid-seventeenth century, was robbed of her Baltic territories by Russia and sank into insignificance. The lesser peoples of Europe, with an equivocal statehood or none, came under particular pressure. The Catalans lost their medieval liberties to the Bourbons. Hungary, emerging from Ottoman thraldom, protested in vain at passing instead under the Habsburgs. On the whole, it was the small nations that fared worse out of all this.

To survive, states had to set clear priorities. For France that meant security to the north and east, where she possessed no historic natural frontiers: an advance to the Rhine, then, already achieved in Alsace though never to be achieved in the Low Countries, not for want of trying. For England the equivalent was to impose a monopoly of power, or at least control, by one single state over the whole of the archipelago she partly occupied in the eastern Atlantic Ocean. Ireland had already been subdued, cleared of Jacobites and placed under a Protestant ascendancy; only Scotland did not so far conform to the strategy. England had an urgent incentive to correct that because she remained inferior in human or material resources to France (which disposed, for example, of four times her population). The French could only be beaten if other nations combined against them. To have, for this arduous project, one of the three kingdoms of the British Isles as a mere passenger might be a fatal handicap. To pursue their aims in Europe, English politicians wanted to be free of that handicap, preferably at the least possible cost, though if need be by unleashing the strength of their state on Scotland, through political pressure or as a last resort through military might.[10]

⁊

Such was the strategic situation of Scotland in Europe as it may be gleaned from any modern history. But contemporaries had no hindsight and it will be interesting to compare what Hooke found to report to the *conseil d'en haut* in 1703. His paper started off from a picture of France surrounded by bitter enemies in a balance of power tilted against her. This was why she had to be protected by the largest army in western Europe and the world's most technically advanced fortifications. Even all that might not be enough to stop England dealing further damage to French trade, prosperity and general ability to wage war. But France did have latent strengths with which to see off the contrary alliance of the English and the Dutch, two nations by nature commercial rivals and united only in enmity to Louis XIV. One prospect on Queen Anne's death was for the Hanoverian succession to bolster the Whigs and renew the Dutch alliance, though Hooke saw this as by no means inevitable. To the Whigs the Hanoverian succession was a mere expedient and the Tories opposed it. Now, with the latter in power at Westminster, was the time to break the anti-French alliance and open up a rosier outlook. The first aim must be to impose an early, favourable peace on the English and Dutch.

This was where, according to Hooke, a restless Scotland came in: 'There is one sure way for France to force English Ministers to the conference table before this costly European war goes any further, and that is to bring Scotland into play.'[11] The Scots hated the English because of Darien and did not want a Hanoverian succession; the notion that they might be reconciled by free trade could be dismissed because this was something the English would never concede (Hooke clearly had good information from Westminster). As to Queensberry's government of Scotland, he could boast of no great following in the country. The Duke of Argyll led the Whigs and Presbyterians, but they were countered by the Duke of Hamilton, by Episcopalians and by others, so that Scottish politics presented a scene of confusion.

In response to Hooke's case, the high council decided it would be worthwhile to play along with Fraser, at least for a little. He was sent back to Scotland to see what he could make of the situation he had so vividly portrayed to the king. He found less enthusiasm for an uprising than he had given out, especially among Highlanders, brave warriors, but chastened by their recent ordeals of failed resistance, massacre and famine. Most chiefs now preferred to protect their interests by keeping the peace and coming to terms with one another rather than by feuding and banditry. Disorder there still was in plenty, but it arose more from landless outlaws than from grasping chiefs. Few of these, however intense their Jacobitism, felt ready to trust Fraser.

So by September and his rendezvous with Queensberry in Edinburgh, Fraser had changed tack. Up to Scotland he carried a package of unaddressed general letters furnished to him by members of the Jacobite Court so he could show them to the Lord High Commissioner. To Queensberry they looked as if they might well have been doctored by Fraser, but anyway were not much use on their own. What the bearer had to say by way of commentary was more interesting. He claimed to have garnered in Paris information which revealed Atholl as a spider sitting at the centre of a web of Jacobite intrigue and aiming to reverse the Revolution of 1688 in order to restore James, the Old Pretender, to the throne of his fathers. When Fraser had earlier related the same story to Argyll and Leven they at once saw its value. Even improbable secret intelligence was hard to rebut so, true or false, it might discredit Atholl. Queensberry seized on this, too, with all the more fervour for the fact that he had been forced the year before to accept Atholl as a colleague in government in deference to the queen's wish for a broad-bottomed Scottish Ministry. One small matter that Atholl as Lord Privy Seal proposed was a more rigorous pursuit of Fraser for his treason. Queensberry and Fraser therefore had a common interest in doing Atholl down.

In return for protection and support, Fraser was ready to offer yet more piquant counsel. In fact he felt happy to broaden his accusations to include as many as might be pleasing to the Lord High Commissioner. An obvious target was Hamilton, Atholl's brother-in-law and leader of the parliamentary opposition. Fraser slipped into his catalogue of conspiracy one or two personal bugbears, Cromartie, of course, then another northern aristocrat who had once snubbed the young Simon – Alexander, Duke of Gordon, a Catholic living in Florence, 'a very fine gentleman who loves his country and his bottle'.[12] Beyond that Fraser named leaders of the Court party, even Seafield. They happened to be men Queensberry eyed as rivals or antagonists. Some of those identified by Fraser did have clandestine links with St Germain, but so had many Scots for purposes of political insurance in an unstable age. If a kernel of truth lurked in his tales, he played it up it with patently faked evidence. So it was rash of the Lord High Commissioner to act the informer on the strength of this tittle-tattle.

The rashness would backfire on Queensberry. Atholl, tipped off from London, would mount a counter-attack which, to cut a long story short, brought him into high favour with Anne. By contrast, the Lord High Commissioner would be the one to find his political credibility in tatters, for a time at least. To brother Scots it would be the last straw that he provoked the House of Lords into setting up a committee of inquiry on the Scotch Plot, as the whole business was called in London, under the pretext that it posed a threat to England. In the wonderful English way, their lordships were at a loss to understand why Scots should object to this interference in the affairs of a neighbouring sovereign nation. After all, Atholl defended himself with vigour and had no trouble refuting Fraser's smears, while the jittery Jacobites rounded up to testify blabbed too readily to sustain an impression of serious intrigue. Under scrutiny the plot would vanish into thin air.

જ

Among the passing comments in the Lords' eventual report, they said a Union of Scotland with England was desirable to put a stop to affairs like the Scotch Plot. Unfortunately for their lordships, the prospect of a Union had meanwhile receded. As the year of 1703 opened it remained just about alive. The Anglo-Scottish commission appointed by the queen negotiated still, though it had become bogged down in fruitless squabbles, first about trade and then about taxation. For five successive meetings in January there was no English quorum, which had accordingly to be reduced from thirteen to seven. The halting pace of the formal sessions was perhaps all to the good because the English, when they privately got together to prepare, were only showing how far apart from the Scots they still stood. At one point the Archbishop of York, John Sharp, held forth 'that now was the time for restoring episcopacy in Scotland, and that, if that was not intended by the Union, both the nation and Church would be the losers by it'.[13]

A crunch had to come. By February 1, the commission got round to the Darien Company. The English, when asked, refused to ratify its privileges. The Scots had a proposal to fall back on, of compensation for dissolving the company. The English refused this too. Yet in a Union the Scots would be obliged to respect the privileges of the English chartered companies. Since the Scots could count among their own assets a perfectly legal chartered company, if somewhat short of cash for the time being, they would have been rash to abandon it as a bargaining counter. Though they could not expect the company to start trading again any time soon they did think the English, who had compassed its ruin, might buy out its rights and compensate its shareholders. For many that was the point of the exercise. Deadlock and breakdown loomed.

While Anne was no expert on the technicalities, she did have some sense of these human factors. Just two days later, on February 3, she adjourned the commission on the pretext it was taking up more official time and effort than could be afforded when both participating nations were at war with France. She made the best of a bad job: 'Though there be some very important matters still remaining to be adjusted yet the great progress you have made beyond what has been done in former times gives us good hope that at your next meeting this will be brought by your good endeavours to an happy conclusion.' She sent the commissioners away to think again on what more might be needed to complete the Union and 'so that you may attend upon our other affairs in your respective stations where our service requires you'. She said she would recall them on October 4 next, but never did. Indeed she never had the chance to because the Scots Parliament meanwhile asserted a role for itself: it decided that any reopening of the negotiations must be subject to a vote in the chamber, rather than a matter of royal fiat. Union was for the time being a dead duck, in essence because the English had shown no interest in it. Against their indifference, pursuit of it by self-interested elements of the Scots political nation counted for nothing.[14]

❧

At home in Scotland, it was now hard to find any further pretext for putting off the election of a new Parliament for a new reign. In the previous summer's final session of the old Parliament, the rump remaining after the walk-out by the Country party had taken measures for securing Anne's succession. It also tried to raise some tax, though many of those liable for it refused to pay their bills on the grounds of the session's illegality. With an end to the only remaining business, the negotiations for a Union, the time had come to find some firmer footing for the government of Scotland. In the first place that meant going to the polls – at what turned out to be the final General Election of the independent nation.

Scotland had a unicameral legislature where the three estates of peers, commissioners for counties and members from burghs sat together. Scots peers numbered over 150. But in 1703 seven suffered exclusion for their Catholicism, a dozen or so were minors and in about fifteen cases the families had become permanently resident in England. Of the last the heads remained eligible to sit in the Scots Parliament but did not in practice do so – though members of the other two estates feared they might turn up in Edinburgh at some crucial juncture to sway the outcome of a great issue, and shortly steps would be taken to disqualify them. Beyond that, numerous peers resident in Scotland never appeared after 1689, most because they were Jacobites unwilling to acknowledge a Parliament not summoned by any royal authority they recognised. That left the effective strength of the peers at something over 80. From the counties came 90 members; every county had originally sent 2 but for larger ones the number was increased to 3 or 4 in 1690. From the royal burghs came 67 members, each being represented by 1 except for Edinburgh with 2. In this last Scots Parliament the maximum attendance from all three estates amounted to over 200, though sometimes less in practice.[15]

It was not a democratic assembly even if since 1689 its own voting procedures had been free and open. All qualified peers could attend in person, while in strict terms the members from the counties represented landed property and those from the burghs represented chartered rights:

not the people, anyway. The franchise was narrow and oligarchical. Voters in the counties probably did not number, even in theory, more than 2,500, and those in the burghs about 1,500: the sum of 4,000 compared with a national population of a million or so, perhaps less after the ravages of famine.

In the counties most voters qualified by reason of being the feudal superiors of their land, under archaic and obscure rules which would lend themselves to corruption as the eighteenth century went on, but had not so far been greatly abused. The effect was to restrict the suffrage to the large landowners and keep out the lesser gentry, let alone the small farmers. Several counties had fallen under the domination of a single noble house and its branches or allies, while others remained in dispute among two or three of them. In others again no commanding interests prevailed and the electors could seek among themselves for worthy figures to speak on behalf of all. Round Glasgow wealthy merchants bought estates and qualified themselves in Lanarkshire or Renfrewshire. So did the increasingly powerful lawyers of Edinburgh in the adjacent Lothians. But in general the representation of the counties devolved on propertied men of good local standing with the weight to get their constituents' interests taken seriously.

As for the burghs, they held their places in Parliament by dint of royal charter, which was sometimes a basis for a degree of independence. Edinburgh, not only the capital of Scotland but also the second city of the British Isles, had a sense of its own importance to match. Its nearest Scottish rivals, Glasgow and Aberdeen, were thriving enough to sustain their own choice of member. Dumfries, busy hub of the restive Covenanting country, could not be controlled from on high. In the same region Kirkcudbright was said to be self-willed. Then there came gradations of diminishing autonomy down to burghs which remained little more than miserable villages, with no chance of escaping the political grip on them of nobility and gentry in the surrounding county. A few could hardly even afford to send a man to Parliament, but would either hire a lawyer in Edinburgh to stand in or not bother at all. The burgh of Cromarty had found the whole business too much of a burden and just relinquished its parliamentary rights in 1672 (which also meant escaping some tax). Members were chosen by the corporations of the burghs, for the most part composed of delegates of the merchants' and craftsmen's guilds. Each council elected its successor, and was naturally inclined to elect itself. So only a tiny fraction of the urban population enjoyed the franchise. The capital itself had no more than thirty-three councillors, while the total sank as low as nine in the smallest burghs.

The system as a whole bore every mark of one originally meant to limit electoral pressure on or in the legislature. That only just started to change after the Revolution of 1688. The polls of 1703 really offered the first chance to see if it was technically feasible for some such pressure to be exerted. In the event, it did turn out to be feasible. Unfortunately, this was also the last chance.

☙

By 1703 the government of Scotland could scarcely have been more unpopular with the electors, and scholars agree it now suffered a huge setback at the polls. This is a little hard to pin down, however. Surviving records of the Parliament, some official and some unofficial, set out at least the bare bones of proceedings: order of the day, motions, often voting lists and so on. They also quote some speeches, but the conventions of the time made them coy about naming the speakers – which is maddening for the modern historian, since many members became passionate advocates for the sentiments they brought with them from their constituencies and little concerned to please the Ministers set over them. In the English House of Commons most MPs sat silent, contented or overawed enough for all the talking to be done by greater men. By contrast the Scottish Parliament in its final, liberated state was tumultuous, its members unable to contain themselves in leaping to their feet to give vent to their injured patriotism, often leavening their outrage with bitter wit. Of course there were others more circumspect (and ribaldly reproached for it): for example, the many members inconsistent in the event who, on venal or other grounds, changed party, or indeed those among the victorious Jacobites of 1703 who chose not to flaunt their allegiance in public, remaining the harder for contemporaries, and for us, to identify with certainty.

Still, from the imperfect muniments of three centuries ago enough emerges to show how the election went. One result was a big turnover of the existing membership, reflecting the voters' fury at the recent conduct of Scottish government. Of the 90 members returned from the counties 58 were new. So were 43 of 67 from the burghs.[16] While a few veterans survived this slaughter of incumbents, it was in the main a young man's Parliament – which no doubt accounts for the frequent 'heats' in its proceedings. High spirits, hot tempers and hard words could and did, this being Scotland, degenerate into brawls. Seafield wrote how, as the new house was still judging disputed elections, Sir Alex Ogilvie, member for Banff, and John Hamilton, Lord Belhaven, had such a sharp exchange that they resolved to fight a duel. When they stormed towards the open air the doors were wisely barred against them, so they started punching and kicking each other in the corridor out of the chamber. The same day an ensign of the guards on duty there decided to pick a bone with Sir Robert Dickson, member for Edinburgh, over the electoral vote he had cast from his rustic seat in East Lothian. This time, says Seafield, 'I took occasion fully to express that nothing would be more displeasing to Her Majesty than that any of the officers of her army should offer to give the least insult or threatening to the members of Parliament.'[17]

The Parliament of 1703, with its membership predominantly drawn from one political generation on after the Revolution, perceived different priorities from its predecessor. That had worked to draw up a new constitution. The seventeenth century in Scotland should perhaps not always be seen as a period only of berserk discontinuity, with bursts of political advance ending in lurches back into black reaction. A line of constitutional progress, if thin and broken, could be discerned by contemporaries. Despite a reputation for Calvinist fanaticism, the Covenanting government of Scotland from 1641 had been good government, reasonably regular and efficient, in particular parliamentary, for some time capable of maintaining the peace and defending the borders, while uniting the nobility with the Lowland middle class. After the horrors of the Killing Time, the Parliament of 1689 followed that lead. It was not at all a bad Parliament. But by the end of its term it had lost political, indeed moral, authority – because it sat too long, because of Darien and in general because it represented first and foremost victorious Whigs never able to reconcile Revolution principles with the Union of Crowns. By contrast the Parliament of 1703 drew together the nation's every strand and displayed all its virtues or vices: courage in contention with canniness, candour with corruption, conscience with calculation. These qualities combined in politics for the first time and, alas, for the last.

The estate of peers saw an influx from families which had, since the Revolution, refused to swear the oaths required to take part in public life – of Jacobites, that is to say. They had scorned to sit in the previous Parliament but events now conquered their scruples and summoned them to the aid of a stricken Scotland. Among the men who thus opted to accept the oaths this time were Lord Balcarres, in resentment at ill-treatment by James VII; Lord Banff, who converted from Catholicism so he could sit; Lord Dunmore, newly pardoned by the queen of high treason; Lord Fraser, a kinsman and crony of Simon Fraser of Lovat (enough said); Lord Rollo, so devoted to any Stewart that, at Anne's behest, he would actually vote for the Union which after her death he tried to undo; Lord Semple, a stripling of eighteen rejecting all blandishments of military promotion if he would turn his Jacobite coat; Lord Wigtown, hotfoot from St Germain; and so on.

When we come to the elected members there is a distinct impression, even from the imperfect evidence, of voters flocking to the polls to throw the rascals of the last Parliament out, at least in those constituencies not under a noble thumb. Otherwise the electors' will could seldom be thwarted – something that would become routine after 1707 once the Scottish was assimilated to the English political practice. Hamilton remarked: 'There seems to be a greater life and vigour in the nation than used to be upon such occasions, if I might judge of the elections through the whole kingdom by those are like to be made in the country I live in.'[18]

All the Ministers of the Crown were either peers or else held their parliamentary seats *ex officio*, so as the results came in the biggest casualty was a figure only of lesser rank, Keeper of the Signet and Receiver-general, Sir James Elphinstone of Logie in Aberdeenshire, noted for a 'pure zeal to King William's government' which he would not now have the chance to display before Queen Anne.[19] Blood-relations of the high and mighty were also targets such as, in Ayrshire, John Campbell of Shankstoun, brother of the military commander, the Earl of Loudoun, part of Argyll's network.[20] Truckling bigwigs toppled too: Cupar, represented by a former Lord Provost of Edinburgh, Sir Archibald Muir of Thornton, got rid of him for a local farmer, Patrick Bruce of Bunzion, from the braes above the Howe of Fife.[21] Chancellor Seafield's native Banffshire slapped him in the face by returning two men opposed to him, Alexander Duff of Braco and James Ogilvie of Boyne.[22]

It was all to the good if a fresh candidate could offer more than youth and impetuosity. In East Lothian, where three of four sitting members went out, a new one was destined to become known simply as The Patriot for his tireless opposition to Union: Andrew Fletcher of Saltoun. In Midlothian, too, three of four incumbents fell; the ablest novice was George Lockhart of Carnwath, forthright Jacobite entrepreneur. Even where no large personalities swayed them, voters diligently replaced the old guard with sturdier defenders of the nation. In Perthshire all the members of the outgoing Parliament were rejected, one a Whig judge, the second a member of the inquiry which had whitewashed the Massacre of Glencoe, the third a persecutor of Episcopalians, the fourth a harmless local worthy, which did not save him.[23] The winners here notched up majorities of five to one over the Court's hapless candidates.

Seldom is any ideological strand to the contests salient, but from the example of, say, Berwickshire, we may be assured it was there: in this county two of the four sitting members went out, with the survivors and their incoming colleagues topping the poll on an explicit Country platform which called for triennial Parliaments, more representation for counties as bastions of independence and property against the peers and burghs, together with consultation of constituents by members before settling the succession or concluding a Union.[24] Again, Angus got rid of three incumbents to return a solidly Jacobite slate of new members.[25] On the other hand Lanarkshire, where Hamilton held sway, returned four thoroughgoing Presbyterians.[26] All would unite in opposition.

It is not possible to draw up a definitive list of gains or losses for the shifting factions. But these straws in the wind confirm the picture of an enormous defeat for the government, with Jacobites the main winners. This proved to be pregnant of the future. English Jacobites were already starting to sink into irrelevance, yet Scots Jacobites offered the most hopeful, logical, patriotic alternative to the superannuated revolutionary generation of 1688. They were coming to stand for the cause of the nation even among those who might have seemed to be their natural enemies on other considerations, whether of religion, of political partisanship, of personal or familial history, of preference for Lowland over Highland values and so on. Jacobitism was above all an ideology of legitimacy – 'the king shall enjoy his own again' – as a guarantee that everybody else might enjoy their own again, if not now then one day. And Scotland as a nation possessed rights too, often trampled underfoot. They represented to many minds old and fine and proven values, in contrast to the ruthless pragmatism of the Whigs (and the English), let alone the muddy self-seeking otherwise prevalent. Here beat the heart of Jacobitism.

∽

Jacobite or not, the fresh parliamentary intake lost no time in making its mark. Fletcher and Lockhart would emerge as outstanding parliamentarians. Fletcher, fifty years old, was in fact a veteran who had first sat for

East Lothian in 1681 but then, like others of independent mind, thought better to seek refuge in Holland. After crossing to England for the Duke of Monmouth's rebellion in 1685, he escaped its savage suppression and set off on travels to Spain and Hungary, where he made a name fighting the Turks. In the Europe of this era the military camps were schools of nations; amid the nightly bonhomie with fellow mercenary officers from every conceivable background Fletcher also acquired a political education which served him well once he could return to Scotland after the Revolution. 'A low, thin man of a brown complexion, full of fire, with a stern, sour look', he preferred pure principle to practical purpose and proved an awkward customer to his fellows in opposition as well as to the powers-that-be.[27]

Yet Fletcher was not a lonely figure. Into a radical wing of the Country party he drew youthful noblemen making a debut in Parliament and known as his 'cubs'. There were two brothers who by a complex succession to their titles bore different surnames, John Leslie, Earl of Rothes, 24 years old, and Thomas Hamilton, Earl of Haddington, 23 years old, the first 'a warm asserter of the liberties of the people', the second an obsessive planter of trees. There was James Graham, Earl of Montrose, 21 years old, not an outright Jacobite as might be expected from his great-grandfather's royalist martyrdom but acquiescent in a Protestant succession and most of all, being poor, eager to recover the money the family had lost at Darien. There was John Ker, Earl of Roxburghe, 23 years old, according to Lockhart 'a man of good sense, improven by so much reading and learning that, perhaps, he was the best accomplished young man in Europe, and had so charming a way of expressing his thoughts that he pleased even those against whom he spoke'.[28] Lockhart himself, if esteeming Fletcher and his cubs, never belonged to their circle. Another golden youth of 22, rich, handsome, sociable, flamboyant, hot-tempered, as well-connected in England as in Scotland, Lockhart played not so much the sea-green incorruptible as the brilliant opportunist ever ready to exploit the weaknesses of government. Yet he had a core of steel beneath his sinuous graces, soldered to his Jacobitism. This it would have been easier and more profitable for him to forsake, as so many others did under official inducements or hopes of them. He, however, stuck to it.

These names do not exhaust the tally of new talent in the opposition. With Fletcher from East Lothian came John Cockburn of Ormiston, aged 23, who in a life devoted more to agricultural improvement than to politics would win the epithet of father of Scottish husbandry. From the burgh of Burntisland came his fellow improver and proto-industrialist, 30-year-old Sir John Erskine of Alva. From Aberdeenshire came William Seton of Pitmedden who, likewise at 30, already saw himself as philosopher of the Country party, advocating in his writings not only economic improvement but also the political preservation of liberty by limited monarchical government, if necessary at the expense of exclusive nationalism. Unusually he thought Union with a more advanced England might promote his causes, and there he differed from other patriots; but Seton's bookish, pretentious manner limited his influence. With Lockhart from Midlothian came Robert Dundas of Arniston, Presbyterian and progenitor of the political dynasty that would rule Scotland, as the Dundas Despotism, later in the eighteenth century. A senior colleague from the same county was Sir John Lauder of Fountainhall, a cultured historian and institutional writer (or codifier of Scots law). From Fife came Robert Douglas of Strathendry, old soldier, gentleman farmer and grandfather of Adam Smith the economist. From Lanarkshire came George Baillie of Jerviswood, 39-year-old scion of revered Presbyterian martyrs, married to Grisell, a Scots songstress. From Perthshire came John Haldane of Gleneagles, aged 43, who had in effect represented the Company of Scotland in the outgoing Parliament – like others, a natural man of the establishment driven into opposition by Darien.

All this is not to say the Court's thinned ranks lacked new talent either. A novice who came in for Whithorn, one of the government's pocket burghs, was John Clerk of Penicuik. Aged 27, he had just got back from a grand tour in Europe burdened with debts that would take him years to pay off. But they were worth it: he turned himself into the first *virtuoso* of the eighteenth century, learned in the law (which he yet disliked), a pioneer of ancient archaeology, a student of Arcangelo Corelli in music (which he also composed himself) and generally an adept in the culture of France and Italy. In Vienna, Clerk met Leopold, the Holy Roman Emperor. In Florence, he befriended Cosimo II de' Medici, Grand Duke of Tuscany, who made him a gentleman of the bedchamber. Clerk had had indeed, uniquely among Presbyterians, an audience of the pope. It was only his running out of money that drove him home and attached him to the coiling Queensberry, to whom he was related by marriage, with a devotion otherwise inexplicable. Clerk's autobiography, in its optimism and self-importance, suggests his sentimental education had still left him an innocent, at any rate easy meat for his cynical patron. But Clerk would make an effective boss of all the backroom boys in the hard graft on the Union. The Court's ranks were otherwise swelled with legmen and placemen, often by the name of Campbell, Dalrymple or Douglas.

Still, as a whole the last Scottish Parliament would turn out to be an able Parliament, not to say an admirable Parliament. Meeting at a fateful time, it was to be deeply divided over many matters that came before it. Its factions, Clerk later wrote, 'rubbed upon one another and with great severity, so that we were often in the form of a Polish diet, with our swords in our hands, or at least our hands on our swords'.[29] Its inexperience and youthful excess did not, however, preclude many of the best of Scotsmen from distinguishing themselves in its hallowed hall on the High Street of Edinburgh. A number of them left a mark on their country or even on their age, if perforce after 1707 outside that hall. This generation of Scottish public men would not be matched till the Liberals' heyday before the First World War – and it still puts to shame the gruesome mediocrities that represented the nation for the rest of the twentieth century, not least in the restored Scottish Parliament of 1999.

℘

On May 6, 1703, old and new members gathered in an Edinburgh where the smell of suspicion and spite spiked the familiar stink of ordure in the closes and wynds. But first came the Riding of the Parliament, a grand public event of the old Scotland. Quite possibly it followed the precedents of a guide to the ceremonial printed in 1681 which prescribed, among other things, different routes to the Parliament Hall for various qualities of citizen, provided that 'the higher degree, and most honourable of that degree is to ride always last'. There survives also an illustration of the riding, with a commentary in French:

> When it pleased the king to convoke a Parliament, the deputies travelled to Edinburgh, capital of Scotland, and assembled at the Abbey of the Holy Cross, or Holyroodhouse, in order to proceed on foot or on horseback, as here represented. Having proceeded in this manner, the Lord High Commissioner seats himself on his throne, and near him the great officers of the Crown, and in two ranks the prelates [no longer present by 1703] and the secular peers, the deputies of the provinces [counties] to the right, and those of the burghs to the left. The Honours

75

are put on the table by the High Constable and the Earl Marischal. After prayers the list of deputies is read. Thereafter, the Lord Chancellor approaches the throne on his knee, and receives from the hands of the Lord High Commissioner the king's commission, which he gives to a Secretary to read. Then is read the formula which is the manner and letter of the assembly, after which the Lord Lyon King of Arms descends from the throne and places the lord and deputies according to their rank. The Lord High Commissioner then declares the intentions of the Crown, which are more amply explained by the Lord High Chancellor, and the oath is tendered to the deputies . . .[30]

For 1703, and what was to be the final riding, the privy council issued orders to ensure it went on 'without disturbance or confusion', marking out parts of the Royal Mile to be cleared, cleaned, roped off and spread with sand to stop horses slipping. There were to be no guns fired, flags waved or drums beaten to demean the solemnity of the occasion.[31] Once the session convened, Her Majesty regretted in the speech from the throne that she could not be there too, adding that 'we thought to have brought you sooner together in this meeting of Parliament, but the great and weighty affairs wherein we have been engaged this winter were a necessary hindrance'. She asked members to protect Scottish rights and liberties, to deal with the problems of the war, to foster trade, to promote religion, virtue and true piety. 'This being your first meeting and we having recommended nothing but what is for your own security and welfare,' Anne went on, 'we confidently expect a suitable return and a dutiful and cheerful concurrence in what we propose and that, all difficulties and animosities laid aside, you will with concord and diligence bring matters to such a happy conclusion as shall establish a lasting Union' – do we hear across three centuries a sharp intake of breath from the new members? – 'between us and our people'. So that was all right, then. Though the queen's message in the event breathed no word of a Union of Parliaments, her bland hope of complaisance soon withered.[32]

In his own speech as Lord High Commissioner, Queensberry praised 'the benign government of a Protestant queen'. Yet he warned that 'we ought not to be too secure, and it were to tempt our enemies to form designs or make insults against us, if they see us in no condition of defence. All Her Majesty proposes to you is for yourselves, without mingling any particular concern of her own.' [33] He had many faults but a saturnine tendency to gloom was not one of them. According to his survey of the prospects previously sent to London, he expected to be able to control this Parliament. The election had, to be sure, gone badly for his government in its loss of so many old stalwarts. Yet he hoped to enter into alliance with the swarm of newcomers known at the time as Cavaliers, emerged from cover now that a real Stewart was back on the throne in the ample, comforting shape of Queen Anne. Some saw it as their plain duty to support her in her broad Tory outlook, others were especially intent on relieving the disabilities of Episcopalians, while others again shaded off into covert or overt Jacobitism. For the moment it struck the Cavaliers that if they went along with the Court and helped Queensberry, this might open the way to more durable influence for themselves.

So Queensberry's sanguine strategy looked at the outset as if it could just pay off. His first business was to ratify the queen's title and to establish the legality of the session of 1702, both of which propositions went through by big majorities. Yet tensions already simmered under the surface. It was actually Hamilton that proposed the ratification. This, the same measure as had passed a year before in the old Parliament he walked out of, could be held to imply the illegality of the session of 1702. Still, he did not press the point. According to Lockhart, Hamilton and his party acted 'considering that this was the particular piece of service the queen demanded of them, in recompense of the great things she promised to do for them; and with what confidence could they have been admitted into her favour, and entrusted with the administration of affairs, if they had opposed her in it'.[34]

There was an awkward moment when the Lord Advocate, Sir James Stewart of Goodtrees (pronounced Gutters), sought to strengthen Hamilton's motion by inserting a clause to make it high treason for anyone to question the queen's title.

This intervention brought an outburst from the testy Belhaven, claiming 'the clause is dishonourable to Her Majesty, seeing it means as if the House was giving Her Majesty an indemnity for her acts since her accession to the throne'.

Stewart suavely replied: 'The words only mean in general Her Majesty's right to exercise her power.'

'Whatever the meaning of those who have offered the clause, yet the words of the clause can admit of no such meaning,' Belhaven insisted.

The Lord Advocate spelled matters out at ponderous length, splitting what hairs he had to: 'By the late Queen Mary's death without heirs of her body, the right of succession came to the queen, upon the prospect of King William's death'. Still, 'the right of exercise did never accrue to her until his actual death, and Her Majesty's actual succession. And it is therefore proper not only to recognise her right of succession, but also to recognise her actual exercise, and to secure both by a sanction of treason.'

Belhaven was not to be put down by lawyer's waffle: 'The Act as first offered by the Duke of Hamilton does fully recognise these and all manner of rights which are, or can be, in Her Majesty's person, but the clause now offered does most dishonourably superadd a ratification and sanction of Her Majesty's exercise.' As he went on to impugn Ministers' motives, he warmed to his theme: 'They themselves must be conscious that contrary to law they have been instrumental in advising Her Majesty to exercise some acts of administration, such as the calling together of a late Parliament, which were plainly beyond the limitations which determined the being of that Parliament and circumscribed its power.' And so he came to his point: 'Being sensible that this their advice may very justly rebound upon themselves, they shuffle in this dishon-ourable clause, very needlessly justifying Her Majesty's exercise of her royal power, hoping under the name of Her Majesty's exercise to shelter themselves who were both the advisers and executors.'

It fell to Hamilton as proposer to cool things down, if not neglecting to put a sting in the tail of his retort: 'I was very hopeful that so dutiful an Act would have passed the vote of this house with all imaginable cheerfulness. And I am both sorry and surprised to find anything thrown in, which can create the least demur to it. But let them answer for it, who are the authors' – in other words, the Lord Advocate and the govern-ment.[35]

So even as some initial measures were comfortably approved, the proceedings took on an edgy, uneasy feel. It did not augur well for the Act of Supply coming up next. Yet if only that could be passed the Court's basic agenda would be fulfilled. Seafield intended to introduce afterwards a proposal for religious toleration, meaning of the Episcopa-lians, which he knew was bound to fail. On this pretext, Parliament could be adjourned after a session conveniently short and to the point, with at least a couple of useful items in the bag and no harm done. The coalition of Court and Cavaliers might then look to the future.

The prospect seemed all the more promising because the opposition was taking time to get its act together, as Hamilton's offhand response to Belhaven's unruly intervention showed. The Country party had come back to this Parliament saying what it was saying on its secession from the old one, that the illegality of the session of 1702 pointed up the need to place Scotland on an equal footing with England. This had already led on to the conclusion that any future Scottish sovereign must be chosen free of English influence and under limitations on the powers of the Crown. It was a plain stance and, to judge from the election, a popular one.

Yet the stance was now muddled by the awkward position of the Presbyterians, a faction sprawling half in and half out of government. Sir James Stewart, Lord Advocate for over a decade now, typified them. Sprung of Covenanting stock and in earlier life an exile, he was the leading lawyer of his generation. A leading lawyer cannot afford too many scruples and he trimmed constantly: he started off and he remained opposed to Union, in the end being dispensed by his masters from voting for a treaty obnoxious to him. Still, he never resigned. Tagging along with him were the Duke of Argyll, who without much in the way of personal religion yet inherited the mantle of secular Presbyterian leadership, and William Johnston, Marquis of Annandale, for the last two years the Queen's Commissioner to the General Assembly of the Church of Scotland. But the waters of pure Presbyterianism had been clouded to the depths by the former Chancellor, the Earl of Marchmont, and his foolish push in the previous session for the Hanoverian succession, which got him the sack instead. Being now split, the Presbyterians faced a risk that the novel conjunction of Court and Cavaliers might turn out a success in ruling Scotland, even offer a permanent basis for ruling Scotland. That could spell doom to the Kirk, and had to be avoided at any cost.

These fears showed the Presbyterians' persistent insecurity. If they were weaker than has often been assumed in retrospect, even their opponents by now often felt ready to settle for presbytery in the Church of Scotland to spare the nation more of the blood and suffering of the last century's struggles over religion; the debate was rather about the latitude for toleration. The impetus for yet another change in the constitution of the Kirk could perhaps only have come from on high, yet Anne, too, was learning to live with an establishment little to her personal taste. A story went the rounds of her asking the politician James Johnston why

Presbyterians did not observe the date of her grandfather's death, January 31, Anglican feast of Charles I, king and martyr. 'Why truly,' he replied, 'they do not keep the day of our Saviour's death or birth, yea, no set days that are not in scripture.'

'That is more than I knew,' said the queen. 'I perceive it's a matter of principle with them and not of pick.'[36] But she had already in February written to her privy council accepting Presbyterianism would remain established by law, and wondering why all the same there could not be some relief of Episcopalians, who were Protestants after all. If these caused no trouble, she urged, Presbyterians should live with them 'in brotherly love and communion'.

One answer to the queen came from her loyal Parliament. where the government obediently introduced a Toleration Act. Quite another came from the General Assembly of the Church of Scotland, which growled that Episcopalians, so far from being tolerated, ought just to conform, since a mere difference on ecclesiastical government was no reason for separation in worship. A louder retort came from Glasgow, where Episcopalians had taken to worshipping privately in the house of Sir John Bell, a former magistrate. There every Sunday morning the magistrates posted guards in case of trouble. Now they got it, when their precaution attracted the notice of 'rude boys' using such 'rough words' as to provoke the guards 'who, chasing them with their swords . . . and violent oaths along the Saltmarket, roused a general tumult'. A crowd gathered in front of Bell's house wielding sledgehammers. They smashed the windows and broke in. At that moment the magistrates arrived with more soldiers, tried to arrest a few rioters and settled for escorting the terrified Episcopalians home. In Scotland, Christians had yet to learn to love one another.[37]

A quirk of the Scots Parliament was that it often seemed to talk in code, deciding one issue by reference to something else. Now the Court's attempt to obtain supply proved to be the test of these religious questions lurking in the background (or vice versa). The Country party preferred to vote no supply at all, not least in the interest of those among its supporters who had been delighted with a pretext to avoid paying tax in 1702 and looked forward to the same in 1703. This sorry state of affairs lay open to factional exploitation. Percipient Presbyterians jumped in ahead of callow Cavaliers. Annandale and Argyll put down a motion to ratify the legality of the Parliament of 1689 and all its subsequent proceedings including, of course, the re-establishment of presbytery in the Church of Scotland. They meant this as a provocation, to flush it out that the Cavaliers could not be regarded as reliable supporters across the whole range of business: so, by implication, their religion should not be tolerated either.

A sharp question exposing this parliamentary artifice came probably from the religious liberal Seton of Pitmedden, calling to mind how his Aberdonian constituents[38] 'were generally disposed for episcopacy'. He went on to ask whether the ratification would mean that if 'any body of men in duty to their own opinion in a very regular way address the Parliament for a rectification of the present Presbyterian establishment, which I consider neither infallible nor unalterable – in this case I ask whether or not such an address would import high treason'. A vehement Calvinist, Sir William Hamilton, judge and member for Queensferry, jumped up to reply that people could address away to their hearts' content, but if after this Act was passed 'anybody owns that he thinks Presbyterian government a wrong establishment of Church government, or that he thinks episcopacy ought to be restored, it is my opinion that by this Act they are guilty of high treason'.[39]

The Country party piled in. One of its leaders, John Hay, Marquis of Tweeddale, moved that the Parliament might widen the proposed ratification and 'proceed to make such conditions of government and regulations in the constitution of this kingdom, to take place after the decease of Her Majesty and the heirs of her body, as shall be necessary for the preservation of our religion and liberty'. What he meant was that the bargaining counter of supply should not be thrown away before settling the succession and considering other reforms.

While the house wondered whether to swallow that copious bill of fare, Annandale and Argyll went to see Queensberry. They threatened him that unless their Act was given priority over the Act for Supply they and all the other Court Presbyterians, up to this point supporters of his Ministry, would desert him and vote for Tweeddale's motion. The government of Scotland would be defeated and left to struggle on as best it could without money for another year. This would be nothing new, of course, but it would mark the Lord High Commissioner's abject failure in what the queen and English government most urgently wanted and needed of him. The choice then facing him was either to adjourn the whole session or to ditch the Cavaliers. He called them in and told them he must let the Presbyterians have their way: Scotland could after all not be run without them. The Cavaliers felt 'much stumbled'. Toleration, needless to say, vanished from the parliamentary programme.[40]

❧

So within weeks the wonderful new combination of Court and Cavaliers had come a cropper, and the government of Scotland was reduced to its habitual haplessness. In anger at Queensberry's surrender the Cavaliers turned against him. But out of this shambles a new prospect arose. While factions of the opposition pursued incompatible ends by hypocritical means, they could agree on one thing, on the need to reduce the English influence in Scotland and its standing offence to Scottish nationhood. The strength of that feeling in this new Parliament next handed the initiative to a man already the rising star of the Country party, admired even by adversaries, Fletcher of Saltoun. He reached for the expedient of an Act of Security. The security he meant was that of the nation – specifically, the conditions for choosing a successor to the Scottish throne, conditions with which he intended to rule out the English influence.

Even in advance of putting flesh on his ideas Fletcher was, as the coalition of Court and Cavaliers faltered, expounding to members the reasons for the confusion and the way to resolve it. First, on May 26, he insisted no supply should be granted till other business was finished: ' 'Tis a strange proposition which is usually made in this House, that if we will give money to the Crown, then the Crown will give us good laws: as if we were to buy good laws of the Crown, and pay money to our princes, that they may do their duty and comply with their coronation oath.' Besides, he went on, 'we have often had promises of good laws, and when we have given the sums demanded, those promises have been broken, and the nation left to seek a remedy; which is not to be found, unless we supply the laws we want before we give a supply'. He explained himself further on May 28, posing a pointed question on executive power, 'whether this nation would be in a better condition, if in conferring our places and pensions the prince should be determined by the Parliament of Scotland, or by the Ministers of a court that make it their interest to keep us low and miserable'. Springing to his feet again on June 22, he specified that 'he who is not for setting great limitations on the power of the prince . . . can act by no principle, whether he be a Presbyterian, prelatical, or prerogative-man, for the court of St Germain or that of Hanover . . . unless that of being a slave to the court of England for his own advantage'. Yet the problem lay not in England, rather here in the Parliament House of Edinburgh. Scotland, with her monarch resident in a foreign country, was being managed by grovelling noblemen for personal and factional gain. The religious or other bickering that took up so much time only made things worse. No wonder the nation looked like a 'conquered province'.[41]

The same day Fletcher introduced his draft Act of Security. It must have been a startling document even to members who had followed his speeches, though its aims were clear. It set out that any successor to the Scottish Crown who was also King or Queen of England would be subject to limitations designed to ensure the independence of the Parliament, the reliance on it of the Scottish government and the defence of the whole nation by the arming of its able-bodied men. There had been no previous parallels to such a programme in any European country but the England of the Civil War, and there the effects were long since overborne by restoration of the monarchy.

Some of Fletcher's proposed limitations seem modern, others inspired by the particular contemporary circumstances of a small country struggling to control its fate. His Act would have had the Parliament elected every year (a demand still being put in vain by British Chartists of the Victorian era). It would have required compulsory royal assent to all Acts voted by the Parliament (which is standard constitutional practice in Britain today). It would have made the government of Scotland not a clique cringeing under the Crown but a committee of an independent Parliament, continuing as such even during adjournments. It would have transferred to this Parliament authority to declare war or peace and to conclude treaties. It would have passed to the Parliament final control over all public appointments. It would have given that Parliament the right to raise the armed forces, and it specified the formation of a national militia. It would have confined to the Parliament the prerogative to pardon. It would have separated powers by abolishing Ministers' *ex officio* votes in the chamber and by disqualifying judges from sitting there. It would have enforced equality in numbers from the estates of the peers and of the commissioners for counties. Any monarch breaking the limitations would forfeit the Crown. All this would have granted Scotland the most advanced constitution in Europe.[42]

Fletcher is to be admired for his persuasive skills as well as his intellectual force. The Parliament had an opportunity, he told it, 'which if we manage to the advantage of the nation we have the honour to represent, we may, so far as the vicissitude and uncertainty of human

83

affairs will permit, be for many ages easy and happy. But if we despise or neglect this occasion, we have voted our perpetual dependence on another nation.' Yet he took care to say nothing hostile to the English by name. On the contrary, he went on, 'the best and wisest men in England will be glad to hear these limitations are settled by us', for they 'will consider that when two nations live under the same prince, the condition of the one cannot be made intolerable but a separation must inevitably follow'.

Even so, perplexities lurked in the limitations proposed by Fletcher. If it was only under them that Scotland ought to accept the same succession as England then, should they be refused, Scotland would logically have to choose a different succession. There was always the Pretender, who some hoped might be persuaded to turn Protestant so as to let the legitimate line of Stewarts be restored. This would in fact never happen. But in 1703, with the boy James aged just 15, the mere possibility remained open: Stewarts had, after all, changed their religion before. So even Protestants might flirt with the Jacobites if another restoration could, like the last, not lead beyond an episcopal Kirk, in any event not to Romanism. As for an indisputably Protestant succession only one other than Hanover was credible – in the House of Hamilton, though this raised as many questions as it answered. Beyond that choices moved off into the realm of fantasy, to the Duke of Savoy or yet more improbable figures. An overriding question was whether the English, after a century with the King of Scots living among them in London, would be at all willing to see a separate monarchy restored in Edinburgh.

Yet the person of the monarch seemed hardly to worry Fletcher. A bit later he was to spell out that 'if we may live free, I little value who is king: 'tis indifferent to me, provided the limitations be enacted'.[43] In other words, he took as his prime purpose what amounted to another new constitution for Scotland, that of 1689 having already proved unworkable. His constitution would still be designed for a Union of Crowns, for it was to that he sought to have his limitations applied; while Seafield tried to smear him as a republican, this was untrue. Scotland had rather to win back the sovereignty lost since 1603 by renegotiating in the first instance the terms of the Union of Crowns, starting with these legislated limitations. Then, Fletcher implied, the precise line of succession became a secondary matter, for Scotland would have constitutional, not royal, government.

Himself anti-Jacobite, and with not so much as a mention of Hanover,

Fletcher therefore set out for the period ahead the means of maximising the Parliament's room for manoeuvre without getting bogged down in the divisive specifics of a particular dynasty. In any imminent crisis over the succession, pressure on the English would be exerted by the fact that, if they spurned a reasonable Scottish offer for the continued Union of Crowns, they would have little choice but to conquer Scotland with men and matériel diverted from the War of the Spanish Succession. That would turn the European conflict into a War of the British Succession too: not a pleasant prospect from an English point of view, for it would hand the Jacobites their chance. The Lord Treasurer of England, Sidney Godolphin, saw this: 'We are now in so critical a juncture with respect to other nations, that all Europe must in some measure be affected by the good or ill-ending of the Parliament of Scotland.'[44]

In fact the Scots Parliament found the limitations proposed by Fletcher too much to swallow at first bite, and rejected them in July. Yet by August it had passed an Act of Security. This Act was not Fletcher's but a different one, if with important points of similarity. Acts of Security became a bit of a fad that summer; when Fletcher introduced his, three different ones lay already on the table. Two came from Sir James Stewart trying to head off the opposition with drafts of his own, the third from young Montrose.[45] The Act of Security at length actually voted by the Parliament originated with another member of the government, the Duke of Atholl.

℘

What happened during long debate and copious amendment was that this Act of Security steadily turned into a statement of the nation's whole predicament, and of a way forward from that, finally formulated so as to command assent from a great majority. Collective compromise was needed to achieve such an outcome without the various factions riding off on hobby-horses of their own and raising matters on which others could not agree, just for the sake of scoring points in the usual manner. This made the Act in its definitive shape and style resemble previous documents pivotal to national history, notably the Covenants, in being uneven and rambling, comprehensive rather than elegant, with the prime purpose of satisfying everyone who could possibly give it support at the expense of being easy or pleasing to read: alas, there had been no Thomas Jefferson at work. Still, the result deserves to stand with the

Covenants as a statement of the nation's aspirations at a turning point in its history.

The debates on the Act of Security proceeded by letting all and sundry propose particular points for inclusion. There were weeks of acid altercations, close-fisted compromises and strained surrenders, as members consulted their interests, listened to the arguments and weighed the pros and cons. That this was a national assembly acting as a national assembly ought to act may be gauged from the fact that the Court soon lost any influence over the process – it just ran away out of official control. Then the members realised they were enjoying themselves. A sign of it came with their indulgence in the Scots sport of pedantic hair-splitting. On July 14 John Allardyce, provost of and member for Aberdeen,[46] remarked that since the wisdom of the house had thought fit to exclude from the throne papists who professed the doctrine of transubstantiation, he saw no reason why Lutherans, who professed the doctrine of consubstantiation, ought not likewise to be excluded: 'And more especially considering that by this course, the family of Hanover would fall to be excluded, which is both proper and necessary, considering that the English have named that family for their successor.' We can almost hear the burst of laughter.

By these convoluted procedures the rickety arch of the Act rose higher and higher. It still needed a keystone. That was set in place with an amendment from Roxburghe. His clause provided that the successor to the Crown of England could not be also the successor to the Crown of Scotland unless Scotland's conditions were met. Following his mentor Fletcher, Roxburghe made no attempt to settle the succession in a particular line, a deliberate oversight which everyone could tolerate for now except the small faction of Marchmont's Presbyterians. Other options remained open – surely the right response to the times. And only contingencies for the future were envisaged. The Act proposed no change in the short term and was not to come into force till Anne's death.

Roxburghe's amendment, put down on July 16, got the debate it deserved. So many members wanted to speak to it that by eight o'clock in the evening Fletcher moved for a vote, anxious lest the chance to firm up a vital limitation be lost by the wiles of Queensberry and Seafield. This over-anxious intervention was a mistake, however: Seafield promptly declared it had grown too late for procedural complication and Queensberry adjourned without allowing a division. His ruling caused 'a great cry and hubbub'. Hamilton, Rothes and Tweeddale protested that it breached parliamentary privilege. Many members, staying in their places after the chair was vacated, vowed to send an address to Queen Anne. 'Afterwards on second thoughts, when the Commissioner was come out they came out, and went to Pat Steil's' (a pub).[47]

In the following session Seafield sought to smooth ruffled feathers. He said he had not wanted to halt debate yet had seen it must go on so long that it would need to resume on another day. Fletcher still accused him of acting illegally, but let the point pass. Meanwhile, Queensberry and Seafield had been racking their brains over Roxburghe's dangerous clause, certain to become law unless they could foil it. Their bright idea was to get the Lord Advocate to propose that 'the successors to the Crown of England be not nominate King or Queen of Scotland unless there be a communication of trade with England agreed to, freedom of navigation, and trading with their plantations, etc, as shall be satisfying at the sight of the Parliament of Scotland'. Here opened a prospect of free trade sure to whet Scots' appetites. Yet the ploy was meant not so much to satisfy their economic ambitions as to scupper the Act of Security. Ministers well knew that the English had not in the slightest degree changed their minds on free trade, namely, that the Scots should not get it, least of all with the American colonies. If a new constitution for Scotland was to be made contingent on free trade, then, it would remain stillborn. Clever as Stewart was, he did not outwit Fletcher, who must have enjoyed standing up to give a welcome to the new clause. He showed Ministers they had not fooled him: as their faces fell, he went on to spoil their stratagem by moving that both clauses, this and Roxburghe's, should be voted on together.

On July 23 Roxburghe, who had been set to burn the midnight oil in compositing the two clauses, moved the result of his work: the Union of Crowns was only to continue under 'such conditions of government, and such settlements in point of liberty and trade secured to us as may preserve our government and Ministry from the influence of the neighbouring Ministry, and such as may extinguish that jealousy which must prove fatal to both, while under the same government'. Stewart had no option but to follow this ardent lead, adding only a minor proviso. After a spirited debate, the composite motion was on July 26 approved by 72 votes. George Ridpath, recording the proceedings, wrote that 'the majority of the House [was] for it, though upon different considerations'; in this it prefigured and epitomised the Act of Security as a whole. Everybody congratulated Roxburghe as hero of the hour, he basking the while in his new repute as 'a young nobleman of great interest and expectation'. There echoed into Parliament House the cheers of a crowd gathered outside in the High Street to hear the result.[48]

Queensberry and Seafield had seen their ploy misfire and knew it meant big trouble for them in London, where even Stewart's clause seemed appalling enough, let alone Roxburghe's. Seafield wrote to placate Godolphin and explain how the nub of his problem lay not so much in any particular proposal as in the now almost impossible task of controlling a Parliament which had made up its mind to snap the neighbour nation's yoke: 'We are environed with resolves, and in anything against the English succession our opposite party are strongest.' Something had to give: unless an Act of Security was passed in one form or other, however unpalatable, there would be no supply and 'great difficulty to preserve authority and government'.

Godolphin still would not listen, deeming unacceptable any legislation which envisaged, even conditionally, a succession to the Scottish throne different from that to the English throne. Yet what was to be done? Robert Harley wrote:

I think it very unfit for anyone here to meddle with Scotch affairs, which are so much out of our way of comprehending. We have had the same speech printed twice in the flying post, besides abstracts of Acts of Parliament and clauses, yet I do not find one person who pretends to understand the proceedings.

In consequence, nobody in London even talked about Scotland, 'less than they do of the King of Sweden and the Pole', though what was happening there could be of vital interest to England. The latest events, Harley gloomily added, 'fill me with grief to see a cloud gathering in the North, though no bigger than a man's hand'.[49]

In Edinburgh debate on the Act of Security continued and amendment too, but its central provisions were now in place. In its final form it provided on Anne's death for the Parliament to meet within twenty days and, if there was no heir apparent, to choose a successor 'being always of the Royal Line of Scotland, and of the true Protestant religion'. The crucial stipulation followed, that this successor must not be the same as in England unless the requirements of Roxburghe's clause were met together with those of the clause on free trade. During the debates on the Act each clause had been voted separately, in line with a general understanding that contributions from every side would always be welcome. It was

Hamilton that proposed the process might be best rounded off if the whole Act finally 'should have the solemnity of a vote'.[50] It took place on August 13, to give a thumping majority of 58.

Scots felt they had done themselves proud. Riven as ever by faction, and faced with a highly complex state of affairs, they yet managed to forge a unity, something so rare in the life of Scotland, and in defiance of hostile manipulation from on high. They at last found a common denominator, a will of Parliament. As Fletcher crowed, the Act of Security was

> an Act that preserves us from anarchy, an Act that arms a defenceless people, an Act that has cost the representatives of this kingdom much time and labour to frame, and the nation a very great expense, an Act that has passed by a great majority and above all an Act that contains a caution of the highest importance for the amendment of our constitution.[51]

In England a different view prevailed. About the kindest comment came from the Anglo-Scot, Bishop Gilbert Burnet, saying of his countrymen: 'A national humour of rendering themselves a free and independent kingdom did so inflame them, they seemed capable of the most extravagant things suggested to them.'[52] Politicians at Westminster saw in the Act only its alarming clause on free trade which, if not conceded, would bring the separation of the neighbour nations on the death of the queen. In other words, English arms were being twisted to the tune of a chauvinist rant. Anne's Ministers in London advised her not to give the royal assent to any clause in any Act for free trade. But why on earth were English Ministers tendering advice on Scottish legislation anyway, let alone getting it heard? Here lay the whole point of the Act of Security.

The Act left the Scottish Ministry in tatters. Never before had the Parliament passed any measure against the wishes of the Court. Up to the Revolution the Lords of the Articles saw to that. No wonder King William wanted to save them from oblivion: look what had happened now. The question arose whether the Crown retained any power to veto legislation by refusing the royal assent. It occurred of necessity to Queensberry, who would have to advise Her Majesty and follow whatever instruction came back from her.

The opposition argued there was no precedent for a veto. Members set out claims, hardly heard before in Scotland, that sovereignty lay with the Parliament. Ridpath, its reporter, published a tract to define its constitutional position in this 'Age of Kings, the meaning of which [is], in plain Scots, an Age of Tyrants; France, Denmark, Sweden, Bohemia, Hungary, Naples and other nations are speaking instances of it'. It came naturally to a Scot to place his country's political problems in a European context, just as others had done for her banking or colonising schemes and her mercantilist laws.[53] Ridpath recalled that during the last century 'the power of the estates in those countries was wholly suppressed by their princes; and had it not been for the late happy Revolution, this ancient kingdom must in all probability have run the same fate'. Such had been the aim of James VII, 'but blessed be God, our Claim of Right in 1689 broke many of the strongest links of that heavy chain which arbitrary princes and fawning courtiers had put about our necks'. Ridpath appealed to the Parliament: 'It is your power fully to restore us to our ancient liberty.' Hence 'there is no reason for a precipitant settlement of our succession without limitations'.[54] Ridpath pointed out how there had been problems over the succession before, and every time from 1318 to 1689 the matter came before the Parliament. However perilous the politics, this was the law: peaceful settlement of the succession without parliamentary agreement there could not be.

The royal assent was by tradition signified when the Lord High Commissioner touched a copy of the Act with the sceptre. He sometimes did so at once, sometimes waited till a backlog had built up and touched several Acts together. Queensberry did not touch the Act of Security when it passed on August 13, or in that week or in that month. He had good reason: he was holding out for an Act of Supply as well. He said nothing, yet by his demeanour sought to convey that he was not merely obstructing the work of the Parliament out of pique. On the contrary, he carried on presiding over the introduction and passage of further measures, from the government and from private members, by no means all of a routine or uncontroversial nature.

One such measure was decidedly odd: the Wine Act, which in time of war allowed a resumption of imports from France of the Scots lairds' favourite tipple (whisky being as yet little known outside the Highlands). They got through amazing quantities of the stuff: the household in Edinburgh of the Dundases, the leading legal family, consumed sixteen hogsheads of claret a year, equivalent to fourteen modern bottles a day. An English traveller in deepest Lanarkshire found, at Crawfordjohn, the people running barefoot but drinking wine and brandy, 'so common are French liquors in this country'. Some members of the Parliament did wonder whether, at such a fraught juncture, they really ought to be bothering about their booze. Tweeddale asked priggishly if the Act might not 'prostitute our character, as a nation unworthy to be treated with, as having no rule in our actings, nor the least regard to our privileges'. Fletcher, not a drinking man, threw vitriol instead: 'It seems no wine will please us but that of a country against which we are in actual war and which uses us ill in peace and war.'[55]

It was in fact the government that proposed the Wine Act, in its need of the revenue from the customs. This explains some of the opposition that it met as well as some of the support that it won – perversely, from members of the opposition protesting against Scotland's forced involvement in a war unlikely to do her any good. The Ministry calculated that many Cavaliers would back a measure they could regard as pro-French, that the Country party would split because it had imposed the ban on imports in the first place and that in the nation at large many might raise a glass to a government doing something popular for a change. Especially 'the peers and barons of the kingdom' ought to drink a health to the Act because they managed to get rewritten into it the exemption from customs on their wine which they had enjoyed since 1582. With that exception Queensberry and Seafield, just this once in the latter part of the session, marked up a success.

The government's general position remained desperate. Frustrated of the Act of Security, the Parliament passed an Act anent Peace and War which in its lesser way was no less striking an attack on the Scottish constitution as it had evolved under the Union of Crowns. Decisions for peace or war belonged, as they still do in the United Kingdom, to the royal prerogative: unlike under the American constitution (at least in theory) the sovereign simply declares war on his enemies. The Parliament at Westminster, while it will doubtless stage a debate, has no actual power here. The Act anent Peace and War moved Scotland from the British to the American constitutional model and, in a matter affecting the basic fate of the nation, abolished the royal prerogative – 'one of the chiefest flowers of the Crown', Godolphin said aghast.[56] The Act still received the royal assent from Queensberry in the hope of obtaining a subsidy for the army. He failed.

Nor were Ministers the only ones to be trampled underfoot by a Parliament cock-a-hoop at having passed the Act of Security. On September 6, Marchmont rose again to propose the Hanoverian succession, the matter he had already botched in the session of 1702. It then cost him his office, but the po-faced Presbyterian was not a fast learner: he explained to friends that he now offered the proposition a second time because he would hate it to be thought he had been less than serious the first time. He even included limitations on the Crown, indeed free trade, though he cast these baits in vain. When his Act was read aloud by the clerk, following the Parliament's regular procedure, none of the members at first knew what was in it and none objected. Then they heard, as the clerk droned on, the name of the Electress Sophia, Hanoverian claimant to the succession. This brought uproar: 'the whole house fell into a flame'. Seafield in the chair had difficulty keeping members quiet long enough for the reading to be completed. Some then moved to get the Act burned, others wanted Marchmont called to answer at the bar of the house while others would have had him locked up in the Castle. By a majority of 57 they voted that not so much as a mention of his proposal should be recorded in the minutes.[57]

The government finally sought to bring forward its Act of Supply. It only provoked another outcry on every hand that the Act of Security must first get the royal assent. The debate threatened to go quite off the rails with a motion from the floor framed to offer a choice between 'liberty or subsidy'. Nobody could doubt which the house would vote for if once given the chance. Seafield therefore tried to avoid a vote. This brought yet stormier protests. Roxburghe, revealing himself to be as headstrong as he was highbrow, declared that if there was no way of obtaining so natural and undeniable a privilege of the house as a vote, they would demand it with swords in their hands. The legislation of supply ground to a halt.

So the tension which had found release in the Act of Security steadily built up again, while it awaited the touch of the sceptre. Queensberry made no direct statement for almost a month. On September 9 he was again pressed from all sides. The next day, he at long last spoke from the chair:[58]

It was with great uneasiness to me that I was forced to be silent yesterday, when so many did appear earnest that I should speak. I have all the inclination in the world to give you full satisfaction, but I thought that I ought not to be pressed to give royal assent or to declare my instructions in Parliament, which I had made known to many noble and worthy members, beside the queen's servants. Now that these instances are let fall, and that you have proceeded to other business, to testify how willing I am to give you contentment in anything that's in my power, I tell you freely, that

I have received Her Majesty's pleasure, and am fully empowered to give the royal assents to all the Acts voted in this session, excepting only that Act intituled Act for Security of the Kingdom. You may readily believe that requires Her Majesty's further consideration.

Though the announcement could hardly have been unexpected, it met stunned silence. Hamilton and Roxburghe wanly moved that 'an address be made to the queen to give orders to touch the Act'. But, if by a small majority, the members voted to proceed to other business. Fletcher rose in reproach: 'I have waited long, and with great patience, for the result of this session, to see if I could discover a real and sincere intention in the members of this house to restore the freedom of our country in this great and perhaps only opportunity.' Yet, he went on, even the Act of Security imposed its conditions for the future freedom of the nation only in 'a general and indefinite clause . . . liable to the dangerous inconveniency of being declared to be fulfilled by giving us two or three inconsiderable laws'. We may wonder how this squared with his eulogy of the Act not long before, but he concluded that the session, 'in which we have had so great an opportunity of making ourselves forever a free people, is like to terminate without any real security for our liberties, or any essential amendment of our constitution'.[59] So he moved his limitations over again. All this, from the visionary untainted by compromise, summed him up better than anything before. His thinking soared high above everybody else's. 'His notions of government are too fine spun,' said one observer, 'and can hardly be lived up to by men subject to the common frailties of nature.'[60] That was why members beyond his yapping circle of devoted pups could not or would not follow him. His motion fell.

By now it had anyway grown clear that few of those taking part day after day in the business of the house were likely to be satisfied with the outcome of its labours. When Lockhart later wrote up his verdict on the proceedings he said: 'And thus I have gone through this session of Parliament which did more for redressing the grievances, and restoring the liberties of this nation, than all the Parliaments since the 1660 Year of God.' Yet it had not assuaged popular outrage: 'Scotsmen's blood did boil to see the English (our inveterate enemies) have such influence over all our affairs, that the royal assent should be granted or refused to the laws Parliament made, as they thought proper.' It still boded ill that there was 'bribing and bullying of members, unseasonable adjournments, and innumerable other ungentlemanly methods made use of, to seduce and debauch people from the fidelity they owed to what which ought to be dearest to them, I mean the interest, welfare and liberty of their country and fellow-subjects'.

On September 16, Queensberry rang down the curtain on this woeful scene. He called for the Acts passed, except the Act of Security, and touched them with the sceptre. He spoke little but his mood sounded sombre: deep matters were yet to be weighed, for which both queen and Parliament needed time. He had hoped to get a quick grant of supply but, seeing there was no chance of this, he would call a short recess and adjourn till October 12. In fact, the session was over and the Parliament would not meet again in 1703.

The whole had ended in catastrophe for the government of Scotland. It finally found itself stripped of all authority, opposed by a great majority in a Parliament that Queensberry had reckoned would be easy to manage. Himself disloyal to those around him, he had provoked them into actively undermining him. Seafield, Atholl and Cromartie by the end turned back to flirting with the Cavaliers, not necessarily out of Jacobite sympathy – though that was the general assumption at the time – but so as to ingratiate themselves with the English Tories who, now ruling the roost in London, might soon attempt some closer control in Edinburgh as well.

When Queensberry made approaches in the same quarter, he was rebuffed. He sent the queen a long, misleading account of his conduct as Lord High Commissioner, casting the blame for his failure on both the opposition and treacherous colleagues; things would go better next time if he could surround himself with cronies, he blithely promised. This showed his order of priorities – in his debacle, to malign opponents rather than to repair the standing of Scottish government. Anne's reply can only be described as chilling: 'It seems the Parliament has conceived a prejudice against you, and that the people slight my authority under your administration, but I will take care for the future, that neither you will be exposed to their hatred, nor my authority to contempt.'

❧

Such was the immediate background to that furtive meeting in the Canongate between Queensberry and Fraser at the end of September. We need not suppose the machinator was taken in by the mountebank. The Lord High Commissioner, after the failure of every other expedient, must have reckoned he had nothing to lose by finding out what was on offer from his twilit visitor. Even false information might be useful for undermining enemies inside and outside the government. In fact the evidence turned out far too thin to convince anybody else. A printed volume of relevant papers was produced for public consumption the next year. Its catalogue of disaffection starts with a letter from one Highland military officer to another telling him to keep watch on a hunting party in Strathspey for Hamilton, Atholl and Grant of Grant, who was to lead 600 clansmen 'in arms, in good order, with tartan coats all of one colour and fashion' (incidentally, this is among the earliest references to a uniform tartan for a particular clan).[61] The writer means to arouse suspicion, but never shows what might render that particular hunting party, compared to others, treasonable. From then on the quality of the evidence deteriorates.

Queensberry anyway made no effort to look into the charges but sent them straight on to the queen. He hoped hints that the entire parliamentary opposition formed a Jacobite conspiracy might win back his dismissive monarch's favourable attention. But he would be foiled by his own partner-in-crime, Fraser, now pub-crawling round London on money paid out to him by the government of Scotland. Somewhere or other he found himself accosted by a man who was a sort of equivalent of Colonel Hooke on this side of the Channel, if anything even shadier. Robert Ferguson, a former minister of the Kirk, had once gone with a boatload of exiled Covenanters to South Carolina. The hard labour of opening up a steamy colony cured him of any concern with principle: after his return he joined so many conspiracies of a turbulent age as to win the nickname of the Plotter. By 1703 he was apparently a Jacobite. On tracking down Fraser, he plied him with drink and pumped him for information, before concluding that the unsavoury Highlander was out only for himself: in that cause he would sell any other, including the Pretender's. Here lay the makings of disaster – a premature rising, no help from France and a meeting with the hangman for many ignorant of the double dealing between Fraser and Queensberry. Ferguson informed Atholl who, once in the know, could put the queen right while covering his own flank. He was not alone in heaving a sigh of relief. Godolphin, too, felt nervous at the prospect of a hue and cry after Jacobites, being himself in discreet correspondence with St Germain.

In Edinburgh the Scotch Plot became known, more accurately, as the Queensberry Plot. The Lord High Commissioner staked most of his remaining political capital on it and lost. Fraser fled back to the Continent lacking redress for the wrongs originally done him yet, having sought revenge instead, destined to languish for a decade as the crushed victim of his foes' enmity before he could get home again. He would finish on the scaffold after the Jacobite rebellion of 1745.

Above all Queensberry sacrificed the confidence of Queen Anne, but she hardly adorned the sorry tale. In her speech to open the next session of the English Parliament on December 17, she complained of 'very ill practices and designs carried on in Scotland by emissaries from France'. Members listening to her took these words as confirmation of some sort of plot. But they knew nothing more than Her Majesty's frets told them. The little news reaching them from over the border had often been distorted in reports from such observers as William Paterson – now, after trailing back ruined and widowed from Darien, at work as a spy in Harley's pay. If there was yet another Jacobite conspiracy afoot, that seemed to ignorant Englishmen to say enough about the Scots Parliament's general posture of nationalist defiance and its consequent spurning of the Hanoverian succession.[62]

English politicians swallowed Jacobite yarns because they were really seeking sticks with which to beat one another. From the fresh Tory majority in the House of Commons arose a litany of complaint about the Whigs' abuses of power, in the past and as now attempted from their remaining bastion in the House of Lords. Whigs gave as good as they got in damning a Scottish policy which, thanks to Godolphin, had only worsened relations between the two countries. This was why the Lords set up a committee on the Scotch Plot. Their prime target was the English government, even if their final report supported in passing 'an entire and complete Union' at some point safely far in the future. While clearing everyone accused of conspiracy, they still pronounced a verdict that 'there had been dangerous plots between some in Scotland and the court of France and St Germain and that the encouragement of this plotting came from the not settling the succession to the Crown of Scotland in the House of Hanover'.[63] Well, they would say that, wouldn't they?

≈

Altogether the winter of 1703 saw Anglo-Scottish tensions still rising, indeed rising faster. Scots gentlemen were yet not deterred from going to London after their own parliamentary session had ended for some well-earned rest and recreation, to sniff the political air, to lobby the government or to seek preferment at court. Lockhart, for example, was among those who went. He dropped in on the levees of Marlborough and Godolphin, 'where I saw the Commissioner, Chancellor, Secretary and other great men of Scotland, hang on for near an hour, and, when admitted, treated with no more civility than one gentleman pays another's *valet de chambre*'.[64]

We get a different taste of the Anglo-Scottish tensions bubbling beneath a polished social surface from a brilliant vignette published the next year. It depicts a dinner in London held in a house surveying the River Thames, with candles lit as winter's early darkness falls on the great city thronged by land and water. Whether it reports some real occasion is hard to say for certain – it reads also like a 'dialogue of counsel', a humanist literary genre devised for putting abstract matter into palatable form for the cultured reader. It has a homeric air: the issue at stake is grave, the protagonists are solemnly courteous yet scornful of prissy dissembling. The best of the conversation, factual or fictional, involves the sharp-tongued Sir Edward Seymour, who had recently insulted the Scots as lousy beggars, and the no less fiery Andrew Fletcher of Saltoun, who was the one to give this encounter its literary cast, addressed to his pups at home in Scotland, in his *Account of a Conversation concerning a Right Regulation of Government.*[65]

Fletcher tells how late in 1703 he went on his own trip to London. One day somewhere about Whitehall he bumped into a colleague from the Parliament in Edinburgh, the Earl of Cromartie, whom we have already met through his hostile designs on Clan Fraser; in the Scots fashion he combined this material ruthlessness with an elegant intellect. When Fletcher met him he was walking along with Sir Charles Musgrave, Tory MP for Westmorland, who had taken a lead in adapting his party to the fraught situation after 1689 which might have killed it off. The pair were going back to dine at Musgrave's nearby lodging. On the spot they invited Fletcher to join them.

The three of them sat down in a room

whence we had a full view of the Thames and the city of London. You have here, gentlemen, said the earl, two of the noblest objects that can entertain the eye, the finest river, and the greatest city in the world. Where natural things are in the greatest perfection they never fail to procure the most wonderful effects.

In his turn Sir Christopher extolled the scene and remarked on the human figures moving across it, but Fletcher broke in to say: 'That which charms me most is the liberty and rights they are possessed of in matters civil and religious.'

Musgrave told him not to be so sure, pointing also to 'the corruption of manners which reigns in this place, has infected the whole nation, and must at length bring both the city and nation to ruin'. There was far too much of what would today be called permissiveness: 'Even the poorer sort of both sexes are daily tempted to all manner of lewdness by infamous ballads sung in every corner of the street.'

Fletcher said he knew somebody else who would agree with Sir Christopher, 'that he believed if a man were permitted to make all the ballads, he need not care who should make the laws of a nation'. This is Fletcher's most famous remark, nowadays admired for getting to the bottom of Scotland's schizophrenia rather than for any reflection on the estuarian underclass.

Then they heard Seymour mounting the stair. He felt amused to find he was to dine with two Scotsmen and set about provoking them. He inquired of Fletcher whether he had been the one 'framing Utopias and new models of government, under the name of limitations', helped 'by several men of quality, of about two or three and twenty years of age, whose long experience and consummate prudence in public affairs could not but produce wonderful schemes of government'.

Fletcher coolly replied that 'the art of government has been looked on as something dangerous to be learned, except for those advanced in years' – Seymour was seventy – 'and this only so far as the experience and practice of those corrupt constitutions and ways of living now in use among men will allow . . .'.

'But pray, sir, what is it in those young noblemen, or in the proceedings of our Parliament in general, that you think deserves so much blame?'

'That they would talk,' said Seymour, 'of such limitations on a successor as tend to take away that dependence which your nation ought always to have on us, as a much greater and more powerful people.'

Refusing to be rattled, Fletcher answered: 'We are an independent nation, though very much declined in power and reputation since the Union of the Crowns, by neglecting to make such conditions with our kings, as were necessary to preserve both.' Scots could hardly be blamed for efforts to retrieve their situation and to 'secure the honour and sovereignty of our Crown and kingdom, the freedom, frequency and power of our Parliaments, together with our religion and trade, from either English or foreign influence'.

Sir Edward, 'all in a fret', would not let this pass: 'Hey day, said he, here is a fine cant indeed, independent nation! honour of our Crown! and what not? Do you consider what proportion you bear to England? – not one to forty in rents of land. Besides, our greatest riches arise from trade and manufactures, which you want.'

Fletcher still heroically declined to be offended and explained how Scotland had enjoyed a prosperity of her own before the Union of Crowns in 1603. He prayed Cromartie in aid, though the earl had by now actually lost faith in his nation's viability: he wished the Scots and the English to unite and regard themselves for the future as Britons.

Fletcher, alluding to the corruption of Scottish politicians as one symptom of their nation's poverty, yet went on: 'I take all this liberty before the Earl of Cromartie, though he be a Scots Minister of State, because 'tis well known avarice is none of his faults, and no person in our government is more ready to promote any new and solid project of improvement.'

'I am obliged for the good character you give me,' rejoined the earl, 'but very sorry I can promote none of your projects; they are I fear too great for our nation, and seem rather contrived to take place in a Platonic commonwealth than in the present corruption of things.' He raised, if ever so politely, the charge of republicanism against Fletcher – as evident in the limitations on the King of Scots he had proposed to the Parliament, which rather seemed likely to destroy monarchy.

Fletcher was not to be put down by mere shibboleths: 'I have always thought that princes are made for the good government of nations, and not the government of nations framed for the private advantage of princes.'

'Right,' said Cromartie, 'but then you must accommodate all monarchical government to the nature of princes, else you will make a heterogeneous body of the prince and the state.'

'I understand you not,' Fletcher came back in response, 'unless you mean that all limitations are contrary to the nature of princes, and that they will endure them no longer than necessity forces.'

Seymour had been quiet for a while, but suddenly spluttered: 'And what hopes can you have of enjoying them long, when your prince may be assisted by the power and riches of a far greater nation to take them away?'

'I cannot think,' replied Fletcher, 'that the people of England are obliged by their interest to oppose these limitations in Scotland, unless they think themselves concerned in interest to make us at all times their secret enemies.'

The conversation moved on to trade, a reason often advanced for the Union of Scotland with England. Yet Fletcher protested: 'Trade is not the only thing to be considered in the government of nations: and justice is due, even in point of trade, from one nation to another.'

The thought alarmed Musgrave the Tory, however: 'Soft and fair, the consequences of these maxims reach perhaps farther than you imagine.' He advised Fletcher not to be too speculative 'or think the world can ever be rightly governed'. They had to take things as they were, while working all the same for their country. 'And if any profitable trade be in the possession of our neighbours, we may endeavour to dispossess them of that advantage for the good of our own society.' It was a statement of the classic mercantilist position that international trade is a zero sum, with one country's gain another's loss.

Fletcher reproached England for applying this to Ireland, and wanting to apply it to Scotland too: 'You must own your way of governing that people [the Irish] to be an oppression; since your design is to keep them low and weak, and not to encourage either virtue or industry.' Yet 'the light of nature teaches, that men ought not to use one another unjustly on any account, much less under the specious pretext of government'.

There is not the space here to pursue these vivid but agreeable exchanges, except to mark how they reveal Fletcher as an acute political thinker with ideas of interest even today – in a world yet more subject than his to commerce (or globalism as the current term has it), with small nations dominated by big ones, with wealth and power unequally amassed at centres rather than peripheries, with political combinations forming and breaking under the resultant pressures. For Fletcher such universal tensions underlay the particular contemporary conflicts of Scotland and England, tending towards some outcome as yet unknown in the range between union and disunion. The outcome Fletcher would have preferred seemed, just as much then as it does now, to be rather in retreat than on the advance. He offered his companions the vision of a kind of European union, not of nations but of city-states defending their mutual interests in league with one another. This was modelled on classical antiquity and, notably, had nothing nationalist about it, though Fletcher stands today as a patron saint of Scottish nationalism. In the

Account he finally proposed that Scotland should herself be divided into two city-states centred on Stirling and Inverness: leaving out Edinburgh, which may reflect his own low opinion of the place.

But the conversation at Musgrave's house, like all the best conversations of intelligent men, could scarcely come to a hard and fast conclusion. As the strong-minded yet civilised Fletcher implied, it was not the winning of the argument that mattered, but the taking part:

I was going on to open many things concerning these leagued governments, when a servant came to acquaint us that dinner was set on the table. We were nobly entertained, and after dinner I took leave of the company, and returned to my lodgings, having promised to meet them again at another time to discourse further on the same subject.

CHAPTER 3

❧

1704

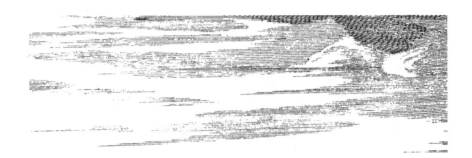

*The burgh of Hamilton, citadel of Presbyterian nationalism
and seat of the enigmatic Duke of Hamilton*

'Hard laws'

On July 19, 1704, an English ship, the *Worcester*, sailed into Fraserburgh, a bleak harbour on the granitic hard shoulder of the north-east of Scotland, to make landfall in friendly, or at least reasonably friendly, territory after an arduous voyage from Calcutta she had begun the year before. The North Sea is treacherous in summer too, when storms no less fierce than those of winter can blow up. But to the 26-year-old master, Captain Thomas Green, that risk seemed preferable to the one he would have faced had he steered directly from the wide Atlantic Ocean for his home port of London, into the English Channel and through the Strait of Dover to the estuary of the River Thames. On this route he would have faced the peril of privateers, especially the fiercest of all, Frenchmen from Dunkirk, who since the outbreak of general European war had infested the narrow seas and menaced any shipping that did not travel in convoy. The thirty crewmen and sixteen guns of the slow and heavy *Worcester*, travelling alone, could have stood no chance against such merciless assailants, who would have felt well pleased with seizing her cargo of exotic goods: pepper, redwood, agla wood, jambee canes, dragon's wood canes, rattans, indigo, cassia lignum, nux vomica and much more.[1]

Instead Green went the long way round, up the Atlantic coast of Ireland, past the Outer Hebrides and Orkney Islands into the North Sea. Even here he could not feel quite safe from attack but at last he might join a regular convoy. Down the eastern seaboard of Scotland the *Worcester* received, along with local vessels, an escort from a frigate of the Scots navy, HMS *Royal Mary*. They proceeded in stages from Fraserburgh by way of Aberdeen and Stonehaven to the shelter of the Firth of Forth, where they anchored on July 31. Green meant to stay here for a while to make the *Worcester* shipshape again after her months at sea and to await another convoy onwards. He and his crew would have been eager to taste the delights of Leith, Edinburgh's salty little port, as raffish then as it is even today. Women and booze were available in plenty, with a ready audience for tales of derring-do in faraway places. The sailors drank too much and talked too loud. So it was that word of their presence soon travelled the couple of miles up the road to the capital and into the ears of Roderick Mackenzie, secretary of the Company of Scotland Trading to Africa and the Indies.

Mackenzie, never fond of the English, had come to hate them for the disaster of Darien. Its sorry consequences flowed steadily across his desk, the latest bad news being but six months old. The Company of Scotland had not quite expired with the hundreds of pioneers it sent on its westward expedition to the Isthmus of Panama. It still hoped to recoup a little of its losses along the eastward trading route round the Cape of Good Hope. The company had sent out three vessels in that direction. The first left in 1700 for Java and China, to be wrecked in the Straits of Malacca on the way home, though its cargo was salved. In 1701 two more set sail. But their captains and crews tired of the journey and turned aside to Madagascar, which offshore at St Mary's Island offered a safe haven for the piracy that European states were now trying to smother in its original Caribbean nests. In this hideaway buccaneers would gather their ill-gotten gains for shipment to America. One of the Scots captains, Robert Drummond, knew of the traffic: a survivor of Darien, he had kicked his heels for a while in New York and perhaps learned of it there. Now, to him and his sailors, freebooting seemed more attractive than the uncertainty awaiting them further east. But when the Scots anchored at the island, the pirates just seized their vessels: these were later lost, though most of the crews survived and a few men returned to tell the tale. That was how Mackenzie gained some inkling of what was going on.

As secretary of the Company of Scotland, Mackenzie had a duty of husbanding what meagre assets still remained to it. One was the cargo waiting in Malacca. In October 1703 the company chartered a vessel to retrieve these goods, the *Annandale*. The captain was brought to Edinburgh to sign a contract while the ship itself still lay in the Thames. Again, sailors' talk was too loud and directors of the East India Company in London got wind of the deal. They had done for the Company of Scotland once before and they could do for it a second time. They held a legal monopoly on trade between England and the Orient. On the strength of that, they investigated whether any Englishman had an interest in a prospective voyage of the *Annandale*, in which case their monopoly was broken and they could claim legal redress. In fact, no

Englishman had: the plan was for the ship to proceed from the River Thames to the River Clyde and load up with trade-goods in Glasgow. Once she set sail at the end of January 1704 the East India Company acted anyway. She was stopped in the English Channel by officers of the revenue who boarded her with an armed guard. They put a pilot in charge and sent the crew ashore. Then they took the ship to Dover where she was declared forfeit to the company.

No wonder Mackenzie felt so angry. But two could play at a game the English had started. The chance arrived with the *Worcester* at Leith. On August 12, the Company of Scotland obtained a warrant for her seizure. Under Mackenzie's personal command a flotilla of small boats went out to her anchorage. They seized her and towed her in custody across the Firth of Forth to a berth in the harbour of Burntisland.

After his tit-for-tat Mackenzie continued to make inquiries about the ships yet to return from the Orient. From crewmen who made it back he began to piece together a plausible picture of how the company's property might have fallen prey to pirates. It was conceivable that Captain Green of the *Worcester* had indulged in a little piracy himself, as was by no means unknown for regular merchant officers to do. In Edinburgh the idea would have been in people's minds after the execution three years before of Captain William Kidd, a Scottish commander sent to the Indian Ocean to suppress buccaneering. Too timid to confront desperadoes sailing under the skull-and-crossbones he had taken to plundering peace-able legitimate shipping he was meant to protect: for which he at length suffered public execution.

Somebody must have come across the missing Scottish ships anyway, Mackenzie reckoned. If sailors home from the Orient denied all knowl-edge of them, it could be because they had taken a hand in wrecking and looting them. On that flimsiest of assumptions, the authorities accused Captain Green and his crew of piracy. They thereby unleashed a chain of events that would send relations between Scotland and England to rock-bottom.[2]

&

It was not as if those relations otherwise looked like improving. They had worsened right through 1703, so far that some remedy for a prospective breakdown had soon to become an English priority – and a higher priority than Union, meanwhile postponed to better times. Scots saw different priorities. And among them Her Majesty's Lord High Commissioner, William Douglas, Duke of Queensberry, saw different priorities from everyone else. He had presided over the last, calamitous parliamentary session and blamed its failure on disloyal colleagues. For the offices of state he told Queen Anne he needed new, loyal colleagues, whose names he would be happy to provide. With their help, he added, he might be sure of success in the session of 1704.

The three Ministers whom Queensberry most blamed were the Chancellor, the Earl of Seafield, the Lord Privy Seal, the Duke of Atholl, and the Secretary, the Earl of Cromartie. In combination they made the trimming Queensberry feel isolated, especially when they flirted with English Tories, to whom he had few links. He was a Whig of sorts, though on the whole a stranger to political principle. Yet the Toryism he alleged of the dissident trio came in handy for him: it meant they might be damaged by Jacobite smears. The false witness Simon Fraser of Lovat bore against them had appeared like manna from heaven to Queensberry, who first squirrelled it away and then, a titbit at a time, spread it forth in the light of day. As that delicate process went on the three Ministers thought to clear the air by a joint meeting with their English colleagues before Her Majesty in London. Queensberry would then have to come clean or shut up.

The meeting followed on January 18. Atholl spoke his mind about the doleful state of Scottish politics. Queensberry by contrast said little. Sir John Dalrymple, Earl of Stair, well used to dirty work as author of the Massacre of Glencoe, did the talking for him and insisted a plot lay at the bottom of his problems. Challenged by Atholl, though, Stair could offer no proof. The meeting turned nasty. Before it ended the queen had to step in to forestall a duel between Stair and Atholl's son. Nobody came well out of it, Queensberry least of all.

Most Scottish politicians were now working on the assumption a new Lord High Commissioner would soon be found. Petty spites apart, it was not just that Queensberry had gone through a bad patch. The mess he faced was a consequence of his whole method of management. Something better was needed for a fraught period ahead during which above all else the authority of Scottish government had to be restored. Queensberry's days were numbered, then. A little English backing would come for him in the report by the House of Lords' committee on the Scotch Plot, written by Whigs, though they felt more intent on promoting the Hanoverian succession. By then none of this much mattered for Queensberry.

Meanwhile, in February, Anne found a chance to sound out a wider range of Scottish opinion than reached her through her Lord High Commissioner when she received a delegation from the Country party, the Earl of Rothes, the Earl of Roxburghe and George Baillie of Jerviswood. They had been sent to London to press the views of the loyal opposition, none being tainted by so much as a whiff of Jacobitism – the two peers were too young to remember the Revolution and Baillie came of stern Presbyterian stock. To the queen's delight they all turned out besides to be gentlemen of upright bearing and courtly manner, unlike so many of their compatriots. They expressed sorrow that Scots at large might be thought capable of treason and hope that this should not bring, as an alarmist Stair was forecasting, the establishment of a standing army in Scotland, paid for by the English, together with suspension of the Parliament. On the contrary, they urged the queen to recall the Parliament so it could look into the Scotch Plot – and sack Queensberry, too, if she wanted an impartial investigation. On him she reserved her opinion but she promised that the Parliament would soon be summoned back and that papers on the plot would be laid before it.

As the Scotch Plot emerged from the shadows, it excited furious indignation in Scotland. In July, Atholl proposed it should be made the subject of an official inquiry. This gave Andrew Fletcher of Saltoun an opportunity to barge in, deploring the Lords' trespass 'on the freedom of this nation' by presuming to probe its politics, 'the greatest step that e'er was made towards asserting England's dominion over the Scots Crown'. And then they had the cheek to recommend the Hanoverian succession! Fletcher thought he might as well try to drive a wedge between English Whigs and Tories too, since the House of Lords was a Whig bastion while in the other place Tories enjoyed a majority – and 'the proceedings of the House of Commons are like those of good subjects to the queen, and good neighbours to us'. Lord Belhaven fumed that he, with the Dukes of Hamilton, Queensberry and Atholl, the Marquis of Annandale, Lord Leven and a Highland chief, Grant of Grant, had all been implicated. Hamilton insisted 'that it was necessary to clear the nation of the plot; that not only those named, but all who voted for the Act of Security last session of Parliament are accused to be in it by a letter from the Duke of Queensberry to Her Majesty last year'. Of this letter, what was more, he had a copy.[3]

The Scotch Plot was causing more trouble than it could ever have been worth to anyone involved. That was why Queen Anne and her English

Ministers at length found reasons for indefinitely putting off an inquiry, to the deep relief of Queensberry, by now urging that further controversy would arouse so much passion as to hinder all other public business. His enemies carried on demanding to see papers on the plot, but with the lapse of time the business was buried – or rather, more pressing matters arose to divert attention from it. Meanwhile it did its damage.

Queensberry, eager as he was at the outset to exploit the spurious plot, in fact ended up its chief victim. Yet he could not have survived anyway. So much had been clear enough at the time of the Country party's delegation to the queen in February. At the end of that sweet-tempered meeting, as the three Scots charmers were backing and bowing their way out of the royal presence, the queen halted them to ask what they thought of the succession in Scotland. It was an awkward question, since none of them had shown enthusiasm for Hanover. So, giving nothing away, they promised to consult their parliamentary colleagues. Anne's query was of interest not for the reply which it elicited but for the thought which prompted it – that there could be a place for the Country party in the conduct of Scottish affairs so long as it seemed sound on the particular point, the succession, of greatest moment to her.[4]

❧

Indeed the Country party – or at least important elements of it – was on its way into office. This cure for the current crisis occurred to James Johnston, a veteran Whig who had served as Secretary for Scotland in 1692–96, ever since then known for his industrious, obsequious manner as Secretary Johnston. Son of Archibald Johnston of Warriston, author of the National Covenant of 1638, he came of an impeccable Presbyterian background. Yet he was a moderate man who had spent his youth in liberal Holland, linking his fortunes to those of the future King William: his house at Twickenham on the Thames bore the grateful name of the Orangerie. For the last few years he had lived in semi-retirement there, while also serving as an adviser on Scots affairs to Sidney Godolphin, Lord Treasurer of England. Johnston was a little out of touch with Scotland, however.

First, Anne had to decide who, other than Queensberry, should be Lord High Commissioner. The choice looked uninspiring. Atholl seemed the best of a bad bunch but, though at the launch of his political career a Revolution Whig, such were the vagaries of Scottish politics that now he could count on no following beyond Episcopalians or Cavaliers; he met a blank response when he put out feelers to the different factions of the Country party. At the opposite end of the spectrum stood the Presbyterians. In the last session one of their leaders, Archibald Campbell, first Duke of Argyll, had often called on government to stand by the Revolution principles of 1689 – which would at least have given him a political programme, if one far from acceptable to the entire nation. The previous September he had died, however, probably of venereal disease and possibly on the very night Queensberry first saw Fraser. The successor to the dukedom was his son John, aged 26, a bumptious young man though a brave soldier. He had set his heart on a military career and was even now away fighting as a brigadier-general in the Dutch service. He remained an unknown quantity in politics.

At home, necessity dictated a quick solution formulated from somewhere in between the Parliament's extremes. Supple Seafield stood ready with a scheme to kill two birds with one stone by bringing together sections of the Court and Country parties. For the Court it was anyway imperative to rebuild itself in a house where during the last session it had lost some crucial votes by a margin of two to one – not least because Queensberry threw away support, notably of Cavaliers, whenever he had to choose between his own and any more general interest. Seafield saw the solution in finding a new Lord High Commissioner while keeping the old Court party so far as possible together. Queensberry's immediate gang of henchmen would be lost with him, no doubt. But more members had backed him for what they could get out of the Court and these might be expected to carry on in the same way, acting with fresh forces fetched in by different factional leaders. The trick was to find a man to manage this delicate coalescence.

Seafield came back from London authorised to offer the job to John Hay, Marquis of Tweeddale, probably on the advice of Secretary Johnston. As a veteran but rather minor politician with not too many enemies, Tweeddale seemed to fill the bill. A crucial condition was to be laid on him, however – that to the coming session of the Parliament he should propose the Hanoverian succession. With this Anne went public as the central aim of policy in her gracious reply to the Lords' report on the Scotch Plot: she would press Scots to legislate it as 'the most effectual means for securing their quiet and that of England, and the readiest way to an entire Union betwixt both kingdoms, in the perfecting of which it was very desirable no time should be lost'. Yet, even as she set out what she wanted, she did realise it was easier said than done. She seems to have been looking for staged progress over some undefined span of time, possibly a long span despite her reluctance to lose time. Johnston recommended also that as an inducement to Tweeddale he should get additional authority to offer the Scots Parliament limitations on the power of the Crown, to come into force on Anne's death. They would more or less restore the Covenanting constitution of 1641: triennial elections; parliamentary control of public offices; legislation to assure impartial justice, presumably by reform of the Court of Session to put a stop, there too, to aristocratic corruption. Bishop Gilbert Burnet, for one, found it a generous offer, 'looked upon by the wisest men of that time as a full security to all their laws and liberties. It did indeed divest the Crown of a great part of the prerogative, and it brought the Parliament into some equality with the Crown.'[5]

It was hoped that, if the ploy worked, the Parliament might forget about the Act of Security, the declaration of Scottish independence still awaiting royal assent after its passage in the previous session. And perhaps then Queen Anne, the Court and the English might for their part forget about Union, since their Scottish problem at its crux – the succession – would have been solved. There could anyway have been no point to limitations if the queen had foreseen that on her death Scotland would no longer be an independent country. To her mind, then, the Hanoverian succession took precedence of Union; and, for now, one need not imply the other. She could have had no idea how the Parliament would mock her good intentions.

The somewhat shy and retiring Tweeddale counted at the age of 59 as one of the older heads in the Scots Parliament if not, it soon appeared, one of the wiser. George Lockhart of Carnwath would judge him to be a 'well-meaning, but simple man . . . forced against his will, by his friends and those he trusted (who made a mere tool of him), to enter into many of the bad measures he pursued'.[6] A large landowner in East Lothian, with an estate running up into the Lammermuir Hills, Tweeddale had done early in life what a Scots laird was expected to do, busied himself with the affairs of his county and served in higher stations when called on. Under James VII he organised defences against invasion, quelled anti-Catholic rioting and bore down on Covenanters' conventicles. It was a good royalist record, yet did not stop him moving straight over to the revolutionary camp in 1688. He had always acted as James wished him to act; now he acted as William wished him to act. Only the enormity of Darien pushed him into opposition. He absented himself with the rest of the Country party from the parliamentary session of 1702. But he came back to play a useful role in the session of 1703 by proposing, at the right moment, a motion to ensure that the bargaining counter of supply was not thrown away in advance of debate on other vital matters.

When Seafield got to Edinburgh, however, he found Tweeddale full of gloom and loth to serve as Lord High Commissioner. He thought too many Country members had been alienated by English handling of the Scotch Plot for the Hanoverian succession to stand a chance in the new session. Yet these members did want their share of such spoils as the government of Scotland might offer – and how were they to get it if not from a Lord High Commissioner drawn out of their own ranks? Tweeddale thought things over and at length accepted the queen's offer. She wrote in relief to say something she would never have felt able to say to Queensberry: 'Your own modesty and backwardness in the concerns of your own family will always be an argument with me to have the more regard to them.'[7]

Yet while Tweeddale could show clean hands, he found them tied in crucial respects. He sought to free them for the conduct of parliamentary business, arguing that amid the habitual hurly-burly he ought not to be bound too tight by London's leading strings. But Godolphin would not hear of it.[8] Nor did he let Tweeddale influence the selection of his colleagues; so far from being united, the reshuffled Ministry was a bag mixed by the need to keep sweet as many factions as might vote for the Hanoverian succession.[9] Seafield stayed on as Chancellor, chief fixer and go-between with the English, while the Earl of Cromartie, Sir James Stewart and even the Duke of Atholl (moving towards Jacobitism but favoured by Queen Anne) also remained in post. Secretary Johnston became Lord Clerk Register. The ministerial personnel had not changed nearly enough to ensure the government's success.

Inside the Parliament, Tweeddale's direct following also showed a character diverse for its modest size, a couple of dozen members merely. To some extent they made up for their numerical weakness with youth and vigour, untrammelled by older links and loyalties. They were soon preening themselves on a patriotism grounded in principle and integrity. Fletcher's cubs figured in this New Party, as it was dubbed. He did not like their leaving his lair,[10] but they had public careers to pursue such as he never could or would have offered them. The Earl of Rothes was an especially valuable recruit to the New Party because, with lands in Fife, he led eight members from that side of the Forth in support of Tweed-dale, including the political clans of Anstruthers and Erskines. And he was a brother of the Earl of Haddington who brought with him another couple of members from the Lothians. Presbyterians also gave support. The more thorough of them, following the Earl of Marchmont, had been advocating the Hanoverian succession for a while, even at the expense of office. Others were leaderless since the death of the first Duke of Argyll but would rally round his son when he came home from the war to lend Clan Campbell's help to Tweeddale; this honeymoon would be brief.

Beyond a core committed to him personally Tweeddale would have to draw on wider support in the Parliament, from those as yet sitting uncommitted on the back-benches. At the beginning of July, with the session about to start, Seafield thought he was achieving this: 'I have disposed the far great part of our Old [Country] party to concur in Her Majesty's measures, and I am not without hopes of success.' Whether he had in his soundings brought up the succession is unclear; for now the one hitch he foresaw was that those calling for free trade or limitations on the Crown (not yet proposed by the Lord High Commissioner) might use delaying tactics.[11] How right he would be.

The basic problem with Hanover was that the Parliament had already shown it meant to hold the succession open till it dealt with other matters. Tweeddale suspected this would not change; so did Seafield. Godolphin, knowing little of their day-to-day difficulties, ignored their advice. He thought his Scottish problem as good as solved now he had swapped a devious for a ductile Lord High Commissioner. He was gung-ho for carrying the succession in this session. When Tweeddale pointed out how various factions still had to be bought off, Godolphin dismissed the hint.[12] The New Party came cheap. A higher price was bound to be demanded by the factions behind Atholl and Hamilton, if they could be purchased at all. Both dukes enjoyed something of a Jacobite reputation and cultivated it for the support it might attract. So in these cases a shift in their alliances – in itself possible and acceptable – could under no circumstances lead to their open commitment to the Hanoverian succession.

Now Queensberry joined his two ducal peers in opposition. The queen hoped to have seen the back of him, yet he showed he was far from finished. Disdaining to attend the session in person, he kept a grip there through a cheerful, dogged aide, John Erskine, Earl of Mar. Mar squared the Jacobites, as wary as Queensberry himself of further exposures about the Scotch Plot. Other factions itched to do down Tweeddale just for having sold out to the Court.[13] If a quick comeback for Queensberry was not on, he still had means to sabotage his successor.

❧

Still, at first the Ministry's position seemed sound enough. Anne gave Tweeddale private instructions to offer the Parliament 'unquestionable proof of our resolutions to maintain the government both in Church and state as by law established in that our kingdom, and to consent to such laws as shall be found wanting for the further security of both, and preventing all encroachment on the same for the future'.[14] No mention of a Union of Parliaments here: the tacit assumption is again that the Union of Crowns will carry on for the foreseeable future.

On the other hand, the queen's public message to the opening of the Parliament conceded the gravity of the crisis between Scotland and England: 'We hoped that the foundation of differences and animosities that (to our great regret) we discovered among you, did not lie so deep but that, by the methods we have proceeded in, they might have been removed.' Yet 'the rent is become wider; nay, division has proceeded to such an height, as to prove matter of encouragement to our enemies beyond sea [sic] to employ their emissaries among you, in order to debauch our good subjects from their allegiance and to render that our ancient kingdom a scene of blood and disorder'.[15]

For this reason Anne was asking the Parliament above all for 'the settling of the succession in the Protestant line, as that which is absolutely necessary for our own peace and happiness, as well as our quiet and security in all our dominions, and for the reputation of our affairs abroad, and consequently for the strengthening of the Protestant interest everywhere'. Delay in this 'may have very dangerous consequences, and a disappointment of it would infallibly make our kingdom the seat of war, and expose it to devastation and ruin'. To encourage decision, 'we have empowered our Commissioner to give the royal assent to whatever can in reason be demanded, and it is in our power to grant, for securing the sovereignty and liberties of that our ancient kingdom'. By the way, she needed supply as well.[16]

In his inaugural speech as Lord High Commissioner, Tweeddale underscored the royal message with stress on its staggering liberality:

In effect nothing hath escaped Her Majesty's care that can any ways contribute to make you a flourishing and happy people, she reckoning the welfare, peace and prosperity of her subjects the only way to her own greatness and happiness . . .

And yet as if all this were too little, Her Majesty extends her care for you further, in recommending to you, as you have heard, the settling the succession in the Protestant line.

He rambled on about it rather more than was necessary at this stage. But if he could get the succession passed then, he repeated, he had the queen's authority to give the royal assent to other Acts for guarding Scotland's liberties, righting her wrongs and fostering her trade. By contrast with the wordy body of the speech his peroration was abrupt: 'I have spoke long, contrary to my way and inclination.'

A final official homily came from Cromartie, who in his turn struck what seems to have been quite the wrong note, seconding the queen's sentiments most smarmily: 'Especially in points of fact, we are bound to rely on her information and judgment more than our own, since what we can but conjecture is obvious to her certain knowledge; and if we should fall into the indiscretion, to oppose our conjectures to her knowledge, that could not miss of dire effects.' He called for common sense, courtesy and coolness in the coming proceedings. Too clever by half, he hardly contributed with his own unctuous conclusion: 'As the Union of Britain is apparently its greatest politic good; so, as certainly, and by the infallible rule of contraries, a division of Britain is its greatest evil. And, it is a necessary corollary, whoever is not for the Union of Britain may be concluded an enemy to it.'[17] Ministers were unlikely to get far with this patronising attitude. It soon became clear, on the contrary, that the Parliament would block whatever they proposed, even when dressed up as compromise.

∽

Unexpected challenges appeared as soon as regular business came on. William Seton of Pitmedden, member for Aberdeenshire, moved for measures 'on such conditions of government to take effect after Her Majesty's death as might best conduce to free [Scotland] from all English influence, to the end the Scots might be in a condition to treat with England, about a federal Union'.[18] He had learned the right order of priorities to win a hearing from this Parliament: frets first, laws later. The kernel of his motion lay in the word 'federal'. Historians point out that at the turn of the eighteenth century this was not a term used with precision, or not with the modern precision, to signify distinct levels of sovereignty, the province of each or relations between them being defined in a constitution. In 1700 thinkers seldom looked beyond a cruder model either of imperial monarchies incorporating older entities or of confederations among still in essence sovereign states, usually for defensive purposes, such as the Netherlands or Switzerland. This was the distinction that had been drawn in one recent analysis by a Scots minister writing from London, the Revd James Hodges; surely the bookish Seton was bearing it in mind. Hodges defined federalism as a system where independent states 'unite their separate interests into one common interest, for the mutual benefit of both, so far as relates to certain conditions and articles agreed upon betwixt them, retaining in the meantime their several independencies, national distinctions, and the different laws, customs and government of each'.[19] As stated, that could have suited Scotland in her future relations with England and in some details it was what the Union of 1707 would bring about. But the Parliament for now felt little inclined to listen to ingenious schemes from clever young men. Seton's motion failed. Perhaps it was this that soon turned him off all forms of federalism and committed him to a Union of Parliaments.

Members wanted to hear, not from brainbox Seton, but from braveheart Hamilton, leader of the nationalist opposition. On July 13 he obliged. He proposed a succinct motion that the Parliament 'will not proceed to the nomination of a successor until we have had a previous treaty with England in relation to our commerce and other concerns with that nation'.[20] In a truculent house this wording almost surpassed that of the Act of Security not just for pithiness (scarcely a hard job) but for unifying force as well – in the previous session the Act, or rather its limitations on the Crown, had put off some Jacobites favouring the royal absolutism which was a hallmark of the House of Stewart. Hamilton's formula, agreed in advance with other factional leaders, could in its mix of compass and trenchancy win over the whole opposition, Jacobites too, let alone Queensberry's bloc of the disgruntled and, according to one estimate, more than thirty members who had by place or pension some dependence on the Court. Lockhart wrote: 'The Court was much surprised and perplexed, not expecting the Cavaliers would have begun so early on that subject; and they hoped to have time to gull over some of the members, with passing a few inconsiderable limitations.' Yet Scotland's greatest expert on limitations, Fletcher, stood up in eloquent support of Hamilton and 'the impossibility of amending and bettering our condition, if we do not take care to prevent any design, that tends to continue the same, without other terms, and better security than we have hitherto had'.[21]

Tweeddale saw Hamilton's game, even while unable to counter it. A duke with dynastic pretensions of his own did not at this stage wish the succession to be settled anyway. But that matter could hardly be spun out by hoo-haa over the flimsy Scotch Plot, which few wanted to be closely scrutinised. What could spin things out was a demand for free trade, because the answer to it lay in the hands not of the aspirant Scots but of the grudging English. Tweeddale said as much to Godolphin, how free trade would be 'the most popular handle to throw off the succession at this time'.[22] Jacobites might concur. Nationalists of any kidney could acquiesce in talks on free trade for the precise purpose of demanding terms 'so extravagant as they cannot be yielded in England'.[23] Complaisance would cloak intransigence.

A vital component of such camouflage was that the Parliament and not the queen (meaning the English government) should name the Scottish delegation to any talks, so as to make sure they did not wander off in search of a Union of Parliaments. It was a position Hamilton had already espoused, as everyone knew. So his nationalist stance remained integral. By supporting his call for a treaty, members were not so much offering an olive-branch to the English as taunting the Court for having fluffed the start of the session. Little did they know that wittingly or no, Hamilton was pointing out a path, stony and serpentine as it would prove to be, not to say strewn with obstacles they made sure to lay, that would at length lead to Union. The Court was to get the last laugh.

Tweeddale may have had an inkling of all this, but what was he to do now? With the session hardly off the ground, his New Party faced a decisive test of its authority. Seafield lobbied behind the scenes. He put to swithering members that a position of limitations on the Hanoverian succession would offer as much bargaining power in talks with the English as one of limitations on an open succession. In the chamber Marchmont underlined the perils of playing with fire: 'There is a popish Pretender, backed with the power of France.' But the government felt its way only warily forward. On July 17, perhaps instructed by Hamilton's turn for simplicity, it prompted Rothes to respond to him, though vaguely rather than crisply: before taking a view of the duke's motion the Parliament should 'rectify our constitution and vindicate and secure the sovereignty and independence of the kingdom'. With that, the Hanoverian succession in effect slipped to the back of the legislative queue: the government had already contrived to reverse its own declared order of priorities.

Members had to decide which of the two motions before them, Hamilton's or Rothes's, to take first. This itself was a test of the government. Debate went on for six hours. It at last reached its conclusion in a proposal from Sir James Falconer of Phesdo, member for Kincardineshire, a crafty old judge who had clawed his way to the bench under Queensberry. With the ironic remark 'that he was very glad to see such an emulation in the house upon account of the nation's interest and security', he proposed to marry rather than choose between the competing motions: he was able to do so just because of Rothes's deliberate vagueness, which meant they did not in their actual wording contradict each other. Other members, fed up with a marathon of procedural wrangling, at once seized on this resolution of it.

Ministers liked the idea not one bit: faced with their first challenge they needed a victory.[24] Seafield from the chair tried to avoid a vote. Lockhart notes that a 'certain member' (presumably himself) recalled an utterance in the session of 1703, that 'if the nation is to be so treated, I know no way to be taken but to demand the vote with sword in hand'. Once again, a hot-tempered house did not have to go so far. Falconer gathered support from the Cavaliers, now working together with Queensberry's dissidents. A vote compositing the two motions was carried by 127 to 79. Then on a substantive vote the composited motion won a majority of 55.

The government did not just lose a battle; it had not even raised an army of anywhere near adequate strength to fight it. Challenged by a combination of Cavaliers and Queensberry's coterie it failed to win over that mass of members in the middle it needed to govern at all, let alone carry the Hanoverian succession. Tweeddale at once wanted to throw in the towel. Of the outcome he wrote the next morning to Godolphin: 'As I have told your lordship in former letters, no other could be expected, considering the ferment the nation is in . . . I see not what can be done but to adjourn till such time as I can have Her Majesty's direction now that the main point is lost.' To his sovereign he also took up his pen, as to one more likely to see sense. The problem was 'the ill temper this nation has been in for some years through the bad usage they have met with from their neighbours in most of these concerns'. This, he added, 'has been of late mightily increased by the House of Lords' proceedings in the matter of the plot, of which great advantage has been taken, to raise such an aversion in them to the settling of the succession at this time that they could hardly bear even the mentioning of it'. He begged the queen to turn to someone 'who may be more capable and so more successful than I have been'. Unluckily for Tweeddale she liked him: he stayed in harness.[25]

To rub in Tweeddale's failure, Scotland at large broke out in rejoicing. This government turned out to be no more popular than the last – in that respect, the New Party had added nothing to the Court. Lockhart wrote how 'after Parliament was that day adjourned, the members that had appeared more eminently in behalf of the resolve, were caressed and huzzaed as they passed in the streets, by vast numbers'. Jubilant crowds followed Hamilton from Parliament House to Holyrood, where as premier duke he lodged, 'and nothing was to be seen or heard that night, but jollity, mirth and an universal satisfaction and approbation of what was done, and that by people of all ranks and degrees'. As usual, the English found the business baffling. Robert Harley, Secretary of State, wondered at the news from Edinburgh 'that men should run into destruction with their eyes open; that the only thing which can preserve them, and unite all of Revolution-principles, is the succession; and yet, because England suggests it, that reason, which were reason enough for it without any other, must be given against it'.[26]

❧

With the Hanoverian succession blocked, and quite off the agenda for 1704, supply was the only other official business. The government had long ago run out of money. A special worry was that the army remained unpaid amid a tense national and international situation. If the English had ever invaded, it is hard to think Scotland's finest could have put up much resistance when their own commander-in-chief, George Ramsay, wrote that 'the small army here is in a manner mouldered to nothing':[27] and this, by the way, in a confidential report to Godolphin. If the general knew which side his bread was buttered, with treason spread thick on top, at least the troops might have redeemed themselves with more fighting spirit. Some in the Scottish government were desperate enough to think the whole army might be paid for out of HM Treasury in London, but Bishop Burnet saw how absurd this notion was: 'An army is reckoned to belong to those who pay it: so an army paid from England would be an English army: nor was it possible to manage such a thing secretly. Neither officers nor men would have taken their pay, if they had believed it came from England.'[28]

The Court being in disarray, the initiative even for supply devolved on Hamilton, who had no mind to be co-operative. He offered a mere two months' supply, if to be voted before anything else, and then linked with limitations. In fact Hamilton had in mind a greater concern in the Act of Security, passed in 1703 to provide either for a separate Scottish succession or for the same succession as in England, but under conditions transferring power from Crown to Parliament, that is, from London to Edinburgh. Now, after its long wait, Hamilton demanded it should receive the royal assent. Tweeddale had no answer. He knew what he might have done if the Parliament had approved the Hanoverian succession, 'but seeing they have entered into a resolve which put that off for this session, things are so far altered, that I know not what I can do, without acquainting Her Majesty and receiving her instructions'. His hope for help from London did not mean, however, he was going to get it.

Given ministerial paralysis, others prodded proceedings forward. On July 21 Fletcher proposed to augment Hamilton's victorious motion of the previous week for a commercial treaty in advance of settling the succession. That motion, perhaps a little too terse for all its acuity, was now to be supplemented with one providing for nomination of eight Scots commissioners from each estate to meet the same number of English commissioners at some place on the border (this to make sure the Scots would not be suborned by temptations of mind or body in London) which they would set about opening to trade. The proposal won support from every side, and notably from Hamilton, who specified only that for the Scots 'the nomination might be in plain Parliament'; in other words, not rigged by royal appointment, as the Anglo-Scottish commission of 1702 had been.

Again, however, the Parliament could not be stopped from haring off on wayward paths of its own. In fact the debate came to turn after all on the Scotch Plot, waxing the fiercer for that. Fletcher himself yielded to a temptation to join in the hue and cry, reviving his charge that the origin of the evil lay in the House of Lords' interference in Scotland, by its inquiry into the plot. Marchmont and Stair argued that the Lords had yet somehow acknowledged Scottish independence and that anyway the plot was a matter for England too. The Marquis of Annandale got nearer the truth in saying the Commons cared not a fig for Scotland. As member after member stood up to speak the house grew rowdy and bitter, coming to the sort of half-baked conclusion no doubt inevitable in the circumstances: it resolved to condemn the Lords but exempt the Commons from censure, as there any Scottish interference in English affairs might be taken amiss! The upshot was that no commissioners could be named – not least because, as Lord Belhaven said, several of the fittest to serve had yet to be cleared of the Scotch Plot. And so the plot continued to exert its ill effects, when its very existence was still to be proved. The queen, on receiving a report of these proceedings, found their tone insolent. Probably they put her off for good from any official inquiry into the plot.[29]

Hamilton had made his contribution to the debate, yet kept his powder dry as it descended into pointless bickering. He stuck by his own view of a way forward, which he had already set out on July 25. He then moved that the Act of Security should be tacked as a clause on to the Act of Supply. In effect, he was saying, the government would be able to get supply only on terms satisfactory to the nationalist opposition.

This business of tacking soon became a matter of hot dispute in both England and Scotland, though at Westminster it was already standard procedure. There an urgent measure could be tacked on to a money bill otherwise unrelated to it because a money bill was something the Lords had no power to block; if a proposal they disliked was thus tacked, they could be forced to pass it. The device had proved useful for English executive government because the two Houses of Parliament might be dominated by different parties, as they were in 1704. Yet that could not be true of a unicameral Scots Parliament. In this case tacking just amounted to obstruction. Secretary Johnston, who dealt with procedural matters, said he thought tacking in England reasonable, 'but here Parliament sits in one house, and tacking of Acts may obstruct voting of them both'. It was anyway 'a straitening of the queen, who may possibly consent to the one, and not to the other'.

The comment made Fletcher lose his always short temper. He flared up to accuse Johnston of having, when promoted to his office or place, sold himself to 'English designs'.

Johnston retorted: 'There can be no influence but the place I have, and it is known I lost a higher place for my concern for my country' – harking back to 1696 when he had resigned as Secretary for Scotland in defence of the Presbyterian interest.

The vehemence of Fletcher's attack shocked many members, who asked the chair to call him to order. His answer, as so often before, was to provoke his critics all the more fiercely. Backed by Hamilton, he widened his accusation to claim that this session's whole agenda had been set in England: 'The letter by the queen to the Parliament was written when no Scotsman was about her, and so behoved to be by English influence.'

Johnston retorted in injured innocence: 'It came up to the queen from Scotland, I believe there is no Englishman would be at the pains to draw a letter.'

The row escalated. Sir James Halkett, the young member of the New Party for Dunfermline, called out that Fletcher was being impertinent. Fletcher snarled: 'He that would call me impertinent is a rascal' – a word which sounded more insulting to contemporary ears than it does to ours, implying that Halkett, a baronet, was a low-born sort of fellow.

Everything threatened to get out of hand. Sir John Erskine, member of the New Party for Burntisland, demanded both men should be censured for unparliamentary language.

From the chair Seafield told them off and they calmed down. They apologised for any offence they had given the house and promised they would not challenge each other to a duel outside – which would have been the normal way to settle the matter.

The tiff brought a decision no nearer. Lord Ross moved the house should vote two months' supply at once and a further four months' supply after the Act of Security got the royal assent. The Earl of Roxburghe moved there should be no action at all till the royal assent was received. The Lord High Commissioner, holding the sceptre which might touch the Act, made a bizarre admission of personal support for the will of the house which it was his official duty to thwart. Tweeddale recalled 'what hand I had in that Act of Security, that I added more clauses thereto than any other whatsoever, and that I am still in my private opinion of the same mind now as then'. Yet once again he would 'have to acquaint Her Majesty before he could do anything'.[30]

It is hard to feel much sympathy for such a feeble Lord High Commissioner, even in this ungovernable house. Lockhart would gloat how Tweeddale and his colleagues 'were obliged to inform the queen, that their measures being quite broke, matters were come to that height, she must either allow the commissioner to grant the royal assent to the Act of Security, or resolve to adjourn the Parliament, without obtaining money to pay her troops'. In private, Tweeddale was himself advising the queen that the time had come to surrender over the Act of Security: on July 22 he told her this 'seems so absolutely necessary to quieten the minds of your people'.

With her Scots advisers at their wits' end, Anne could only turn back to her English ones. If imperious Godolphin remained unwilling to surrender, he was astute enough to be looking for a way out. And quaking Tweeddale managed to gather his thoughts so far as to put an idea in the Lord Treasurer's head. The Parliament, he wrote, remained so insistent on an Act of Security that it 'seemed willing to accept [one] without the clause of communication of trade', that is, without stipulating free trade between Scotland and England. He possessed no authority at all to say any such thing: the Parliament had not voted to amend the Act in this sense nor even discussed doing so. Godolphin – or at least somebody in London – took the hint, though. Given the wider political necessities of the moment (with dramatic moves in the European war, to be dealt with below) there was something here that might at a pinch be presented as a bargain between the Court and the opposition in Scotland, though for preference not an explicit one. Anne's advisers in London agreed it would be 'better to satisfy the desires of the people, by allowing that Act the royal assent, than by refusing it to increase the divisions, and be obliged to disband the army'.

What followed was a sin against parliamentary sovereignty, but a sin of omission rather than commission. Nothing of it can be detected from the official record of the *Acts of the Parliament of Scotland*, not published till 1824. Here the Act of Security has no clause on free trade, though we know beyond doubt from earlier texts that it had been in the legislation of 1703. John Clerk of Penicuik recalled that 'the clause relating to the liberty of the plantations was by some trick or other left out, for though it was voted and agreed to, as will be found in the minutes, and though it was perhaps read with other clauses in the Act in order to have the royal assent, yet it seems it never had it'. And Clerk must have looked, for he noted also that 'in none of the printed Acts does it appear, though by the by it was chiefly to obtain the benefits of the plantations that the Union was agreed to in Scotland, at least it was the chief instrument used for the settlement of the question'.[31]

The Crown exercised by stealth what in the United States is known as a line veto, a power presidents often wish they had, if so far withheld from them. In Scotland this constitutional innovation – to put it kindly – took a week to concoct, with the session adjourned meanwhile.[32] Once it resumed on August 5, Tweeddale announced he was now under instructions 'to pass an Act of Security that might sufficiently secure the nation'. Had Hamilton gained an inkling of manoeuvres behind the scenes? He stood up to say 'it was not *An* Act of Security, but *The* Act of Security that they were for'. If there had been a change to the text, the duplicity of it perhaps did not escape the duke. Or else, was there some tacit accord in the house that the Act would be worth having even without its clause on free trade? In this case, we can at least surmise that the politics rather than the economics of the matter stood uppermost in members' minds.

Anyway Hamilton's caveat was passed over. The Act received another reading, was then approved – and this time touched by Tweeddale with the sceptre. Now it had become law that Scotland would choose for her next monarch one different from England's unless meanwhile satisfied in her conditions. Daniel Defoe would write in his *History of the Union* that 'the measures taken in Scotland seemed to be well grounded, and their aim well taken . . . This effectually settled and declared the in-dependency of Scotland, and put her in a posture fit to be treated with, either by England, or by any other nation.' At once the Parliament passed unanimously an Act for six months' supply.[33]

❧

What official business the session could do was now, a week into August, done. Yet, sweaty and bored, it meandered on to little purpose for the rest of the month as different factions took a chance to show, even now, how bloody-minded they could be. There was a tally-ho after Queensberry when a committee of inquiry into public expenditure revealed he had spent £Scots 42,000 on some murky 'secret service'. That prompted an Act anent Misapplying Public Funds. Other legislation was less useful – for example, a provocative measure to forbid imports and promote exports of wool, which the English saw as a sanction on their most lucrative trade: it invited retaliation on Scotland, which came along in due course. Not content with castigating Ministers past and present, members sought diversion in falling out with one another, even over trifles. Hamilton and Fletcher, at some mere difference on the order of business, challenged each other to a duel before Tweeddale exacted of them a promise that they would make no more of the squabble outside the house. Yet they did not speak to each other for months.[34]

The whole session ended in grudge. It passed a remonstrance to the queen over the misbehaviour of her English House of Lords, for good measure voicing dismay at not having even yet had sight of papers on the

Scotch Plot. She was asked, since interference from Westminster infringed Scottish independence, 'to take such measures as may effectually prevent such meddling in the future'. While on the remonstrance Queensberry's supporters abstained – all they decently could do – the New Party still failed to muster enough votes to block it. Here was a final reminder how impotent Scottish government had become. During the session of 1703 the Court's more resolute approach had brought humiliation; during the session of 1704 the alternative of wary accommodation to Scottish interests equally finished in abject failure. The question of the succession remained as open as ever and the rest of policy in disarray while the Anglo-Scottish crisis deepened. At the end the Scots stood angrily defiant of England. England would not fail in firm response.

On August 28 Tweeddale adjourned the Parliament for six weeks, though in fact it was not to meet again till the summer of 1705.[35] He laboured under no illusions about the mess he had made of it. Instead of excuses he offered his resignation. The queen again refused him but, too late, let him bolster his position with a ministerial reshuffle. Atholl was put out: while loyal to the queen he could summon up no allegiance to the Hanoverian succession, and this proved to be his downfall. It was more generally a parting of the ways for him and others tempering an inward Jacobitism with deference to the person and policy of her present Majesty.

Tweeddale also used this brief bout of royal indulgence to weed out men still wedded to Queensberry and bring in supporters of his own. Roxburghe became Secretary, a post he held jointly with the veteran Seafield, whose own office of Chancellor went to Tweeddale: a mistake, for he found its administrative routines irksome. But at least a little was done to tighten management of Scotland after a spell of hopeless drift. With supply granted it grew possible to buy some support too, so long as it came cheap. The young Seton of Pitmedden, for example, had approached Seafield for a pension of £100 a year, promising 'he will be your servant and give you a suitable return'. Seton now got his money, and so offered a practical demonstration of what he preached in his jeremiads on the enervation of public virtue.[36]

❧

Scottish government somehow staggered on, then. But if it was one thing for the Parliament to vote supply, it was another to raise supply. Land-owners liable to tax had to pay in specie, in gold or silver coin: there was, with an exception shortly to be noted, no other means of doing so. Availability of specie depended as much as anything on the balance of payments. When Scotland had a surplus on trade, specie came into the country; when she had a deficit, it went out. John Law of Lauriston, the political economist, reckoned just one-sixth of more than £Scots 2 million issued after a recoinage of 1686 remained a couple of decades later in circulation. At least since King William's Ill Years, specie had been going out, now faster, now slower. It had gone out of necessity to buy food during the famine. Yet recovery from this crisis of subsistence did not halt the flow. And of Darien we need not speak. A pamphleteer concluded in 1704 that 'the want of money has been gradually growing for some years past'. Among the causes, 'a balance of trade hath had a principal share, for want of being duly regulated'.[37]

If Scots had a chronic and growing problem with the balance of payments it was rather because they could not produce many of the things they wanted to consume, let alone the things they needed to progress. A recurring problem in Scottish history is how the intellectual developments run ahead of the material conditions. One piquant example from this last epoch of the independent nation came in a difficulty discovered by James Gregory, inaugural professor of mathematics at the University of St Andrews. In setting up Scotland's first astronomical observatory there he had been obliged to get every single thing he needed from abroad, not only all his scientific instruments, but even the paper on which to write out his calculations. At best he could buy this from a bookseller in Edinburgh who imported it from Holland, at worst he had to do his sums on blank spaces in letters he received.

On a broader scale it would still be too much to claim the condition of the economy was past remedy, though the useful innovations tended to offer a future potential rather than an immediate prosperity. For now, the press of problems had the net effect of inducing a protectionist mentality among the leaders of Scotland. True, a few were waking up to the advantages of free trade which would in the end, if not without difficulty, save the nation from its backwardness and set it off on its modern evolution. But more typical was a petition to the Parliament that the plethora of mercantilist regulations already in place 'in no ways answered the design or obtained the end, for which they were made, which was to curb prodigality, improve our own product and discourage all foreign import'. For example, 'it is evident from practice and experience that foreign silks of all sorts, and stamped calico and linen were never more frequently worn and . . . hundreds of ells are worn, for one ell made in the kingdom'. This was not just a commercial but also a moral concern, as 'the trade of silk from abroad is carried on by unfreemen, strangers and smugglers, of mean fortune, and desperate, who run the silkstuffs free of duties and all public burdens, and sell them clandestinely, to the ruin of the merchants and retailers'. It comes as no surprise to find this petition had been sent in by the merchants of Edinburgh. But lest anyone think them self-interested they cited a risk to every fellow citizen of 'draining the kingdom of money, for all smugglers only deal with money in specie'.[38]

Not least because of the monetary problem, the Scottish state had carried out several inquiries into trade in the seventeenth century. Since the state lacked an efficient customs and excise, the data turned out to be of dubious value. In 1704 it undertook another survey. A copy is preserved in Fletcher's papers, presumably for use as ammunition in parliamentary debate.[39]

Fletcher's own economic ideas were always hazy, yet he did not dissent from advocates of Union that Scottish trade had decayed and was still doing so; since he supposed this to have gone on since 1603, he concluded the Union of Crowns was at fault. In his cause of a decentralised, quasi-republican constitution he proceeded to call for reforms at least as drastic as any unionist's. He would have begun with government and foreign policy, to shift relations with England on to a more even footing and reap the benefits of neutrality in her wars. If his wider international vision had ever come near realisation, it too would have brought a commercial effect in ending mercantilism.

But Fletcher's whole outlook rested rather on a fancy that commerce created corruption and conflict among the nations. He wanted instead to found the economy on agriculture and to curb commerce, at least beyond what the sumptuary expenditure of the nobility and gentry might permit. To put it another way, in order to defend the rights and interests of her people, Scotland would have to reject the path of capitalist development England was laying down as an example before her. In that vivid *Account of a Conversation concerning the Right Regulation of Governments* which Fletcher published in the spring of 1704, he wrote:

> If the governments of the world were well regulated, and men might have the liberty of choosing, they would not be confined to such narrow, barren and unwholesome places, nor live so much at sea, or in the exercise of a sedentary and unmanly trade, to foment the luxury of a few; but would

disperse themselves over the world in greater or lesser numbers, according to the goodness of the soil, and live in a more free and manly way, attended with a more equal distribution of riches than trade and commerce will allow. Trade is not the only thing to be considered in the government of nations.[40]

Fletcher here presents the prospect of a national economy where trade and manufactures are not large or vital elements. So far as derived from the Scotland of his own day the prospect is perhaps not altogether perverse, yet it would be dispelled by her actual development in the eighteenth century. He saw how this might come about and accepted it was a goal for many of his countrymen, yet that did not alter his view of it as unnatural. By this he meant it would skew the distribution of wealth and drive men into a crude, licentious materialism hostile to the public good. He could not demonstrate that was an inevitable mental or practical progression from his premises. He just drew, by way of contrast, his Platonic picture of a perfect alternative. Founded on agriculture, it would assure more equal distribution of wealth, eliminate social tensions, restrain anarchy and vulgarity, lead people to their duty.

In short, Fletcher could not reasonably claim to be defending the Scotland of his day against the menace of Union. On the contrary, he stressed he was seeking changes at least as drastic as Union might ever bring. He started from the point that the primitive agriculture practised by Scots was 'the principal and original source of our poverty'. He wanted radical reform of it through introduction of long leases, enclosure and freehold, with payment of rents in money rather than in kind and formation of a class of sturdy peasants perhaps not unlike that which, a century later, Thomas Jefferson would wish on the American prairies. But Scotland was mountainous, and along Fletcher's path the Highlands, containing half the population, had yet further to go than the Lowlands. As a first step towards peace and security he called for the chiefs to be stripped of their feudal power over the clansmen. Again the long-term solution lay in better husbandry, in moving on from the pastoral life of the glens. While Fletcher did not want to abolish trade and commerce, the sole scope reserved for them in his vision of the future lay in their underpinning the structure and values of an ideal agrarian society. All this is set out in his *Second Discourse concerning the Affairs of Scotland*.[41]

It was in that cause Fletcher collected his statistics. Contrary to a naïve view among Scottish academic historians of the present day, statistics do not guarantee absolute knowledge free of bias. They often if not always reflect prejudices, assumptions and wishful thinking among those who gather or deploy them. Fletcher's show that in 1704 the four largest exports from Scotland were linen, to the value of £Scots 480,000; wool and herrings, to the value of £Scots 300,000; and black cattle, to the value of £Scots 240,000. Together they accounted for well over half of exports. On the other hand the largest imports were of linen and leather, about one-quarter of the total. Then there followed a long list of every kind of consumer good available in northern Europe at the time. This being Scotland, alcohol, tobacco and 'drugs' figured prominently, accounting for more than 15 per cent of the total. With trifling exceptions, all glass and metalware in Scotland were imported, and so was much even of the earthenware, not to speak of more elegant furniture, mirrors and clocks, let alone porcelain, tea, coffee and chocolate, or prunes, dates, raisins, figs and currants, or olives, capers, anchovies and pickles (some of these items, it must be said, not easily found in the average Co-operative supermarket even today).

The really dismaying statistic emerged when all the figures were totted up. The value of the country's exports came to something over £Scots 2 million and imports to over £Scots 4 million. Here, with the imports worth almost double the exports, lay the source of a constant drain on the nation's money which in the end must have squeezed Scotland whether or not a third of her liquid capital had vanished into the jungles of Darien.

It did help Scots that the economy of England forged ahead about the turn of the eighteenth century with a vigorous expansion of foreign trade and a burst of construction, of which the finishing of St Paul's Cathedral in London, the noble architectural composition at Greenwich and the royal palaces at Kensington and Hampton Court are permanent memorials. Here was an economy mature enough to experience cycles, however. The boom flipped over into bust after a cyclone in November 1703 blasted the coasts of the English Channel and sank ships in large numbers. The losses compounded the soaring expenditure on war with France. Money tightened, and the effect spread from London to Scotland. While London was already a financial centre with mechanisms to cope with contraction, by a fall in the stocks and a rise in the rates of interest, Scotland again remained backward, with no financial markets and far less coin.

❧

Yet, as memories of Darien began to fade, Scots still sought a magic wand to wave and raise their penurious place among the nations. They did have a bank, the Bank of Scotland, founded in 1695 by, among others, William Paterson, colonial pioneer and now in his ruin an English spy. For its time unique in Europe, a joint-stock corporation formed from private capital for making a business of banking, it remained, except in the legislation creating it, unconnected with the state. By contrast the contemporary Bank of England was chartered by the state as a machine for raising money. The Bank of Scotland did not lend to the state, indeed was forbidden to do so – though this perhaps had less to do with the condition of the bank than with the condition of the state, in its fiscal feebleness.

So all the bank's innovations arose from private enterprise, often needing a period of trial and error before their worth could be proved, or not, as the case may be. One of the earliest was the Scottish pound-note, still with us today, thanks not least to the success a century later of Sir Walter Scott in making of it a nationalist icon. At first the bank had issued notes only of larger denominations, usually £5. The circulating currency in Scotland remained the coinage, the very medium of exchange likely to vanish in a crisis. Here was a reason why pound-notes proved so useful. The bank thought long and hard before it issued them, but in 1704 it decided to. The move was timely because a paper currency turned out to be one means of dealing with crisis, by smoothing peaks and troughs in demand for cash. If coin vanished, external payments to cover a trading deficit had to be made clumsily with plate or bullion; but internal payments, even of taxes, could be made with a note. Once this realisation struck home a great expansion of the issue followed, with displacement of specie in smaller transactions.

The pound-note was, after logarithms, the Scots' second great invention for the modern world, harbinger of tarmacadam and anaesthesia. Like other inventions it needed careful management at the outset, more careful than Scots knew. They had to undergo a learning process before a stable monetary system could emerge. Eventual success here is to be admired as all the more remarkable for the fact that no state became involved.

By the autumn of 1704 the Bank of Scotland reached a crucial stage in the learning process. War was draining the country, indeed the British Isles, of specie. Rumours spread that the Scottish government was about to revalue the currency, that is, declare coins to be worth more than their face-value.[42] That response would be taken by modern economic theory as bizarre; but these were early days in demand management. Anyway, with gains to be made in holding specie for a rise, who would hold notes? Directors of the bank complained that the rumours of revaluation 'occasioned a very great, unexpected and unaccustomed demand'. By December people were rushing into their office in a close off the Lawnmarket of Edinburgh and clamouring after coin in exchange for handfuls of notes they brandished. Coin ran out. The bank's charter did provide for such a contingency in allowing it to raise further capital from subscribers, and the directors tried to. They also sought to make themselves more liquid by calling in loans, but that would take weeks or months and could be of no use on the morning the bank's tills emptied.

A huge row blew up. Customers complained that directors 'entrusted with the nation's money' were for 'love of gain' lending it out and 'never concerning themselves whether it was to stay in the kingdom or not'; so much departed that it 'in a manner left us beggars'.[43] The bankers just saw themselves as engaged in a harsh but necessary duty, forcing the system to contract after over-expansion. Perhaps the basic problem was that events moved too fast. On December 18 the directors ruled no more coin should be paid out for notes. The bank stopped.

A few days later Lockhart of Carnwath happened to pass by the sanctuary at Holyrood where debtors could take refuge from creditors: 'Money is a great rarity and the Abbey Close is as thronged just now with broken lairds and tradesmen as if Her Mejesty's Commissioner were there with his court.'[44] The impact on propertied Scots explains why, though the bank and the state were independent of each other, the state found itself unable to ignore the bank's stop. Its governor was David Melville, Earl of Leven, not at all a banker to trade but rather a soldier, one of several who had been drawn by troubled times into politics, as an Old or Revolution Whig, and so now into Scottish high finance, such as it was; this canny Fifer showed himself also a kindly soul – 'the civillest man alive', according to Lockhart.[45] His prisoners in Edinburgh Castle once thanked him for his gentle treatment of them. Could depositors at the Bank of Scotland expect the same mercy?

To Leven at any rate it fell to receive a committee of privy councillors who stomped up the Lawnmarket to look into his books.[46] They satisfied themselves that, while the bank might have turned for the time being insolvent, its true assets exceeded its liabilities. This was convenient for Tweeddale, a shareholder himself. Now he could feel justified in arranging a rescue to tide the bank over while it got more capital subscribed and pressed its creditors to repay their loans, meanwhile offering interest on bank-notes to deter holders from redeeming them. The stop would last for five months, but the bank escaped collapse and its close shave led rather to the refinement of banking principles in Scotland.

An underlying problem was the recurrent one in modern society of what to employ for money in all its many uses, as not only a medium of exchange but also a measure of value and a store of wealth. Ever since ancient times the answer had been to employ gold and silver. But when gold and silver ran out, or were in short supply to start with, then they could not be used for the whole gamut of monetary tasks, which therefore could not be performed. This was the problem Scotland had faced before establishing a bank. The problem was eased by issue of notes convertible on demand into the precious metals, but the financial crisis of 1704 showed the problem was far from solved.

If people wished to move away from the rigid system of controlling credit according to a stock of gold and silver, they had to find alternatives. Scotland was precocious in proposing them. One idea came in the form of a land-bank, a mechanism for turning into current money the future rents from land or revenues from tax on it by an issue of notes based on these prospects. The notes would not be redeemable in gold or silver on demand, so the backing for notes was an abstraction rather than precious metal, if an abstraction potentially realisable – in the last resort, by sale of the land. Credit might then be provided beyond what the cautious banker held in his vaults.

The idea as yet bristled with difficulties. There had to be rules of some sort, because the procedure of monetising rents or revenues in itself set no definite limit to the issue of notes, unlike a system of convertibility into precious metal. Also, the state would have to intervene to the extent of making non-convertible notes acceptable by law, to create a principle of legal tender in other words. But if proper controls and safeguards could be put in place then Scots, not to speak of the rest of humanity, might at last find that means to fulfil their dreams which we see on every hand today – by creation of credit, in other words of money they do not as a matter of fact have.

Scottish debate over all this began with Hugh Chamberlen, the obstetric surgeon who in 1688 delivered the Old Pretender to Queen Mary of Modena and King James VII. In his spare time Chamberlen dabbled in finance. Here he was in some ways strikingly modern, anticipating arguments in the twentieth century of the Nobel prizewinner in economics,

Friedrich von Hayek, who sought to deter governments from debauching the currency by interposing a private interest in its issue.

Both started from the fact that money is more than precious metal. Anything can be monetised: to quote Chamberlen, 'all materials, when made money by a government, whether silver, gold, tobacco, leather, fishbones, shells, credit, etc. becomes current living pledges, and therefore requires no interest, though some of them are more fit than others, and none more so than land credit'. He went on: 'It is indifferent of what material, weights and measures are made, provided they agree with the public standard.' This could be especially useful for Scotland: 'Credit upon land, which Scotland does not want, may be made as useful as real money, as any of gold or silver, which Scotland has not in plenty.'[47] A friend of Chamberlen's in Edinburgh, the lawyer James Armour, now in the crisis of 1704 offered advice to the directors of the Bank of Scotland. The country needed 'circulation within itself, independent of the foreigner' – so not subject, like specie, to pressure from the balance of payments. She also needed a bank resting on 'the public faith of the nation', issuing notes with the status of legal tender.

The debate widened. The Scot who won his intellectual spurs from it was John Law. He had returned home after several years on the run in Europe for killing a man in a duel. During a spell in Amsterdam he lived off the gaming tables. In the cold light of morning he would ponder problems of the money he had staked and in large amounts won the night before. Back in Scotland he began to publish his conclusions in tracts addressed to the Parliament.[48] He advanced contemporary thinking through his advocacy not only of paper money guaranteed by the state but also of a public body to spend it on promoting progress. He believed that the Bank of Scotland was in principle a 'very good thing' yet that it had misdirected its efforts.[49] Without some matching economic development to soak up the issue of pound-notes, 'almost all use for money' had vanished. Money instead emigrated, 'for our imaginations were so blinded with the notion of there being great sums of specie in the bank that we thought the national stock of money secure and satisfied ourselves with pieces of paper which either were readily exchanged for specie or circulated amongst us upon the credit of the managers'.

Law, aware that his bright ideas might be tarnished by his shady past, also understood how few go far in Scotland without political patronage. His choice of patron proved shrewd too: he teamed up with the young Duke of Argyll, himself just back from Europe and ready to make a mark at home. Lockhart could look down from the height of his sterner principles on the upstart financial wizard who 'lived by gaming and sharping'. This 'cunning fellow, and lively expert in all manner of debaucheries, found a way quickly to get into my lord Duke of Argyll's favour'. Once successful in that, he 'presented a very plausible scheme all the Court . . . espoused because it was so found that in process of time it brought all the estates of the kingdom to depend on the government'.[50] Such creative accounting might well have beguiled the ambitious and autocratic Argyll, who would have felt in general impressed by Law's renowned mathematical virtuosity, or maybe just by his tips on sex. Or again, it may have been the duke's younger brother, Archibald, later Earl of Islay, that lobbied his less cerebral sibling on Law's behalf; Islay at length became a patron of science and collected a library of 1,000 mathematical volumes, with fourteen editions of Euclid alone, to serve a range of his hobbies from classical architecture to scriptural chronology to general improvement of Scotland.

In course of time such improvement turned into the great cause of Whigs of the Enlightenment, as opposed to Whigs of the Revolution, who had been more concerned with the condition of their souls than with mathematical (or sexual) ingenuity. By this change of heart enlightened Scots would be depoliticised; they argued no longer from partisan positions, in the state let alone in the Church, but on an altogether more abstract and ultimately consensual level, concentrated on the right role of the ruling class in a framework for progress. In a sense, economics became the politics of Scotland.

This change of heart was owed not least to Law, with his innate carelessness about loyalties. Once Scotland lost her independence he would depart for France and, after converting to Catholicism, find a new benefactor, the Duke of Orleans, regent during the minority of King Louis XV. Under such exalted patronage, which also made him Duke of Arkansas, Law set up a bank to implement his principles. The result was the ruinous Mississippi Scheme, leading in 1720 to one of the greatest collapses in financial history. Yet Law cannot have been wholly wrong to reject the straitjacket of liquidity imposed by specie, and seek instead the foundation for a managed system of money and credit: this is, after all, what he have on a global scale today.

How far John Law advanced financial thinking even in his own time may be gauged by comparing him with William Paterson, his rival as the Scots' economic guru. Paterson belonged to the older world of mercantilism, though he had taken its thinking in new directions by his personal interest in loosening the ties that bound commerce, its expansion and so its proceeds. Yet his aim was still to accumulate gold and silver, as he made clear in a tract, *The Occasion of Scotland's Decay of Trade*. 'The balance of trade will never be on our side', he said, 'unless, by our frugal management, we export more of our native commodities, and import less of superfluities; otherwise the nation will be impoverished, and drained of its wealth.' He took care to distinguish his position from his rival's: 'Although Law should settle an imaginary credit on tallies or notes, it would not have the desired effect . . . This imaginary credit would not be received in payment, though Law should establish the same, and order their currency.'[51] Here Paterson was setting out a case for full, instant convertibility of paper money to precious metal. In his view a forced circulation of paper money would cause precious metal to be hoarded, then to go to a premium against notes and thus to be exported. As financial transactions ceased, real transactions would follow, for precious metal would have passed out of circulation and the only other legal tender would be all but worthless.

The Scottish debate turned out amazingly precocious, even if, like many precocious debates, it was conducted without much experience and on a limited fund of hard evidence. The outcome did err for now on the side of caution: after the crisis had been mulled over in the chamber of the Parliament, counting houses and taverns, the government decided to keep the Bank of Scotland as a private corporation and withhold from its notes the status of legal tender.[52] Still, in its official aspect the affair reminds us how the proceedings of the last Scots Parliament attained a level of economic, as well as political, interest often going well beyond the matters on hand. Members understood land and business from personal experience. The Scottish debate combined that experience with the rationalising speculation of public intellectuals. Then, as now, it was a formula for deepening insight and improving practice, a procedure that, once learned, would continue in Scotland long after the demise of the Parliament. Here, at least, she was not a backward nation. On the contrary, she led the whole of Europe.

❧

If Scots were laying up treasures in some intellectual heaven, in stubborn reality their domestic scene still looked bleak. Under a powerless government the internal problems multiplied, while the external situation grew more complex and demanding too. The European war went on, with fortune now smiling on English arms. In May 1704 one expeditionary force of Queen Anne's landed in Lisbon, then another near Barcelona to help the Catalans in defence of their liberties against the Bourbon, Philip V, installed on the Spanish throne in Madrid. Two months later Admiral George Rooke seized Gibraltar. 'It has been much questioned by men who understand these matters well,' wrote Bishop Burnet, 'whether our possessing ourselves of Gibraltar, and our maintaining ourselves in it so long, was to our advantage or not. It has certainly put us to a great charge, and we have lost many men by it.' But he consoled himself that the Spaniards were prepared to lose just as much in soldiers and silver in order to take the Rock back.[53]

As for the other theatre of war in Germany, the imperial capital of Vienna came during the summer under threat from an offensive by French and Bavarian forces. Meanwhile, from the opposite direction it was menaced by a rebellion under Ferenc Rákóczi of the Hungarian Calvinists, about one-third of the population, indignant at having swapped Turkish for Austrian rule only to find themselves persecuted by the Catholic Habsburgs. The English and Dutch had made representations on their behalf to the Emperor Leopold, with little effect.[54] When he now begged help from the Duke of Marlborough, still bogged down in the Low Countries, there came a prompt response he did not deserve. But the duke saw a chance to exercise the independent command of which he had so far been frustrated by the demands of the grand alliance. He led an astounding march of his mainly Anglo-Dutch army, 40,000 strong, over 250 miles eastwards to join forces with Prince Eugene of Savoy, who himself had 20,000 men. They covered the distance in 21 days, in a feat of both physical stamina and logistical organisation: a further harbinger of modern warfare.

Scotland too was a member, however grudging, of the grand alliance. To this campaign she sent three regiments, the Cameronians, Royal Scots and Scots Greys. The Cameronians were recruited from among the Covenanters, fierce men sustained by a conviction of fighting the good fight. One, John Blackadder, wrote on the road from Low to High Germany how he was 'marching all this day, my frame serene and spiritual, singing hymns and psalms'. He and his mates must have made an odd contrast to the usual riffraff of European soldiery – 'a sad place to be in an army on sabbath,' he added later, 'where nothing is heard but oaths and profane language'.[55]

When the allies reached the River Danube, still in fine fettle for a fight, they surprised the forces of the French Marshal Camille Tallard and Elector Charles of Bavaria, which were larger and ought to have been fresher. Marlborough and Eugene launched an attack on August 13 near Blenheim, properly Blindheim. Marlborough's men overran both the left and right of the enemy's line so that the centre crumpled and fled, while Eugene routed the cavalry. Not for fifty years had the French suffered such crushing defeat. It brought rapid, far-reaching results. Vienna was saved and Bavaria overrun. King Louis XIV had to abandon any idea of conquest in Germany and look to the defence of France. With the triumphs of a single season the War of the Spanish Succession, inconclusive so far, took a sharp turn in favour of the grand alliance. Marlborough got the reward of a baroque palace in Oxfordshire paid out of public money and named after his famous victory.

One of the Scots Greys, James Campbell, wrote a couple of days after the battle to his brother at home 'to give you an account of the most glorious victory that ever we heard of'. He describes the overnight march which brought the allies within striking distance of the enemy, then their lying in wait for a whole morning under a hot sun. Lapsing in his excitement into Glaswegian, Campbell recalls that 'between twelve and wan the attack began'. He goes on: 'We went through the water that was in their front with little opposition and took ane piece of cannon. After that we made a little halt and attacked the village that was upon their right which they had all pallisaded. They received us with so fast a fire that they killed and wounded twenty officers.' But the allies charged on to disperse the enemy: 'The twenty-six battalions of foot and six regiments of dragoons which was surrounded was obliged to surrender prisoners of war. In short we have got ane entire victory, we have twelve thousand prisoners and Monsieur Tallard and several other generals prisoners.' George Hamilton, Earl of Orkney, commander of the Royal Scots and brother of the Duke of Hamilton, personally took the surrender of those cornered foes, though at that moment facing them with only a fraction of their strength. 'Without vanity, I think we did our pairts,' he said drily.[56]

In England, Blenheim brought a burst of national self-esteem which turned the European conflict into a popular struggle. That overbore the inscrutable news from Scotland, where the war won little support or interest from a nation engrossed in its own affairs. Not till English martial euphoria died down a bit, in November, did politicians at Westminster look north.

❧

The chauvinism boiled up afresh once it was seen what the Scots Parliament's Act of Security might mean, now it had the royal assent. Wild stories swept the country. Scots were supposed to be on the point of invading, and the queen received a parliamentary address asking her to fortify Newcastle and Tynemouth, repair works at Carlisle and Hull, arm the militia of the four northernmost counties and march regular troops to the border. French money was said to be flowing into the Pretender's coffers. Once Louis XIV's army landed in Scotland, so rumours ran, its operations would be succoured by the many Scots in French pay, some of them members of the Parliament.[57]

For this and other reasons the session at Westminster which opened in the autumn of 1704 turned out among the liveliest of the reign. Still, the most controversial business was domestic, not foreign, the Occasional Conformity Bill. It offers an example of how the English Parliament set about its business in this period of transition between the seventeenth and eighteenth centuries, between an age where it had often been at odds with the Crown and an age where executive government would come to depend on support at Westminster. In Anne's time it was she that appointed Ministers and it was her confidence that sustained them, rather than a parliamentary majority – though they would obviously want to cobble one together, if measure by measure rather than through anything that could be called a legislative programme. But laws would as likely start from the floor of the house. Such was the case with the Occasional Conformity Bill.

It was an issue on which Tories in the Commons waxed fierce. The problem they wanted to tackle arose out of a practice among dissenters of occasionally taking communion in the Church of England to qualify themselves for national or local office under the Test and Corporation Acts of Charles II. Devout Anglicans thought this blasphemous. Among them was William Bromley, MP for the University of Oxford. His august institution told him to find a different seat if he could or would not put a stop to the scandal. He felt indignant at it himself, but other Tories were rather looking to what political advantage they could reap.

Victors in the last General Election, Tories now sought to secure their majority by cutting back the large number of Whig votes cast by dissenters, especially in English boroughs. Bromley brought in a private member's bill to disfranchise these electors, among a range of sanctions, if they only occasionally conformed. Two similar bills had been defeated in the Lords in previous sessions. This time Bromley won support from some

Ministers, but the queen and the rest of the government doubted if it could be wise to deal with dissenters in such a way. As autumn wore on, tensions grew. In November about 150 high Tories resolved to do what the opposition in the Scots Parliament had done if faced with official obstruction, and block supply till the bill was passed. In London, unlike in Edinburgh, this move was thought provocative by Tory leaders.[58]

The high Tories in the Commons hoped to get the Occasional Conformity Bill through now by tacking it to the Finance Bill, so the Whigs in the Lords could not reject it. The war was half fought on English money, and to the queen, after such triumph in the field, this appeared a ploy of unbelievable recklessness. Godolphin agreed and so did the moderate Tories led by Harley, who thought it foolish to make a partisan issue the pretext for a constitutional battle. Theirs was, then, a patriotic stance. They assembled strong support. It included the Whigs. A new constellation of forces emerged to isolate the high Tories, and in no uncertain fashion. The tacking motion, put forward by Bromley, was thrown out on November 28 by 251 votes to 134.

It proved to be a turning point. The Court and the high Tories from now on took divergent paths over defence of the Church of England, a divergence so wide that they could not get back together again. The high Tories had shown how dangerous they might be if the Court indulged them. In their ardour for the connection of the English Church and state, they threatened to repeat the worst of its champions' past mistakes – and did not seem to care. In England the fear was that they could give dissenters needless grounds of disaffection. For Scotland, too, the rashness of the high Tories in England sounded an alarm against tolerating their Episcopalian brethren, let alone admitting these to any privilege of established religion or even contemplating re-establishment some day of an episcopal Kirk. It seems unlikely those high Tories spared more than a moment's thought for Scotland. But their folly meant that, if Union was to come at all, it could not come while they remained in a position of influence in London.

Apart from anything else, it was to the English Whigs that the Court had now to look for support in voting supply. So the Whigs, out of office since Anne's accession to the throne, began to find their way back into royal favour and potentially into government. This was a signal achievement by the Junto, that inner circle which had dominated moderate English Whiggery for a decade: John, Lord Somers; Edward Russell, Earl of Orford; Thomas, Earl Wharton; Charles Montagu, Earl of Halifax;

Charles Spencer, Earl of Sunderland. They were Court Whigs *par excellence*, who had first got together in support of William of Orange's war effort and not relished being cast out in the cold by Anne. As they came back in from the cold again, Scotland moved up their agenda. They had earlier offered Queensberry what support they could, if diminishing over time. The Junto's shift back closer to the centre of power in London had a further effect in setting limits to the options, at least the constitutional options, available to Tories in Edinburgh or Scotland generally.

ℭℌ

Scots Tories had, given their chance by Anne, been unable to exploit it to the full. They had their trimmers, such as Seafield, a courtier rather than a partisan, or Cromartie, who trod a unionist tightrope of his own. But they never quite took over government despite a strong position in the Parliament, if one short of matching the Tory majority in the Commons at Westminster. From that match, in any case, too little meeting of minds emerged. For example, the English Tory leadership did not, at least openly or for the time being, contest the Act of Settlement and the Hanoverian succession it fixed. There had arisen in England a distinction between constitutional Tories and Jacobites. It originated in the disfavour for Anglicans of James VII and II. It showed itself yet in the inability of the Anglican queen to reconcile herself with her Catholic brother, the Pretender. Observing all this on a visit to London, a disgusted Lockhart wrote: 'They don't so much value in England who shall be king, as whose king he shall be.'[59]

Lockhart shows why most Scots Tories could never bring themselves to assent to the Hanoverian succession, not in conscience nor even out of expediency. As long as that succession remained the main aim of official policy in Scotland, they had to remain shut out from control of government by reason of their Jacobitism. The chance of political accommodation between Scotland and England on Tory terms passed. The English Tories, as we saw from the example of Sir Edward Seymour, anyway never showed the slightest interest in it.[60]

Scots Tories who remained stubborn on the succession found more room for manoeuvre on the religious establishment, while among English Tories that order of priorities was reversed. Their hostility to the Presbyterian settlement of 1690 remained rigid while Scots Tories were learning to live with it, and would have done so happily enough in return for the little bit of toleration the Episcopalians never got before 1707. Anglicans rather expected the Church of Scotland somehow to conform again one day to the Church of England (perhaps after the fashion decreed by Charles I). They did not pause to note that even Episcopalians refused for their part to concede that the Kirk was anything less than an independent national institution with its own tradition, not just a factitious trifle of history. Patriots in their own way too, these Scots insisted on a historic difference and historic equality of the two national Churches, so that neither might prescribe for the other.

And despite their political eclipse those Episcopalians were still an intellectual force to reckon with in Scotland, not mere English lackeys. The patronage of James VII had brought among them a cultural flowering which foreshadowed the Enlightenment. Its versatile leaders remained two decades later active in public life, though not in public office. Archibald Pitcairne was both pioneering physician and polemical playwright, diffusing the new scientific spirit of his age while sending up the restored religious establishment of his country. His fellow boffin Sir Robert Sibbald, familiar of antiquarians and natural philosophers at home and abroad, wrote tracts tracing the history of Scottish religious independence and, for good measure, appealing for pity on the parlous plight of Episcopalian priests. 'I am sure their pressures that I ever heard of were but flea bites to the scorpions wherewith they oppressed others', snapped back his Presbyterian friend, the Revd Robert Wodrow of Eastwood.[61]

But if canny Scots inclined to let sleeping dogs lie, there were silly Englishmen who sought to goad them into howling hostility. One got right up Scottish noses, with a parade of claims dating back to King Edward I's medieval aggressions about an alleged feudal superiority of England over Scotland, matched by an authority of the see of Canterbury over the Kirk. William Atwood, a Whig, found time from his day job as a lawyer to write these anti-Scottish ravings. He had just published the latest, *Superiority and Direct Dominion of the Imperial Crown of England over the Crown and Kingdom of Scotland*. It reached two verdicts of current relevance, that Scotland as a fief of the English Crown was bound by the Act of Settlement passed at Westminster in 1701, and that the Archbishop of Canterbury had a right to summon 'the bishops of Scotland to a national synod'.[62]

Presbyterians ought to have been able to laugh off such nonsense but their sense of humour remained stunted so long as they felt insecure in their hold on the Kirk, and did not much improve afterwards. At any rate they seemed unable to overlook the most distant threat to their authority. Of hacks set to cobble together a riposte to Atwood, the most cogent was James Dalrymple, showing how the Church of Scotland had always been separate from the Church of England, either self-governing or else dependent on Rome, though St Andrews had not been erected into a metropolitan see till 1472.[63] All this may now appear impossibly anti-quarian, yet the Parliament felt jealous enough of its authority to take the debate seriously. It voted money for works vindicating Church and nation. It ordered Atwood's book to be burned by the public hangman.[64]

In short, the religious situation circumscribed what the Scots Tories could attain, despite royal indulgence and electoral success: just one among the many messy compromises of Scottish politics. And because Tories were not able to take their chance to plot a path for the nation out of the morass of its multiple dilemmas, the job would have to be left to Whigs.

ℰ✺

That now grew clear, or at least in convoluted fashion clearer, as in London the consequences of the Scottish Act of Security sank in. The Act laid down procedures by which the Union of Crowns might be dissolved unless Scotland's other demands had been met by the time of Anne's death. English reaction to it waxed furious, and turned against Godolphin for having advised the queen to give it the royal assent. He and his policy came under close scrutiny as the Parliament at Westminster held in the autumn of 1704 its first big debates on Scottish affairs, at least since the War of the Three Kingdoms.

The House of Lords turned to Scotland on November 23. Godolphin, sensing his job was on the line, asked the queen to come down to Westminster in person, then and a week later when the debate resumed. Such regal attendance was a usage which has since fallen out of favour (except at an actual opening of Parliament), because the Hanoverians later on were unable to follow proceedings in English. Though a tradition not unknown before 1714, it had been little observed and signified the seriousness of the occasion. Anne, as ever, did her duty to the best of her ability. The weather outside was so cold that she moved from her throne to sit by the big open fire that in those days kept the house warm.

The debate was opened by John Thompson, Lord Haversham, a short, stocky, red-faced, contentious Cockney improbably ennobled for his revolutionary principles by King William. He was now, with chirpy opportunism, moving towards the Tories. Known for wordy speeches which yet could score telling points, Haversham gave a good account of the state of Scotland. He deplored failure to settle the succession and blamed it on Tweeddale's motley Ministry, beside a lack of application by English and Scottish Ministers alike. It was no surprise Scots had turned so awkward: 'I think every man wishes these things had not been; and, in my opinion, there is no man but must say they should not have been.' Yet Haversham did not blame the Scots: 'There are two matters of all troubles: much discontent and great poverty; and whoever will now look into Scotland, will find them both in that kingdom.' The discontent existed among the nobility and gentry, 'as learned and as brave as any nation in Europe can boast of'. The poverty existed among the people, 'very numerous and very stout'. In all this lurked peril to England. The aim of Haversham in praising the Scots was to damn Godolphin for making a reality of the peril: 'By yielding to the Scottish will, the Minister has betrayed the Crown's interest in favour of Hanover.' In the debate this case against Godolphin received no adequate answer. It was not the Lord Treasurer's day.

The second debate on November 30 dealt with the Act of Security as such. A Tory, the Earl of Rochester, proposed to have it read out to the house, but Godolphin and the Whigs opposed this as sure to anger the Scots by an assumption of the right to review proceedings of their Parliament. Bishop Burnet was hauled in to harp on Scotland's hardships since the Union of Crowns and English severity towards Darien. He feigned surprise that the house had never been so exercised by the Act anent Peace and War of 1703, something 'of infinite more consequence to England than the Act of Security'. But Burnet could not deflect the assault. Tories denounced the Act of Security as an Act of Exclusion in effect, cutting off the Hanoverian succession and threatening England. There had to be doubts about the loyalty of a Minister who advised the royal assent for it.[65] Godolphin might count his lucky stars that, with its clause on free trade deleted, at least he did not have to face attacks on economic grounds too. Instead he was able to concentrate his return of fire round the fact that, without the Act of Security, the Scottish army could not have been paid. He had acted to stop relations worsening, possibly to the point of war. And the story was far from over: 'whatever ill look it might have at present, it is not without remedy'. That remedy lay in Union.

The Tories berating Godolphin had no majority in the Lords. So a crucial question was what line the Whigs would take. At first they seemed unhelpful too. One of the Junto, Halifax, launched his own scathing attack. In a case where Anne had such guidance as she got from Ministers over the Act of Security, 'it becomes the greatness of the Queen of England to refute their advices'. Yet Halifax, it turned out, was not representative of his party. Burnet wrote of Godolphin's plight at this point: 'The Tories resolved to attack him and that disposed the Whigs to preserve him; and this was so managed by them, that it gave a great turn to all our councils.'[66] Nor did Godolphin himself sit passive under the blows. Before he found the whole house ranged against him, he had the presence of mind to stage a dramatic gesture. He sat beside two lords of the Junto, Somers and Wharton, and consulted them in stage-whispers.

What on earth were they saying? To the rest of the chamber this piquant tableau hinted at compromise to save a man seeming all but sunk. According to one sour Tory onlooker, Godolphin 'delivered himself entirely into [the Whigs'] management, provided they brought him off' from the pressure he was under. His wish to conciliate them had no doubt come over him less abruptly than this comment suggests. If often blinkered and dictatorial, not least in respect of Scotland, he was never a strong partisan, rather the contemporary equivalent of a senior civil servant, even in his irascible manner ready to work with politicians of different hues while keeping the ends of the state in view. That meant, at this juncture, victory in Europe. His prime purpose was to fend off criticism of the war while he got supply for Marlborough. Whigs who would support that in return for concessions on lesser issues became friends of Godolphin. In fact, they were now of more use to him than Tories.[67]

☙

With the Tories going into eclipse at Westminster, what difference to Scotland would a rise of the Whigs there make? They remained far from agreed on any need for Union and overall cool towards it: Scots MPs might turn out to be Jacobites or else, on account of their poverty, creatures of the Crown. English Whigs felt much more intent on the alternative of the Hanoverian succession, not least as a promise of power to themselves. Their motives were assessed on December 7 in a report back from the Earl of Roxburghe, who had been sent by the government of Scotland to keep an eye on things in London: 'The design of the Whigs, in this matter, is to force us into the succession.' If that was the aim, a question arose whether it would more likely be fulfilled by a prior treaty between Scotland and England to resolve other differences between them. Roxburghe put his own view: 'I am only afraid that . . . this bustle make the Scots Parliament positive to have a treaty first.' The reason was clear: 'How shall we be sure but hardships be put upon us, so soon as the succession is over, if we be not secured against them antecedently, as much as a poor nation can be secured against the oppressions of a richer, since it is always in their power, and since they already seem to threaten us with it?'[68]

Altogether, though approaching the matter from a different angle, this came to much the same conclusion as Anne had: the essential was the Hanoverian succession, and the question of a treaty, of a nature as yet unspecified, fell to be judged according as it promoted that succession or not. On this line of argument, trade would pose for Whigs a problem equally subordinate to the succession. Though it was they, more than Tories, that represented the commercial interests of London, a city with a delusory vested interest in mercantilism, Whigs were still prepared to open up trade with Scotland because after it 'the succession cannot fail to be settled'.[69]

Succession, treaty, trade, usually in that order, if with numerous individual variations on it:[70] these were the three related questions Scots and English politicians alike found themselves having to grapple with as the turn of another year loomed. At different stages of a process of trial and error they hit on different drafts of the right answer they sought. The first English stab at it was to be the Alien Act.

This infamous Act originated with one of the Junto, Somers, who had been Lord Chancellor under William of Orange and now, of all his colleagues, lay furthest out of favour with Anne. A self-made man, he had matured into an able, circumspect, eloquent lawyer, at present making good use of his enforced idleness in opposition. First he wanted to get his new friend Godolphin off the hook of furious Tory attacks on him. In its wisdom the House of Lords decided to take no collective view of the Act of Security but rather to deal with its results. Somers led in this and struck a chord among his peers. They saw that his proposals were not the only ones open to them, but that they did offer a course worked out towards goals which appeared attainable. Rochester remarked: 'The Scotch are brave and stubborn, and therefore, I do not think to threaten them is the way to persuade them, which makes me have a very bad opinion of the [Alien] bill; however, I submit to the opinion of others and vote for it.'[71]

Somers's gambit was that England should brandish both carrot and stick at Scotland, while knowing that even the carrot of Union was not for the moment to the Scots' taste and the stick of sanctions would be stuck with painful spikes. In practical terms the queen would be asked on the one hand to appoint commissioners to negotiate Union for England. On the other hand economic penalties would be imposed on the Scots if they made no equivalent move. This latter was the point that most struck home north of the border, to produce popular fury. Yet there seems no doubt that, to Somers's mind, it was a subordinate matter: the Hanoverian succession remained the prime aim, to be achieved by what blandishments it took, if not in a more friendly, then in a less friendly fashion. Altogether he did seek to force the settlement of the succession, but softly-softly, making it the subject of negotiation and indeed offering Union (of a sort as yet unspecified), if that was what the Scots should prefer.

Somers at any rate did not sound like the Seymour who had dined and cavilled with Fletcher of Saltoun the previous winter. The English Whig now played the good guy where the English Tory had then played the bad guy. The one disclaimed any wish to meddle in internal Scottish affairs while the other had dismissed them as of no account. To prickly Scots, though, Englishmen who ventured to interfere in any way were obnoxious.

Another Scottish Minister reporting back from London was Secretary Johnston. He got down to, as his own people saw it, the nitty-gritty: the English plan was for 'a law to make the Scotch aliens, and to forbid the coming in of their cattle – this law to commence after some time, and to determine whether the succession should be settled'.[72] At that point in a rolling programme of pressures, assuming the prior postures had exerted no effect, the draconian aspect would kick in. All Scots not resident in England, Ireland or the American colonies, and not serving in the English army or navy, would be declared aliens unless Scotland accepted the Hanoverian succession or entered into negotiations for Union by a date to be set; so they would become subject to the English Navigation Acts and be penalised with economic sanctions. On December 12 the Lords agreed with Somers and resolved to introduce two bills giving force to his scheme, while keeping the House of Commons informed.

In England this line united Whigs and Tories; such was the first result there of the Act of Security. The line therefore united both Houses of

147

Parliament. The Commons caused no ill feelings in shortly taking the legislation over, judging it improper for a bill with financial implications to be initiated in the Lords. The Commons' version called in its preamble for 'a nearer and more complete Union' and, asking the queen to name commissioners, imposed no prior conditions on the project. It did set a limit of time for Scots to ponder their prospects, at Christmas Day, 1705. Goods which they as aliens would then be banned from selling in England were also designated: cattle and sheep, coal and linen, their four most valuable exports. In case they wanted to pick a fight over it, the Act besides forbade export to them of English horses, arms and ammunition.

It was in this clause, tucked away in the body of the Act, that a hint of something more menacing lay. The implication could be readily followed. Any hostilities between Scotland and England would be sure to bring in the Pretender and Louis XIV; in other words, to start a war of the British succession as part of the general European war. Once a theatre of conflict, Scotland would face a yet grimmer future. To this sequence of tacit threats Scots responded in outrage, with invocations of Robert Bruce and William Wallace.

There was already a war of words being waged in pamphlets, to generate a literature about the Union of durable interest. This war carried over into the early Scottish newspapers – the *Edinburgh Gazette*, founded in 1699 by an old soldier turned entrepreneur, James Donaldson, and the *Edinburgh Courant*, first brought out in this winter of discontent by Adam Boig. The pair hit at each other as well, Boig coming off the better with his deeper coverage and wider circulation. The law jumped on both when he carried a notice of a book published in England by the Scots author, James Hodges, *War betwixt the British Kingdoms considered*. It actually urged Scotland and England not to fight, since this could only benefit France. But the privy council in Edinburgh was too jittery to look beyond a title lurid by contemporary standards. It suspended both newspapers for a while, though afterwards Donaldson and Boig were able to resume their feud. England had grown more accustomed to public polemics, at least of a secular kind, and there the authorities did nothing to check a rush of publications fanning tension between the two nations, scaring the English, goading the Scots.

Jacobites spoiled for a fight anyway. Lockhart gave, as ever, a red-blooded response to the situation: 'This was a strange preamble and introduction towards an agreement, first, to propose an amicable treaty to remove grudges and animosities between the two nations; but at the same time threaten the Scots with their power and vengeance, if they did not comply with what was demanded of them.' It came as no surprise that 'all true Scotsmen looked upon it as a gross invasion on their liberties and sovereignty, and an insolent behaviour towards a free and independent people'. The English 'could not have proposed a more effectual way to irritate the Scots nation . . . and I look upon it as the first rise and cause of the general, I may say, universal aversion, that afterwards appeared to the Union'.

Some Presbyterians, those of the Covenanting tradition, rattled their sabres with little less relish. In the south-west, hotbed of that tradition, bitter memories of the Killing Time still lurked beneath the surface. Only in February there had been fresh trouble in Dumfriesshire on the rumour of a Jacobite conspiracy. Gangs broke into the houses of certain gentlemen and ransacked them in search of popish baubles, of religious books or images. Under arms they marched to the county town to make a bonfire at the market-cross of what they had found. If zealots could act like this towards a cowed minority, they would surely stand up to English aggression.

Elsewhere, less militant Presbyterians viewed the prospects more soberly. Even nationalists among them, George Ridpath as well as James Hodges, called on the Scots to keep the peace. They pointed out how for a century war had brought nothing but harm to Kirk and people. And they warned England that this time war would inflict damage on her too, since the standing army needed to occupy Scotland would subvert her own liberty.[73] Yet from the sentiments of Ridpath there emerges also a weary resignation to the eternal arrogance of the English on behalf of all minorities in the Atlantic world, an augury of the future: 'Thus the Scots, thus the Irish and thus their own American plantations do all of them complain of their too great narrowness of soul, that while they pretend to fight for their own liberty, and that of all Europe, they are very niggardly in dispensing it to any people over whom they can have influence.'[74]

Still, not everyone in Scotland strutted or swaggered, panicked or quailed. Roxburghe, Tweeddale's nephew and agent, was a young man of twenty-five, losing his illusions as in London he came face to face with hard facts of politics. He, too, disliked English arrogance: 'Instead of proposing us favours, as a separate kingdom, if we do settle the same succession with them, they make hard laws upon us, if we do it not within such a time; nor without an entire Union will they ever give us any favour in trade.' He could not exclude the eventual possibility of war between

Scotland and England, though not while the fighting in Europe went on: 'I am thoroughly convinced that if we do not go into the succession, or an Union, very soon, conquest will certainly be, upon the first peace.'[75] This might be none of it pleasant to contemplate, yet it was the reality. At least, for Scots at large it made basic choices clear: 'you may settle the succession upon limitations' or else 'you may accept of a Union'. The sole alternative to those courses, plain besides to the toadying Secretary Johnston, was this: 'If you will do neither, you may expect all the mischief that can be done you; for . . . you and your independence are not so great but that you must depend either on France or England, and sure they will not suffer you to depend on France.'[76]

Indeed, England would allow no readjustment in boundaries set by 15 years of unforgiving struggle with France, between herself as an insular power and the aspirant hegemon of the Continent. To put it another way, the English could permit no resurrection of the Auld Alliance between the Scots and the French. A deep, durable cleft opened in European geopolitics, cutting through more traditional or more congenial Scottish connections and loyalties. The modern world severed from an older world. Scotland found herself left teetering on one side. She might leap back across, only with peril. Or else, if she did not dare, how was she to find her footing?

CHAPTER 4

❧

1705

The Castle broods over Edinburgh, seen from the south, with St Giles and Parliament House on the right

'Scotland's ruin'

Nightfall on August 31, 1705, found the 47-year-old James, fourth Duke of Hamilton, waiting on a visitor in the apartment at the Palace of Holyroodhouse which he had the right to occupy by virtue of being the premier peer of Scotland. Nathaniel Hooke was due to appear there after dark. The pair of them had first got to know each other during the Revolution back in 1688, while both being held prisoner in the Tower of London for refusal to forsake their allegiance to King James VII and II.

Their ways had then parted. Hamilton became, on succeeding to his dukedom in 1698, one of the great noblemen of Scotland – if, like some others, rather poor. He still had a name, associated with two things: the Hamiltons were always loyal to the Stewarts, but in everything else they vacillated and masked their vacillation with duplicity. The duke had grown into an oddly unpatriotic patriot, with an open preference for the society of Paris or even of London over that of Edinburgh; his return home after a grand tour in his youth was, his father observed, 'much the same to him as to go to the galleys'.[1] By now there was more in Scotland to disgust him even than her Whig politics and Presbyterian religion. In his private affairs he had been beggared twice: by the fiendish complexities of feudal inheritance, which kept the revenues of his estates in the hands of his mother, the Duchess Anne; then by his hefty subscription to Darien, which, so far from offering a quick cure for his penury, left him worse off than ever. Whether Hamilton possessed or ever could have found the moral, mental or material resources to deal with his problems remains an open question.

One or two small parallels may be drawn between the duke and Hooke, now aged forty-one, who had come in a peculiar way by his own loyalty to the Stewarts. Born an Irish Protestant, he went like many of his race to finish his education at the University of Glasgow. From there his life took more unusual turns which successively made of him a Roman

153

Catholic, a Jacobite and so now an exile with the rank of colonel in the army of King Louis XIV of France. He too, then, was a man of duplicity. He had arrived in Edinburgh as a spy, charged with assessing the chances for a French invasion of Scotland.

This meeting with Hamilton would be the fourth since Hooke's secret Scottish landing on August 7, after a long wait at Dunkirk because of contrary winds and then a stormy passage across the North Sea which laid him low with sea-sickness. At last he had reached his destination, Slains Castle on Cruden Bay to the north of Aberdeen, seat of the Earls of Erroll and in later times reputed by Bram Stoker to be a haunt of Count Dracula. Hooke travelled south to meet the Revd Thomas Nicolson, Roman Catholic vicar apostolic in Scotland, who lurked incognito in the capital when not touring the remote communities still faithful to his Church to oversee the couple of dozen priests that ministered to them. Nicolson found lodgings for Hooke with Lady Comiston, who had an old house containing a priesthole; he emerged only at night accompanied by a servant of Erroll's. Though unable to catch him, the government of Scotland knew of Hooke's presence. So did the government of England. 'He is a bold, dextrous man, and if he could be taken knows very much,' Robert Harley, who ran the secret service, would longingly write.[2]

As Hooke was guided about Edinburgh, he found many of the people he had come to see reluctant to meet him face to face, so that they might if necessary be able to swear afterwards that they had never set eyes on him. Some of these encounters verged on the bizarre. When Hooke wanted to speak to the Earl of Aberdeen he had first to make his way to the residence of the Earl Marischal. There he was asked to hide in a closet till Aberdeen came and made himself at home in the chamber outside. The Earl Marischal and his lady carried on the discussion between their two visitors by passing back and forth to repeat to the other what each had just said.[3]

For his initial rendezvous with Hamilton, Hooke had brought with him a token, a guinea cut in half, to match one in the duke's hands. Their later meetings, too, carried on in this spirit of skulduggery. Hooke entered Holyrood by a back-stair and talked in the dark to the duke, who in his turn wanted to be able to swear he had never seen any French agent. By August 31, he had so sworn and this time they met by candlelight. Hooke could now take in the slight, swarthy figure he had known in his youth. They stood ostensibly on the best of terms and often broke off their exchanges to recall mutual friends and days gone by. Yet neither quite trusted the other.

Hooke had one single aim in coming on his mission: to foment revolt in Scotland and restore to her throne the legitimate line of the House of Stewart in the person of the Old Pretender, James VIII *de jure*. Assuming Hamilton still to be a Jacobite, the Irishman was puzzled and annoyed that the duke would not, as leader of the patriotic opposition in the Scots Parliament, commit himself to that project. As he had spoken out in consistent opposition to the Hanoverian succession on the death of Queen Anne, why could he not go the whole hog, openly back the Pretender and so win vital support from France as well?

There were good reasons why Hamilton kept his counsel. Out of the mess in which Scotland found herself, he saw a way which at one fell swoop would solve all his problems as well as hers. It was that he should himself become James VIII, first King of Scots from the House of Hamilton.

The Stewarts' blood ran in his veins from the marriage of his ancestor, James, Lord Hamilton (1423–1479), to Mary (1452–1488), daughter of King James II. It was not a wonderful claim, yet quite as good as certain others touted in recent times. If the legitimate line of Stewarts excluded itself by reason of its Catholicism, and if the Scots were not willing – as the English were – to be ruled by a German or some other foreigner, then Hamilton stood next in line.

But Hamilton had to find powerful backing, or else he would just provoke his brother Scots, the jealous and peevish nobles, to dispute his claim. Backing powerful enough could come only from France. To the duke, Hooke's arrival out of the blue was a godsend, the chance to establish contact with Versailles. Yet their talks had led nowhere. Hooke responded to none of Hamilton's ploys. Instead he made clear that Louis XIV wanted nothing but a Jacobite restoration. He required of the duke only a pledge to support it. Hamilton also asked for money to bribe members of the Scots Parliament, but constitutional battles were not what the French had in mind and the request went unanswered. Now, on a sweaty summer's evening, Hamilton and Hooke again talked for a long time at cross purposes.

'I have one thing to add,' said Hooke, drawing the verbal jousts to a close, 'You have said you intend to take up arms. When will that be?'

'At the right time,' replied the cagy duke.

'When will that be?' insisted the Irishman.

'I cannot say. Who can predict the course of events? If they turn out happily, we will profit from them. But you can count on it that we will act when Queen Anne dies.'

Hamilton mused for a moment, then came out with something from which with hindsight we may discern that, after exploring every other avenue, he had made up his mind: 'Perhaps I will be obliged to support the measures put forward by the Court, but my purposes are still the same.'

Hooke was not a spy for nothing: 'It is said that you have come to an arrangement with the Earl of Stair' (an arch-Whig acting for the government of Scotland) 'but that your supporters will not follow you.'

'I will act as necessary despite what my party think,' retorted the duke. With that Hooke flounced out the door and left him for good.[4]

⌘

What Hamilton meant by these cryptic comments grew clear the very next day, September 1. He was lodging at Holyrood in order to attend the current session of the Scots Parliament. The great question it had at this point to decide was what response to make to the pressure from the queen, and behind her from her English Ministers, that Scotland should open negotiations for Union.

The plan enjoyed the formal support of the government of Scotland but, since it had seldom controlled the Parliament in recent years, that might not mean a great deal. Whatever a treaty promised for an England at war with France, by closing off a potential threat from her northern border, hardly a soul in Scotland would agree to it just on those grounds. Of course the Parliament might feel bound to receive Anne's wish with outward respect and pass an Act authorising the start of talks – but then would surely see to it that nothing came of them.

On that September 1, the proceedings started with a motion from Andrew Fletcher of Saltoun to omit from the negotiating brief any guarantees for the Church of Scotland. Since with this he clearly meant just to goad the Presbyterians, he found no support. Next came William Murray, Duke of Atholl, calling for a condition to be set that no negotiations should start till the English Parliament had repealed the 'menacing clauses' of the Alien Act, which were due to impose economic sanctions on Scotland from the end of the year unless she accepted the Hanoverian succession. As the Scottish government had no control over that it was obliged to fob Atholl off with a compromise after a series of wearisome divisions.

So it was well on in the evening before the next item on the agenda could be taken, whether the Parliament or the queen should nominate the Scots commissioners for drawing up a treaty. The government expected to lose this vote. Chancellor Seafield yet set off to do his best, displaying the options as if he really believed the members might choose between them on their merits. By tradition the Crown ran foreign policy, he pointed out, appointing the embassies and the envoys, a royal prerogative always respected in England. But since 1603 Anglo-Scottish relations had been divorced from foreign policy as such and placed on a footing of their own. In consequence, practice here could be said to favour the Parliament as much as the Crown: in 1604 or 1689 nomination of negotiators had been left to the Parliament, but in 1670 or 1702 the Crown exercised that right. Naturally Seafield wished the house to go for the latter option once again. But he knew the precedent freshest in members' minds, that of 1702, was a bad one. As far as could be assessed in advance, a great majority would want the Parliament to choose the commissioners, so it could select men certain to block every English move and ensure the negotiations proved abortive. After Seafield sat down, some argued just that point. Yet most, thinking there could be no time for much more debate at the end of a long day, had with rumbling stomachs gone out to dinner.

In a thin chamber, this was the moment Hamilton seized to get to his feet 'with his usual haughty and bantering air' and propose that the queen should nominate the commissioners – which meant all talks must be a sham, conducted on both sides by creatures of the English Ministry. 'The Parliament is too much in heats and feuds,' said the duke, 'and can never agree on proper persons, but the queen, who is free from partiality, may doubtless make a good choice. But if she shall make a bad one, we will be safe, for all must return to us again, and we may send the Act back to the place whence it came.' The government, unable to believe its luck, called a snap division which it won by four votes. A fortnight later it would adjourn the session, so the opposition could not undo what had been done. It was now much more likely, as something requiring not the active consent but only the passive acquiescence of the nation, that the Treaty of Union would be written by Anne's English Ministers and rammed through the Scots Parliament.[5]

Some members had detected a deep sarcasm in Hamilton's words on that fateful night of September 1 but, whatever he meant, he horrified those on his own side. George Lockhart of Carnwath later recalled how 'about twelve or fifteen of them ran out of the house in rage and despair, saying aloud it was to no purpose to stay any longer, since the Duke of Hamilton had deserted and so basely betrayed them. From this day may we date the commencement of Scotland's ruin'.[6]

Hamilton's behaviour has been a puzzle ever since. Leader of the Country party, darling of the nationalist crowds outside the Parliament, he had so far done his best to frustrate Union by demanding strict conditions on every single move that might conceivably lead to it. As he assured his mother, 'Nobody needs take any pains with me' about the form a treaty with England should assume: 'what has been the source of our ruin since our kings became theirs' was the fact 'we had not stipulations made with them'. In consequence, that which is 'now called a treaty of Union is a treaty of subjugation and not of Union'. Unless the basic approach changed for the better, he was saying, he would not hear of a treaty or countenance progress towards one.[7]

What made Hamilton change his mind? An obvious possibility was that he had been bought or otherwise suborned by the English. The government in London wanted Union but no real negotiation for it. This might give Scots opinion too much influence and produce terms unaccept- able at Westminster. So it was vital that the Parliament in Edinburgh should let the queen and her English Ministers name the Scots commis- sioners. Patriots knew this and stood ready to foil the ploy. Fletcher had remarked of the prospective nomination: 'You had as good leave it to my Lord Godolphin, and we know that our queen is in England, under the influences of an English Ministry, and 'tis not to be expected that the interest of Scotland should be so much considered by her as the inclina- tions of an English Parliament'.[8]

How, then, could Hamilton have fallen for just that? There were sensitive points at which the English might put pressure on him: his debts, his lands in Lancashire acquired by marriage to a local heiress, his dealings with Jacobites which, however obscure and irresolute, laid him open to a legal reckoning. Private correspondence of the time contains hints that he had in secret been offering whatever services it might take to get money and favour out of the government in London. As early as December 1704, the Earl of Roxburghe, writing on the prospects of Union to George Baillie of Jerviswood, reported: 'I have been told by a friend of Duke Hamilton's, and one that knows him well, within this eight-and-forty hours, that if the queen has mind for this business, Duke Hamilton was vain and necessitous.'[9] Secretary Johnstone noted on January 13, 1705: 'I have had suspicions, but now I am certain, that Duke Hamilton is tampering by the means of Harley with the Lord Treasurer [Godolphin] . . . He must have his debts paid.'[10] Johnstone observed again on February 15: 'Duke Hamilton's friends are so gross as to intimate to great men here that he is a *chambre à louer*. But for all that's to be done now, I find it's thought scarcely worth the while to make the purchase.' At any rate Sidney Godolphin felt able to give out by mid-July that 'Duke Hamilton will not oppose a treaty.'[11] Others heard how 'Duke Hamilton has positively engaged to bring it about'. As part of the deal, the Earl of Mar told the Duke of Argyll, Hamilton would leave to the queen the nomination of the Scots commissioners to negotiate a Union.[12]

But none of this is absolutely conclusive and a case may be made on the other side too. The duke vindicated his own conduct, to Hooke as it happens, in a letter written a couple of weeks after the vote on the nomination. The Irishman, after completing his mission, was by this time again at Slains awaiting the ship that would carry him back to France. Word from Hamilton reached him through a third party with this brief excuse for what had transpired: 'I went into the measure of giving the nomination of the treaters to the queen, for if they had been chosen by the remaining majority of the States [Parliament] it had been yet worse.' Hamilton knew the Cavalier party was angry at his behaviour, 'but when they cool, and find good effects from it, I hope they acknowledge they have been in the wrong, to me as well as to themselves, for censuring so rashly'. He had rather tired of the whole business, yet 'if by my giving this single vote to the queen I come to be upon the treaty, which was not practicable any other way, you shall see that if they don't previously rescind their Act in so far as we are declared aliens, there will be no more treaty'. In other words, to get on the commission negotiating the Union, and to make repeal of the Alien Act a condition of opening talks, was Hamilton's aim (in which he would not succeed).[13]

Hamilton could have had a number of possible purposes. Either he meant to block the negotiations, or else, he had already in his own mind accepted that Union was going to happen and sought to make the best of it: a position consistent with his frustration of a Crown. Again he may have believed, as many did in both England and Scotland, that Union was a chimera, that it could just never happen, in which case it might be safely invoked to hinder the Hanoverian succession. This was the line some

Jacobites actually took in the belief they had means to wreck any serious negotiations, by their strength inside the Parliament or in the last resort by armed revolt outside.

Later, Hamilton threw more light on the matter. Hooke, home in France, received a message by the same channel to supplement the one handed him at Slains. It showed the duke worried at bitterness in Scotland over his actions. He still asserted that, in giving the queen the nomination, 'he did well because she cannot choose worse than the Parliament would have done, for in that case there would have been at least two for the Court against one for the Country, because each state choosing their own members, the nobility and burghs are for the Court, and only the barons for the Country'. If this was what Hamilton really thought, he had made another mistake. In the end, commissioners were selected on account of their support for Union, though in some cases the Court may have erred in its assessment.[14]

Later still, one more account reached Hooke. Again, it was a mysterious third party that wrote from Edinburgh, this time on current relations between Hamilton and the rest of the Country party. The letter pointed out that, the morning before the vote on September 1, Hamilton had come to an agreement with the Earl of Home, leader of the Cavaliers, that they should each, together with their followers, vote for the nomination of commissioners not by the separate estates but by the Parliament as a whole, in which the Court could not be sure of a majority. Yet between that deal and the opening of the session in the afternoon the Cavaliers somehow changed their minds. And they only told Hamilton 'as he was going up to his seat, that they had altered their resolutions, and would vote for the separate states, that each should choose their own commissioners'.

Lockhart, as it happens, left a record of the same encounter. He and two colleagues had gone to see Hamilton about the Tories' position, 'and desire his opinion, but his Grace being abroad when they came to wait upon him, the message was not communicated to him, till just as the Parliament sat down'. The duke assured them nothing would be decided that day. According to Hamilton's own memory of the exchange, though, he found time only to say he would not go along with the Tory change of mind before the proceedings got under way, 'and because the second overture would have been the nomination to full Parliament or separate estates, therefore at the first overture, whether queen or Parliament, he gave his vote to the queen, at which his whole party rose in such a rage that they are not fallen yet'.[15]

By such nuances of intention, or the memory of them, may the fate of men and states be decreed. The whole business tends to confirm the theory of a cock-up rather than a conspiracy. Yet we know what Hooke's correspondent did not know, that the duke had had in mind to win a throne for himself. If there was a motive of any consistent kind in his confusing behaviour, chagrin at his frustration on this head can perhaps supply it.[16]

☙

Much as the reasons for Hamilton's volte-face may interest us, on account of the chain of events it brought in its wake, they were not quite so fascinating to Hooke. He naturally felt more concern about the actual purpose of his mission, to assess the chances for a French invasion of Scotland. Back in Paris he sat down to write a report for his employer, Jean-Baptiste Colbert, Marquis de Torcy, the French Foreign Minister. To some extent Hooke tacitly admitted the prospects were none too bright: he had found a political nation in disarray, and it was sometimes hard for him to draw firm conclusions from conflicting evidence he culled. For example, one peer he encountered was the Duke of Montrose, who 'had reconciled himself with the Court, after declaring to his friends that, as he could see nothing to be done for the Pretender or his country, he was going to think of his own interests'. Yet this does not seem to be an accurate account of the position of Montrose, who in spite of a right royalist heritage was never that much of a Jacobite, except perhaps for cosmetic purposes. Hooke tended to overestimate the commitment to the Stewarts' cause of most he met.

As for Hamilton, Hooke had found that he only deepened the disarray, 'that he was obviously going to go his own way; that the others were not all happy with what he had done; and so everything languished'. Apparently the Duke of Gordon had earlier in the year organised a Jacobite circle intent on entering into some sort of bond to combat the Union, which Hamilton agreed to join. But he proposed the formalities should be left till the next session of the Parliament convened, when they would all have the chance to get together and firm up their plans in Edinburgh. Yet after the other conspirators arrived there he neither made a move to meet them nor gave reasons for his inaction and reticence.[17]

Hooke had learned from Erroll that many Jacobites harboured deep suspicions of Hamilton: 'They would indeed risk everything to bring back their legitimate prince, but they would not lend a hand to put the duke on the throne.' They feared Gordon's scheme for a formal agreement among conspirators would place all their military resources under the command of Hamilton, and that 'afterwards he could use them for his own elevation'. So far they had complied with the widowed Queen Mary of Modena's instruction to obey him, yet did not like it that he 'required them to follow him blindly'. Since then the exiled court had taken to complaining he did not even answer letters. Now things had come to the pass, in Scotland too, 'that the more enlightened . . . did not tell him what they were doing and that he did not want to listen to their reasons'.[18]

At this point in his report, Hooke recalled some sentiments of Hamilton's he had noted down from one of their interviews: 'What we want is not to be English slaves, and we believe that if Queen Anne comes to die without having the Hanoverian succession accepted in Scotland, then it will be easy for us to separate ourselves from England, or to make them grant us the conditions that we demand.' Perhaps that offered the key to understanding what the duke was up to.

In answer to those words, Hooke remembered, 'I was non-committal. I only asked him if the Scots would then be strong enough to resist, alone and without help, the might of England.' The duke had replied that Scotland could find enough men and provisions, but needed money, arms and munitions. These he was sure France would not fail to supply, as it must always be in her interest to support Scotland against England.[19]

At a later meeting, Hamilton had said the more he reflected on things the more he saw the problem of doing anything for *le roi d'Angleterre* (the name which he and Hooke used for the Pretender throughout). This was because of James's Catholicism, obnoxious in England. Even if he should be welcomed on landing in Scotland, he would be repulsed by superior force once he tried to cross the border. But a King of Scots supported by the French might hold off the English. Hamilton stopped there and asked Hooke what he thought.

Hooke had replied that he thought as Hamilton did, that it would be better for the Pretender to be King of Scots than to remain without a kingdom.

'Yes, but it would be impossible for him to maintain himself here for reasons I have just told you,' Hamilton had retorted testily, 'while a Protestant prince with no pretensions at all to the Crown of England would meet fewer obstacles.'

Hooke had agreed, adding that this was something the English themselves must take account of. If their feelings could be judged by what they said of Hamilton, then they believed he was working for himself with just that aim.

'Yes, they call me Stanislas in England,' Hamilton had chuckled – in reference to the Polish aristocrat, Leszczynski, who in the Warsaw of this very September 1705 was in the act of overthrowing Augustus the Strong, his elective sovereign from the Saxon dynasty, whom he would replace. 'And by that they mean that I dream of the throne. But they are wrong,' he insisted, 'I am seeking the restoration of the *roi d'Angleterre*.'

'And if you cannot bring him back?' Hooke asked.

'If we cannot bring him back I would prefer anyone to be king rather than submit to Hanover; and the *roi d'Angleterre* cannot think that a bad thing. It must be a matter of indifference to him who fills the throne if he cannot occupy it,' Hamilton had cryptically replied.

It should be borne in mind yet again that Hooke remained at bottom uninterested in Hamilton for himself, only in the extent to which he could further French designs. The main question the Irishman had set himself to answer was whether or not France should foment a Jacobite revolt in Scotland. He finally judged any such revolt would win wide support there: in that he was only telling the truth, beside saying what his masters at Versailles wanted to hear. Yet he also, in the vividness of his depiction, let them know just who they were dealing with in the man they expected to step forward as native leader of an uprising. Hooke captures with something approaching genius Hamilton's duplicity. The duke's declarations of loyalty to the Stewarts are in these accounts constantly subverted out of his own mouth, in words betraying how his personal ambition for the Crown lay always at the back of his mind. If this was the key to it all, then the best explanation of his conduct in the Scots Parliament on September 1 is that he had come to the conclusion the French would never give him the help he needed. His loss of his illusions was followed the next morning by his betrayal of his country. That country could well be won for the Jacobites, Hooke had for his part determined; yet it would be won despite, not because of, their native leadership. It is hard to envy the Ministers at Versailles the decisions they would have to take on the basis of such a shrewd but unsparing judgment.

✑

The political reality for Scotland, it is clear from all this, was by the autumn of 1705 even more complex and unreadable than it had been just

163

at the turn of the year. Then matters remained in their way simple, with Scotland screaming defiance of England. Still, the nadir in relations had yet to be reached.

On February 5, Anne gave the royal assent to 'the Act for the effectual securing of the kingdom of England from the apparent dangers that might arise from several Acts lately passed in the Parliament of Scotland' – to the Alien Act, that is. It set out how, unless the Scots accepted the Hanoverian succession or gave a sign by Christmas of their willingness to talk about Union, they would be penalised. If not already domiciled in England or her possessions, they would be treated as aliens, while trade to England in their main exports would be banned.

Almost certainly this Act was unconstitutional, though it never underwent a test in court. If Scots had to be declared aliens in England from Christmas 1705, they obviously could not have been aliens in England already. There, by common law, their naturalisation followed from the precedent of Calvin's case, the judicial ruling after 1603 that the *post-nati*, Scots born later than that date, might on the same terms as Englishmen live, work, own property, buy and sell in every dominion of James VI and I, on both sides of the border and ocean. This ought to have lasted so long as the Union of Crowns did. But whatever the standing of the Alien Act it had the effect of concentrating the Scots' minds by its threat of sanctions. As that threat loomed Joseph Taylor, an Englishman returning from a trip to Edinburgh in September, chanced near the border on 'a prodigious number of Scotch cattle, coming from the mountains to be sold, before our Act of Parliament passed' [sic].[20]

The real target of the Act's menacing clauses was the Scottish ruling class, those who would decide the fate of the nation. Only the nobles and gentry ever had much to do with England. Some already owned property or had been married there – and more hoped to do both, a prospect which would recede if they became aliens. They were besides the ones that created the deficit on the balance of payments with their conspicuous consumption. They paid for it too, in some sort, with the export to England of their livestock, coal and textiles: the proceeds of the first went largely to Highland chiefs, of the second to the landowners in the Lothians and Fife who sat on the seams, and of the third often to other Lowland lairds whose tenants handed over their rents, not in money, which they seldom saw, but in kind, in linen woven by the fireside during the long, dark winters when they had no work in the fields. One implicit long-term English aim was to absorb the Scots ruling class and cure its anarchic instincts. This was sometimes what the noblemen and gentlemen of Scotland wanted too, but so they could turn the improved relations to their profit. They only asked the starting price. The queen had told them the Hanoverian succession would do for the time being. Even that seemed to certain of them too much; yet it might not be enough.

For now, though, the salient feature of relations between the two countries was Scotland's fury at England's law. This, intended to sway attitudes on the Scottish side, there only caused watchful distrust to lurch into incandescent hatred. It stirred up talk of war all over again. In Ayrshire 7,000 men were said to be drilling, including the Cameronian fanatics. In Dumfriesshire, according to an English report, the people 'are all in arms and exercise their men once every month, and there are a considerable number of gunsmiths come lately from France, so they are equipping themselves might and main to force a trade with England if the Union does not succeed'.[21] This was alarmist: whatever the motive of the training, it had become official and legal under the Act of Security. Still it scared the English. Thomas Coke MP had a letter from a constituent in Derbyshire: 'It's not the first time the Scots have invaded this nation with success; there's some alive that don't forget Leslie's coming into England, which gave so much encouragement to the late unhappy Civil War. The French king, I suppose, won't let them want money to go through with it.'[22] But he would have to wait till 1745 to see Scots in his county again. In reality it is hard to believe Scotland posed much of a threat to England. The commander-in-chief of the Scots army, General George Ramsay, was himself a traitor in touch with Godolphin. That problem solved itself when, later in the year, the general drank himself to death with another old soldier, the Earl of Kincardine; a third, the Earl of Balcarres, just survived their three days of a bender. It hardly speaks for a high state of military preparedness in Scotland.[23]

More likely was an English invasion of Scotland, though it would probably have led to French intervention in favour of the resistance. Louis XIV, tiring of Jacobites and their fatuous plots, actually hoped events would follow that course. In the end it did not greatly matter to him whether Stewarts or Hamiltons emerged with the Crown of Scotland in hand, but a war on two fronts for England would do nicely. On the English side Godolphin, as ever, preferred to threaten rather than be threatened. 'England is not now in the condition it was when Scotland used to make inroads on us,' he wrote to Seafield. 'We have the power, and you may give us the will to return those visits. And supposing the

French are more able to assist the Scots than I hope they are, the French have the character of being very good servants but the worst masters upon earth.' It sounds less like an imminent threat of invasion than sound, if gruff, advice to Scots to choose their friends with care. Much has been made of such sabre-rattling by the nationalist historian, Paul Scott.[24] Yet, as we see, the English also had their fears. And the man who might have led their invasion, Marlborough, spoke always of Union rather than war. A politician too, not just a soldier, he knew war was a perilous and precarious means of palliating political problems. Even conquest of Scotland would hinder his campaigns in Europe by diverting his forces, and possibly dry up his indispensable flow of Scots recruits. Not least, the queen avoided all talk of war, and constantly urged her two kingdoms to come to terms.

℘

Big talk in Scotland is even today just part of the ritual preliminaries to combat, familiar in the streets any Friday night, which now as then leave any actual ignition of fighting still a good way off. But the tinder was there, certainly. During his tour, Joseph Taylor had found even 'the children, which can but just speak, seem to have a natural antipathy against the English'.[25] What were they saying? One pamphlet gave a downright peasant's view of the neighbour nation: 'a pack of pock pudden, pork eaters, belly-god tykes . . . the refuse of the whole earth, a hotch potch of bastardy, dastardly scum, sprung from the armies that subdued England from time to time'.[26] Themselves an unconquered race, of course, Scots also disliked pigs and pork as creatures of Satan; Sir Walter Scott was still writing about this *curiosum* a century later. One of the most virulent anti-unionist pamphlets, bent on stuffing nasty facts down the Auld Enemy's throat, came out under the title, *A Pill for Pork-eaters*. English consumption of and consequent likeness to pigs apparently explained much about them.[27]

A virtue in some of these attempts to put across a popular view is that they offer early representations of vernacular Scots. Court Scots, the language of James VI's Castalian poets, for example, was still used in speech and writing by a toff like Seafield, and 150 years later Lord Cockburn could recall from his youth its cadences on the lips of genteel old ladies. But the voice of the people from the turn of the eighteenth century echoes down to us less often: it had not yet, though it would soon, come to be prized as a fund of authentic Scottishness, of a sort vanishing from other walks of life. The aim now of employing it in print was to stress that the high-heid-yins hobnobbing with the English did not speak for the nation.

One tract puts this in a peasant's mouth: 'I find the maist part of fock here-awae against it, and sayen wee greeten faces, they're fly'd at the heart, it'll be a black bargain for Scotland.' The country should not be overawed by its neighbour's wealth: 'As the fool thinks the bell clinks, but Engles merchants is better stocked nor ours, and I doubt nae, an there be onny gear gaen, but they wad lick the butter off our focks bread.' All the same, it was advisable to look for the iron fist in the velvet glove: 'But than another wrack will fallow, whan we hae it nae to pay, they'll send dragoons to quarter on us, and tack awae a' we hae, and that will raise great murmur and ill blood, and wha kens what this may drive our poor fock to.' That might even bode a return to the Killing Time: 'And what will come of us an we get some new sort of aiths amang us that honest fock will startle to take, and something or other that will puzzle or learned ministers themselves what to do about it?' Above all, 'I wiss my een may nae see the ald episcopal wark of hangen and headen amd persecuten come into fassen again, the Engleses will neer bear wee mony things that our awn fock thought fit to wink at.' This sturdy character concludes: 'I'm neither prophet nor prophet's son, but I speak out what many fock thinks. A' is like to go to the pot together.'[28]

❧

The traditional trading of insults was as nothing to the tidal wave of wrath risen among Scots now. It left their own leaders aghast. The wobbly Lord High Commissioner, John Hay, Marquis of Tweeddale, found his position further undermined, while his New Party quite lost its bearings: how could such disinterested patriots think of yielding to the English in this their latest haughty guise? If they did, they would just ape the self-seeking of the great nobles they condemned and thought to have superseded, men like the Dukes of Hamilton, of Argyll and of Queensberry. Yet they were soon angling for some accord with such figures. The too searching test of the New Party's good intentions and strength of character only went to show why it had failed so miserably in the previous parliamentary session.

An already depressing record was about to sink to rock-bottom in the conclusion to the affair of the *Worcester*. It would end with the judicial murder of Captain Thomas Green and two of his men. They and the rest of his crew were brought to trial on March 14 before the Court of Admiralty in Edinburgh on a charge of having destroyed a ship belonging to the Company of Scotland Trading to Africa and the Indies. The jury consisted of five skippers from ports along the Firth of Forth and nine merchants of Edinburgh under the presidency of Sir James Fleming of Rathobyres, a former Lord Provost and a shareholder in the company. Though the evidence remained flimsy, Green and 17 others, all but one of those in the dock, were found guilty and condemned to death. The verdict embittered Anglo-Scottish relations as never before in peacetime. Secretary Johnston reported the reaction of people in London: 'They lay it entirely at Tweeddale and the New Party's door . . . The Whigs make a national Jacobite business of it and it will be trumped up at all the elections.' An incensed English public opinion demanded reprieve of the queen, who found herself in two minds. For her to overturn due legal process in Scotland could only add to her difficulties there. It would have been asked why she had not done as much in England in the corresponding case of the *Annandale*. All that occurred to her was to hint to her Scots privy councillors that they might weigh the quality of mercy while she turned the matter over in her thoughts, rather slowly. She sent them a message to that effect but not in such terms that they felt obliged to do anything about it.

The real problem for the Scots privy councillors lay not 400 miles away in London but under their noses. Panic-stricken at the cry in the streets of Edinburgh for blood, they lacked the guts to defy it. Half of them did not even turn up to their meeting scheduled for April 10 which had reprieve on its agenda. Prominent among the absentees, on a range of feeble pretexts, were the privy councillors from the governing New Party. Seafield, back as Chancellor, attended – but his resolve, privately in favour of reprieve, failed him too. He had, on the contrary, written to Godolphin that the convicted sailors would have to be sacrificed to the mob. In fact, and shamefully, the government of Scotland hoped to profit from their fate. The ill-will it was generating on both sides of the border bid fair to ruin any project of Union, so getting Ministers off that hook. Worse, they thought pandering to the outcry would win them the popularity they had lost, or never gained, by espousing the Hanoverian succession. Baillie of Jerviswood wrote to Secretary Johnston on March 28: 'If the queen shall grant them remissions, it will spoil the business of

Parliament.' On March 31 he added: 'Go the matter as it will, we shall by it have the country.' He was wrong. Politicians fanned the flames of nationalism at the cost of innocent lives, but all to no purpose in the end.[29]

Without a reprieve the condemned men were due to be executed on April 11. At the last minute a good deal of ministerial toing and froing continued under the vigilant gaze of vast crowds bent on vengeance which had gathered in Edinburgh from miles around. This was a final deterrent to political interference with the course of the law. 'As we went along the streets,' Seafield reported to Godolphin, 'the whole people and mob were crying for justice, and desired we might grant no reprieve. After we were some time in council, we came to be convinced that there was no possibility of preserving the public peace without allowing some that were thought most guilty to be executed.' The lily-livered decision did not spare Seafield unwelcome popular attention. The rabble brought his coach to a halt before the Tron church under a hail of stones. 'At last, I was forced to come out and expose myself entirely to their fury, but, when they saw me, they fell immediately calm, for I did not seem in the least discomposed, and they separated to each hand, and I went into a friend's house, and none of them offered to follow.' Others thought his exit from the scene more hasty and undignified than his own account suggests. At any rate the rioters lost no time in smashing his coach to smithereens.[30]

Another huge throng had gathered on Leith Sands, at the place of execution for pirates between the high and the low water-mark. These people were threatening to come up into the city unless the captives soon appeared down there. Meanwhile the mob in the High Street yelled it would tear them from the tolbooth and string them up on the spot. All the privy councillors would do to salve their consciences was decide there should be no instant massacre of the whole hapless crew. Just three would be hanged that day, with the rest to follow in weekly batches. Captain Thomas Green, the mate John Madder (a Scot) and the gunner James Simpson were to die first.

A grim procession set off from the tolbooth, with the three prisoners surrounded by the town-guard. They marched down the Canongate, then round towards Leith. The Revd Robert Wodrow of Eastwood, who happened to be on business in the capital, followed and came on 'the greatest confluence of people there that ever I saw in my life, for they cared not how far they were off, so be it they saw'. At the sands a battalion of foot-soldiers and some horse-guards were drawn up underneath the scaffold. The prisoners mounted it in turn, each protesting even yet, with the rope already round his neck, that he was guiltless. 'This indeed put all people into a strange demur', Wodrow says, 'There's only this to alleviate it, that they confessed no other particular sins more than that, even when they were posed anent their swearing and drunkenness, which was weel known.' Right by the gibbet stood a twenty-year-old student of law, Duncan Forbes of Culloden, a boozer himself and otherwise filled by fellow feeling for the condemned: 'I put myself in deep mourning and with the danger of my life attended the innocent but unfortunate men to the scaffold, where they died with the most affecting protestations of their innocence. I did not stop here, for I carried the head of Captain Green to the grave.'[31] Forty years on as Lord Advocate, Forbes would in his treatment of Jacobites after their final, failed rising earn a durable reputation for the instincts of clemency he here first showed. Scots like the doomed to die well, and as the executions went on the victims' courage aroused misgivings in the rest of the onlookers too. Popular hysteria at once subsided afterwards, giving way to shame and remorse. In September all remaining captives from the *Worcester* were freed without fuss – proof enough of the injustice done to the dead.

૭୬

For the New Party the sequel was not cheap popularity but its fall as the government of Scotland. It had neither won over the people nor fulfilled even the minimal expectations of the Court; if anything it left even more of a mess than before. Queensberry stole out from the shadows to suggest that Seafield should next star as Lord High Commissioner, presumably on an assumption he might himself be able to control the performance from the prompt-box, but it was too early for a comeback by the old actor-manager. Seafield as well, after squaring Godolphin, pressed openly for a change of cast.

Nosey Lockhart accosted Seafield one day, though he would give nothing away. His interrogator mused: 'I suppose they find they're engaged to loose so ravelled a knot that they know not at which end to begin.' But a solution might lie in the young Duke of Argyll, 'who as far as I can understand knows nor proposes no way to loose such Gordian knots, but like Alexander the Great to cut them with his sword'.[32] The correspondent favoured with such speculation was Hamilton, though he remained preoccupied by his poverty. He was now in touch with the Earl of Mar, Queensberry's crony, and appeared to stand with him in 'great familiarity and confidence'. Lockhart would at length conclude that was the reason why Hamilton showed 'less zeal and forwardness in this ensuing than in former Parliaments'.[33]

The brightest youngster in the New Party, Roxburghe, also hoped Argyll would be the next Lord High Commissioner, as a man 'with abundance of zeal'.[34] Several of Roxburghe's colleagues seconded him in their hurry to get off the sinking ship of Tweeddale, a pleasant old buffer but now revealed as useless in a crisis. Argyll could at least keep out Queensberry, and it was hard to see who else might. Every other candidate would be bound to meet some objection either from the Court or the Parliament. Godolphin, too, decided Argyll must be the man.

Argyll was politically an unknown. But already, at the age of twenty-five, after an education at Eton and Christ Church, Oxford, he bestrode several worlds: from the military camps by the River Rhine to the courtly coteries of Anglo-Scots by the River Thames to the Presbyterian Lowlands to the barbarous Gàidhealtachd. With the mark he made elsewhere it is easy to forget how the Highlands may have been the most potent of all those early influences on him, making him proud and prickly though slightly fey. Free of Hamilton's pretensions to the Crown, Argyll was yet the holder of a regality, where under Scots law the feudal superior wielded a king's powers, notably that of 'pit and gallows', the right to try his vassals and condemn them to durance or death. While clans were entering on their historic decline they had not fallen so far as to deprive the duke, as chief of the Campbells, of command over more men than there were regular troops in Scotland, and better fighting men too. Among his own people he stood out as a great warrior – MacChailein Mòr, to give him the traditional heroic epithet, or Red John of the Battles. And his regality had remained (unlike that of Atholl, for example) under a single family for centuries, whose name many of its people took as their own in immemorial allegiance to the petty kingdom of remote Celtic antiquity from which it had grown: Earra Ghàidheal, coastland of the Gaels.[35]

Callow as Argyll was, a high title and electoral interests in a swathe of counties made for much in Scottish politics. His awareness that he could boast bluer blood than almost anyone he ever met – and so to his own mind was entitled to address even Queen Anne as a virtual equal – informed his behaviour right through his public career. Though the last Scots Parliament was a young man's Parliament, a cockpit of passion and intensity, he had not been there when it first convened as he was then on active service in Europe. When he got home his rough edges had yet to be smoothed; he still itched to take embattlements by storm. He remained hard to fathom, all the same, now as later – disinterested but covetous, eager for power but, according to his eulogist Sir Walter Scott, 'free from the ordinary vices of statesmen'.[36] Proud, fretful of nonsense, unimpressed by rank (at least civilian rank), he was a man others never really knew how to handle. He had the same trouble with them.

Argyll was not so callow as to be incapable of elementary political gamesmanship, such as playing hard to get. All his life he would remain absolutely shameless about money, because of the huge debts his family had run up in surviving its last, sombre century.[37] Anyway, being broke did not make him an exception among Scots noblemen. He now demanded £20,000 for his coming political struggles, ostensibly to pay arrears of salaries or pensions and make sure of at least a little personal following in the Parliament. But the Treasury in Edinburgh was empty and the Treasury in London, run by Godolphin, refused to cough up. The duke also asked for an English peerage, which had the virtue of coming cheap; this, the Earldom of Greenwich, he did get.

Once in office MacChailein Mòr proved irksome both to those above and to those below him. Probably he still saw himself first as soldier rather than statesman; an observer remarked that 'his head ran more on the camp than the court'.[38] At the court smarmy accommodation may have been the rule but in the camp things took on a different air: Red John's reaction to lip was to bawl it out. As for his supposed superiors in London, he only baffled and annoyed them. While previous Lord High Commissioners had been supplicant, he was importunate. If Seafield insinuated himself with sure-footed deference, and Tweeddale never had the force to match his sense, Red John shook things up. Hamilton – higher than Argyll in the order of precedence, and not even a member of the government – said after hearing from him that his letter 'was in such a strain as if he had been writing to one of his chamberlains in Kintyre'. He addressed English Ministers, indeed Her Majesty, in much the same tone. At least he dispelled some of the naïvety in London about the weird and wonderful ways of politics in Scotland. And right through his term as Lord High Commissioner, he insisted on a free hand, repeatedly threatening to resign otherwise. With little luggage, he would continue to travel light. Soon after the session was over he left for the battlefields of Europe with barely a backward glance.[39]

Argyll arrived in Edinburgh a fortnight after Captain Green's execution. He had intervened in that affair from a distance and asked Seafield to reprieve the crew of the *Worcester*; no doubt, had the Lord High Commissioner been earlier on the spot, he would not have dithered in defying the mob or dispersing it by force. He came now with an escort of clansmen armed to the teeth, sufficiently daunting to the canaille of the capital. With him he brought also the dim view he had meanwhile formed of Tweeddale's Ministry. From the New Party and the Old Whigs, though without Queensberry, Godolphin hoped Argyll could forge a coalition, and so did Seafield. But MacChailein Mòr would have none of this mending and making do. He preferred a strong team, which to his mind meant ruling out even those in the New Party, notably Roxburghe, who had helped him to office. 'A faithless friend is worse than a professed enemy,' he said; he wanted men 'such as have always been firm to the Revolution'. Nor did he fancy being stuck with the Hanoverian succession as his pivotal policy. Yet Anne trusted Tweeddale and refused to abandon the New Party. Seafield supported her. The retort from Argyll was to tender his resignation, brazenly adding: 'I hope your Majesty will not think I resign my post of Commissioner in order to persuade you to make the alterations I proposed.' He got his way and consented to carry on.[40]

Once he had slapped some squaddies into shape and marched them up to the top of the hill, Argyll then had to march them down again into the Parliament House of Edinburgh, where small matters such as majorities counted. The thing he had yet to achieve was just such a majority, to replace the one thrown away in getting rid of the shirkers in the New Party. A solution was not easy. For reasons slightly obscure, Argyll turned back to the nonpareil of seasoned Whiggery to complement his own brasher version. Any arrangement with the old Court party which ignored Queensberry was probably doomed anyway. He, backed by the Junto in London and still disposing of a good number of votes in Edinburgh, had already shown he could trip up a rival. What he could not in fact offer (and for now did not especially want to) was a secure majority in the Parliament.

All the same it was Queensberry that Argyll chose to bolster his position, as a man still with a lot of chips to cash and favours to call in; he had outstanding expenses to collect, too, as he did not hesitate to remind the new Lord High Commissioner. The olive-branch must yet have come as a bit of a surprise to Queensberry if we may judge by the fact that he had never ceased to plot – for example, by trying to set Argyll and the New Party at odds (something unnecessary in the event) while angling for fresh support from the Junto. Argyll does not seem to have taken this amiss, so long as he could look forward to lining up behind himself the train of trucklers trailing after Queensberry. Waifs since his dismissal, they had been reduced to voting with Jacobites to do down common enemies. Now, on his return to office, they would surely rally round. He probably saw Red John not merely as a Highland marauder but also as a potential fixture at the top of the greasy pole, a rival for permanent leadership of the Court party. That would explain his continuing duplicity towards Argyll, if explanation is needed for what came as second nature to him. Still, return to office made risk for the future worthwhile. Queensberry accepted both.[41]

The one problem lay with Anne, who flatly refused to employ Queensberry again, as 'a thing I can never consent to, his last tricking behaviour having made him more odious to me than ever'. Godolphin was called in to urge her to give way, but she replied: 'It grates my soul to take a man into my service that has not only betrayed us, but tricked me several times, one that has been obnoxious to his own countrymen these many years and one that I can never be convinced can be of any use.'[42] So there was nothing for it but that Argyll should again deal with the matter in person. He went to see his sovereign and, presumably more in sorrow than in anger, browbeat the poor woman into complaisance.

By sheer effrontery, then, Argyll was able to form a government largely drawn from the old Court party, supplemented by some of his own kin and by those Presbyterians still looking to his family for leadership. The Ministry contained two joint Secretaries for Scotland, the Marquis of Annandale, a sidekick of the first Duke of Argyll, then another Campbell, the Earl of Loudoun, a fervent advocate of Union. Lord Privy Seal was the office allotted to Queensberry while his principal man of business, Sir James Murray of Philiphaugh, became Lord Clerk Register. Adam Cockburn of Ormiston, a stern Presbyterian, was Lord Justice Clerk. The evergreen Earl of Seafield blossomed forth again as Chancellor.

The reorganised Court party, representing a sharp swing back towards the Revolution Whigs, would face an opposition consisting of the Cavaliers and the New Party. These refused to co-operate, having fallen out too far in the session of 1704. Since Court and Cavaliers remained evenly matched in the Parliament, the New Party held the balance of power there. In contempt Argyll dubbed it the 'half a dozen';[43] yet it still could count on a score or more of votes and made a habit of casting them tactically. It was a flying squadron, then, and won the jocular name of Squadrone Volante (it will be so called here from now on).

The nickname announced both a modish keenness for Italian culture in one nucleus of the party, flocculent young noblemen not long back from their grand tours in Europe, and a more serious aim of judging issues on merit rather than according to dogma. The Squadrone was nationalist, standing for an independent Scotland with a Hanoverian succession under limitations, though it found difficulty in remaining firm on that. In his memoirs, John Clerk of Penicuik was one to give it a bad press in consequence. Its members had been 'all Whigs in their principles, but who herded together, and kept little or no communication with the Duke of Queensberry and his friends'; nor indeed were they fonder of Argyll. While from opposition they vaunted their patriotism, 'in their hearts they were known to have Court preferments and places in the chiefest degree of veneration'. A little more positively, 'such a Squadrone Volante in any Parliament seems always to be a happy means in the hand of Providence to keep the several members of an administration in their duty'. Its leader, Tweeddale, was 'a very good man, but not perfectly qualified for Court intrigues'.[44] Anyway, he hardly bridled his followers' quest of a role above all profitable. Even a balance held by this wayward minority, however, put Argyll in a better position than Queensberry and Tweeddale had faced, or contrived to create, during their own terms as Lord High Commissioner. With no burning enmity to contend against, MacChailein Mòr had to that extent a free hand – the more so as the Court, chastened by the experience of 1703 and 1704, did not know what to do this time.

❦

Argyll's freedom of action was yet, on the major matter before him, curbed by the English Alien Act. It offered two choices, one of which the Scots Parliament was invited to take by Christmas: either the Hanoverian succession or the naming of commissioners for a treaty. Unlike the succession, the nature of a treaty had yet to be spelled out in detail and would remain vague for some time to come. All it meant for now was a package to improve relations between Scotland and England by what means came to hand. This stood the better chance in the Parliament as it might attract the votes of a variety of interests, while the Hanoverian succession was too specific and narrow in appeal. To go instead for a treaty, with other benefits that might accrue (free trade and so on), could hold the succession open, as most members wished. Bishop Gilbert Burnet pointed out how even Jacobites might in good conscience vote in this sense for a treaty, as it 'kept the settling the succession at a distance, and very few looked at the motion for the Union as anything but a pretence to keep matters yet longer in suspense'.[45]

As the opening of the session neared, Hamilton made his entry into Edinburgh with customary panache, amid crowds cheering him through the portals of Holyrood. Atholl ordered his clansmen to accompany him, and they tramped the streets armed to the teeth. Argyll was not to be outdone with his own escort of cut-throats but, more to the point, he had political wares to put on display. He obtained two addresses from the queen, corresponding to the Alien Act's alternatives, one stressing the succession, the other a treaty. She told him he could use which he liked, but he made a fuss and insisted on firmer instructions. When she opted for the one giving priority to the succession, in line with her own previous pronouncements, he replied that this made it harder to fulfil either aim. What an infuriating young man! In the end he conflated the addresses and recommended both policies to the Parliament, with a slight preference for the succession. It would be as accurate to say he left everyone in the dark.[46]

Among Argyll's colleagues the succession, obviously the more trouble-some alternative to carry, was the preference of only two Ministers, Annandale and Cockburn. Seafield advised Godolphin while the queen's message received its finishing touches: 'I know the succession is most desirable, but I am very afraid it will not succeed at this time . . . whereas that of a treaty seems more probable to succeed.' Like last year, a new government would find the wind at once taken out of its sails if it tried and failed to get through the main item on its programmme. While it controlled the parliamentary agenda, there was always the risk of ambush by the opposition. Seafield wrote again as members were arriving in Edinburgh: 'Those lately turned out seem to be for limitations, others are for a treaty and a great many against both. I am only afraid that they join in some previous resolve; if not, it is probable either the limitations or the treaty will carry.' He, at any rate, seemed resilient as ever.[47]

At the opening of the Parliament on July 3, the final version of the queen's speech plunged straight into the succession and 'the great inconveniency of the matter's continuing in suspense'. Anne wished members 'to go to the settlement of the succession before all other business', and herself stood 'ready to give the royal assent to such provisions and restrictions as shall be necessary and reasonable in such a case'. But she did not fail to give Union an honourable mention too, and in this more conciliatory tone: 'We earnestly recommend to you to pass an Act for a commission to set a treaty on foot between the kingdoms, as our Parliament of England has done, for effectuating what is so desirable, and for such other matters and things as may be judged proper for our honour.' Besides, 'great benefits would arise to all our subjects, by an Union of Scotland and England, and nothing will contribute more to the composing of differences and the extinguishing of heats, that are un-happily raised and fomented by the enemies of both nations'. The letter also asked for supply, as the money granted in the last session had already run out.

Argyll in his speech as Lord High Commissioner gave no more than a succinct résumé of the queen's letter. Seafield in his turn echoed its sentiments: 'It is unquestionably the interest of both nations, that they were more closely united, and that there were an entire communication of advantages and privileges, and that they both had the same interest, which would make this island secure at home, and formidable abroad.'[48]

Yet the house remained unimpressed. Most members preferred to avoid any decision on the alternatives before them, whatever the English Alien Act might have to say. This rather smug show of the opposition's strength would turn out to be an error, however, as Lockhart later admitted. While always possible at the start of a session, he explained, in time the members would find other diversions or even go home to see to their own business – and the opposition would falter. Besides, it would in the current case be able to count only for a little while on Queensberry's faction, which omitted to come to the government's aid only because its leader had not yet got back to Edinburgh and set it right (the muddle, by the way, suited him down to the ground). A stop was put eventually to this but it took time and, Lockhart observed, 'the Court, who had the purse and the power, were still gaming upon the Country, who had no arguments or persuasives to induce members to stand firm'.[49] A campaign of attrition by the government was to prove all too feasible.

At the outset Argyll and his Ministers were still struggling to get their act together. During the first regular sitting of the Parliament on July 6, Annandale took everyone aback, his own side included. He stood up to propose limitations in advance of settling the succession, though nothing of the kind had been mentioned three days before in the queen's speech on behalf of the government he was serving in. And then he called for a committee of the house to consider the economic situation, which offered enough grief for members to witter about for weeks on end without ever getting round to the official agenda. It would have been no surprise if Annandale's bright ideas had come from the opposition. But here was a Minister moving measures going well beyond what had just been announced as policy.

Annandale was, like Argyll, often a pig-headed and ill-tempered fellow, but Bishop Burnet offered a deeper reason for the *faux-pas*. He reported there had already been discord among Ministers. Annandale was for an immediate attempt to secure the succession, with more limitations if need be, but others felt sure it would fail and preferred to concentrate on Union instead, since that 'seemed to be a remote thing; there would be no great opposition to a general Act about it'. As such it would also be the most painless method to get Scotland off the hook of the penalties due under the Alien Act at Christmas. Talks on Union might drag out for years, so there would be short-term gain well in advance of any long-term risk. Such was the view expressed by the majority in the privy council, but Annandale felt so offended at his rebuff that he took no further part in the discussion and left his colleagues to it. In Scottish politics such behaviour was normal. This Lord High Commissioner, however, took exception and dismissed Annandale, to his surprise and chagrin. In as a replacement came Mar, Queensberry's legman.[50]

Yet Argyll's assertion of collective responsibility did not prevent the passage in the chamber of Annandale's proposals, and by 'a vast plurality'.[51] In the last session the house had shown it contained no majority for the Hanoverian succession. Now the same seemed true of a treaty, despite the threat of sanctions. A conceivable if still hazardous way forward was to postpone any and all debate on the alternatives. That might nullify official policy and render another session futile: the Parliament would not decide anything but then it would not reject anything either. Left in limbo, the Ministry could just crumble as its forerunners had done. One route to such a happy state of affairs (from the opposition's point of view) was to put the economy at the top of the agenda. This might be a legitimate concern of many members anyway, yet it also had the potential to take up infinite time without reaching any definite conclusion, since no cure for the nation's ills was easy or obvious.

It is hard to say from the bare record if what followed was intelligent debate or evasion of issues. One day members got down to discussing a scheme from John Law for a solution to the nation's running financial crisis. If the Bank of Scotland was back in business, recovery from its stop last winter had otherwise barely begun. A current pamphlet on the problem started from the cheerless view that 'the extreme poverty and misery which this poor nation at present groans under, wanting both coin and trade, sets . . . a great many heads a work to find out some proper means to supply the defect of coin'.[52] Under Law's proposal, the bank was to be taken over by the state so it could issue credits for economic development. The notion gained authority from the fact that his patron, Argyll, sat in the chair. But to many this just meant the duke and his chums were out to get their hands on brother Scots' money or property, which may well have been true. Members would have none of it. 'The forcing of any paper credit by Act of Parliament is unfit for the nation', they resolved, not to say 'prejudicial to this kingdom and of very dangerous consequence'.[53]

It was a debate less single-minded than its subject merited, however. Fletcher of Saltoun, not a hard man to rile, at one point interrupted it to denounce George Baillie of Jerviswood, member of the Squadrone for Lanarkshire, who was just speaking in favour of Law's scheme. Fletcher said Baillie was talking 'gibberish' and accused him of 'a contrivance to enslave the nation'. Baillie, a 'grave, silent and thoughtful' fellow[54] with no gift of repartee, shrank under the attack. So bold Roxburghe sprang to his defence and upbraided Fletcher with a reminder that 'a gentleman ought at least to be treated with good manners'. Fletcher, needless to say, 'fell into a passion'. From the chair, Argyll ordered him and Roxburghe to be confined to their lodgings. In the next session the row escalated. Now the Patriot issued his former cub with the inevitable challenge to a duel. They were locked up once again at the Lord High Commissioner's command. But they slipped down to Leith Sands early next morning. There Roxburghe suddenly announced he could not fight with swords because of a bad leg. Never at a loss, Fletcher whipped pistols from his pockets. Suddenly the cavalry rode to the rescue: a platoon arrived down from Edinburgh Castle on a tip-off and took the pair back into custody. The seconds composed the quarrel by firing the pistols in the air.[55]

⁓

For a while these diversions went on from debates that seemed to be leading nowhere anyhow. At some point a crunch had to come. Mar forecast it would arrive on July 16, when 'we'll be busy upon what carried, either treaty or succession. We have trifled all this time . . . This is like to be a hot day in Parliament.'[56] Hamilton, leader of the nationalist opposition, had again been biding his time to strike. But now his proposal was curious: that the house should once more adopt the motion passed a year ago to the day, 'that this Parliament will not proceed to the nomination of a successor till we have a treaty with England in relation to our commerce and other concerns with that nation'. Only this time it came with a rider: 'And further, it is resolved that this Parliament will proceed to make such limitations and conditions of government for the rectification of our constitution as may secure the liberty, religion and independence of this nation before they proceed to the said nomination.'[57] The rider was odd too, in saying nothing new, for surely in the Act of Security the Parliament had already voted limitations to its heart's content. The Squadrone, supposedly holding the balance of power, opposed the duke. Other members protested in all innocence that they had not yet finished with the economy. But Hamilton's motion passed by 43, a majority little less ample, than he had won in his coup a year before.[58]

That is to say, the house had not changed its mind and was not going to change its mind about the Hanoverian succession. In 1705 as in 1704 and 1703, such settlement of the succession could just never get through this Parliament. The Court suffered yet another defeat on the central aim of its policy, and at the same crucial juncture – the start of the session – as governments before it, with the same risk that all official business might grind to a halt. When would the Court learn? The humbled Seafield only regretted his side had not been better whipped. He reported to Godolphin on the post-mortem carried out by Argyll and other Ministers: 'We all agreed that there remains nothing now to be done concerning the succession in this session of Parliament, and that we ought to endeavour to have ane Act for a treaty in such terms as that we might hope to have some success.' Seafield said he would propose to the house that the queen should name the commissioners for a treaty, though not in terms suggesting he had much hope: 'and if we cannot prevail in that, to join that there will be a good nomination. If this cannot carry, we will be necessitate to bring the session to a close as soon as we can.'[59] They had been here before.

Yet there was one difference from previous years, in the absolute absence of Queensberry: more absent now than in the session of 1704 because then he had just hung about down the Canongate, whereas now he lingered in London, waiting on events and keeping his counsel.[60] All inquirers, even Godolphin or Argyll, were told he lay ill in bed. From under the covers issued forth the odd tremulous message exhorting them to be 'unanimous and positive', with a wish that 'having so fair a game before them they may not sniffle it, but play it boldly home'. As for himself, 'I shall care very little whether I am concerned in the public or not, but in whatever capacity I am I shall always be ready to serve those who have continued their kindness to me' – by which he meant not sweeties and flowers but reimbursement of his official expenses, still a sore point.[61] Yet he was supposed to be Lord Privy Seal in the government of Scotland. While in his own previous ministerial role he too had faced stubborn obstruction of the Court, this evidently did not cure him of any urge to make life awkward for his successor by every means to hand, even from 400 miles away. Now Queensberry was wheedling his way back into favour, or at least place, he would still suit himself rather than the latest Lord High Commissioner or anybody else.

On July 23, just days after Hamilton's motion had won its thumping majority, Queensberry reached Edinburgh. Lockhart suggested he wanted to test 'how affairs were like to go, and whether or not he might venture himself in Scotland'. More than this, surely, he meant to show the Parliament could not be managed without his help, now Argyll had run into such trouble. Lockhart himself acknowledges, if with dismay, how Queensberry's influence remained real even 'over men of sense, quality and estates; men that had, at least many of them, no dependence upon him'.[62] He had waited to see what would come of the Hanoverian succession. Since this was the Court's priority, Argyll would have won a feather in his cap if he had got it through. As things turned out, he was beaten. The cocky young duke might stew for a while in his own juice.

Nothing suited Queensberry better. He could hold up his hands and deny all blame for disloyalty on the part of his followers, since he had not been in the chamber or even in Edinburgh at the moment the Lord High Commissioner was drubbed. Whenever later correspondents brought up the defeat, Queensberry stressed it all happened before he got home. MacChailein Mòr's Ministry had, despite his martinet's methods, achieved precious little up to now. Once Queensberry was back some prudence entered into policy, if seldom without a puff of perfidy about it. Lockhart wrote that Queensberry used Argyll 'as the monkey did the cat in pulling out the hot roasted chestnuts'.[63]

∽

The reality of the situation after July 23 was this: since the Parliament had rejected the Hanoverian succession then it would have to fall back on the alternative of a treaty with England, assuming it wanted to avoid the penalties on Scotland due from Christmas under the Alien Act. The government undertook to impress the fact on the many members who still preferred to put it out of mind. Lockhart thought that if the opposition had forced the treaty to a vote early in the session, 'they might easily have either rejected it altogether, or at least framed and clogged it as they pleased, and chosen such members as they had a mind to be commissioners for meeting and treating with the commissioners from England'. As it was, matters had been allowed to drift and quite other consequences would follow.[64]

For anyone able to read the runes, Queensberry had already turned his mind to those consequences. On July 20, three days before his arrival back in the capital, his subaltern, Mar, proposed to the Parliament an Act for a Treaty. This was in fact, despite its initial rejection and later ups and downs, to form the basis for Scotland's negotiating brief with England. It sought to make the prospects acceptable to as broad a range of opinion as possible. It emphasised to Scots that this was something their gracious monarch wanted, 'considering with what earnestness the queen's Majesty has recommended the settling of the succession and also a treaty as the most effectual way for extinguishing the heats and differences that are unhappily raised betwixt the two nations'. It stressed that negotiation would be between equals, 'her two independent kingdoms of Scotland and England'. It anticipated Presbyterian misgivings by excluding 'any alteration of the worship, discipline and government of the Church of this kingdom as now by law established'. To cap all, it provided that nothing proposed or agreed would take effect till confirmed by an Act of the Parliament of Scotland.[65]

Still, even the most sanguine observer would not have expected Scots to opt for this or any other treaty without squeezing out of it every last drop of recompense. Hamilton had demanded yet more limitations, and perhaps a way forward was to let him have them. By August 1 Seafield reported to London his colleagues' accord in council that they 'should try if we can gain a majority for a treaty, and that in order to have time we should proceed to some Acts of trade and limitations'. Naturally, when they first returned to the chamber with this resolution in mind, 'we met with nothing but high and studied speeches complaining of the English Act of treaty, and that it was inconsistent with our sovereignty and independency to treat until the menacing clauses in the English Act were rescinded'.

Others suggested the way to get rid of the menacing clauses was to start a pow-wow rather than carry on with the war-dance. Seafield protested his personal concern for the honour of Scotland yet he 'could never be for a separate king or a separation from England so long as there was any possibility of getting our differences removed'. And he gave more solid reasons for 'conjoining with England'. It would defend the Protestant religion. It would open trade. Besides, 'England has freedom and liberty, and . . . the joining with it is the best way to secure that to us'. It would be in any event the only way to secure peace and foil foreign plots against both nations: 'Therefore, I was for a treaty.' But Seafield took care to say nothing of a Union of Parliaments.[66]

There was no way except by trial and error that the Court could learn what mix of limitations or commercial concessions might produce the desired outcome: 'If this can result in obtaining ane Act of treaty and a supply, it is well, but, if not, we must give it over for this time,' Seafield wearily wrote. Impenetrable wrangling followed on how a treaty might be linked with limitations or free trade and, if so, which head should be debated first. At one point the opposition extracted a promise that limitations were to be taken before a treaty, only at once to demand another promise that trade was to be taken before limitations. So it went on, but at length all sides agreed to spend four days of debate on trade and four on limitations. By accepting this, Seafield felt, 'we may at last carry the Act for a Treaty and a supply'.[67]

Those who swung the procedural compromise were the members from the Squadrone, or at least most of them. They consented that 'if limitations on the successor be voted, though not passed, they will then be for the treaty'. This peculiar but in the event successful device gave rise to a bizarre procedure under which in advance of any consent to talks with the English the opposition would draw up a wish-list to be voted on item by item; yet any approved would not actually come into force, merely be given a tick of approval, as it were – and perhaps appear in the eventual treaty, though that was never spelled out. The approved items would meanwhile hover in a legislative limbo, neither lawful nor unlawful, awaiting redemption of the pledge which had helped to get them passed. Lockhart dismissed the entire business as 'wheedling', while ruing that the Court 'had the power and the purse' for it. It surely bore Queensberry's fingerprints all over.[68]

So far the Ministry had still been losing the votes, though, if by smaller margins than the 42 which rejected the Hanoverian succession. All the same it was the opposition that found the greater difficulty in co-ordinating itself now, some demanding this and others that. In the habitual wheeler-dealing it sacrificed any unity and became susceptible to growing firmness on the part of the government: Argyll and Queensberry, the dictatorial and the devious duke, began to pull together rather than apart. At the end of a long, dark tunnel, a majority for a treaty slowly swung into view.

Anyway, members of this Parliament were never backward in coming forward with limitations on the Crown. Fletcher brought in again the whole package of those, a dozen in number, he had proposed in 1703. They would have transformed Scotland into a constitutional monarchy – or a republic, according to Seafield. Though Fletcher had failed that first time he got much credit for the effort, which formed a basis for the Act of Security. Now he urged his limitations to be passed as a Claim of Right, on a par with the defining document of the Revolution as a sort of fundamental law rather than just common-or-garden legislation. To his incredulous horror, he failed to find a seconder. It marked a caesura in his influence. One of the most active in the house, he would remain so as long as it yet sat. He had often been able to convince it with his eloquence, if by no means always. But suddenly not to find a seconder was a humiliation. It showed members turning away from the politics of gesture to the politics of substance. While they remained tolerant of Fletcher's foibles they would no longer follow his lead.

In reaction, Fletcher seemed to lose his own bearings. His interventions in debates grew erratic. At one point he would suggest Scotland should look for the succession to Prussia, on the grounds that this was a state ruled by a Calvinist rather than, like Hanover, a Lutheran dynasty. But there could be no franker admission of the humbug in calls for an alternative to Hanover than his plan for the most ancient kingdom in Europe to be offered to this house with a royal dignity four years old: it was only in 1701 that the Elector Frederick III of Brandenburg-Prussia had got himself crowned Frederick I, King of Prussia, at Königsberg beyond the bounds of the Holy Roman Empire so as not to annoy the Emperor Leopold. Let us be thankful Prussians and Scots never got a chance to bring out the worst in each other.

In contrast to Fletcher's failure, a further proposal from the floor of the house proved a success. This was an Act, introduced on August 9, for a

Designed by a committee – the various contemporary ideas for a flag to represent the Union of England and Scotland

LEFT.

The military mentality of John Campbell, second Duke of Argyll (likeness by William Aikman), proved useful for bringing the Scots Parliament into line (© *Scottish National Portrait Gallery*)

BELOW.

The old castle of Inveraray, built about 1450 and demolished in 1774, was the home of the Duke of Argyll and citadel of Clan Campbell

ABOVE.
All passion spent: the deserted
and echoing chamber of the
Scottish Parliament as it appeared
in Victorian times, from Robert
Billings, *The Baronial and
Ecclesiastical Antiquities of Scotland*
(1852)

RIGHT.
The 'thin, sour look' of Andrew
Fletcher of Saltoun, the Patriot,
defender of the last ditch of
Scottish independence, after
William Aikman (© *Scottish
National Portrait Gallery*)

A flattering portrait of Queen Anne, contrived
by the Dutch art of Willem Wissing and
Jan van der Vaardt (© *Scottish National Portrait Gallery*)

LEFT.
William of Orange, King of Scots, caught in a rare good mood, by Anna Maria Braunim (© *Scottish National Portrait Gallery*)

BELOW.
The entrance in the Canongate of Moray House, residence during parliamentary sessions of the Lord High Commissioner (© *Rory Cooper*)

OVERLEAF.
The traditional Riding of the Scots Parliament in 1681: the scene was repeated for the last time in 1703 (© *Trustees of the National Museums of Scotland*)

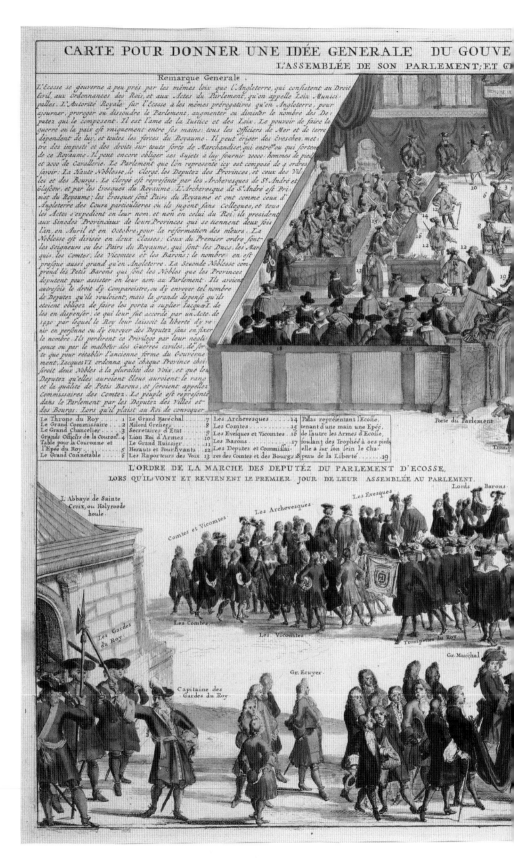

Remarque Generale

L'Ecosse se gouverne à peu prés par les mêmes loix que l'Angleterre, qui consistent au Droit civil, aux Ordonnances des Rois, et aux Actes du Parlement, qu'on appelle Loix Munici-palles. L'Autorité Royale fur l'Ecosse a les mêmes prérogatives qu'en Angleterre, pour ajourner, proroger ou dissoudre le Parlement, augmenter ou diminer le nombre des De-putez qui le composent. Il est l'ame de la Justice et des Loix. Le pouvoir de faire la guerre ou la paix est uniquement entre les mains: tous les officiers de Mer et de terre dependent de luy, et toutes les forces du Royaume. Il peut eriger des Eveschez, met-tre des impests et des droits sur toute forte de Marchandise qui entre ou qui fortent de ce Royaume. Il peut encore obliger ses Sujets à luy fournir 2000 hommes de pied et 2000 de Cavallerie. Le Parlement que l'on represente icy est compose de 4 ordres favoir: La Haute Noblesse, le Clergé, les Deputez des Provinces, et ceux des Vil-les et des Bourgs. Le Clergé est represente par les Archevesques de St. André et Glasgow, et par les Evesques du Royaume. L'Archevesque de St. Andre est Pri-mat du Royaume; les Evesques sont Pairs du Royaume et ont comme ceux d'Angleterre des Cours particulieres ou ils jugent sans Collegues, et tous les Actes s'expedient en leur nom et non en celui du Roi: ils president aux Sinodes Provinciaux de leurs Provinces qui se tiennent deux fois l'an en Avril et en Octobre, pour la reformation des meurs. La Noblesse est divisée en deux Classes; Ceux du Premier ordre sont les Seigneurs ou les Pairs du Royaume, qui sont les Ducs, les Mar-quis, les Comtes, les Vicomtes et les Barons; le nombre en est presque aussi grand qu'en Angleterre. La Seconde Noblesse com-prend les Petis Barons qui sont les Nobles que les Provinces deputent pour assister en leur nom au Parlement. Ils avoient autrefois le droit d'y Comparoistre, ou d'y envoyer tel nombre de Deputez qu'ils vouloient, mais la grande depense qu'ils etoient obligez de faire les porta à suplier Jacques I. de les en dispenser; ce qui leur fut accorde par un Acte de 1430 par lequel le Roy leur laissoit la liberté d'y ve-nir en personne ou d'y envoyer des Deputez sans en fixer le nombre. Ils perdirent ce Privilege par leur negli-gence ou par le malheur des Guerres civiles, de for-te que pour retablir l'ancienne forme du Gouverne-ment, Jacques VI ordonna que chaque Province choi-siroit deux Nobles à la pluralité des Voix, et que les Deputez qu'elles auroient Eleus auroient le rang et la qualité de Petis Barons, et seroient appellez Commissaires des Comtes. Le peuple est represente dans le Parlement par les Deputez des Villes et des Bourgs. Lors qu'il plaist au Roi de convoquer

Le Throne du Roy ... 1	Le Grand Maréchal ... 7	Les Archevesques ... 14	Pallas représentant l'Ecosse,	
Le Grand Commissaire ... 2	Milord Grenier ... 8	Les Comtes ... 15	tenant d'une main une Epée,	
Le Grand Chancelier ... 3	Secretaires d'Etat ... 9	Les Evesques et Vicomtes ... 16	de l'autre les Armes d'Ecosse,	
Grands Officiers de la Couron ... 4	Lion Roi d'Armes ... 10	Les Barons ... 17	foulant des Trophée à ses pieds	
Table pour la Couronne et	Le Grand Huissier ... 11	Les Deputez et Commissai-	elle à sur son sein le Cha-	
l'Epée du Roy ... 5	Heraults et Pourfuivants ... 12	res des Comtes et des Bourgs 18	peau de la Liberté ... 19	
Le Grand Connetable ... 6	Les Raporteurs des Voix ... 13			

Porte du Parlement

Tromp

L'ORDRE DE LA MARCHE DES DEPUTÉZ DU PARLEMENT D'ECOSSE,
LORS QU'ILS VONT ET REVIENNENT LE PREMIER JOUR DE LEUR ASSEMBLÉE AU PARLEMENT.

L'Abbaye de Sainte Croix, ou Holyroode houle.

Les Gardes du Roy

Comtes et Vicomtes

Les Archevesques

Les Evesques

Lords Barons

Les Comtes

Les Comtes

Les Vicomtes

Trompette du Roy

Trompettes du Roy

Gr. Maréchal

Gr. Ecuyer

Capitaine des Gardes du Roy

...MENT D'ECOSSE; L'ORDRE DE LA MARCHE OU CAVALCADE DE
E LA SÉANCE DE CET ILUSTRE CORPS.

Tom. 2. N.º 56

Suite de la Remarque.

*son Parlement, Les Deputez s'étant rendus à Edimbourg Capitale de l'Ecosse, ils s'assemblent
à l'Abbaye de S.te Croix, ou Holyroode houle, pour proceder à la marche, ou Cavalcade, tel
le qu'on la represente ici: s'étant rendus au Parlement en cette cerïmonie, le Grand Commissaire se place sur son Throne, et près de lui les Grands officiers de la Couronne,
et aux deux costez les Prelats et les Pairs seculiers: Les Deputez des Provinces à la
droite et ceux des Bourgs à la gauche. Les Ornemens Royaux sont mis sur une
table par le Grand Connétable et par le Grand Maréchal. Apres la priere faite
par l'Evesque d'Edimbourg, on fait la Lecture de la Liste des Deputez: en suite le Grand Chancelier s'aprochant du Throne se met à Genoux et reçoit des
mains du Grand Commissaire, la Commiffion du Roi, qu'il donne à un Secretaire
pour en faire la lecture. On lit en suite la Formule qui est la maniere et l'ordre de l'Assemblée, apres quoi Lion Roi d'Armes descent du Throne et place
les Seigneurs et Deputez selon leurs rangs. Le Grand Commissaire declare
en suite les intentions du Roi qui sont plus amplement expliquées par le grand
Chancelier; on fait prêter serment aux Deputez et on nomme des Commissaires pour dresser la reponse à la lettre du Roi. On procede en suite à
l'Election des Commissaires, appellez Seigneurs ou Lords, des Articles
pour dresser les Actes qui doivent estre proposez au Parlement:
pour cela on choisit 8. Evesques; 8. Milords, 8. Chevaliers et 8. Bour-
geois pour les 4. ordres du Royaume. Voicy la manière de proceder à cette Election: Les Evesques choisissent les Seigneurs qui
sont 1 Duc, 1 Marquis et 6. Comtes. Les Seigneurs nemment les
Ecclesiastiques qui sont ordinairement les 2. Archevesques avec
6 Evesques. Ces 16. Commissaires avec les Grands Officiers de
la Couronne qui sont Commissaires dans toutes les affaires, choisissent les 16 autres, savoir 8. pour les Provinces, et 8. pour
les Bourgs. Tous ces préliminaires étant achevez, on re-
conduit le Grand Commissaire dans le même ordre: on
vrient les autres jours au Parlement sans Cérmonie.
Il y a encore un Parlement fixe à Edimbourg qui
fut établi par Jacques V. avant celui-ci: il y en avoit
un mouvant qui alloit par les Villes rendre Justice
et interpreter les Loix. Les Ecossois ont encore quel-
ques Cours souveraines de Grands Justiciers pour les
matieres criminelles de chaque Province. Outre ces
officiers ordinaires, il y a encore un Vicomte here-
ditaire qui juge les causes civiles et criminelles.*

Les Commissaires des Comtes, et des Bourgs, et des Villes.

Poursuivants

Lords Advocats

Les Commissaires des Comtes, Bourgs, et Villes.

Herauts d' ....mes.

Lyon Roy d' Armes.

Le Grand Huissier

Marq. qui porte la couronne du Roy. *Massier*

1 Massier

Grand Commissaire.

Gr. Connetable.

Celui qui .... porte la Commiffion du Roy.

C.... port: l'Epée du Roy.

C.... port: le Sceptre du Roy.

A charming portrait in childhood of
James, the Old Pretender, and of his
sister Louise. Scots were not charmed.
(© *Getty Images*)

LEFT.

Queensberry House (1695), today a portal to the new Scottish Parliament, built by the Duke of Queensberry and modelled on the Parisian *hôtel particulier*, it exhibits the primarily French taste of the Scots ruling class. (© *Rory Cooper*)

BELOW.

Not a man to mess with – Sidney, Lord Godolphin, architect of Union from the English side, by Sir Godfrey Kneller (© *National Portrait Gallery*)

Portrayed by Sir Godfrey Kneller,
the greatest soldier of the age,
John Churchill, Duke of Marlborough,
advocated conciliation of the Scots
(© *National Portrait Gallery*)

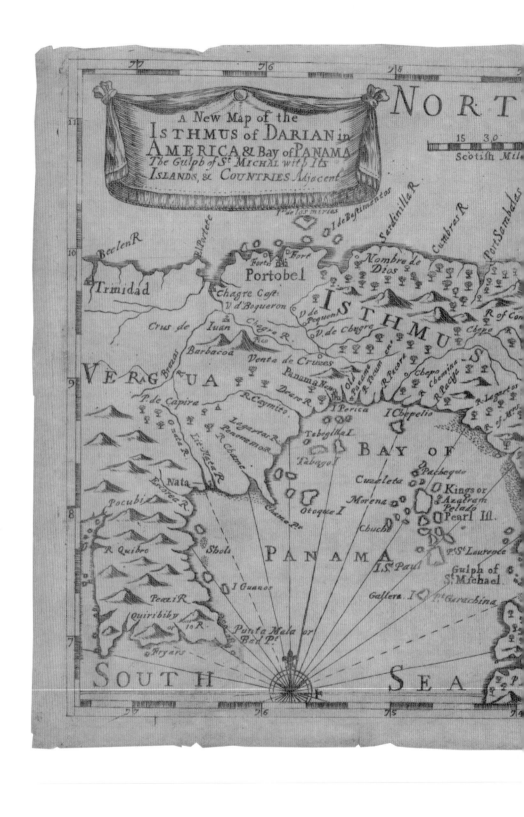

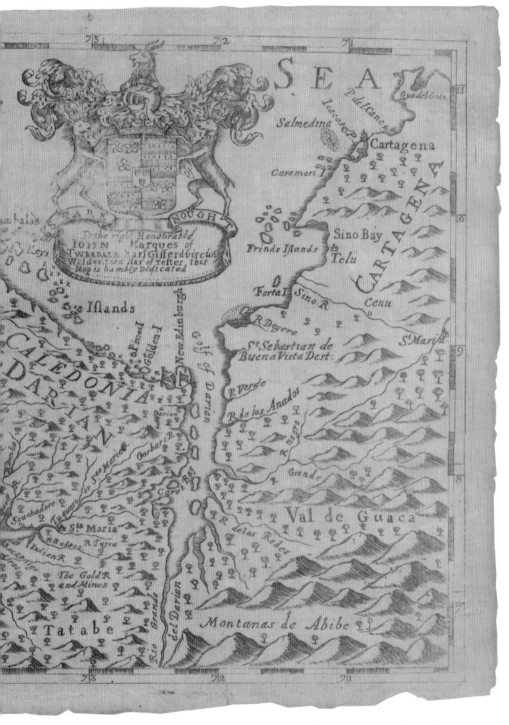

Depicted as a land flowing with milk and honey,
the colony of Darien was wormwood and gall to
the Scots (©*Trustees of the National Library of Scotland*)

The Palace of Holyroodhouse acquired its present external
appearance under the later Stewarts but was hardly ever occupied
by the royal family till the reign of Victoria (© *Rory Cooper*)

The east front of Edinburgh Castle frowns
down on the Scottish capital, but its citizens
were seldom overawed (© *Rory Cooper*)

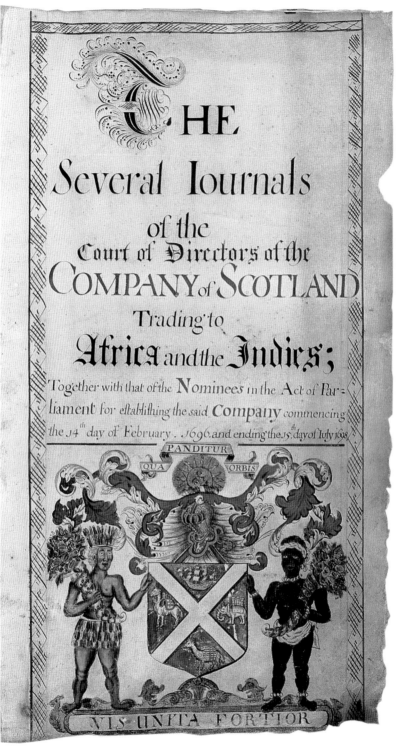

The vivid coat of arms of the Company of Scotland Trading
to Africa and the Indies betrayed nothing of the dismal reality
of Darien (*Courtesy of the Royal Bank of Scotland*)

James, Duke of Hamilton, as shifty as he was
swarthy, let down the Scottish opposition to
Union he was supposed to be leading
(© *Lennoxlove House Ltd. Licensor www.scran.ac.uk*)

council of trade. The idea had been espoused by the political economists, William Paterson, Hugh Chamberlen and John Law, in order to start tackling the deficit on the balance of payments. Now it was taken up by William Seton of Pitmedden – a unionist, though it remained unclear (maybe even to himself) what kind of unionist he might be. A council of trade anyway presupposed that Scotland would have in future some semblance of an independent economic policy, which could be formulated only in a continuing Parliament. The Act was passed.

But as so often, the item on the agenda proved to be the test of an unrelated issue, here the will among members to exert control over public appointments. Two immediate procedural points arose, whether appointees to the council of trade should be nominated by the Parliament or by the queen, and whether the Parliament should vote for them in a body or by estates; the government preferred in both cases the second option. And it lost in both, as expected. But in the first the hostile majority came to a mere nine: a vast improvement on previous divisions and, by the low standards of Scottish government, not a bad result at all. When later the house actually nominated the members of the council, the government surpassed itself to win a majority of them, except among the delegates of the counties. By the peers Hamilton was kept off. In private Seafield taunted him that he might not in future be able to win the places he coveted on other bodies, such as a commission for Union. This was not nice of the Chancellor; but it is another plausible reason for the imminent reversal in the duke's commitments.[69]

The next limitation on the agenda provided for officers of state to be named by the Parliament and not, as the current formula had it, by the king in Parliament. The Court proposed an amendment changing this to 'the king, with the consent of Parliament'. Members were urged not to go beyond the Covenanting constitution of 1641 which gave the Parliament only the right to take or leave a list of nominations from the king or the Lord High Commissioner. 'To lodge the nomination in the estates,' Seafield contended once again, 'was to divest the sovereign of all power and to extirpate the monarchy and constitute a republic.' Yet he thought the contrary argument worth reporting to London, and in less than damning terms: 'There was a great deal said for lodging it in the estates as the only remedy to prevent English influence on the successor and to prevent the nobility and gentry going up to London to seek places, which did ruin our private estates and fortunes, and exhaust the wealth of the kingdom.' Though Seafield was seeking to be flexible, his defence of the official position in the house, that nomination by the Parliament would 'run ourselves in all confusion and disorder', failed to convince. Still, the majority against him was only 16: again, not bad.[70]

The fate of a further proposal confirmed the trend of the votes. It was a double limitation, setting a term for the Parliament of three years and excluding from its membership anyone employed in the public revenue. The government argued that it restricted the royal prerogative in a way deemed unconstitutional in the past. Both Cavaliers and Squadrone supported it, yet their combined vote drooped – now on an amendment that the limitation should take effect before, not after, the death of Anne. Here the majority was again only 16, so the previous improvement in the Court's position held. The opposition unwisely pushed its luck. Hamilton proposed further that the present Parliament should be dissolved after just one more year, rather than three as the government wished. This he lost decisively, by a majority of 32. Still he did not take the hint. He pressed again for exclusion from the chamber of officials of the revenue: all assumed he meant Sir Alexander Ogilvie, member for Banff and, as receiver-general of taxes for Scotland, one of Seafield's trusties, apart from being his kinsman too. If members started hunting down one another's relations, where would it all end? Hamilton's motion suffered yet heavier defeat. On peripheral issues, at least, the opposition's majority was slipping away.[71]

℘

The house had spent so much and could have spent still more time dreaming up limitations. But the direction of the divisions indicated that a moment had to come for it to turn to the one thing that really ought to be decided in the current session: a treaty with England, and if or how to open negotiations for it. By the last week of August this necessity was becoming clear even to the diehard Lockhart: 'The Cavaliers and Country parties observing that there was a great inclination in the house to set a treaty on foot, thought it improper to oppose it any longer, in general terms.' Instead, they would seek to 'clog the commission with such restrictions and provisions as should retard the treaty's taking effect'. Atholl and Belhaven, Fletcher and Hamilton began, in no great hurry, to turn their minds to a treaty too, or at least to the spanners that might be thrown in its works. As ever, a question arose whether the grant of supply should precede or follow it. If not that, there was always a question whether the Alien Act ought to be rescinded first – such a 'scurrilous and haughty procedure', as Fletcher denounced it, which should rule out a treaty 'until it were proposed in more civil and equal terms'.[72]

At last, on August 25, the house got down to the treaty as such. It broached the question by taking up that draft Act which Mar had tabled the month before, bending over backwards to meet reasonable objections: if there could be no treaty on these terms, there could be no treaty at all. The relentless Fletcher, even so, proposed an address to the queen that 'out of the sense of duty we owe Your Majesty we do declare that we shall always be ready to comply with any such proposal from the Parliament of England, whenever it shall be made in such terms as are no ways dishonourable and disadvantageous to this nation'. He complained once again of 'the unneighbourly and injurious usage received by ane Act lately passed in the Parliament of England'. Yet, he held, the Parliament was still ready, in order to promote a good understanding between the two nations, to enter into a treaty with England. It would be, however, inconsistent with the honour and interest of Scotland to appoint commmissioners before the English Parliament had made a proposal 'in a more neighbourly and friendly manner'. The change in the house's mood can be gauged from the fact that it ignored Fletcher's ramblings. Instead it called for the reading of Mar's draft of an Act for a Treaty.[73]

The Jacobites managed this stage of the debate with more skill, while still dragging their own feet. Atholl posed the awkward question whether the Parliament's commissioners could in effect be asked to negotiate under duress, that is, to engage in discussions with English commissioners which must surely go on beyond Christmas, the deadline for Scots to be declared aliens in England and suffer the penalties. He proposed to prohibit any Scottish commissioners from crossing the border before the menacing clauses in the Alien Act had been rescinded at Westminster. This was trickier for the Court to deal with. Atholl had a point to which no instant response could be given, at least from Edinburgh. What the government managed to do was put off answering him till September 4, by which time the situation had wholly changed.[74]

The debate on Mar's draft resumed on August 31 and reached a crux. A third heavyweight from the opposition, Hamilton, proposed an additional clause, 'that the Union to be treated on shall not derogate any ways from any fundamental law, ancient privileges, offices, right, dignities and liberties of this kingdom'. The clause would have been familiar to cognoscenti of a century's stillborn attempts at Union: it had been included in identical terms in every Scottish Act to start negotiations with England since the reign of James VI.

But this time the clause was 'vigorously opposed' by the Court, for behind the catch-all safeguards clearly lay an intention of ruling out a Union of Parliaments in favour of some federal arrangement. Seafield claimed this showed disrespect for the queen, who had sworn with her coronation oath to do just what the clause called on her to do. Hamilton snapped back that 'she is not in a capacity to know the interest and circumstances of Scotland, so well as that of England'. It was also objected that the English at large might take the clause amiss, but he thought this unlikely when they had themelves set out to protect their valued institutions as a precondition of any treaty; sauce for the goose was sauce for the gander. For example, 'before they advised with us, [they] restricted their own commissioners from treating on any alternative of the Church government of that kingdom,' said Hamilton, angling for Presbyterian support. One answer might be made to all objections: 'we are a free, independent people, and have a power to give what instructions, powers and restrictions we please to our commissioners.' Who could disagree with that? The Cavaliers did not. Nor, after a pause for thought, did the Squadrone. Yet in the house as a whole Hamilton lost his clause by two votes.

༄

Here at last was the punch, right to the opposition's midriff, that the government had been manoeuvring to land. Lockhart put all blame for the blow on a handful of irresponsible absentees: he could only 'lament the woeful fate of this nation; for though it was well known, that the house was to be that day upon this grand affair, and the Court have mustered together every individual of their party; yet seven or eight of the Cavalier and Country parties were absent, and thereby lost this clause'. If it had passed, it 'would have proved a mortal stroke to the Court; they being resolved to have laid aside the Treaty of Union, and adjourned the Parliament; by which means the nation had been free of that fatal thraldom, to which 'tis since subjected'. The majority of two was the Court's first real victory on a matter of any substance in three sessions of the Parliament. It led straight on to the extraordinary events of the following day, September 1.[75]

Despite its defeat, in the morning the opposition still seemed full of fight. The Cavalier party counterattacked to recover the lost ground with a motion spelling out how talks must be for a federal, not an incorporating Union. The Court replied that the powers of the Scots commissioners ought to match those of the English commissioners (which were not restricted), so all options should remain open; here Seafield for the first time let slip the words, 'ane entire Union', taken to mean a Union of Parliaments.[76] But he won the point.

The next crucial issue was the procedure for choosing the commissioners. Indeed, all now hinged on it. And so we arrive back at the point from which this chapter set out, Hamilton's meeting with Hooke and motion for the queen, not the Parliament, to name the commission for a Union. It passed by four votes but, as Lockhart wrote, the English, 'knowing the backwardness of the Scots nation to enter into an incorporating Union, would, if there had been but two or three members [of a majority] that opposed it, have been so far from pushing it as they did, that the treaty would have been advanced no further than those others that had been set on foot formerly'. So finely indeed was the question poised.[77]

Instead, with Hamilton's aid the Ministry won sweet reward for its tranquil tenacity and adroit adjustment in a cause it had been as likely to lose. There were even yet supporters of Union in doubt it could ever be accomplished, who thought the Parliament had voted for negotiations to waste time and stall. This was the view among sections of the opposition too.[78] But Seafield, for one, saw just what had happened. He wrote: 'I am very hopeful, if rightly managed, this may be the foundation of a lasting settlement between the two nations.' In the same mood of quiet satisfaction he reminded Godolphin there was still a long way to go, not least in London: 'I am very hopeful that the English will make a right use of this opportunity, and that your lordship, under Her Majesty, will have the honour to establish what hath been so much desired and difficult to obtain.'[79]

It seems amazing that Hamilton continued to head the patriotic opposition in the Parliament. Even if we sift word by word what he and others had to say about his behaviour, it still resists explanation. Perhaps the key lies not in any internal logic but in the external reality that he had just suffered a double disappointment: refusal of the Parliament to show support for the federalism which might have left scope for his own dynastic ambitions, accompanied by failure to elicit any hint of French support for them. Such setbacks would have been enough to knock anybody off course, certainly a pussyfoot like him.

Indeed, Hamilton never really knew what to do at crucial points in his own and the nation's life. Vacillation led him into self-contradiction as a feckless form of insurance. Yet otherwise his standing, prestige and abilities meant the opposition could not do without him, even when floored by his behaviour. Often his methods of leadership did prove adequate, not to say skilled – for instance, his habitual biding of time, in which was he always at his best rather than, as in moments of decision, at his worst. Clerk said: 'The Duke of Hamilton was the head of the Jacobites, and indeed, a man every way fitted to be the head of a popular discontented party. He was a man of courage, and had a great deal of natural eloquence, with much affability in his temper.'[80] From the opposite political pole Lockhart agreed: 'Never was a man so well qualified to be the head of a party' with his nerve and his 'clear, ready and penetrating conception'. While always cautious of any course proposed to him, after the duke opted for one 'nothing could either daunt or divert his zeal and forwardness'.[81] Yet these skills were tactical, seldom strategic. At Hamilton's most fateful hour so far he had fallen short of all hopes vested in him. If inadequacy is not the explanation, there is only one other. He had done enough, and no more, to end Scottish independence. Had it been able to serve his purposes, he might have saved it. As it could not, he at least secured his pickings in a United Kingdom.

This session of the Parliament continued for a further fortnight or so. The government had two main items of business left, to obtain six months' supply, which was done in short order, then to answer the ticklish point earlier proposed by Atholl, that the English must rescind the menacing clauses in the Alien Act before negotiations could usefully start. Seafield told Godolphin on September 3 how 'we found that all the parties were like to be united not to treat whilst we were declared aliens'. Therefore 'we found it necessary to agree that by an address or instruction we should so order it as the commissioners should not enter on the treaty till the clause declaring us aliens be rescinded'. In other words the question was to be raised with the English in either a more or else in a less combative form, either by inserting a special additional clause into the Act for a Treaty or else by just addressing the queen. The house settled for an address.[82]

While loose ends were being tidied up Fletcher appeared to go slightly off his head, and no wonder. He now proposed, in further riposte to the Alien Act, a total ban on English imports. Since Scotland ran such a huge trading deficit with the neighbour nation she might have drawn some benefit from this drastic measure, but it seemed less attractive once the costs were counted too. For instance, Hugh Montgomerie, member for Glasgow, a city already addicted to nicotine, pointed out that while much of the tobacco consumed in Scotland came smuggled direct from America, a certain proportion also arrived by a legal channel, that is to say, re-exported through English ports. If that channel was cut off, then at the least the price of tobacco in Scotland would soar. Thoughts of gasping unsatisfied for a smoke proved too much for members. They voted against banning imports of tobacco from England. They then consigned the whole question of future cross-border traffic to the new council of trade where Fletcher, not being a member of it, would have no say.[83]

Another private member's initiative was an Act for Sending Ambassadors to Foreign Treaties, proposed by a Jacobite, the Earl Marischal, and given a first reading. Though it would never receive the royal assent, it usefully reminds us of one or two neglected aspects of the controversy on Union, not its depressing realities but its interesting terminology. The first is the contemporary usage of the word 'treaty' or 'treaties', such as the treaty with England which the Parliament had just voted to essay. In his own writings Paul Scott has rightly stressed that in this age a treaty could mean not only a solemn accord between states but also the negotiations leading up to it. It was clearly in this sense that the Earl Marischal employed the term 'treaties' for the title of his Act. The point allows us to make plain also that those members of the Parliament who on September 1 had voted for a treaty were not necessarily voting for Union, even if the Court meant the one to lead to the other. A further linguistic nuance is that the negotiators could be referred to in contemporary parlance as 'treaters'. In Scots, this was a homophone of 'traitors'. Lockhart and others made gleeful use of the pun.

On a different tack, the Earl Marischal's Act also reminds us that Scotland, though an independent state, had no diplomatic relations with any other except England, and then only in the odd form of ministerial traffic to or from the fount of sovereignty, a monarch resident in London. The tiny exception to this was the office of conservator of Scots privileges at Veere in Zeeland, which in the Middle Ages had been Scotland's staple for the Netherlands, a port where her commerce enjoyed special concessions. These were by now falling into disuse, and in fact most Scottish trade went through Rotterdam, but the conservator's post at Veere would be maintained till swept away by the Batavian Republic in 1799; the *schotse huizen*, the emporium where Scottish imports could be purchased, still stand there to this day. The lack otherwise of direct foreign relations had been a severe handicap to Scotland during the century since the Union of Crowns, as she was dragged into English wars. The remedy would, however, be rather different from that envisaged by the Earl Marischal in his hope of a Scots *corps diplomatique*.

At this tail-end of the session the old Scots Parliament again showed its habitual generosity to authors, something the new Scots Parliament re-established in 1999 has yet to match. It awarded a gratuity of £630 to John Slezer for his *Theatrum Scotiae*, a lavish volume of attractive engravings with useful commentary which offers practically all we know of how Scottish towns looked in this era. Slezer, a Dutchman settled in Scotland, replied that after 'the usual civility and kindness strangers are treated with amongst them, it is no wonder if I am tempted to leave some little marks of gratitude behind me, in transmitting to posterity those venerable remains of former ages, and oblige other nations with the prospects of so many considerable places'.[84] Finally an Act passed for the payment of £15,000 owed to Queensberry: sign enough, surely, of who was now running the Parliament again.

On September 21 Argyll touched with the sceptre the Acts for a treaty with England, for the council of trade, for supply and for four further economic measures. He ignored the other Acts voted, on limitations, on appointing officers of state, on triennial Parliaments and on Scottish representation in foreign treaties.[85] Baillie of Jerviswood complained to Roxburghe: 'You cannot conceive how much all sorts of people grumble at refusing the Acts, and what odd reasonings they have upon it. Some say it is now evident nothing is to be expected from England, and that Scotland cannot be happy till a separation; others that the Court is not in earnest.'[86] But it was too late for afterthoughts. Argyll promptly adjourned the third session of Anne's first and last Scots Parliament. It had been brought round to approve what her governments had sought ever since she came to the throne. The question of the succession was solved if the treaty on foot should end by incorporating Scotland into a unified Great Britain.

಄

Meanwhile the political situation in England was changing too. A General Election had taken place where the Tories suffered a setback. A grumbling crisis preceded it. Already by the spring of 1704 those closest to the queen, Godolphin and Marlborough, were fed up of ruling with the Tories, in particular with the high Tories. They decided to get rid of some Ministers and rebuild the government round a coalition of friendlier figures – their cronies, other placemen or pensioners and the Court Tories headed by Harley. A deal was also sought with the Whig Junto. The new alliance had begun to gell by the turn of the year during the row over the tack, the abortive high Tory attempt to force through a measure against occasional conformity in the Church of England by tacking it to a money bill.

So things went on up to the election of 1705. Then many Tories, turning against the reconstructed government, campaigned on the slogan of 'the Church in danger', of its subversion by dissenters and their parliamentary accomplices; nor did they forget the plight of Scots Episcopalians under the Presbyterian yoke. In retort Godolphin and Marlborough endorsed Whigs in many seats. On both sides propaganda waxed fierce, Tories playing on the threat to the religious establishment, Whigs urging that the real issues at stake lay in the prosecution of the war and the future assurance of a Protestant succession. The result was a hung Parliament, not least because Harley's Court Tories retained official support. Observers calculated the outcome in terms of Tories, Whigs and 'Queen's servants'. One wrote, 'by the nearest computation [that] can be made the Whigs and Tories are equal, so that the placemen will turn the balance'.[87] Anyway the Tories lost their majority. The outcome was bound to affect Scotland too, because of the religious issues, but more because there actually lurked a little subtlety beneath the Whigs' sponsorship of the Alien Act: they soon showed they were willing to use it as a lever, not just a bludgeon.

On October 28 the new Parliament met at Westminster in buoyant mood. In foreign affairs the war continued to go well, if with no further victory on the scale of Blenheim. Conflict in central Europe rather wound down. It shifted instead on to the territories of the Bourbons. Queen Anne approved the transmission of £10,000 to the isolated Protestant insurgents of the Cevennes in south-eastern France. There the so-called Camisards, poor Calvinist peasants clad in smocks, had endured frightful persecution ever since the Revocation of the Edict of Nantes in 1685. But they had mounted, and were still mounting, a heroic resistance. This, Bishop Burnet wrote in awe, was at first 'looked on as the effect of oppression and despair, which would quickly end in a scene of blood, but it had a much longer continuation than was expected'. He had found means to keep in touch with the rebels and concluded from their messages to the outside world that they were 'full of a sublime zeal and piety, expressing a courage and a confidence that could not be daunted'. At any rate, they bogged down French troops who might have been deployed on other fronts.[88]

James Stewart, Duke of Berwick, bastard son of the late James VII and II and now a general in the service of France, arrived in the Cevennes in the early autumn of 1705 to take command of a new offensive and bring this costly, embarrassing affair to an end. The best way, he decided, was to disarm the locals, including those who had feigned submission and conversion to Catholicism. Now anyone at all found in possession of weapons would not just be sent to the galleys, as before, but executed on the spot. This would supplement the normal burning alive and breaking on the wheel of captives who had refused to surrender. It made Bluidy Claverhouse's treatment of Covenanters look a model of mildness, though the dirty business was ultimately directed by bigots at the French court. Berwick could not really object because, as a mercenary, he needed the work. He just wondered: 'It is astonishing that the English and Dutch, who fomented this revolt underhand, never sent the Cevennois any capable leaders, or even gave them any better counsel.'[89]

Yet Berwick failed to crush the Camisards. They survived his brutality and carried on, not in open rebellion, but as an underground Calvinist Church, till at the end of the century the French revolutionaries drove the Most Christian Kings from Versailles and ended all religious persecution in their realm, only to substitute political persecution. As for Berwick, he had soon, at a fresh Spanish crisis, been transferred to command of the French forces on the further side of the Pyrenees. His assignment was to repel the invasion by which the grand alliance hoped to put its own candidate, the Archduke Charles of Austria, on the throne in Madrid. Charles III of Spain, as he called himself, had arrived with an English fleet off Barcelona and prepared to lay siege. A gloomy Berwick believed this to be the prelude to loss of the whole country of Catalonia for, as soon as the allies landed, the people would go over to them.[90]

In October, Barcelona indeed fell to a popular revolt and Charles III entered it in triumph at the invitation of his loyal subjects. They also sent to Queen Anne thanking her for the fact that the Catalan nation was 'free from the heavy yoke suffered by the violent oppression of France, and restored to the centre of its felicity, under the easy and desired dominion of our adored monarch'. Now they lay 'prostrate at the feet of Your

Majesty for the quality, number and goodness of the troops which have acted with singular regularity, punctual obedience and inimitable valour'. Nobody seems to have reflected how it might seem strange for Anne and her English government to be upholding the rights and fulfilling the aspirations of the Catalans just at the moment when their efforts to do the opposite for the Scots were entering a crucial phase.[91]

❧

As for English domestic politics, the new Parliament ought to have looked kindly on the prospect of a treaty with Scotland. The Tories who disliked the whole idea now sat chastened in opposition. The queen's speech recommended Union. Yet the loyal addresses in reply from Lords and Commons alike avoided any reference to the topic. Whigs ruled the roost in both houses and saw no reason to do favours for a Tory queen who had so far done none for them. She needed their support but felt a deep distaste for any degree of dictation from them.

Scotland became a term in these conflicting calculations. An end to the toils of Scottish management would be a boon, yet bring to Westminster a band of MPs likely not just to go along with the Court but to grovel to it. To Whigs, the prospect threatened that their present ascendancy could vanish through no fault of their own, still less by defeat at the polls, just by arrival of the interlopers, both in the Commons with its fine balance of parties and in the Lords for which 150 down-at-heel Scots peers might conceivably claim eligibility. The Whig majority there had allowed the Junto to change the entire political outlook in England by neutralising Anne's dislike. A Scottish influx might put them back to square one.

In the particular matter of Union, the English Whigs could show no history of strong commitment. Under King William of Orange they had espoused it, but only as a part of general support for the Court. When driven into the wilderness by Anne they turned against it, since few Scots MPs at Westminster seemed likely to be Whigs. But now they were hoist on their own petard by the fact that one of the Junto, Lord Somers, had offered the second choice of a treaty to Scotland if she preferred not to accept the Hanoverian succession yet to escape sanctions under his Alien Act. He and others seemed surprised when the Scots Parliament opted for this second choice – which shows how little they knew about Scotland. At any rate, instead of a smooth Hanoverian succession they were now to be saddled with a tiresome negotiation, and one quite likely to boost the Court. In fact they felt so irked that at first they wanted the royal assent withheld from the Act for a Treaty on its arrival from Edinburgh. It was not that the lords of the Junto ruled out a treaty. It was rather that they wished to take it on at their own pace, and with a view to squeezing from it the maximum of political gain.

For a while it looked as if they might for the present coldly obstruct a treaty by refusing to repeal the menacing clauses in the Alien Act. That could have helped them in England, but a moment's thought showed it would quite likely cause Scotland to explode. Here was a powder-keg that ought to be rendered secure rather than lit with a blue touchpaper. So by November the lords of the Junto changed their minds. They were pushed by the Tories who, recalling the Alien Act was a Whig measure, thought they could win back some credit with the queen by proposing its repeal. Not themselves caring for Union, they did so simply to embarrass and discredit the Whigs. But these foiled the ruse by accepting the proposal for repeal.[92]

In the Lords, Somers himself, author of the Alien Act, was the one who stood up to advocate its repeal 'except the clause that empowers Her Majesty to appoint commissioners to treat of a Union'. The measure went to the Commons and was unanimously approved there on December 20.[93] If Whigs had played things well, raptures over their statesmanship are uncalled for. Rather they decided their interests would be better served by going along with a treaty, then using their parliamentary majority to make sure they appointed the English commissioners. Since they also had a friend in Queensberry, whose fortunes were taking such a turn for the better, a way opened by which on both sides of the border Union might strengthen Whiggery.

Yet all this was not just a matter of high or low politics. Burnet tells us the repeal of the menacing clauses in the Alien Act met a warm welcome beyond Westminster as well. People in the north of England, 'which had been disturbed for some years, with apprehensions of a war with Scotland, that would certainly be mischievous to them, whatsoever the end of it might prove, were much delighted with the prospect of peace and Union with their neighbours'.[94] And in Scotland, too, the repeal convinced some that an equitable Union was sought not only by the Crown but also by the English Parliament. Of course, Union still would not follow of itself, only at the end of a tortuous tussle. Huge obstacles lay ahead, on any one of which it might stumble and fall.

Many remained pessimistic that it could ever be negotiated, let alone approved by the two Parliaments.

ഹ

In politics, words and actions, convictions and votes, do not always move in tandem, and on this occasion they did so still less than usual. In the Scots Parliament there actually sat Jacobites who had come out in favour of the Act for a Treaty in the expectation either that it would get nowhere or else that they could still thwart Union if it did pass. Even from the imperfect records emerges the fact that a certain number of these loyalists to the House of Stewart went on to cast a series of tactical votes in the same sense: the member for Kilrenny, James Bethune; for Inverness, Alexander Duff; for Angus, James Haliburton; for Kincardineshire, Sir David Ramsay; for Rothesay, Dougald Stewart; for Elgin, William Sutherland. There were probably more.

At the opposite end of the spectrum the house also contained convinced advocates of Union, such as the Earls of Cromartie and Stair, together with their connections. Even these do not seem to have assumed that Union must now come as a matter of course. Stair told Mar he feared the two nations might be plunged at any time into crisis by premature death of the queen and the 'great mischiefs' that might follow – so in the first instance the aim of a treaty should be free trade in return for the Hanoverian succession, with Union only as a more distant goal. It is true at the same time that Mar, on a visit to London, gave an early warning of greater ambition on the English side: 'I find here that no Union but an incorporating relishes.' Up to the end of 1705, however, this remained something to which only insiders of the Court were privy.[95]

In between stood the Squadrone. It now entered on an agonised reappraisal of its position, which was awkward. Its members had posed as upright patriots and almost believed their own propaganda; in fairness to them, they did dislike the idea of Union. Yet now they feared it might come anyway and leave them out in the cold. Baillie of Jerviswood wrote to Roxburghe on December 15 that the best thing would still be some federal arrangement: 'But it being more than probable that England will only treat of an incorporating Union, what's most advisable I cannot say . . . I cannot satisfy myself which would be more for the New Party's interest.' Still, there was a nation to think of too, and on an incorporating Union, or Union of Parliaments, 'it's hard to know that such ane Union can be good for Scotland, which must be attended with the greatest inconveniency that, if hurtful, there can be no retrieving of it. No wise people would willingly run themselves into such a condition.' Yet that condition was no longer a mere theoretical possibility, considering 'the temper of this nation, how averse they are to limitations, and how willing to truckle under England for private advantage, I believe wise men will be forced to drink the potion to prevent greater evils. Some that were no friends to it, seem inclined to go along rather than struggle without hope.'[96]

Towards New Year, Baillie's views hardened. He wrote to Roxburghe on December 29: 'The Union is certainly preferable to our present condition. Therefore it ought to be tried; for it will either succeed, or force them that are against it to be for the [Hanoverian] succession with limitations.' Yet still he could not make up his mind. He mused that even Cavaliers might see something in the Squadrone's stated position, of a Hanoverian succession with limitations, as an alternative to the end of national independence which would cut off their hopes for ever. So that succession, though repeatedly and emphatically rejected in the Parliament, might even yet unite different factions, if only they would take a long view of the good of Scotland: a tall order. 'I know not which would be best, that both a federal and incorporating Union be treated of, or that of an incorporating Union only,' Baillie brooded on. In the first case, 'there may be too much ground for the Parliament to go upon for to postpone their determination, and perhaps to throw both out, together with the succession'. In the second case, 'they'll probably reckon it a prescribing by England of terms, and of the way and manner of uniting, which will be a popular handle to break it off'.[97]

So things stood by Hogmanay, not much further forward, in the mind of a man whom Lockhart called 'morose, proud and severe, but of a profound solid judgment'.[98] At least amid gathering gloom on the last night of the year a way had opened before the Scots where there had been only stumbling blocks before. Yet it was as yet by no means clear if they would take it, or if it could lead anywhere they wanted to be.

CHAPTER 5

❧

1706

Dumbarton Castle guarded, often ineffectively, the western Lowlands against Highland marauders

'Blinded nation'

c/

On an evening in October 1706, Robert Harley, the English Secretary of State, sat down to write out instructions for a mission on which he was about to send one of the spies he employed. Harley, a 45-year-old Londoner, had been born into a family of Presbyterians who fought against King Charles I in the War of the Three Kingdoms. So it was by a circuitous route that he had risen to his present eminence under the martyred monarch's granddaughter, Queen Anne, as leader of the moderate Tories in the House of Commons and keystone of the coalition run by her favourites, Sidney, Lord Godolphin, and John Churchill, Duke of Marlborough. To his moderation Harley added the priceless parliamentary quality that, as an observer put it, 'no man knows better all the tricks of the house';[1] he had won the nickname of Robin the Trickster. This quality served him well as Speaker from 1701, a post in those days partisan. From the chair he supported his sovereigns' measures, William's then Anne's. Indeed he piloted through the Act of Settlement fixing the Hanoverian succession for England. Now he set about winning Union with Scotland too.

Harley's schemes had reached a crux, and he needed ears and eyes of his own among the Scots. So, he said to the agent he was sending to Edinburgh, 'you are to use the utmost caution that it may not be supposed you are employed by any person in England, but that you come there upon your own business, and out of love to the country'. Once he got there, 'you are to write constantly the true state how you find things, at least once a week, and you need not subscribe any name, but direct for me under cover to Mrs Collins at the Posthouse, Middle Temple Gate, London. For variety you may direct under cover to Michael Read in York Buildings.' This second fake addressee was, according to Dean Jonathan Swift of Dublin, 'an old Scotch fanatick, and the damn'dest liar in his office alive',[2] Meanwhile Harley's spy in the Scottish capital should 'assure those that you converse with that the queen and all those who have credit with her are sincere and hearty for the Union'. More, 'you must show them, this is such an opportunity that being once lost or neglected is not again to be recovered. England never was before in so good a disposition to make such large concessions.'[3]

The recipient of these instructions was Daniel Defoe, another Cockney, but one taking a rockier road through life and for the time being dependent on Harley's patronage. In the three centuries since their time, however, Defoe has gained by far the greater fame. He achieved this above all with his tale of *Robinson Crusoe*, based on the true story of a Scots sailor who at that moment in 1706, half a world away, was marooned on an uninhabited island of the South Pacific Ocean, wandering amid its jagged precipices, clad in goatskin, gun on shoulder, the loneliest and most forsaken of all Queen Anne's subjects. His name, Alexander Selkirk, from Largo in Fife, had not yet even become known to the man who would immortalise his adventures, but Defoe's literary output was already prodigious. He really ought to be canonised as the patron saint of freelances, having in effect founded the profession in England and proved himself so versatile in it as to be the envy of his remote successors in the United Kingdom he played some part in creating. Harley might rather serve as a model of the commissioning editor, exacting and hard to please, then slow to pay the agreed fee however faultless the eventual execution of the work.

Defoe was of an age with his employer but from a humbler background. A self-made man of incredible energy, he turned during a long and complex career as adventurous in commerce as in literature. He began by investing in ships and expanded this line of business into import-export of wine, spirits, tobacco, textiles and logwood. He speculated in anything from civet cats to a diving bell. In 1692 he had gone bankrupt for £17,000, equal to £680,000 today, but managed to worm his way out of debtors' prison. He put all his colourful experience to use in his writings, which demonstrate a precocious understanding of banking, credit, transport and other emergent facets of the modern economy. He was remarkable also for his awareness of the social problems of capitalism, and for his sympathy towards its victims, especially widows and idiots.

Above all Defoe revelled in controversy. He may have been the instigator, by attacks on a Lord Mayor of London for 'playing bo-peep with God Almighty', of the divisive political battle over occasional conformity in the Church of England. Yet when the Tories took up that cause he turned against them for trying to make of it a pretext for persecution. His satire on the subject, *The Shortest Way with Dissenters*, won him national notoriety. It also got him in trouble with the law again. Sentenced to stand in the pillory, he could count on enough friends to gather round and shield him from the insults, or worse, of the mob. Anyway, Defoe's fellow Londoners turned his punishment into a party. They threw at him not rotten eggs but flowers. He still had to go back to prison during the queen's pleasure, which might have meant ruin by halting all his ventures unless he could shorten his term by making a deal with some politician. His release came through the good offices of Harley, who recognised talent going to waste. Instead he recruited it for the state.

So Defoe started to work for Harley. Both were men kindly and temperate by nature but also secretive and shifty. In tandem they made a good controller and agent, each after his own way considerate of human nature while harbouring no illusions about it. Run by his boss, Defoe inaugurated official surveillance of individuals in England. He earned a reputation as a pioneer of counter-insurgency, with some professional practices surviving to this day.[4] The intelligence was also, needless to say, grist to the mill of his pamphleteering and journalism, which provided his cover. Before being sent to Scotland, he went in the summer of 1704 on tour round England to survey public opinion, report popular fears or doubts, infiltrate local institutions of civil society, identify leaders and differences among them, write tracts to win support for government from those suspicious of or uncommitted to it. His contacts continued to send him reports and in return broadcast his own writings to a wider public. He was collecting so much material that with it he could launch *The Review*, forerunner of similar journals and periodicals down to the present time, often under some variation of this original title. Most have been partisan. Yet in an era of ferocious political rivalry, *The Review* espoused Harley's watchword of 'moderation'. It helped that Defoe seems to have believed personally in the principle he supported editorially.

One reason Defoe had been selected for a mission to Scotland was that another spy posted there before him made such a hash of the job. William Paterson, also still on his uppers, perhaps not yet recovered in his mind from the searing experience of Darien, was sending back some dubious dispatches. Harley passed them to Godolphin, who said: 'His notions seem to me for the most part to be very confused.' Paterson talked up the Union's chances, yet anyone could see it was far from in the bag; he seemed just to be reporting what he thought his controllers wanted to hear.[5]

An altogether superior service would be offered by Defoe. Once in Edinburgh he showed his habitual resource. He did not just collect intelligence but also made sure Scots knew of his own opinions. As ever, he sought to make money on the side, with speculative investments in saltworks and weaving shops. He soon found good contacts in the Parliament, in the Church of Scotland, among merchants, tradesmen, sea-captains and many others. He ran some risk in the volatile capital, but he was discreet, dauntless and determined. He left vivid accounts of a turbulent time.

Defoe's earliest extant letter from Edinburgh is dated October 24. He reports 'a most confused scene of affairs' with the government having 'a very difficult course to steer'. He has seen two riots and expects another. The remark was ironic: one riot had been a meeting of the commission of assembly, which ran the Kirk in between General Assemblies, held to consider the recently published terms of the Treaty of Union. Defoe was there, of course, and found 'very strange things talked of such as put me much out of love with ecclesiastic Parliaments'. Still, all this only came 'from some tumultuous spirits who are overruled by men of more moderation, and as an Assembly they act with more wisdom and honesty than they do in their private capacities'. Yet 'they contribute too much to the general aversion which there is to the Union'. Defoe at once understood how misgivings among Presbyterians arose from the fact they felt 'unsafe and uneasy in their present establishment'. Not to worry, he assured Harley, 'I work incessantly with them.'[6]

The reports from Defoe turned out to be of great value in the achievement of Union. It cannot be said English Ministers were well-informed about Scotland or Scottish Ministers, for reasons of their own, felt eager to enlighten them – indeed George Lockhart of Carnwath wrote at this time that the latter 'had heretofore been at great pains to conceal the true state and inclinations of the people from their friends in England'.[7] To a man in Harley's job some objective, reliable intelligence was like gold-dust. Now he learned, as he could have learned from no other source, how the project of Union might be going awry even at this late stage, with the treaty complete and about to be legislated in Edinburgh. The first thing to have struck Defoe, arriving as a stranger there, was the vehemence of Presbyterian opposition to it. This must have surprised Harley too, as he tried to see through the self-serving of Scots politicians, when up to now he had had only Paterson's placebos to guide him. Yet Harley was nothing if not sharp, like Defoe himself. Time remained to save the situation.

Big trouble was breaking out in Edinburgh – and, as Defoe said, 'a Scots rabble is the worst of its kind'. One night the mob as usual cheered James, Duke of Hamilton, down from the Parliament to his lodgings at the Palace of Holyroodhouse. This time when they came up again they threw stones at the town-guards and broke windows along the Royal Mile. 'I was warned', Defoe went on, 'that I should take care of myself and not appear in the street.' He heard a bunch of thugs say as he went into a stair: 'There is one of the English dogs.'

The next night the crowd vented its wrath on Sir Patrick Johnstone, Lord Provost and member of the Parliament. He always supported the Court and had served on the commission for Union. While following the official line there he also worked to get special concessions for Edinburgh, such as continuation of a local duty on ale; thus far the capital stood in his debt. But its citizens remained unimpressed. Defoe told how at the height of the riot they attacked Johnstone's home: 'the mob came upstairs to his door and fell to work with sledges to break it open, but it seems could not.' He made his escape, but 'his lady in the fright with two candles in her hand that she might be known, opens the window and cries out for God's sake to call the guard'. A passing apothecary heeded her distress and went over to the guardhouse in the middle of the street: he 'found the officers very indifferent in the matter, whether as to the cause or, is rather judged, through real fear of the rabble'.

Defoe took the chance to slip back to his own lodgings. The tumult was far from over, however: 'I had not been there long but I heard a great noise and looking saw a terrible multitude come up the High Street with a drum at the head of them and swearing and crying out all Scotland would stand together, No Union, No Union, English dogs and the like.' By now the whole city was in a 'terrible fright' and everyone had put out their lights for fear of provoking more vandalism. The town-guards 'were insulted and stoned as they stood'. So it went on for hours: 'They are a hardened, refractory and terrible people,' Defoe concluded.[8]

Yet a man in contrast so emollient, agreeable and charming was not to be put off extolling the benefits of Union to both Scots and English. 'The advantages are infinite, unaccountable and as times go, incredible,' he wrote, 'but to say on which side the greater, I will not undertake to determine.' Only bigots or blockheads would believe anything else, only rascals or rogues deny it: 'To the Scots they cry out that the English will enslave them, that the English want a Union and they do not; that the English will make a mere conquered kingdom of them and the like.' Defoe bent every effort to disprove this.

With his straight reporting of the agitation in *The Review* Defoe mixed editorials. He took nationalist claims one by one and sought to show how each arose from misunderstanding or malice. He would sum everything up in a *History of the Union* which he was putting together now though he would not publish it till 1709. The book showed his knowledge of Scotland to be limited and in some ways defective, yet beyond doubt he made the biggest contribution to unionist propaganda on either side of the border. He found answers to the common English objections to Union and the economic or religious dogma behind them. His answers to the Scottish objections, if not quite so watertight, have proved durable in the basic argument that any prospect of a rich, happy Scotland depends on Union: that was the case still being put in favour of the settlement of 1707 during the campaign for the referendum on devolution in 1997. Unlike his modern counterparts, Defoe did feel able to concede Scots might also lose out a little, 'yet this the most prejudiced man in Scotland *must acknowledge they have an exchange*, and which *if they know how to value it*, is worth all they have paid, or can pay for it; I mean Liberty, in its due and best extent, religious and civil.' Curmudgeons 'should do well to look back upon the days of cruelty and persecution, when the jails were filled with their citizens, and the places of execution covered with the blood of their ministers, when their Church was trampled under foot'. Now, 'the interests of popery, tyranny, French usurpations and spurious succession received a mortal stab by this Union'.[9]

෴

Partisans of those hostile interests must by this time have been wondering if Defoe's bold claims might be right. From the turn of the year English unionists had embarked with assurance on the groundwork of their project which, it soon emerged, required Scots to go further than any overt commitment by their Parliament in the Act for a Treaty passed last session. Hans Willem Bentinck, Duke of Portland, King William's old comrade in arms, had stayed on in England after the death of his sovereign, keeping in touch with the Revd William Carstares, now principal of the University of Edinburgh. To him, from London in January, Portland reported simply this: 'People expect a total union.'[10]

On February 27, Queen Anne named thirty-one commissioners to represent Scotland in the negotiations with England. Most were friends or allies of James Douglas, Duke of Queensberry. With his political reha-bilitation well under way, he could strike deals, line up likely candidates and advise the queen just who to pick, in most cases at least. Less could be expected of the outgoing Lord High Commissioner, John Campbell, Duke of Argyll. He hurried back from the politics of Scotland to the battlefields of Europe. Asked after a month or so to return and lend his aid again, he retorted: 'It is surprising to me that my Lord Treasurer [Godolphin], who is a man of sense, should think of sending me up and down like a footman from one country to another without ever offering any reward.'[11] His presence and support behind the scenes were still judged indispensable so Marlborough, who hated him, was detailed to talk the insufferable fellow round. Not till awarded promotion to major-general did he deign to come home and help out.[12] The Earl of Marchmont, the Presbyterian leader meanwhile, had urged that commissioners for Union should be chosen from a wide spectrum of opinion: 'My advice would be to make a mixture with due regard to a just balance.'[13] Then no party could complain of exclusion and a fair wind for parliamentary passage of the treaty might be assured. But the English government showed not the least interest in maintaining a just balance, only in producing the sort of treaty it wanted. So far from eliciting the mind of Scotland, the purpose was to prepare her compliance with what now crystallised as the English goal, a Union of Parliaments.

For example, the most senior legal figure in the government of Scot-land, the Lord Advocate, Sir James Stewart, was left off the commission because of his aversion from Union. There was no chance either for the Duke of Hamilton, leader of the nationalist opposition in the Parliament and eager to serve, even though the Duke of Argyll had promised him a place for his role last September in handing the Crown the nomination of commissioners. Argyll gave this double-cross as a pretext for his own departure from the domestic scene, though he probably preferred killing Frenchmen anyway. Leaders of the Squadrone Volante found themselves barred as well, but at least were represented by a couple of backbenchers, Sir Robert Dundas of Arniston and Sir James Smollett of Bonhill. While the Squadrone had done as much as any party to bring Scotland to the negotiating table, senior figures were unsure whether to feel enraged or relieved at being kept away from it, since nobody could see how the talks would end this time: in 1702, after all, they had failed.

Instead the Scots commissioners were drawn mostly from the Duke of Queensberry's faction, plus a few of the Duke of Argyll's. The latter, while not serving himself, put up his younger brother, Lord Archibald Campbell, with two kinsmen, Hugh Campbell, Earl of Loudoun, joint Scottish Secretary, and Daniel Campbell of Shawfield, merchant in Glasgow and member of the Parliament for Inveraray. An automatic choice was that complaisant fixer, the Earl of Seafield, Chancellor of Scotland. Half the commissioners held public office, including four judges of the Court of Session. A couple of others, the Earl of Sutherland and William Seton of Pitmedden, had given proof enough of readiness to be bought. Yet not all the candidates eligible on these or other grounds felt eager to oblige. John Clerk of Penicuik stated in his memoirs that, though he himself was a unionist, he had been slow to accept a place on the commission because of the 'great backwardness in the Parliament of Scotland for a Union with England of any kind whatsoever'. He thought in the end nothing would come of it and he would be left whistling for his expenses. But he was a client of Queensberry and in this enterprise the great man could not be thwarted.[14]

Eyebrows might still be raised at one or two of the Scots selected.[15] Viscount Dupplin figured among those spotted as Jacobites by the French agent, Colonel Nathaniel Hooke (who did, though, tend to exaggerate the disaffection of people he met). Dupplin was anyway to be arrested during the rising of 1715, so he must have given somebody grounds for distrust. Doubtless he got on the commission for Union because he was father-in-law to John Erskine, Earl of Mar, a crony of Queensberry; in fact Dupplin would not rock the boat. The Lord Provost of Glasgow, Hugh Montgomerie, was nominated but attended not a single meeting and finished up voting against the treaty in deference to his nationalist town council. Lockhart of Carnwath, alone of all the Scots commissioners, opposed Union in any shape or form. He must have been chosen either to give the commission some air of balance or else in the hope his ways might be mended by Lord Wharton, his uncle, member of the Whig Junto and an English representative. Lockhart's first reaction had been to refuse a role so obnoxious to his patriotism but he consulted Andrew Fletcher of Saltoun, the Duke of Hamilton and others. They advised him to go ahead, keep his head down and act as informer on the rest of the commissioners so 'he might make discoveries of their designs, and thereby do a singular service for his country'.[16] The Scots delegation was indeed weighted in favour of Union yet not quite as heavily as has often been suggested.

The English commissioners, also thirty-one in number, were named on April 10 with the same end in view of pushing a treaty through their Parliament, where the Court now relied on the Whigs to get things done. The nominees included Godolphin, Harley, all five lords of the Junto, but no Tories other than one or two junior politicians and John Sharp, Archbishop of York, an anti-unionist. Godolphin was still getting over the opprobrium he had attracted by advising the royal assent for Scottish legislation offensive to the English, and found in the project of Union oil to pour on these troubled waters. He had no great zeal for it, all the same. He told Marlborough: 'The settling of the government of Scotland and the management of the revenues there is a grievous burden, and the uneasiness of people's laying weight upon every trifle after one has overcome the greatest difficulties to satisfy makes me weary of my life.'

By now there was greater interest in Union among the Whig Junto, as insurance for the Hanoverian succession which would at length hand them power in the state. The hard work put into the commission by one of them, Lord Somers, gave him the greatest influence on the English side. Contrary to the agreed mode of procedure, designed to keep the two sides apart, he kept in touch throughout with leaders of the Scottish delegation. He hoped to steer the deal in such a way that Scots MPs, when they finally appeared at Westminster, would strengthen the Whigs rather than the Court. His commitment might have been calculated yet his application and adroitness contributed much to the outcome.[17]

The agreed mode of procedure was a bit of a sham, then, but it followed the precedent of the abortive negotiations of 1702. That is, the two nations were supposed to sit separately, address each other in writing and observe strict secrecy. For most Scottish commissioners it was no mere formal separation; Lockhart would recall how 'none of the English during the treaty had one of the Scots so much as to drink a glass of wine with them'.[18] When the English wished to put something forward they would ask their opposite numbers to meet them in the chamber set aside for the commission at the Palace of Westminster, the Cockpit, where their papers were given in by Lord Somers or Lord Cowper, keeper of the great seal of England. When the Scots had something to say, or answers to make, these were presented by Seafield. In the Cockpit stood a table, 50 feet long, with space round it to seat all the commissioners of both kingdoms. At the head, under a canopy, was placed a chair ornamented with gold lace and crimson velvet, for the queen when she came, to sit with Seafield on her left and Cowper on her right. She attended thrice, at the inaugural meeting to brief the commissioners on her aims and wish them all the best for their success and unanimity, a second time to monitor progress and have the minutes read to her, the third time to approve the result.

The English were clear in both aims and procedures. The position they staked out on an incorporating Union, a Union of Parliaments, and what followed straight from it gave every sign of being well-prepared. Even Lockhart conceded they 'cannot be blamed for making the best bargain they could for their own country, when they found the Scots so very complaisant as to agree to everything that was demanded of them'. The Scots' performance was less structured and less effective. Outside the formal sessions they gathered at the houses of the joint Scottish Secretaries, the Earls of Loudoun or Mar. This pair, Lockhart says, ran the delegation almost as a private club, 'so that when the Scots commissioners met amongst themselves, a paper containing an answer to the last demand of the English commissioners was presented by the Chancellor or one of the two Secretaries, which being read, was immediately approved of'. Then it would be handed into a formal session 'without being discoursed upon (as matters of such weight and importance did require) and the commissioners allowed copies or the least time to consider what was contained in it; and thus they drove on headlong to a conclusion'. No welcome awaited dissent, then, even reasoned dissent. 'We must not differ', said the Earl of Leven, one of the Scots commissioners, 'for, if we do, we shall appear to be a very insignificant party.'[19]

❧

As for the substance of the discussions the commissioners worked on the agenda pursued, if never to the end, in 1702. One question left unanswered at the adjournment, and recommended for further study before any resumption, was this time apparently excluded by the terms of reference of the new commission. It had no brief to do anything about the Church of Scotland or Church of England – implying that, in the event of Union, the two countries would each retain their own religious establishments.

After inaugural formalities, working sessions began on April 22. The Scots commissioners opened with a proposal for federal Union. Few of them wanted it, yet many people at home in Scotland did: these had to be given an impression it was being taken seriously. Perhaps some vestige of a regional assembly might have been preserved with limited powers, the rest being passed to the Parliament of the United Kingdom, in a kind of reversal of the devolutionary settlement of 1999.

Discussion on these lines had taken place among the Scots commissioners because several were wary of hastening towards a Union of Parliaments – notably the Earl of Stair, who, despite favouring it in principle still thought it would have to come about in easy stages.[20] He had repeated to Mar in January that, while he believed in an incorporating Union, the commission ought first to tackle free trade and the succession since no more than slow progress might be expected towards the greater goal. But to this Mar rejoined, for example in a letter to Carstares, the self-appointed guardian of Presbyterian interests, that Union and Hanoverian succession as alternatives were no longer on offer. He wrote from London: 'Your friends here tell us plainly that they will give us no terms that are considerable for going into their succession, if any, without going into an entire Union; and if we insist upon that, they will never meet with us, for they think the notions about federal Unions and forms a mere jest and chimera.' Mar added: 'You see what we are to treat of is not our choice.' He, for one, did not mind.[21] Nor, if truth be told, did others. As Clerk of Penicuik recalled, 'after all the trouble we have given ourselves, we knew at the time that it was but losing our labour, for the English commissioners were positively resolved to treat on no kind of Union with us but what was to be incorporating and perpetual'.[22]

On the English side Godolphin, Harley and Somers made that plain from the start, indeed before. They disliked the idea of federalism not least because of the problems England had found fighting a war in alliance with the United Provinces of the Netherlands, a federal state. The Dutch diffusion of authority among different levels of government gave Marlborough endless headaches. On hand to underline the point was the Dutchman, Portland. He wrote: 'An entire Union is contemplated . . . I do not comprehend the mutual benefit for the two kingdoms of a federal Union, nor the means of arriving at it'.[23]

So, to the English, federalism implied a degree of weakness they could not afford in an age of fierce international rivalry. They remained uninterested in discussing if one or other variation on a federal theme might be more or less feasible. None would in a future Great Britain avoid

friction or quash the risk of vetoes from Scotland. Godolphin rattled his
sabre again, hinting the English might fight for a Union of Parliaments as
worth the blood and money to keep foes from their back door. His heavy
hints would gain credibility after Marlborough's smashing victory in May
at the Battle of Ramillies – where young Argyll, having a whale of a time,
was 'the second or third man who with his sword in his hand broke over
the enemy's trenches and chased them out of the village of Ramillies;
he received three shot upon him, but happily all blunt'. This huge defeat
for King Louis XIV of France ended any chance he might hold on to
the territory he had occupied in the Spanish Netherlands, present-day
Belgium. Though he was far from finished, there could be no more danger
for the time being of diversionary landings round British coasts by the
French or their Jacobite stooges.[24]

Yet, as a concept, federalism would continue to hover in the background right till Union was all but concluded (it still does today). The
House of Lords debated it in the course of passing the treaty in 1707, but
decided it would be too inefficient and cumbrous a system without
offering any guarantee of permanence to Union or, yet more important,
to the succession. The issue is no further forward 300 years later. Seafield
at the outset of these negotiations anyway saw that the English 'have not
the least notion of the nature of federal Union'.[25]

In the event the Scots barely tried to make a sticking point of
federalism. To kick off, the English proposed that 'the two kingdoms
of England and Scotland be forever united into one kingdom by the name
of Great Britain; that the United Kingdom of Great Britain be represented
by one and the same Parliament'; succession to the Crown would be as in
the English Act of Settlement. The Scots countered with a different
agenda, but 'faintly', according to Lockhart: Hanoverian succession;
reciprocal exchange of rights and privileges; free trade; repeal of laws
contrary to these other provisions. This was what Stair had pressed for,
out of fear the nation could not for now be brought to accept a Union of
Parliaments. The proposals made no mention of merging the two kingdoms or legislatures. It would be excessive to describe them as federal,
bearing in mind how little precise meaning the term had at the time. They
would have amounted to a renewal of the Union of Crowns, now in the
House of Hanover, with free trade in return, including free trade to the
colonies, and its counterpart, repeal of the Navigation Acts: back to 1603,
in fact. A brusque retort came from the English. They were 'so fully
convinced that nothing but an entire Union of the two kingdoms will

settle perfect and lasting friendship between them, and they therefore think fit to decline entering into any further consideration of the proposal now made' by the Scots. Instead they asked for a reply to their own.[26]

The Scottish reply was acceptance of the English agenda, with a proviso of 'full freedom and intercourse of trade and navigation and communication of privileges and advantages'. The English said not to worry because this would be a 'necessary consequence of an entire Union'. So the talks were, after a bit of preliminary sparring, single-mindedly directed towards a bargain by which the Scots' agreement to abolish their Parliament would be set against the one real concession the English had to offer, or the sole item of the slightest interest to Scotland: free trade. That deal was at least coherent. To enjoy free trade with England and her colonies, Scotland would paradoxically have to be absorbed into the protectionism of the Navigation Acts. She would then be subject to England's central regulation of trade. That had to mean a single Parliament. Yet it seemed a high price to pay when trade made up only a small part of Scottish political business. Anyway, the elements of the package were inscribed in the first four articles of the draft Treaty of Union. By the nature of the case, they still left out a lot.[27]

ℰℐ

The Scots then sought what more they might extract, and not without success. The effort first focussed on finance. To strike a balance between a rich country and a poor country the commissioners had to resort to a good deal of fiscal jiggery-pokery. The main sources of revenue for both governments were customs and excise and then a land-tax. England did levy further forms of taxation, in particular several temporary imposts to pay for the war, which Scotland did not levy. It was agreed Scots would be exempt from these, most due to expire in a few years' time anyway. A greater problem lay in the fact that in England taxes were efficiently collected, in Scotland hardly at all sometimes. Mere installation of a uniform system would make Scots pay more than they were used to. Even so, their relative burden was to turn out light: against £2 million of land tax in England, Scotland would be assessed at £48,000, a proportion which did not alter for the rest of the eighteenth century.

More disagreeable was that higher taxes would include a share in redemption of the English national debt, rocketing because of the war. With some high-powered calculation from David Gregory, the expatriate

Aberdonian serving as Savilian professor of astronomy at Oxford, and with technical advice from the ubiquitous William Paterson, a number could be put on this share: £398,085 10s. By Scots' standards it was indeed an astronomical number. They had shown sense enough to keep their kings so poor as to lack the credit even to start accumulating a national debt. It was agreed the English would hand the calculated sum, known as the Equivalent, back to the Scots.

The Equivalent would then be used for sundry deserving purposes in Scotland, at the least to compensate individuals who suffered losses from Union. Weights and measures differed in the two countries, and the money could first make good the costs from reduction of coin to the English standard (the pound Scots was in the event not to vanish completely, but to maintain a ghostly presence as a unit of account into the nineteenth century). Next the Equivalent would refund capital and interest due from the Company of Scotland Trading to Africa and the Indies, Darien's losers being such a broad cross-section of the Scottish ruling class that there could be no chance of Union without compensation to them. The *quid pro quo* (resisted briefly but vainly by the Scots commissioners) was that the Company of Scotland would be dissolved as a threat to the East India Company's monopoly. Last but not least, other outstanding claims on the empty Treasury in Edinburgh were to be met, such as arrears of pay to the employees of a penniless state. A further part of the Equivalent, expected to arise from brisker trade and higher revenue in Scotland, would be set aside for promotion of domestic industry: Scots' own money was to be hypothecated for their own purposes. In short, none of their resources could be transferred to England – an academic point, perhaps, but worth setting down in black and white.

These terms were not bad from the Scottish point of view. Clerk of Penicuik hailed them as a great victory, won by titanic struggle, though with his embroidering of the reality he surely had in mind a coming campaign of unionist propaganda. Yet even Lockhart could hardly argue that the financial provisions were stingy, just that they were a 'mighty bait, a swingeing bribe to buy off the Scots members of Parliament from their duty to their country'.[28] It all took a month of haggling. Anne must have fretted a little, for she visited the commission on May 23. Clerk felt shocked at her appearance: 'Her Majesty was labouring under a fit of the gout, and in extreme pain and agony. Her face, which was red and spotted, was rendered something frightful by her negligent dress, and the foot affected was tied up with a poultice and some nasty bandages.'[29] She managed to pant: 'I am so much concerned for the Union of the two kingdoms that I could not satisfy myself without coming before I went out of town to see what progress you have made in the treaty, and to recommend very earnestly to you the bringing it to a happy conclusion.'[30] Progress was in fact being made, and she hirpled off contentedly enough for a holiday at Windsor Castle.

☙

The next knotty subject to come up before the commission, in the first days of June, was the laws of the two kingdoms, different not only in particular but also in general. Scots had a logical legal system derived from Roman law, augmented from other sources yet all drawn together in a structure of noble elegance by the great work of Viscount Stair, Lord President of the Court of Session, in his *Institutes of the Law of Scotland* (1681). By contrast the English system was a hotch-potch, the random work of centuries. An advantage for Scots lay in the fine but clear distinctions their system let them draw. One was between civil and criminal law, where in England jurisdiction had degenerated into a mess. The other was between private right and public right, the first of which could remain separate in the two kingdoms and the second of which could be unified – as to laws of the past by cancelling Acts of Parliament inconsistent with the treaty, as to laws of the future by joint legislation. The English, having no better idea, agreed.

The counterpart was that each country should also keep its own courts and jurisdiction. The civil Court of Session and the criminal Court of Justiciary were to retain after Union the authority and privileges they had enjoyed before (subject to such regulations for better administration of justice as might be made by the Parliament of Great Britain). All other Scottish courts were to continue too, on the same condition. Scots laws, except those for trade, customs and excise, would stay in effect unless inconsistent with the treaty. And laws concerning private right were not to be altered unless for the 'evident utility' of Scots. No legal cause in Scotland would go to any English court, not even the highest, such as 'any court in Westminster Hall'. No English court could review or alter acts or sentences of Scottish courts, 'or stop the execution of the same'.[31]

The Scots thought they had won watertight guarantees for their legal independence, but in one point they erred. Nothing was said in the draft treaty about a right of appeal from the Court of Session in Edinburgh to the House of Lords in London. It may just not have occurred to the commissioners that any Scot might want to take a civil appeal there. Yet within a few years this was what happened and a right of appeal was then, if after a huge row, assumed to exist. The effects have been damaging, not only to Scots law. This departure twisted the terms of the deal struck by the commissioners. They could have transferred appellate jurisdiction if they had wanted, but never did. The argument later put forward to justify the transfer, that the British Parliament inherited all rights of the Scots Parliament, was fishy. Nobody could be sure the Scots Parliament did have an appellate jurisdiction over the Court of Session, a matter in dispute before 1707. However that may have been, the Lords, not learned either in Scots or in Roman law, would prove themselves unfit to act as a civil court of appeal for Scotland.

❧

Untidier yet was the next topic to try the commissioners, the parliamentary representation of Scotland. It brought under unsparing light the hindrances to anything that might be called an entire Union, for Parliament was the centrepiece of the project, the place where, if anywhere, it ought to attain entirety. Yet the two nations remained too unequal and too disparate in too much of their past and present for total integration, as they still are even after 300 years.

For the franchise, Scottish rules were to continue as part of the general preservation of domestic law – it would take a century before the eccentric native suffrage came to seem, for all its venerable ancestry in chartered or feudal rights, intolerably restrictive. That still left the question of how many seats Scotland should be awarded at Westminster: if the tally was set too low the Scots might reject it, if too high the English might. The opening English bid ran a risk of wrecking the whole project. It rested on Scotland's taxable capacity, compared to England's. The ratio lay 40:1 in favour of England. It implied adding a mere 13 Scots to 513 MPs in the existing House of Commons. Even the English commissioners did not expect this to be accepted. They suggested 38, a figure still below the 50 MPs the Scots commissioners asked for. The gap yawned wide enough to prompt the sole joint session of the two sides on June 12.

There the Scots argued 'that in the best models of national unions the make-up of the Parliament has been determined partly by population and partly by the dignity of the participating nations' (in obscure reference, presumably, to the fact that Scotland was not actually being conquered by England). Given how messy the rules in both countries were, the commission could either start again from scratch on some rational principle, or else just merge the two legislatures, with all Scots peers going to the Lords and all other Scots members going to the Commons. It was a good try, but the English would have none of it. They retorted that Union would prove impossible if, as a result, 'the ancient constitution of England were to be changed in any way'. They felt it incumbent on them to 'preserve in its entirety a parliamentary structure that has stood the test of so many centuries'. They could only consider 'adding to our ranks a certain number of Scots to form the Parliament of Britain'. This was the nearest the English came to saying in so many words what would prove in practice to be their view, that a Parliament of the United Kingdom would not be a new Parliament at all, but an old Parliament with Scots roped into it. In any event, as England meant not to reform her own representation – far from it – she had no motive to dream up an ideal scheme for Scotland.[32]

Population would have been one means of determining the 'certain number' for Scotland. The Scots commissioners believed their country accounted for a sixth or seventh of the population of Great Britain, and even proposed an official census to arrive at an accurate figure. Yet neither nation was a democracy. And proportional representation had not even been thought of, so in the distribution of constituencies they were unused to counting heads. The English system had again evolved into a hotch-potch, a chaotic if not bizarre product of history: Cornwall alone, with forty-four MPs, boasted about as many as Scotland could expect.

So the commissioners fell back on a fiscal criterion, which could at least produce something countable, not for its intrinsic virtue but to justify a proportion of English to Scottish seats deemed acceptable on vaguer grounds. They hit on a proportion of 12:1. The fiscal criterion was applied just to Scotland and not, now or later, to England and Wales: taxable capacity, if rational, never became a general principle of representation. It was a device to reach compromise, pushed by Somers with an eye to future league with the Scots. It yielded forty-five MPs for Scotland. In the Lords there would be sixteen representatives elected by the body of Scots peers. These terms were not, according to modern conceptions, generous. They cut the number of parliamentary constituencies in Scotland by two-thirds, and in practice excluded from Westminster nine in ten of her noblemen.

လၢ

Once the big issues of finance, law and representation had been slapped on the canvas of Union with a broad brush, the remaining detail proved less irksome. For example, there was ready agreement on the flag of the United Kingdom, conjoining the crosses of St Andrew and St George; it could have been a vexed question, as shown by some of the weird and wonderful designs drawn up, but it turned out simple, if inelegant.

A few provisions went perforce into particulars. One concerned the future status of ships belonging to the queen's subjects in Scotland, many up to now owned jointly with maritime capitalists in Amsterdam or Rotterdam. Scotland belonged to the Dutch rather than to the English commercial system, with 16,000 Scots serving in the merchant fleet of the Netherlands.[33] Care had to be taken to avoid causing problems for this, and so for the world's carrying trade, the economic prop of a military ally. The nub of the problem really lay on the English side, for the Navigation Acts forbade Englishmen to buy or own ships built abroad. In the end (and after amendment during the legislative process) the clause permitted ships built abroad, if owned by Scots at the time of the treaty's ratification, to rank as ships of Great Britain on condition of being so registered after oath taken; this meant Dutch joint owners had to be eased out, but time was allowed for complex foreign contracts to be untangled.

Yet much weightier if less technical matters were waved airily away. One the Scots had disputed among themselves was whether the Kirk, while not included in their negotiating brief, should all the same be safeguarded by a specific article. Somers did not like the idea at all. It looked to him like a gift to the Tories at Westminster, who were bound to raise a rumpus about toleration for Scots Episcopalians and so throw a spanner in the Union's works. Better, as the Scots at length concurred, for silence to reign on religion in the treaty but, in supplement to it, for the two Parliaments respectively to pass Acts of Security in favour of the Church of Scotland and the Church of England.

In this and other ways the final draft of the treaty turned out, it must be said, English in its essential character. The Scottish method of tackling complex issues was, as in Stair's *Institutes*, to set out general principles then derive particular applications from them. The English method was to adjust all details in pragmatic terms and leave general principles to look after themselves. The two sides in effect wrote a constitution for a new state yet made no effort to define the standing of its central embodiment, the Parliament of Great Britain. The English already possessed a doctrine of the sovereignty of the Crown in Parliament. The Scots had heard of it, but their own Parliament found itself amid such headlong, if not tumultuous, evolution from its previous lowly status that its doctrine of sovereignty was hard to fathom. Did the Parliament of Great Britain just cut across the process and impose the doctrine of the English Parliament, now itself to be superseded? Whatever the answer to the question, the commissioners never asked it. They had done trade, finance and law – no mean feat in itself. It was enough: the relative status of the Parliaments of Scotland, England and Great Britain interested them no longer.

A Union of the two nations posited on total integration was anyway impossible either in theory or in practice. A drive to impose it might well have crashed, so the commissioners never tried. The term 'incorporating Union' often used of the result, was and is not a good one, for except of the Parliaments little incorporation took place. Such as that was, it began to unravel before the treaty even passed into law, as we will see. The English had their own illogicality to blame, after seeking a quick fix, concentrated on some big issues (though not the very biggest), going only selectively into detail, with no co-ordination of the whole. A quick fix let the Scots slip in a range of safeguards for themselves, agreed more or less on the nod. This implied that they were the weaker partners, yet it would be shown, in the gap between negotiation of the treaty and its entry into force nine months later, that if Union was to take effect their very weakness could be turned to greater account.

It was on July 22, 1706, three months to the day after the commissioners convened for their first working session, that they approved the twenty-five articles of the draft Treaty of Union.[34] Four copies were made, one each for the queen, House of Lords, House of Commons and Scottish Parliament. All the commissioners signed them except a single Scot, Lockhart, and a single Englishman, the Archbishop of York. The next day they went in procession to St James's Palace to announce to Anne the success of their labours.

In the queen's presence Lord Cooper claimed, for the English side, that they had averted war: the 'great and main consequence of the treaty' would be 'continuation of peace and tranquillity in this island upon a descent of the Crown, instead of the bloodshed and distraction which would probably follow upon the fatal division of it'. Lord Seafield, for the Scots, agreed. He praised the treaty as 'necessary for establishing the lasting peace, happiness and prosperity of both nations'. This speech, Clerk of Penicuik thought, 'excelled the other' because Seafield spoke fluently and Cowper was 'miserably mangled in the delivery, and at last . . . forced to draw it out of his pocket and read it'. The queen scanned the treaty and answered: 'The particulars of it seem so reasonable, that I hope they will meet with approbation in the Parliaments of both kingdoms. I shall always look upon it as a particular happiness if this Union, which will be so great a security and advantage to both kingdoms, can be accomplished in my reign.' The Earl of Mar later wrote to the Earl of Cromartie that they had done their best and hoped the Scots Parliament 'will think it for the interest of the nation, and so ratify it, by which there would be an end put to all our divisions, and honest people would get leave to live at peace and ease, and mind their affairs and the improvement of their country – a much better employment than the politics'. Here was an agenda for the enlightened Scotland of the future.[35]

$$\mathcal{C}\mathcal{D}$$

For now, though, politics could not be dispensed with. Clerk of Penicuik recalled how the Scots on their way home 'fancied themselves that they had been doing great service to their country in the matter of the Union, so they would be acceptable to all ranks and degrees of people'. He would soon learn better. 'The whole nation appears against the Union,' said Lockhart on his return, 'the ministers roaring and denouncing judgments on those that [are] for it.'[36] It was one thing to write a treaty, in other words, another to pass it – and through two Parliaments. The Court saw the Scots one would be the harder to handle. So it was decided the treaty should first undergo ratification in Edinburgh before being so much as introduced at Westminster. The text would not be published till October, only just in time for the session of the Scots Parliament. The motive for the caginess was to frustrate the concerting of opposition.

The key to the struggle, as seen from both capitals, lay in the Scots nobility. Scotland, state and nation, was dominated by men of blue blood. An observer noted the government 'had no confidence or hopes in the affections of the people, knowing that all this whole affair would turn upon the votes and power of the nobles of Scotland'. And Bishop Gilbert Burnet later wrote: 'It was the nobility that in every vote turned the scale for the Union: they were severely reflected on by those who opposed it; it was said, many of them were bought off to sell their country and their birthright.'[37] The common Scotsman, a peasant in a feudal society, readily acknowledged dependence on his superiors, indeed sought to affirm and exploit it in order to protect or advance himself. Only in the emergent urban communities of Edinburgh, and to a lesser extent Glasgow, were Scots to some degree liberated from those chains of dependence, in the latter city also through links to Covenanters in its hinterland who placed their religious above any other obligations, if by now often in no more than a quietist manner – that is to say, not in any way readily translated into political action.

Nationalist historians stress how little support Union found among the Scots people. This is true, yet at the time it did not much matter. Nobody then thought the Scots people had a right to decide. Scotland could boast a 'Gothic' constitution, a picturesque survival from the Middle Ages when, as in several other European countries, it grew out of royal summons to the estates, the different social orders; now Scotland (with England) possessed just about the sole surviving example of a Gothic constitution, elsewhere superseded by absolute monarchy. The estates had conformed to no theory of popular sovereignty but derived their legitimacy from the Crown, in its patents of nobility or other grants of privilege. If the Declaration of Arbroath spoke in 1320 of the community of the realm of Scotland, and if in the sixteenth century George Buchanan dusted off that concept in defining the nature of Scottish kingship, it is not clear these high authorities meant anything more than the local variant of a Gothic constitution. A right to decide on Union has been imputed to the Scots people only by later generations of nationalist writers. It rests on an ahistorical assumption.

℃

So the treaty paid every possible regard to the noble estate, in economic and other provisions, as one which did in theory have a right to decide – beside in practice dominating the other estates. Clerk of Penicuik thought, when listing for himself the components of potential opposition to Union, that the key to victory over them must lie in the aristocracy. What this might mean in real life was pandering to 'a great many disobliged courtiers and self-conceited men who could relish nothing but what was of their own contrivance'.[38]

Management of them could not be certain of success, however. The Marquis of Annandale offered an example. Starting off an opportunistic supporter of the Court, and appointed a Minister under Argyll in 1705, he was soon sacked after trying to subvert his colleagues' preference for a treaty over the Hanoverian succession, in the days when these had still been alternatives. The testy Annandale erred off further and further into opposition till in the end he would vote against a Union securing the Hanoverian succession he said he wanted. Little less perverse was a nationalist hero, Lord Belhaven, a 'rough, fat, black, noisy man, more like a butcher than a lord', who at his outset bid fair to do well in his career. His industry and eloquence put him on the first rung up the official ladder when Tweeddale made him a commissioner of Treasury. But Belhaven, too, bit the dust once Argyll took over, and struggled in vain to recover. The umbrage of a frustrated seeker after office should be borne in mind when he is recalled as the silver-tongued patriot.[39]

There were two baits for hooking slippery noblemen to Union: status and money. The Court dispensed both, but found from bitter experience they could not be doled out indiscriminately. For example, the Duke of Argyll had demanded and got an English peerage for his services as Lord High Commissioner. Not that this sated his greed, with which he could still panic government any time he liked. He was already looking to the place he would take in the future Great Britain. He demanded his wee brother, Lord Archie as he called him, should be created an earl in his own right and so become eligible as one of the 16 representatives at Westminster. Mar wrote: 'He is very desirous to have his brother made a peer of Scotland, and made us all promise to write to the Treasurer [Godolphin] of it, which I have done.'[40] The queen's advisers were in a fix; they had a long list of such supplications and feared to pique the patient queue. But the Campbells remained implacable, and the government had to give in.

It remained for Lord Archie to select his territorial title. He had the gall to propose Earl of Dundee. It was a title the Grahams regarded as their own (John Graham, Bluidy Claverhouse, had been Viscount Dundee); no doubt the Campbells sought to appropriate it out of spite, recalling the mortal rivalry of the Marquis of Argyll and Marquis of Montrose 60 years before. The present Marquis of Montrose, a member of the Squadrone, had just gone over to the Ministry, bringing a few of his clients with him. He did so on the offer of a post, Lord President of the Council, which a small financial inducement made all the more acceptable. Suddenly he found honour more important than money and threatened to defect back to the opposition. Ministers kowtowed to both antagonists. Not till Loudoun, cadet of the Campbells, interceded with Argyll and his brother would they see sense. Lord Archie emerged as Earl of Islay.[41]

To others less carping, promises could be kept vaguer. Many needy Scots nobles hoped faithful service now to the Court would later be rewarded by a British peerage, that is, a hereditary seat in the Lords with its ready access to official patronage. In fact no cornucopia would ever be offered. After Union, only six such promotions came to Scots before a barrier fell with a crunch in 1711. It was then the Duke of Hamilton, just created Duke of Brandon in the peerage of Great Britain, was disqualified for the Lords in a case contrived to set an adverse precedent for future promotions. Those Scots who did get a step up into the British peerage were then denied an automatic place at Westminster, which destroyed the whole point of the exercise. The restriction was not to be lifted for 70 years.

As for money, there was a problem that the Scottish state had no money, there being little money in the country to have. Its revenue depended largely on the customs, so if there was no trade there was no revenue. Loudoun's depute in Edinburgh, George Dalrymple of Dalmahoy, member of the Parliament for Stranraer, wrote to him as the negotiations in London were drawing to a close: 'Except you great men bring a vast deal of ready along with you when you come to Scotland I believe you will not find people so well inclined to the Union as I would wish.' The dearth affected the Secretary himself. Loudoun drew a salary of £500 a quarter. But early in 1706 the Bank of Scotland still declined to pay cash over the counter except at 14 per cent interest, so he preferred to do without till the rate fell. At that point he was in fact owed two instalments of salary, yet the bank just refused to release the second on any condition. In general, public expenditure was becoming all but impossible, even for a government of Scotland used to handing out far more than it took in. Collection of taxes had been farmed, to use the contemporary term – contracted out to private entrepreneurs as agents of government; they were called tacksmen. In Dalrymple's words, 'tacksmen pretend that they have advanced so much money already upon the public account that they can give no more without danger of breaking themselves'.[42]

If money did not come from Scotland, it would have to come from somewhere else. Scots were never particular, so that taking money could look awfully like treason. Lockhart condemned it as 'abundantly disgraceful' and in noblemen still worse: 'for persons of quality and distinction to sell, and even at so mean a price, themselves and their posterity, is so scandalous and infamous that such persons must be contemptible in the sight of those who bought them, and their memories odious to all future generations'.[43] This was something most could live with, yet the effects remained unpredictable. Hamilton had asked Hooke for money from Louis XIV and probably got some, for the ostensible purpose of buying votes in the Parliament – though, heaven knows, he needed it himself. Years later, James 'Ossian' Macpherson in a 'secret history of Great Britain' referred to 'large sums of money which [Hamilton] laid out during the sitting of the last Parliament of Scotland'.[44] French and then English money did change hands, but whether it changed minds is a different matter; in the eighteenth century personal sweeteners were routine lubricants of politics, just as collective subsidies are today.

What came home to people in Scotland now was a tightening in the Court's management, compared to its fecklessness during previous sessions of the Parliament. It helped that a clearer goal had been set of building a majority for the Treaty of Union. So a better reason existed, beyond routine, for putting resources into purchase of support. While Argyll as Lord High Commissioner had failed to get the £20,000 he wanted for that, now the sum was forthcoming. As it could not be found from the empty Scots Treasury, it had to be sent from HM Treasury in London – meaning, in turn, with connivance from Godolphin and permission from the queen. It arrived in Scotland in between the end of the negotiations for Union and the convening of the parliamentary session to debate the terms. It was advanced to pay debts on the civil list. Presumably these would at length have been paid anyway, from the Equivalent or some different fund. The dubious aspects of the transaction lay in bringing it forward to just before the session of the Parliament, and in meeting a Scottish head of expenditure from England. Perhaps nobody in the end got more than he might have by other means (on a heroic assumption every claim was genuine). Yet it would be naïve to see all this as just a handy way to square accounts.

The business is muddied by the huge 'bygones', or arrears of salary to holders of Scottish offices. In the eighteenth century many public servants received no regular payment of salary, not even in England, let alone Scotland. The government would give them money if it had money, which in Scotland was seldom. Anyone could be affected by this public parsimony. Towards the bottom end of the scale the commander of artillery at Edinburgh Castle, Captain Theodore Dury, put in an official complaint that he had not been paid in full since 1693. At the top end the Earl of Cromartie wrote: 'I borrowed no money whilst I was Secretary, but what I was necessitate to do, in consequence of that employment wanting the ordinar dues thereof, so now must sell some little part of my great heritage, to pay the absolute necessars of that post, which perhaps was not deserved.'[45] At least a few were in a position to cover professional expenses out of their own pocket and get them back later; it was only human for them then to put in claims generous to themselves, as modern journalists will see. Now, in a crackdown, the Court would make or withhold payment depending how the claimant voted on Union, even in cases of legitimate debt.

Nothing was known outside a closed circle about the £20,000 sent north for these purposes in the autumn of 1706. The first hint of it came five years later, recounted in an appendix to Lockhart's memoirs.[46] He was by then MP for Midlothian at Westminster. He chanced on proof of something amiss while serving on a parliamentary commission for the public accounts, and resolved to expose it. It is easier to dismiss Lockhart as partisan (which he was) than to explain away the evidence he presents. He shows Queen Anne had on August 12, 1706, authorised HM Treasury to lend £20,000 to pay debts on the Scottish civil list. A correspondence followed between Godolphin on the one hand and several Scots on the other, the Duke of Queensberry together with the Earls of Seafield, Mar, Loudoun and Glasgow; the last, treasurer-depute of Scotland, was the man who actually handled the money. He, with Loudoun, acknowledged receipt of it in two instalments of £10,000. Glasgow insisted this had to be kept secret in Scotland, otherwise it 'might probably make some noise if the letter were read in the Treasury before the meeting of the Parliament and before the treaty is well-received'.[47]

Corroboration of what Lockhart exposed in his memoirs is found in two letters in private archives of which he could have had no sight. In the first, written to Queensberry on July 20, 1707, Seafield and Glasgow say they are getting the £20,000. They suppose it to be part of the Equivalent, which they clearly see as a slush-fund, whatever higher purposes it might have. Their letter is to be read to Godolphin who is worrying if the money will be well-spent. The delicacy of the matter is implied in the postscript: 'Your Grace may be pleased to burn this letter when you have read it to my Lord Treasurer.' Godolphin, however, kept a copy which two centuries later passed into the public records: meanwhile, he might produce it as a receipt if challenged and it gave him a hold on the two Scots noblemen.

The second letter, of March 22, 1711, is from Glasgow to Harley, by then Earl of Oxford and Lord Treasurer in Godolphin's stead. In a blue funk Glasgow begs Harley's protection from a parliamentary inquiry (the one where Lockhart was serving). He has no receipts or vouchers for disbursement of the £20,000, and is being asked by the MPs for his comments. He admits he might have broken rules but pleads secrecy had been vital.[48] The money made no official appearance in the Scottish Treasury, 'for if it had been known that there had been a farthing sent from England to Scotland it would have totally disappointed the carrying on of the Union'. He followed orders – that is, from Queensberry – in handing out cash, 'I being enjoined to carry on this matter with the greatest secrecy and privacy, for if ever it had been in the least discovered during the haill session of the Union Parliament, the Union had certainly broken.' Glasgow also believes he would have been lynched by the mob. He asks for Harley's instructions, which he will 'punctually obey', and ends with one of the passages of grovel so noisome yet so frequent in letters at that time from Scots to English politicians.[49]

As for spending it, £12,325 went to Queensberry 'for equipage and daily allowance'. So he took the lion's share, but he did have genuine debts from his time as Lord High Commissioner and beyond doubt was due something. Whether he fiddled his claims is another question. According to Lockhart, the duke – and not only he – got paid twice; later he offered to repay part.[50] At the opposite end of the spectrum stood the £11 2s. to Lord Banff, a man so poor he deserted his Roman Catholic religion in order to attend the Parliament and desert his country too – at least he came cheap. There are further awards that seem trifling; yet most Scots peers were broke, and what look like trifles now appeared like manna from heaven then.

Otherwise, according to Glasgow and Seafield, payments had gone to those helpful with the treaty, to Atholl, Balcarres, Dunmore, Marchmont, Roxburghe, Tweeddale and so on: all did indeed vote for it except Atholl, who was unlikely to do so however much he got. The transactions still held their little mysteries, then, yet it remained impossible to provide a full

account 'without discovering the haill affair to every particular person
that received any part of the money, which hath been hitherto kept
secret'. In any event, people would 'refuse to give assignations if they were
demanded of them, so the discovering of it would be of no use, unless it
were to bring discredit on the management of that Parliament'.[51] As the
sordid business receded into the past, men thought better not to light up
the encircling murk. The best general judgment is that, while the dues
may have been in the main just, the way they were met still smacks of
corruption.

If motives among some of the bribed remain blurred, there is no doubt
the bribers sought to squeeze a return even out of sound claims on the civil
list. Mar reported how he had discussed with Tweeddale his arrears from
service as Lord High Commissioner 'and I assured him of all the
assistance in my power, and that much would depend on himself to
make it in my power or not'. Atholl was told his debt would be paid if he
kept away from the Parliament while the treaty was going through; he
spurned the offer, continued to oppose Union and afterwards was still
trying to get his money. The Earl of Rosebery had received a peerage as
well as a pension of £300 a year, yet could not have his money till Mar
saw how he acted in the Parliament; he at last judged Rosebery had
performed 'very honestly and firmly', so deserved his reward. When the
Earl of Glencairn proved less reliable, Mar noted he 'had not got his letter
of pension, and now we must think before it be given'.[52]

಄

Anyway, the Scots people would see none of what money was going –
while, to add insult to injury, on their Parliament the English exerted
more influence than they did. Yet the people's influence was not non-
existent either, or else there would have been no point in keeping official
secrets till the session convened. Dalrymple gave one reason to his boss,
Loudoun: 'I am sure it is strange madness to be against an Union before
they know what the terms are. It hath been a long time a maxim in
Scotland to be always against the Court, without ever considering
whether they are right or wrong.' At the end of September, James Brodie
of Brodie reported from faraway Moray: 'I find all here, both laics and
clergy, much in the dark about the matter of the Union.'[53] Yet anybody
acquainted with George Lockhart of Carnwath or with Adam Cockburn
of Ormiston, Lord Justice Clerk, could just go and ask them, as they were

happy to leak the terms. Some inkling of them spread abroad, even if details remained hidden. Mar's brother, James Erskine, wrote of the treaty in the summer: 'There are certainly a great many violently against it, and though there are severals [*sic*] for it too yet they don't seem to be half as zealous for it as the others are against it.' At the same time Mar told Godolphin he had 'conversed with a great many and I found most of them prepossessed against the Union'.[54]

The terms, once published in October, aroused popular fury. As Defoe wrote soon after arriving in Edinburgh, if not yet with complete accuracy, 'till the printing of these articles, the people were generally very desirous of the Union, as that which tended to the putting an end to all former animosities, burying the ancient feuds between the nations, and removing the apprehensions good people on both sides had justly entertained of a new rupture'. It surprised him 'to find a nation now fly in the face of their masters, and upbraid the gentlemen, who managed it, with selling and betraying their country, and surrendering their constitution, sovereignty and independency to the English'. Still, 'nothing was to be heard now, but of slavery to the English, running away with the Crown, taking away their nation, and the like'. Anger drew together 'parties and peoples whose interests and principles differed as much as light and darkness', Presbyterian or Jacobite, Cameronian or Catholic. 'And such was the clamour against the treaters, that I verily believe, had the articles of the treaty been published before the treaters came home, there was not many of them would dared to have gone home, without a guard to protect them.'[55]

From his opposite, nationalist standpoint Lockhart viewed the outrage with relish: 'During this time the nation's aversion to the Union increased; the Parliament Close, and the outer Parliament House, were crowded every day when the Parliament was met, with an infinite number of people, all exclaiming against the Union, and speaking very free language concerning the promoters of it.' While Queensberry faced insults and curses in the street, Hamilton as leader of the patriotic opposition was 'huzza'd and conveyed every night, with a great number of apprentices and younger sort of people, from the Parliament House to the Abbey [Holyrood], exhorting him to stand by the country and assuring him of his being supported'.[56]

Clerk of Penicuik regretted the 'triumph in our streets of wilful ignorance, contradictions and inconsistencies'. But for a sober fellow he managed to paint a vivid picture of it: 'Here you may find several persons exalting an Union of confederacy, and at the same time exclaiming against that article of the treaty concerning equal duties, customs and excises as if there would be an Union of confederacy without equal burdens.' Down the road, 'others quarrel, amongst other things, with the charges the nation will be put to in sending up 16 peers and 45 Commons to the Parliament of Great Britain, and at the same time, in both words and writings, they cry out against that number as a small, dishonourable representation'. Further along, 'some are regretting the extreme poverty of the nation and scarcity of money; yet, notwithstanding, they exclaim against the Union as a thing that will ruin us' – though Clerk believed ''tis scarce conceivable how any condition of life we can fall into can render us more miserable and poor than we are'. Finally, 'you may see a Presbyterian minister, a popish priest and an Episcopal prelate all agreeing together in their discourse of the Union, but upon quite different views and contradictory reasons'.[57]

&

The hostility could not have surprised the government of Scotland, yet some of it did come from unexpected quarters. Of 25 articles in the draft treaty, 15 dealt with economic topics. These were for unionists the main selling point, given Scotland's backwardness, with a poor population, no capital, no currency and crippled commerce. In the circumstances it seemed easy to urge the benefits of free trade with England, still more tempting to go further and laud the transformations Union might bring. Thorny problems still littered the road, but these the commissioners had taken trouble to clear aside.

Today one school of Scottish historians draws the conclusion the economy must have been the basic motive of Union. But it is then difficult to account for some awkward facts – for example, that the royal burghs, at national level the one institution of Scottish society with an explicit commercial function, in a plurality opposed the treaty. Their stance seems on the modern determinist view to run counter to their interest. Yet the contradiction is not hard to resolve. The royal burghs had little to do with the awakening enthusiasm of Scots for free trade, evidenced by writings of John Law or William Paterson and by the practical activities of entrepreneurs. The function of a royal burgh lay in regulating, not deregulating, commerce. It was a medieval relic, not a harbinger of modernity, a retarded, not progressive element in the life of Scotland.

The sole exceptions to that outlook could be found in Glasgow, which profited from smuggling as the one form of free trade available under a national system of regulation, and to some extent Edinburgh, which had a more diverse economy and otherwise was cosmopolitan and open-minded beyond the horizons of smaller burghs.[58] Unlike Glasgow, Edinburgh never presented an address against Union, yet the real contrast lay between these two and the rest – say, a burgh like Montrose, conservative in both trade and politics. There the town council now sent a letter to its member of the Parliament, James Scott of Logie, rich merchant and supporter of the Court. The bailies first sought to soften him up by conceding the advantages of Union were 'many and great'. But they went on to press an overriding wish for him to protect their interest in the manufacture of linen, lest they 'be deprived of the only valuable branch of our trade' and find themselves falling in with the 'fate of this poor, miserable, blinded nation'.[59] Such sentiments bespeak no animal spirits buoyed by a vista of free trade. But they were typical of the royal burghs.

Every year these discussed matters of common interest in the Convention of Royal Burghs. Like some other public bodies it sent in an address against Union, approved by 24 against 20 of the delegates to it, with 22 abstaining. Those drawing up the objections first put a point often made by others that they had nothing against 'an honourable and sole Union with England, consisting with the being of this kingdom and Parliament thereof without which we cannot conceive neither our religious nor civil interests and trade, as we now by law enjoy them, can be secured to us and our posterity'. But they preferred some form of federalism, with a Scots Parliament retained, given the prospect of English levels of taxation, 'which is a certain insupportable burden', and of English bias in regulation, 'considering that the most considerable branches of our trade are differing from those of England, and are and may be yet more discouraged by their laws'.[60] The men behind this were clearly uninterested in free trade either. They worked rather on the assumptions of what is known today as 'capture theory', the idea that regulation secured through lobbying a government will always be sought by interested parties for their own selfish benefit, at best thinly disguised as public good. This is economics ruled by politics: again, not the spirit of *laissez-faire* in action.

In fact any liberal impulse, like other advanced ideas in Scotland, came from the nobility, the most progressive class, from peers who were entrepreneurs with estates sitting on natural resources. A typical example, the Earl of Wemyss, looked to Union with England because his markets for coal and salt in Europe were being squeezed by foreign protectionism; by contrast, his family had fond memories of a fortune made from free trade within Great Britain under Oliver Cromwell. Industrialists remained a small minority of this class but in agriculture, too, only large landowners could afford the improvement which was a key to higher productivity and income. That would be desirable whatever view the laird took of Union: the nationalist George Lockhart of Carnwath developed and exploited his lands with no less zest than the unionist Earl of Cromartie (who was, however, also a shameless importuner of government).[61] Bailies of the burghs lacked the social or economic standing to follow the quest for change, except through noble patrons who had often placed them where they were. Closed minds preferred closed markets.

જી

In any event, to many more Scots the economics of Union just did not matter. Jacobites would oppose the treaty come what may, even if a few had once cast tactical votes in the Parliament to open negotiations for it. Such opportunism could be justified so long as no treaty specified the Hanoverian succession; yet this one did, in validating for Scotland the English Act of Settlement. The sole hope of succession by the Stewarts would then lie in a still independent Scotland; even so, succession and independence would probably have to be vindicated by war. Scots Jacobites remained ready to fight, as they had fought during the Revolution while English Jacobites dithered.

Only exceptionally, as in Cromartie's case, was it possible in Scotland to draw a distinction now possible in England between Tory and Jacobite. His thinking continued to develop, and further in the direction of Union: 'Unless we be a part of each other,' he told Mar, 'the Union will be as a blood puddin to bind a cat – that is, till one or the other be hungry, and then the puddin flies.' He became in fact the original North Briton and may have been the first, apart from that perverse pedant, James VI and I, to resurrect the word 'Britain' or its derivatives, all properly pertaining to a province of the Roman Empire which had never conquered Caledonia. 'May we be Britons,' Cromartie all the same wrote, 'and down go the old ignominious names of Scotland and England. Scotland and England are names unknown in our native language [meaning Gaelic, his own mother tongue]. England is a dishonourable name, imposed on Britain by Jutland pirates and mercenaries usurping on their lords.' He is the true ancestor of the modern Scottish Tory or Unionist or Conservative party, which only gelled at the end of the century under Henry Dundas and appears today to have reached its sorry end. A problem for it has been that the English never agreed with Cromartie. They still used the word 'England' not just for their own country but also to include Scotland, Wales, even Ireland, and Britain or the United Kingdom as a whole.[62]

For the rest, Scots Tories were Jacobites. They had been managing to behave themselves more or less, at least to the extent of accepting on the throne a sovereign other than the heir in direct line of the House of Stewart, and even taking oaths to sit in her Parliament where they could amuse themselves tripping up the Court. Clerk of Penicuik wrote of them: 'As they were very numerous even in the Parliament of Scotland they could not think of embracing a system for the Union of the two kingdoms wherein succession to the Crown was to be settled on the House of Hanover.'[63] The one useful distinction to be drawn among them lay between those preferring to work by constitutional means, which had meant watching and waiting on the death of Anne, and those who did not rule out plots or rebellion.

Most of the Cavalier party in the Parliament stood, at least for now, on the constitutional side of the divide, in loyalty to the queen without prejudice to their views of the succession. Typical was their leader, the Earl of Home, but he died in August 1706 and deprived them of trusted if mediocre management. Atholl was their most interesting figure, having arrived at the Cavalier position from an original stance as Revolution Whig, impelled as far as can be seen by patriotism. His personal evolution gave him a claim to represent an alternative national interest, not just identified with dynastic legitimacy but also balanced by Country positions, such as vigilance against executive abuse – even if that should sound hollow in a Cavalier party which had supported royal absolutism in the past and might be called on to do so again. Yet, by later in the century, Jacobitism could be identified with redress of Scots' grievances.

Atholl's positions assumed clearer outline when he came up against the machinations of Queensberry. The Scotch Plot would hardly have been worth the candle unless contrived against a man whose politics of continued national independence under a fair-dealing Stewart was becoming more rather than less coherent and attractive. Atholl saw the bogus plot raise his standing in the queen's eyes, only to find it deflated again when her insistence on the Hanoverian succession got too much for him and he resigned from government. His snooty air put people off; now it seemed not to be balanced by any tactical finesse. The Cavaliers faced problems not just of leadership. Their whole political position won since 1702, so far proof against malice and blandishments of place or patronage, would dissolve with the Scots Parliament. Was a time not approaching for Jacobites to fight?

৶

The Jacobite political faction and the Episcopalian religious faction overlapped without being coterminous. The insecurity and bitterness of Episcopalian ministers deposed in the 1690s did sharpen Jacobitism among them. Yet Charles II and James VII had never defended an episcopal Church of Scotland to the last ditch. From time to time they offered a little indulgence to Presbyterians, if only to isolate the fringe of Covenanting fanatics. Once fidelity to the true Kirk was no longer a sentence of death, the faithful might hang on against a day when they could take over the religious establishment again – just what had happened in 1690. The Episcopalians then sold out turned into mouthpieces for the exiled Stewarts: such are the ironies of history. Even now the king over the water and the Church in the wilderness did not see quite eye to eye. The Pretender was a Catholic and Catholics were by definition not Episcopalians, whose mode of worship in Scotland remained anything but popish (in fact it was thoroughly Reformed). And in their politics such people, for example Hamilton, might take up causes for their own reasons, not all congenial to Jacobites: in the duke's case, his own succession to the throne.

Union suddenly there as a practical proposition altered the outlook for Episcopalians too, and for the worse. In general, they could hardly support it. While the Kirk had been excluded from the draft treaty's purview, Union was meant to establish Presbyterianism beyond recall – Clerk of Penicuik wrote indeed 'of a first intention which many of the members of Parliament had of making the Presbyterian government and its security the basis of any Union between the two nations'.[64] So far the cleft between Episcopalians, whether conciliatory or resentful, and Presbyterians, whether triumphant or edgy, had proved unbridgeable. It even ran deeper than any division during the Reformation more than a century before, when clergymen unable in conscience to break with the old faith had been cushioned with modest stipends and left to live out their days at ease, though not in priestly office. Scotland could no longer afford that, in her pocket or in her head.

So the recent experience had proved more harrowing. Over a decade after the Presbyterian settlement of 1690 many hapless Episcopalians still suffered persecution, with meeting houses shut up at random and priests beggared by punitive fines. The Revd Alexander Ross, Bishop of Edinburgh, protested to Loudoun: 'God forgive those who not satisfied with the desolation of our Church and the establishment of your own also can and do bring many poor churchmen already overwhelmed with trouble unto the last extremities of misery.'[65] Expelled from their manses and forced to cast themselves with their families on the charity of an often hostile populace, they would cling to any patron willing to look after them. Their only requital lay in fortifying Jacobitism among the landed class. Their only hope was that Presbyterianism might be overthrown again one day by return of the Stewarts. But that could never happen if Union took place.

ↄ

While all official favours were being showered on the estate of the nobility, in fact the estate of the clergy (excluded from the Parliament since 1690) would prove just as crucial to Union. If Scots at large could exert little political pressure, through presbytery they might still make a case. Presbyterianism was, after all, a religion of the people. Since an Act of Security for the Kirk had been specified in the deal with England, the Act might, by the agency of clerical surrogates, give the people a say before Union stilled their voice for a long time to come.

A point the commissioners in London had preferred to skate over, while being bamboozled into a quick fix by Somers, was that a Union of states without a Union of Churches made to the mind of the age a contradiction in terms. National religion and national identity blended all over Europe, the first often determining the constitutional or political content of the second. A single established religion was the norm, in both unitary kingdoms and composite monarchies. Only in looser Unions hardly counting as such, Switzerland or the Holy Roman Empire, could room be found for differing establishments. The Dutch granted a degree of toleration, yet no nation had more than one established religion. If Great Britain was to try, it would run counter to all thinking of the time. That the experiment could work was by no means clear. If not, the Scots

Presbyterians would be the likely losers. Their dilemma went to the nub of the treaty and its meaning: was it a binding international agreement which constituted a new state, or did it just preserve and enhance an old state in disguise, to maintain in practice the absolute sovereignty of the English Crown in Parliament?[66]

Presbyterians themselves did not espouse any single, collective, let alone favourable view of Union. Economics cut no ice with them; some modern scholarship has sought to equate Calvinism with capitalism, yet the ultra-orthodox Revd Robert Wodrow of Eastwood denounced 'the sin of fondness upon trade'.[67] It was in any event on a different tack that the Duke of Hamilton set off to rally Presbyterians against the treaty, with the help of the minister in his home parish, the Revd Robert Wyllie, who acted also as his agent in the General Assembly and correspondent with other senior clerics. Wyllie improbably joined this aristocratic favour with esteem from colleagues of the cloth; according to Wodrow, he was 'a man of shining piety, fine taste, excellent sense and singular accomplishments in every branch of valuable knowledge and learning'. His attributes seemed especially valuable now that a stumbling block to Union could be discerned in the Covenanting current of Presbyterianism, whether brought back into the body of the Kirk in 1690 or soldiering on in the sect of Cameronians, small but fierce, refusing all compromise with an uncovenanted state – which in return eyed it with bottomless suspicion.

That Covenanting current remained strongest in the West of Scotland. There the presbytery of Hamilton sought, at Wyllie's behest, to speak for all: 'As to the disposition of the people, the plain truth is, that they are generally most averse from the Union.' The presbytery would take in time a line still stronger – indeed 'of an extraordinary nature' according to Defoe – that no Union of Parliaments should be concluded till a General Assembly had been called: 'the national Church established by law hath an undoubted right to be consulted'.[68]

Such Scots saw in their history a work of Providence. It gave them a religion of apostolic purity, to pollute which would be a sin crying to heaven. Yet that was the likely result of Union with an England where the religious establishment, erected round unscriptural bishops, had so compromised with a secular state as – horror of horrors – to let them sit in the Lords. 'There is twa kingdoms in Scotland,' the reformer Andrew Melville had said, 'the kingdom of Jamie the Saxt and the kingdom of Jesus Christ'. Here lay the Scots' own constitutional doctrine of two swords, one brandished by the state, the other by the Kirk, institutions complementing or correcting each other without vesting supremacy in either; hence the Covenants' anathema on civil office for clergymen. The philosopher George Davie has traced the conceptual lineage of this constitution balanced between Church and state, by means of which the Scots 'would govern themselves through the co-operation of a pair of mutually critical but mutually complementary assemblies, the one concerned with politics and law, the other with the distinguishable, but nevertheless inseparable sphere of ethics and faith'.[69]

To militant Presbyterians the only possible compromise with England would have to come through a return to the Solemn League and Covenant of 1643, drawn up at Westminster by commissioners of both nations. It had sought to extend Presbyterianism all over Great Britain. Needless to say, the false English soon abjured it. No Scot should be surprised if such a forsworn people sought to force bishops back on their godly neighbours. Pulpits rang with philippics against the prospective prelacy. 'We incorporate with a nation deeply guilty of many national abominations, who have openly broke and burnt their Covenant with God, and league with us,' preached the Revd James Hepburn of Urr in Kirkcudbrightshire: they have 'their public and established worship corrupted with superstition and idolatry'.[70]

But one problem was that Covenanters and fellow travellers had turned so apolitical. After the older generations' ordeals of persecution and martyrdom, many now combined in touching fashion a heroic piety with a rustic charm, as Sir Walter Scott was to bring out with his novels, in the character of Davie Deans and the like. True, Hepburn of Urr stood ready to raise armed volunteers – and against the Jacobite rebellion of 1715 he would do just that, under a banner bearing an inscription 'For the Lord of Hosts'; yet he also wrote a book called *Humble Pleadings for the Good Old Way*.[71] Clerk of Penicuik, who had Cameronians in his constituency of Whithorn, thought them 'a wild, vain and conceited set of men. Instead of minding their own business as farmers or manufacturers, they amused themselves chiefly with their own schismatic scholastic divinity.'[72]

For these people, religious obligations took precedence over all political commitments whatsoever. They saw it as their true task to rededicate Scotland to her 'national engagements' with God and to uphold 'Christ's rights in Scotland'. The sole test of Union, or any political measure, was whether it furthered this aim.[73] It would be hard to argue the treaty did. A leading Covenanter inside the Kirk, the Revd James Webster, minister of the Tolbooth in Edinburgh, rejected the draft as a 'manifold breach of the

Solemn League', where in the first article Scots had sworn to 'reform England in worship and government'. Since Union was to comprehend two national religious establishments, there would be 'an eternal embargo upon all such endeavours'.[74]

Webster's hard line found an echo among others by no means to be dismissed as backwoodsmen. Wodrow was, on the contrary, a scholar of 'curiosity and Athenian spirit',[75] member of an international intellectual community. He desponded at Union too: 'I have a great many melancholy thoughts of living to see this ancient kingdom made a province, and not only our religious and civil liberty lost, but lost irrevocably, and this is the most dismal aspect any incorporating Union has to me, that it puts matters past help.' In 1572, 1638 and 1688, he recalled, Presbyterians had managed to get their lost rights restored, 'but now, once lost, ever lost'.[76] Nor were the clerical misgivings always so narrowly religious. The Revd James Hodges, minister of a Presbyterian congregation in London, was one taking a more political line, if still on a stark contrast between the English 'slackness of ecclesiastical discipline, drinking in of false doctrines and spreading of erroneous opinions' and the Scottish resolve to hold 'Satan's kingdom' under 'powerful and awful checks'.[77] Hodges warned Scotland that Union with such a sinful and depraved nation as England would call down a divine judgment. Whatever safeguards might be written into the treaty, a British Parliament was bound to create one British Church or cause woe for the Scots by trying to. So Hodges thought federal Union, if any, was preferable.[78] The old spirit of Presbyterian nationalism lived yet in him.

Now came its last fling before it was to die away harmlessly during the eighteenth century. Presbyterianism had at this juncture been re-established in Scotland just sixteen years and its defensiveness still showed. Hence the fears which, once they burst to the surface on publication of the treaty, politicians found themselves obliged to assuage as an urgent priority. When the commission of assembly first saw the articles of Union it recoiled in horror. It found in them not even minimal safeguards for Presbyterianism. Seafield wrote to Godolphin: 'There have been several addresses against the Union presented to the Parliament, but what troubles me most is that from the commission of the assembly, which declares the Union inconsistent with their principles.' Mar underlined the point: 'One thing I must say for the Kirk, that if the Union fail it is owing to them.'[79]

❦

Yet militant Presbyterians were not running the Church of Scotland. Wodrow, for example, might have been of a calibre to join the men who were – but he always declined to move from his backwater in Renfrewshire (though it was no idyll) to Edinburgh or even Glasgow, where he might have made a difference at national level to the politics of the Kirk. It has for most of its history been kept in order by cautious clergymen in the capital who, while far from impious, take this world at least as seriously as the next, on a priority of maintaining the religious establishment by accommodation to the civil power where feasible. A *curiosum* of Presbyterianism is that, so long as not established it erupts in revolt and rage, yet once established it turns as douce and docile as can be.

The men in charge of the Church of Scotland were all for Union. That held true of every Moderator of the General Assembly during the years covered here: in 1702, the Revd David Cuthbertson of St Cuthbert's, though he once had been a Covenanter; in 1703, the Revd George Meldrum of the Tron, also professor of divinity at the University of Edinburgh; in 1704, the Revd Thomas Wilkie of the Canongate; in 1705, the evergreen Revd William Carstares; in 1706, the Revd William Wishart of South Leith. Venerable figures, some the victims of persecution long ago, they did command genuine personal authority and could sway doubters. It was probably on account of their efforts that Lord Selkirk at length complained to his brother, the Duke of Hamilton: 'I am extremely scandalised with the Presbyterian ministers . . . for several who both prayed and preached against the Union are now come over to the measure'.[80]

Among the clique in control of the Kirk, Carstares had acquired or assumed special eminence. It would have been easy enough for him to treat his appointment in 1703 to the post of principal at the University of Edinburgh – a post soon joined with the parochial charge of Greyfriars – as a sort of lap of honour after his years close to the heart of royal government under William of Orange. But Carstares set with no less energy and creativity about his academic duties. He put into permanent form a provisional arrangement for diverting former bishops' rents to finance the four Scottish universities. At Edinburgh in particular, he mended relations with the town council, damaged by frequent disputes with this municipal college over its right to elect professors. He not only reformed and ran the place but also himself gave weekly lectures and saw to the discipline of the rowdy students, while not neglecting parochial duties either. Hamilton called Carstares a 'bishoprick'[81] – yet no man did more to make Edinburgh a cradle of Enlightenment.

Carstares took the lead in delicate adjustment of the Church of Scotland to Union – and, more important, *vice versa*. He could rely on his clique in Edinburgh ('the most grave and judicious ministers here'), for those with reservations were ready to swallow them. All along he pulled secular strings as well. He had kept in touch with the commissioners for Union – for example, urging Loudoun to scotch rumours that ministers as a body disapproved of the negotiations: 'So far as I can observe, they trouble none with their opinion or advice as to what should be the nature of the Union, but leave that to those whose proper work is to adjust it.'[82] His reward came in the fact that continued establishment of a Presbyterian Kirk was taken as read, by the English too, and the assurance in the treaty of the Hanoverian succession would keep the biggest threat to it at bay. It then fell to Carstares to head off a clash between the treaty as it had been written and the conflicting claims of Presbyterian nationalism, made flesh in young hotheads preaching against the betrayal of Scotland to English apostates.

It was not a time for the Kirk to hang back. The week after the treaty had been published, the commission of assembly drew up a wish-list of safeguards. Seafield saw that 'without some security to the Church the whole Presbyterians will be dissatisfied'.[83] As if to underline the point to London, Defoe was reporting that 'Church men in particular are going mad. The parsons are out of their wits and those who at first were brought over, and pardon me some of them my converts, their country brethren being now come in are all gone back and to be brought over by no persuasion'. He took a personal hand as self-appointed delegate of English dissenters to the Scots clergy, urging that defence of the entire Protestant interest in Britain counselled passage of the treaty. Meanwhile the commission of assembly set October 18 as a national day of prayer in the light of 'the great and weighty affairs now in agitation'. On October 22 it sent out a circular asking presbyteries to fix another day for 'solemn public prayer, fasting and humiliation'. At a special service in St Giles' on October 31, Ministers of the government assembled with members of the clique in charge of the Kirk to pray for divine guidance. They needed it.[84]

From the points made by the commission of assembly, three stuck out. First, as Seafield tried to explain to a bemused Godolphin, it was 'contrary to the Covenant that the bishops sit in the Parliament'. The commission wanted to dig in its heels over this, or at least call for some guarantee against the baleful parliamentary influence of English prelates. But the government of Scotland could not legislate for England, and any effort to build more elaborate religious conditions into the treaty might kill it off. Seafield had to argue again and again to his countrymen that 'it is most reasonable to leave it entire to the Parliament of England to secure the Church there'.[85]

Presbyterians had another bone to pick, with the English sacramental test. Hamilton jumped in to condemn it as 'an inequality, whereby Scotsmen are barred from employments in England, but Englishmen are not barred from employments in Scotland'.[86] That was not just a niggle. A prospect of the treaty more mouth-watering to Scotsmen than to Englishmen lay in its opening public office to all citizens of Great Britain. Yet there was a hitch: such office in England remained open only to those who took communion in her established Church under the Test Act of Charles II which, to be sure, dissenters had learned to get round by occasional conformity. This sort of pragmatic artifice did not appeal to the Caledonian cast of mind. Scots moving south would be subject to the test, but might not wish to take an Anglican communion and perhaps might not be admitted to it. Still, assuming they were members of the Kirk, they could not be defined as dissenters; on the contrary, they belonged to an established Church themselves. It seemed, then, that loyal Presbyterians might be held ineligible for office in England: what sort of Union was that? One answer would have been to declare communion in the Church of Scotland as effective for Scotsmen seeking office in England as communion in the Church of England would be for Englishmen in Scotland. This proved too logical for the English. They could not be pushed beyond conceding that the sole valid religious test in Scotland should be the Kirk's Confession of Faith. Their own dissenters lived with the test, which did not do them too much harm. Scots would have to put up with it as well.

A third Presbyterian cavil was with the chance the British Parliament might legislate toleration in Scotland – meaning of Episcopalians. Webster of the Tolbooth in Edinburgh said: 'A legal toleration in Scotland will be very prejudicial to this Church and nation. Every thinking man knows that such a toleration will certainly follow on the Union, and 'tis as certain that it will bring along with it very mischievous effects, and have a malign influence on all the branches of our Reformation.' On this point the militants did approach closer to the clique in charge of the Kirk. Meldrum in particular ranted and raved at any hint of toleration, blaming Episcopalians for his own deposition as rector of Marischal College, Aberdeen, back in 1681. In aims and outlook different from Carstares, he was yet a definite Scottish type, not a discreet backrooom boy but a diligent manufacturer of grievances: for the guidance of the public he had just published a manifesto for sneaks and spies on 'the lawfulness of inform-ing against vicious and profane behaviour before the courts of immor-ality'. But Carstares, free of such defensive intransigence, knew no English guarantee against toleration could be won anyway. Presbyterians would just have to take the matter on trust. In fact, in 1712 their fears would come true, when the British Parliament passed a Toleration Act for Scotland, a deliberate Tory provocation. Even then it would neither revive the Episcopalians nor fatally erode the established status of the Kirk.[87]

In sum, Carstares and his colleagues had not got far towards meeting the technical Presbyterian objections to the treaty. His line to his reverend brethren was reported like this: 'Our Church did not fare too well in the old days when ministers were overmuch involved in politics. Civil administration is best carried on by the king and his Parliaments. We churchmen should leave the job to them and get on with our own, religion and the cure of souls entrusted to us.'[88] But an old man's sage advice was in danger of being drowned out by the public clamour. Mar wrote to Godolphin: 'The humour in the country against the treaty or Union is much increased of late . . . the ministers preaching up the danger of the kirk is a principal cause of it.'

℘

Uproar had broken out as soon as the treaty's terms became known, with little need of incitement from pulpits. In taverns, coffee-shops and streets, people were heard 'all exclaiming against the Union, and speaking very free language concerning the promoters of it'.[89] In Edinburgh the crowd had in recent times assumed a political role in history, almost consciously, like crowds in other European capitals. It stemmed from a medieval tradition but here took a modern turn in 1688, the winter of the Revolution, when the crowd mobbed Ministers and aspired to hold the government of Scotland to account, much as the crowd in Paris would do after 1789. More recently the people of Edinburgh had forced the judicial murder of Captain Green, and now they meant to stop Union. A law-abiding observer felt shocked at the 'disorderly and insolent convocations, and gathering of commons, filling the streets with clamour and confusion, and insulting not only peaceable persons but also some of the members of our high and honourable court of Parliament, presuming to threaten and invade them in their very dwelling-houses'.[90]

Public order in the capital was the task of the town-guard, wheezing old soldiers who now, not for the first time, showed themselves useless in a crisis. They were nowhere to be seen when the mob hammered on the barred and bolted door of Parliament House. Instead the government had to summon regular troops from the Castle. Horse-guards came clattering down under the Duke of Argyll to occupy the High Street and Parliament Close. Inside the chamber the opposition denounced the deployment as tyrannical. Annandale intoned: 'Shall we, who live in a free kingdom, put up with this barbarous restriction even before we have agreed to join our kingdom to another? This Union spells death to our nation's liberty, but not until it is passed into law should we be ringing our Parliament with troops.' Yet most members, not wishing to be roughed up or worse, supported a proclamation to condemn the riots as 'contrary to the very being and constitution of government, and destructive of the chief ends thereof, the safety and security of men's lives and fortunes'.[91]

Still, with nobody willing or able to do more to stop them, riots became daily events. They were often sparked off by Hamilton as he made his way back and forth between the Parliament and Holyrood amid a rowdy though still good-humoured throng, 'shouting and crying out, God bless his grace for standing up against the Union, and appearing for his country and the like'. Having worked themselves up into patriotic mood they would turn nasty when Queensberry's coach galloped past with horse-guards in front and panting footmen behind, these then the targets for volleys of stones from onlookers and 'all the insults, reproaches and indignities offered him that they durst'.[92] The word 'indignities' was a euphemism for the 'flooers o' Edinburgh', turds lying about streets and closes after being thrown from high windows of tenements with no other sanitation. Upper echelons of society did not usually deign to venture forth on foot. Now they had to walk rather than draw the mob's fury against their carriages.[93] That went on for weeks. In the Parliament, Lord Provost Johnstone was, on November 19, summoned to the bar of the house to answer 'why nothing was done against them who were prisoners for the last mob' – meaning the one which had attacked his own house, whence he fled and left his wife to face it. There was not much he could say.

Meanwhile, on November 6, disorders broke out in Glasgow as well. They were sparked off by a fiery sermon from the minister of the Tron, the Revd James Clark, exhorting his flock to put no trust in Parliaments or princes but to be 'up and be valiant for the city of our God!'[94] The next day a new Lord Provost, John Aird, was walking towards the cross for a coffee when he found himself accosted by merchants and tradesmen demanding the town council should send a nationalist address to the Parliament. He refused for himself, but said he would have no objection if others drew up an address. Glaswegians thought this not good enough: 'Within a short time there was a great confluence of people about the coffeehouse, young lads and women of no good lives, and with stones brake all the windows and came searching for the provost who had escaped, and went to divers houses and to his own which they spoiled and brake the windows.' In the end Aird had to get out of town to Edinburgh. He came back after a few days but was forced to flee again. In Glasgow, too, the mob had the run of the streets for more than a month.[95]

Glasgow was a Presbyterian stronghold, but a scary turn of events came when Jacobites – 'those from the country, demanding money and arms' – arrived to join in the incitement. A working alliance between them and the locals would make a formidable nationalist force, Jacobite and Presbyterian at once. There was a chance here of turning riot into rebellion, seized on by two men of the people, Findlay and Montgomery (Lockhart calls them 'mean artificers' and does not trouble to give their full names).[96] They led the mob in an attack on the tolbooth, where arms were stored. It failed, but they all set out for Edinburgh anyway. Along their route lay Kilsyth, a weaving village and hotbed of Covenanters. They paused to wait for supporters to arrive from the country around. Not enough did. Meanwhile news came that a force of 200 dragoons had left the capital on the way to nip this uprising in the bud. The Glaswegians turned south to Hamilton, another old citadel of fighting Presbyterianism, where a greater rebel force was supposed to be mustered.

Nearby stood Hamilton Palace. The duke's mother, doughty Dowager Duchess Anne, was in residence. A patriot, she was urging Presbyterians to resist Union. But she could find no common cause with Jacobites; on the contrary, she detested them. Findlay and Montgomery, drawing a blank here too, fell back on Glasgow where with other ringleaders they were arrested once the troops arrived. These did not stay long. Riots broke out again as soon as they left. A rattled Ministry blamed the bailies and threatened to suspend the town council unless it at once restored order. It imposed a curfew on 'women, boys, young men and servants'.[97] The disorder died down yet seemed to exert an effect, if we may trust

Defoe's testimony. He reported to Harley as the dragoons rode west that 'these tumults and terrors have brought all the mischiefs on and 'tis impossible to avoid the amendments' – amendments, he means, to the Treaty of Union by then on its way through the Parliament.

Ripples ran through the Covenanting hinterland. In Lanarkshire, at Shotts, Lesmahagow and Stonehouse, handbills appeared urging a march on Edinburgh by the people in arms, 'to disturb the Parliament'. Presbyterians were to gather and be 'ready on a call with ten days' provision'. Lockhart reported leaders of the people were meeting to form fighting units, to choose officers, to find horses and arms. Riots broke out at Kirkcudbright and other places right in the south.[98]

Then, on November 20, 300 armed men entered Dumfries. They fixed to the market-cross a call to arms: 'We are confident that the soldiers now in martial power have so much of the spirit of Scotsmen that they are not ambitious to be disposed of at the pleasure of another nation.' They denounced the politicians who 'shall presume to carry on the said Union by a supreme power over the belly of the generality of this nation'. They burned a copy of the treaty as 'utterly destructive of the nation's independency, Crown rights and our constitute laws, both civil and sacred'.[99] Townsfolk joined in, crying 'Thus may all traitors perish!' The government had lurid reports that 5,000 men were occupying Dumfries, with 7,000 more bivouacked roundabout ready for a march on the capital. A proclamation in the queen's name condemned the 'insulting to magistrates, attacking and assaulting the business of our peaceable subjects, and marching in formed bodies through the country, and into our burghs, and insolently burning, in the face of the sun and presence of the magistrates, the articles of the treaty betwixt our two kingdoms'.[100] But in the event it all amounted to little. The supposed leader, James Cunningham of Eckatt, was an old soldier, a survivor of Darien, who ever since had scratched a bare living and was now in the pay of the government. He would get £100 with command of a company of foot as his reward for having flushed out what disaffection there was in these parts.

Glasgow abuts on the Highlands too, with the hills visible from the streets. To the west, Dunbartonshire ran up amid mountain and flood, and farms in its lower grasslands were often raided for cattle by clansmen. A member for the county, William Cochrane of Kilmaronock, factor to the Marquis of Montrose and a relation by marriage of Bluidy Claverhouse, offered funds to foment rebellion and sought to liaise with Atholl and Lockhart. To the north of Glasgow, Stirlingshire contained villages full of fierce Presbyterians but then fertile carses with often Jacobite lairds, merging further off into the territories of the clans. Bailies of the burgh of Stirling sent an address to the Parliament calling on it so to 'settle the state of this nation as the hopes of all popish pretenders whatsoever may be forever defeat', then 'maintain and support the true reformed Protestant religion, the government of this national Church as now by law established', finally linking both causes with 'the sovereignty and independency of this nation'.[101] In contrast to that Covenanting spirit the three members of the Parliament for the county of Stirling, James Graham of Buchlyvie, John Graham of Killearn and Robert Rollo of Powhouse were, according to the Duchess of Atholl, 'such violent Jacobites that they have never been at church since the Revolution'; she also dropped a dark hint that in the current crisis 'what was concerted was not stood to'. Another neighbour confirmed the trio 'never appeared much in the world' and were 'of very indifferent fortunes'.[102] Whatever the reason, they made no response to the nationalism of their constituents. An officer at Stirling Castle reported on December 4: 'This day at twelve o'clock I was standing near the cross of Stirling and there came some ruffians out . . . kindled a fire and threw the articles in it with several huzzas. The guard that is kept here is good for nothing but to raise tumults, for the whole town are every night drunk.'[103]

At the same time, back in Edinburgh, there seemed to be an 'unusual number of Highlanders around', or so Defoe thought. It made him nervous: 'They are all gentlemen, will take affront from no man, and insolent to the last degree . . . a man in his mountain habit, with a broad sword, target, pistol or perhaps two at his girdle, a dagger and a staff, walking down the street as upright as haughty as if he were a lord, and withal driving a cow'.[104] But the question how the Highlands reacted to the prospect of Union is otherwise bedevilled by lack of documentation, for their language was Gaelic and their culture oral.

One clear voice from the North was bardic. The greatest Gaelic poet of the age, Iain Lom, aged over eighty, had been hymning the bloody exploits of his clan, the MacDonalds, ever since they followed the Marquis of Montrose in wasting the rival Campbells in 1645; his praise of their victory then at the Battle of Inverlochy was especially gruesome. He wrote a poem against the Union where he states he witnessed a gathering of the clans held to contest it, at some date and place unspecified. He blames Viscount Dupplin for being bribed by the government not to bring orders from the

Duke of Atholl that would have sent the Highland host south, first to Stirling to seize this gateway to the Lowlands.[105] Something of the sort may be confirmed by a report from Mar on October 29 mentioning stories, which he hoped were 'brags', that the nation would rise and never let the Parliament finish legislating Union: 'I'm credibly informed that the Duke of Atholl's men are to muster this week.'[106]

There seems also to have been some more formidable plan for clansmen to join with Covenanters in a tryst at Hamilton Palace, whence they would march on Edinburgh. According to Lockhart the idea fell through because the Duke of Hamilton, leader-in-waiting and prospective link between the two forces, cancelled the orders just before the appointed day; 500 men still turned up, but as a *coup d'état* it all fell flat. Of Hamilton this is easy to believe, not least because he was in touch with Godolphin. Amid the unrest, on November 14, he sent to London a typically ambiguous letter: 'A good Union should be with the hearts of the people; but as this has been managed, I may take liberty to say, our people have taken great umbrage at it, which nothing but time or altering the nature of the things seems a remedy.' He wants Godolphin to do something, but quite what remains obscure: 'I must acknowledge the ferment increases, and I pray God, speedy measures may be taken to allay the minds of the people, who are under the greatest apprehensions, from what is now before us.' Seafield noted with truth that Hamilton 'knows not how to unite his pairtie'. What the duke did now know – more to the point and on the word of Colonel Hooke – was that France would never support his claim to the Crown of Scotland. Given this indecision and incoherence at the head of resistance to Union, it was easy for the Parliament on November 29 to pass an Act forbidding all assembly in arms during its current session: and to get itself, more or less, obeyed.[107]

If a *coup d'état* never happened, it does not mean there had been no chance of one. English counter-measures give an opposite impression. Secretary Johnstone informed George Baillie of Jerviswood about the nervous mood in London: 'Orders are sent down to the Ministry to dispatch the business of the Union one way or other, and to assure them that there shall be troops at hand on the borders and in Ireland, and from Flanders too, if they need them, and it's said ships of war too are ordered to your coasts.'[108] Invasion of Scotland would also have found some internal support from creatures of the Ministry, at least in offering *points d'appui*. From Edinburgh Castle its commander, Leven, wrote to Godolphin: 'I humbly conceive it would be of great advantage to have some forces in the North of England near the border, for the troops here are few in number.' Lockhart confirms there were 'not 7000 standing forces in all Britain, of which these that were in Scotland were so dissatisfied with the Union that everybody knew, and the officers had acquainted the government, that they could not be trusted'.[109]

English forces indeed mobilised on the border. At the end of November the Scottish Secretary-depute, Sir David Nairne, told Mar of the presence of 'three regiments of foot, and in the North of Ireland, three of horse, one of foot, and one of dragoons, and they have the necessary orders; but all relating to this affair must be kept very private'.[110] Nairne wrote again from London a fortnight later: 'There is 800 horse marched from this to the borders by advice of the Duke of Marlborough, for he thinks they will be more useful than thrice their number of foot.'[111] The strain threatened to get too much for Queensberry, yet Godolphin and Marlborough urged him to hang on without calling in English troops. They were right to keep cool. Despite rumours of risings, only local disturbances took place – and never that revolutionary alliance of Lowland Covenanters and Highland Jacobites which might, by very reason of its disparate nature, have saved the independence of a disparate nation.

CHAPTER 6

ε𝕤

1707

*The Bass Rock, sentinel of the Firth of Forth and
prison of Covenanters*

'Auld sang'

∽

In London the day of the Union, May 1, 1707, was one of rejoicing. John Clerk of Penicuik had arrived there as a member of the official Scottish delegation to celebrate the inauguration of the United Kingdom. He found the English not just welcoming but overjoyed to see him and his colleagues. They had been lionised at Berwick, Newcastle, Durham and further stages on the road south. Especially James Douglas, Duke of Queensberry, dubbed the Union Duke and soon to be Duke of Dover in the peerage of Great Britain, 'was complimented and feasted wherever he went, and when he came within 20 miles of London the whole city turned out to meet him'. On April 16 he made a public entry into the English capital with 46 coaches and several hundred horsemen. That night all the members of the Ministry fêted him, led by Sidney Godolphin, Lord Treasurer. Of other Englishmen close to events, only the spy, Daniel Defoe, was taking a more jaundiced view. From Edinburgh he had reported to his controller, Robert Harley: 'The great men are posting to London for places and honours, every man full of his own merit and afraid of everyone near him: I never saw so much trick, sham, pride, jealousy and cutting of friends' throats as there is among noblemen.' Noting how the contagion had spread down the social scale too, Defoe concluded: 'In short money will do anything here.'[1]

Before he set off from his lodgings in Whitehall to the jollifications on May 1, Hugh Campbell, Earl of Loudoun, no longer joint Scottish Secretary (for that job was now abolished), posted a letter he had written the night before to the Revd John Stirling, principal of the University of Glasgow. Loudoun was reporting back Queen Anne's response to a loyal address from the Church of Scotland, just voted by its General Assembly. He had in person handed over the address 'which Her Majesty received very graciously and ordered me to renew to you the assurances of the continuation of Her Majesty's protection and favour. I am very glad to know by the accounts I have from you and others that there appeared in the proceedings of the assembly so much moderation and calmness.'² This had been quite a relief.

Of May 1 itself Clerk of Penicuik would recall: 'That day was solemnised by Her Majesty and those who had been members of both Houses of Parliament with the greatest splendour. A very numerous procession accompanied the queen to the cathedral church of St Paul, at least 300 or 400 coaches.' Godolphin told the Duke of Marlborough: 'The streets were fuller of people than I have seen them upon any occasion of that kind.' The Bishop of Oxford, the Revd William Talbot, gave the sermon on a text of Psalm 133, 'Behold how pleasant it is, for brethren to dwell together in unity.' Prayers of thanksgiving followed and 'a fine piece of music closed the solemnity'. Clerk found 'real joy and satisfaction in the citizens of London, for they were terribly apprehensive of confusions from Scotland in case the Union had not taken place. That whole day was spent in feasting, ringing of bells and illuminations.'³

Edinburgh, by contrast, seemed in no mood for celebrations. But the Union Duke's eldest son, James, held one of his own at Queensberry House in the Canongate, also with feasting. This heir apparent to the ducal title, to which in the end he would never be permitted to succeed, suffered from gigantism and was a homicidal maniac kept under lock and key at all times. In the absence of his father, however, he managed to escape. He caught and killed a kitchen-boy, then roasted him on a spit. The deed was discovered as he sat down to his horrid repast. Scots said it was judgment on the father for his part in the Union.

Official gestures, at least, were made towards marking the occasion in Edinburgh. In the morning the bells of St Giles' rang out the tune, 'Why should I be sad on my wedding day?' Guns later fired a salute from the Castle. That was about it. People paid more heed to news of whales beached at Kirkcaldy across the Firth of Forth. A pod of the species known to Scots as the ca'ing whale, each about 25 feet long, had arrived 'roaring, plunging and threshing upon one another, to the great terror of all who heard the same'. Even today whales penetrate the firth, apparently because they have taken a wrong turning; in despair of finding a way out to open sea again, they kill themselves by swimming on to dry land. A contemporary account says: 'Thirty-five of them were run ashore upon the sands of Kirkcaldy, where they made yet a more dreadful roaring and tossing when they found themselves aground, insomuch that the earth trembled.' Fifers murmured that this, too, was an ill omen of Union.⁴

The air seemed full of foreboding in more distant parts of the country as well. Many Presbyterian parishes declared the day of the Union to be one of fasting and humiliation. From another point of view, up in the Highlands, the Bard of Keppoch, Iain Lom, could not restrain himself from lamenting the blow to the Jacobite cause. It is hard to date exactly his poem *Òran an Aghaidh an Aonaidh*, Song against the Union. But, assuming he had composed it by May 1, he would surely then have been singing it round the foot of Glen Spean, where his chief had his seat. The bard shows his contempt for a corrupt pseudo-Jacobite, Viscount Dupplin, *Dh'èirich rosgal ad chridhe 'n uair chual' thu tighinn an t-òr ud*, 'turbulence rose in your heart when you heard that gold coming'. As for the Duke of Queensberry he is *mar fhear-stràice cur thairis*, 'a measurer raking off the surplus from the bushel', and as for the Duke of Hamilton he is just *dùbailt*, duplicitous. Iain Lom reserves his bitterest venom for another renegade Jacobite, the Earl of Seaforth: *Is dearbh gu leaghainn an t-òr dhuit, a staigh air faochaig do chlaighinn gus an cas e do bhòtainn*, 'truly I would melt gold for you, and inject it into the shell of your skull till it would reach your boots'. The bard consoles himself that rebellion must be imminent against their betrayal of the nation.[5]

Back in Edinburgh, across the Canongate from Queensberry House, Harry Maule was staying at Panmure House, his family's residence in the capital; years later, after its sale had been forced, it would become home to the father of economics, Adam Smith. Maule was a foe of Union too, who as member for Brechin had walked out of the Convention in 1689 when it declared James VII forfeit of the Crown. Maule never wavered in devotion to the Jacobite cause either. In 1715 that loyalty would send him into exile, but meanwhile a gentleman like him had time on his hands. On the day of the Union he wrote to the Earl of Mar, a neighbour from Angus, saying the people of the capital seemed morose at the event, if not indifferent. Maule was also the author of a *History of the Picts*, published a year before. By modern standards it had little scholarly value, though it offered one proposition novel at the time yet today accepted as the standard view: that ancient Caledonians, Britons and Picts had been of a single race, so Scotland could boast an indigenous stock dating far back into the mists of time, before any written record.

∾

The publication of Maule's work was a cultural event of note. It marked a further stage in Scotland's Jacobite or Episcopalian tradition, which rested on a claim that the country had been from time immemorial not just occupied by a single race but also ruled by a single royal line, from Feargus mac Erc in 330 BC down to the Stewarts of the present day. That tradition was defeated in a political sense in 1688, yet it continued to flourish on this cultural level: it can even be defined as the main bearer of Scottish culture for some way into the eighteenth century. Philistine Presbyterians, with their suspicion of secular learning, could not compete with it and did not want to.

Thomas Carlyle, the Victorian sage, once remarked that Scottish culture up to the Union and for quite a way beyond it had been in essentials French. The great literary controversy in France at the turn of the eighteenth century divided *les Anciens* from *les Modernes*. The former, cultural conservatives respecting the authority and example of classical letters, took up cudgels against the latter, who claimed autonomy for modern civilisation and justified it by an appeal to the concepts of progress and of natural law, which would equally become founding principles of the Scottish Enlightenment. Already that French controversy was finding a parallel in Scotland in variant guise, one aspect of which lay in the choice of linguistic vehicle for bearers of the culture, between a venerable Latinity or a vernacular Scots; the alien English of England would not do.

To the older generation of Maule's circle in Edinburgh there belonged Archibald Pitcairne, eminent not only as a surgeon and not only as a playwright in Scots but also as a poet in Latin; and then Sir Robert Sibbald, antiquarian and polymath, author of a *Scotia Illustrata* and many other Latin works. The tradition they represented had enough life left in it to carry over into a younger generation.

For example, Robert Freebairn was a publisher and editor, notably of the *History of Scotland* by Robert Lindsay, a humanist of the sixteenth century. Freebairn would issue a new edition in 1728 with a didactic introduction, picking out from it 'those great and good qualities' which 'ought to be employed in the public service' as a guide along 'rugged paths of virtue'. Here Renaissance and Enlightenment became linked. And there is a forward as well as a backward link. Freebairn, with some companions, formed the Easy Club, one of many clubs for serious debate and even more serious drinking which were to become vehicles of Enlightenment and which indeed adorn social life in Edinburgh right down to the twenty-first century. The Easy Club subsidised publication of Alan Ramsay's poetry, a bridge between the golden age of Scots literature and its modern revival.

Thomas Ruddiman had arrived in the capital from Aberdeen, bringing with him a blend of Jacobitism, Episcopalianism and passion for the classics typical of the culture of the north-east of Scotland. He sought to revive the Scots-Latin literature which had given the nation a European standing in the sixteenth century. Actually it was on its last legs, and his Scots rather than Latin accomplishments furnished him with his claim to fame. A protégé of Pitcairne, Ruddiman became keeper of the Advocates' Library, forerunner of the National Library of Scotland. He republished, under Freebairn's imprint, a translation into Scots of the *Aeneid* by Gavin Douglas, dating from 1513. To it Ruddiman added a long glossary which, as Freebairn remarks, 'may serve for a dictionary to the older Scottish language'. In his notes Ruddiman maintains that Middle Scots generated a classic corpus of works on a par with the Middle English literature of Geoffrey Chaucer or John Gower and displayed linguistic riches un-matched except by Greek or Latin, superior anyway to the weak, dilute quality of English. Ruddiman also suggests the living speech of the 'vulgar' is the modern representative of this Middle Scots. He added his stone to the cairn of literary prestige which Scots was again to erect by the late eighteenth century.

James Watson came of a nest of rare birds indeed, Orcadian Catholics. His father had moved to Aberdeen, being known in the city's couthy fashion as the Papist Printer. But the younger Watson spent all his working life in Edinburgh. He used the early newspapers in the capital to advertise for the manuscript or otherwise unknown Scots poetry he wanted to publish. He would produce three volumes of it between 1706 and 1711, his *Choice Collection of Comic and Serious Scots Poems*. This sets out what was still then known of the older Scottish literature, at risk of being lost because the royal court had long gone from Edinburgh and the Parliament, also a patron of culture on a modest scale, was preparing to follow. The preface boasts it is the first printed anthology of poems 'in our own native *Scots* dialect'. It, too, contributed to the vernacular revival which led on to the poetry of Alan Ramsay, Robert Ferguson and Robert Burns. Each delighted to find in Watson's collection traditional genres and metres with which to enrich his own work.

That line of intellectual descent shows how, as if by some intuition, Scotland prepared for her extinction as a state with revival of her culture. Indeed the Scots have endured, to the present, as a cultural community sustained by recurrent revivals, which also laid the foundation for their re-emergence as a political community 300 years later. Andrew Fletcher of Saltoun had said: 'If a man were permitted to make all the ballads, he need not care who should make the laws of a nation.'

❦

Fletcher seems to have stayed away from the Scots Parliament during its last few weeks of life after losing hope the Union could be stopped. Beyond New Year, 1707, records refer to just a single intervention by him. On January 20 the government proposed that the 16 peers for the House of Lords and 45 MPs for the House of Commons should be chosen from the present chamber, a tacit admission that election of them by the new constituencies would have been a gift to the opposition. Fletcher moved that no peer or eldest son of a peer should be eligible to sit for a county or burgh, with a view to restricting a little the influence of the unionist aristocracy. But his motion was defeated by 13 votes.[6]

The Patriot is said to have left Edinburgh, and probably Scotland, as soon as the Parliament was adjourned for the last time on March 25. Friends crowded round, begging him to stay. They asked, as he stood poised with a foot in the stirrup, 'Will you forsake this country?' He cast a cold eye on them and said, 'It is only fit for the slaves that sold it.' Then he swung into the saddle, spurred his horse and rode away.[7]

Fletcher went first to London. From there he wrote to David Gregory, who had worked out the Equivalent for the Treaty of Union. Gregory, professor of astronomy at Oxford, had earlier taught at Edinburgh, distinguishing himself as the first man in the British Isles to give public lectures on the revolutionary teachings of Sir Isaac Newton, another friend. Not content with mere exposition, the best of Newton's disciples lost no time in applying his findings to sundry sciences which started to develop much faster and to change human conceptions of reality. Gregory remodelled his own discipline in that way. He cast off its doctrinal past, its mumbo-jumbo of empyrean spheres and the like, to render it consistent with Newtonian physics. Vital to this was his interest in geometry, manifested in his edition of Euclid in 1703. In those changing conceptions of reality, geometry no longer served as just a formal exercise, a part it had played in western learning since antiquity. With Newton's revelation that physical bodies were related by mathematical law, geometry became a key to understanding the universe. In his turn, Gregory made it central to Scottish intellectual tradition. This, though, he had not stayed to develop himself. A royalist, he found life in Scotland too fraught after the Revolution, which was why he emigrated in 1692 to Oxford.

The letter from Fletcher to Gregory begins by referring to his interest in the design of St Paul's church in Covent Garden, London, and mentions a response from no less than Sir Christopher Wren to a related technical question concerning construction of some outbuildings at Saltoun. The letter continues: 'Dr Arbuthnot and I are very much obliged to you for your kind remembrance. We miss no opportunity of all grateful remembering you and hope to see you here for all that has happened, and if you are resolved not to come to London, I hope to see you at Saltoun.'[8] Arbuthnot was another Scottish émigré in the English capital, a fashionable physician, indeed personal doctor to Queen Anne, renowned also as wit, author and satirist. He boasted among his circle of friends Alexander Pope, John Gay and Jonathan Swift. Fletcher's sentiments showed he stood on terms with two Scotsmen moving in the highest literary and intellectual circles of London, the sort of people who could ask Wren for a building estimate. In keeping that kind of company Fletcher prefigured one aspect of the Enlightenment, its easy contacts with England entailing no sense of inferiority; the philosopher David Hume scarcely did better. Truly, the native roots of the Scottish Enlightenment go back far beyond 1707.

ɛʊ

The final session of the Scots Parliament had opened on October 3, 1706. Clerk of Penicuik would remember it in melodramatic terms: 'Never in the whole history of Britain had any event so stirred expectation. Everyone knew that on that Parliament depended the destiny of the island, the queen's authority, and the religion, prosperity, welfare, peace and security of the entire British people.'[9] Queensberry was again Lord High Commissioner. Having done all that might be asked of him to produce the Treaty of Union, he was the man most likely now to carry it. Anne had to swallow her personal dislike and political distrust, but this time she gave him more precise private instructions than before. He was to go all out to get the treaty through with as few changes as possible; any particular change should be referred to her. No other result than a Union of Parliaments would be acceptable. In case of deadlock Queensberry was to adjourn, and not for a moment entertain proposals for a federal Union or for the Hanoverian succession in lieu of the treaty. The security of the Church of Scotland, however, could be left to the Parliament.[10]

The Earl of Seafield carried on as Chancellor, with two Secretaries of State. The Earl of Loudoun, a soldier by profession, dealt with everything arising from the war, including foreign trade, and with taxation (which meant finding means for an empty Treasury to tick over), together with the Church and the universities, where he would be found 'abundantly civil and discreet'.[11] On the Earl of Mar, not a bright but a diligent fellow, devolved all other business. He took it on himself to help in daily management of the Parliament and to keep London informed of its debates, as of the general situation in Scotland.

When Mar conferred with Godolphin on prospects for the session, it was if anything in a downcast, diffident mood. He felt especially worried about the Lord Advocate, Sir James Stewart, the one member of the government hostile to the Union. Mar suggested Godolphin might write a letter to be shown to Stewart saying 'that the queen expects all in her service would act vigorously for the Union, else they cannot expect her favour, nor to continue in her service'. This kind of heavy hint usually brought people to heel, since she was the fount of patronage. Stewart's colleagues pressured him too. Yet 'notwithstanding of all the commissioners and the rest of the queen's servants can say to him, he continues of his own opinion, and argued against it to us all together'. If he had to resign, he answered, he would do it 'freely without any grudge'.[12]

Despite its misgivings, the government of Scotland was in fact managing to build a broader base than before. It could count on Queensberry's and on Argyll's factions, with rather less reliable support from the Squadrone Volante. Their *ménage à trois* was, to be sure, more marriage of convenience than love-match. This time round, Queensberry would maintain better discipline over the Court party. He was yet obliged to accept it could not control the Parliament, even in the alliance with Presbyterians which had carried the Act for a Treaty last time. Presbyterians, too, were learning the virtue of cohesion, less from experience of Argyll's erratic leadership than from realisation that in order to safeguard the Kirk they must take an active part in legislating any Union. As for the Squadrone, its claim to disinterested patriotism had grown threadbare but it still felt keen to reap rewards from holding the balance of power. This was what kept it together as a faction, when it might have been absorbed by another; in fact it hoped that way to win higher rewards at Westminster than it ever enjoyed in Edinburgh. Each party still kept an eye on the main chance, then, though with skilful handling might be persuaded to march in step with the others. All the same, the Court's managers felt by no means confident the Union would pass.

The queen did her best, as ever. Her message to the opening of the Parliament commended it in the most glowing terms, if with little regard to accuracy: 'The Union has long been desired by both nations, and we shall esteem it as the greatest glory of our reign to have it now perfected, being fully persuaded that it must prove the greatest happiness of our people.' She forecast not only that peace would follow but also that religion, liberty and property would be secured, while strength, riches and trade would increase 'and by the Union the whole island being joined in affection and free from all apprehension of different interests, will be enabled to resist all its enemies, support the Protestant interest everywhere and maintain the liberties of Europe'. Further, she renewed her assurances for 'the government of the Church as by law established in Scotland'.

After the queen's letter had been read Queensberry spoke in his own capacity as Lord High Commissioner, and in his turn praised the terms of the Union. Seafield next stood up to call them 'just, honourable and advantageous'. He concluded: 'I am hopeful that you will proceed to the consideration of the articles of the treaty in such a manner as shall bring it to the desired conclusion, and it cannot but tend to the lasting honour of this session of Parliament to have so happily finished this most weighty and important matter.'[13]

❧

The Parliament got down to work on the treaty as soon as it could, on October 12, 1706. Many members, according to Lockhart, thought this 'too hasty a procedure in so momentous an affair'. Sir Thomas Burnett, Presbyterian member from the Mearns, moved they should first consult their constituents now they had sight of the articles of Union. There 'arose a hot debate whether or not the Parliament without particular instructions from their constituents could alter the constitution of the government'. Ministers said 'the members had ample commissions to do all things for the good of the country'. But, came the retort, no word of Union had been uttered at the first election of this Parliament in 1702: 'besides it was so long ago that it was not strange the barons, freeholders and burghs expected their representatives to advise with them; and since they were not allowed to have a new election, that thus their sense of this weighty affair might be known in Parliament'.[14]

On October 15, after the usual procedural wrangles, the house resolved by a hefty majority of 66 to proceed to a first reading of the treaty. Just for a change the government of Scotland had succeeded in launching a parliamentary session with a show of strength. A euphoric Seafield wrote to Godolphin: 'What occurred yesterday gives so good hopes of success that we thought it necessary to acquaint you with this by flying packet.' Seafield felt especially pleased at the conduct of the Squadrone. Its stance had been in doubt but it voted with the government to give a majority much bigger than expected.[15]

Still, battle was not joined yet on the substance of the treaty. The government thought it preferable for the house to spend a week or two digesting the articles before definitive votes on any of them. That would give both sides a chance to size each other up. It would allow time for waverers to be won over. Anyway, there was little point in trying to move forwards in advance of an Act of Security for the Kirk; without that, the project of Union could go no further. This process, as set out in the last chapter, continued yet. Not till November 1 did the Earl of Marchmont, leader of the parliamentary Presbyterians, signal success for the efforts to square the Church of Scotland. Such was the implication of his motion on that day for 'the Parliament now [to] proceed to the further and more particular consideration of the Articles of Union, in order to approve them or not, and to begin with and read the first article'.[16]

&

The first article provided for the Union of Scotland and England into one kingdom, Great Britain. Here was the principle of the whole treaty: if it passed, surely the rest should fall into place. Yet it was not a straightforward matter. The opposition raised two caveats even to proceeding with the article. First, there was no sense in a vote on it till all details had been adjusted. And yet again, many members wanted a chance to consult their constituents. Debate on that took hours, so was adjourned till the morning. Then a militant Presbyterian, Walter Stewart of Pardovan, member for Linlithgow, urged the house to make certain the Church of Scotland was out of danger before it dealt with any article of the treaty – this in doubtless disparaging reference to the imminent appearance of the Act of Security for the Kirk, which he was to think too feeble. But the house remained unimpressed. It voted by a majority of 36 to move on to the first article.[17]

The opening debate on November 2 proved to be the best of the whole session. It inspired several good speeches yet the crux came in a four-way exchange, on the unionist side with William Seton of Pitmedden at length and the Earl of Marchmont succinctly, on the nationalist side with the Duke of Hamilton at his most eloquent and Lord Belhaven still more memorably.

'What!' demanded Hamilton, 'shall we in half an hour yield what our forefathers maintained with their lives and fortunes for many ages? . . . Where are the Douglases and the Campbells?' Well, one Douglas, the Duke of Queensberry, was sitting in the chair as Lord High Commissioner and one Campbell, the Duke of Argyll, was aiding and abetting his scheme of Union. Hamilton found so much to harp on here that, in Lockhart's words, he 'outdid himself in pathetical remonstrance'.[18]

That set a scene for the rhetorical fireworks which followed. Seton, for his part, poured scorn on the main alternative to the Union, Hanoverian succession under limitations: 'I conceive such a state of limitations to be no better for Scotland than if it were entirely separated from England, in which case there's little appearance of procuring any remedy to our present circumstances.' He cited the examples of England, France and Spain which had to their own good transformed their disjointed provinces into unitary states. But his argument hinged more on economics: 'This nation being poor, and without force to protect its commerce, cannot reap great advantage by it, till it partake of the trade and protection of some powerful neighbour nation, that can communicate both these . . . By this Union, we will have access to all the advantages in commerce the English enjoy.'[19]

Belhaven answered with a speech which has been held up as a masterpiece, though more to the taste of his own age than of ours. It built up its effect by striking tableaux of a future Scotland: 'I think I see a free and independent kingdom delivering up that which all the world hath been fighting for since the days of Nimrod, to wit, a power to manage their own affairs by themselves, without the assistance and counsel of any other.' Proceeding to religion, Belhaven went on: 'I think I see a national Church, founded upon a rock, secured by a Claim of Right, hedged and fenced about by the strictest and pointedest legal sanctions that sovereignty could contrive, voluntarily descending into a plain, upon an equal level with Jews, Papists, Socinians, Arminians, Anabaptists and other sectaries.' Turning to address his peers he said, 'I think I see the noble and honourable peerage of Scotland now divested of their followers and vassalages and put upon such an equal foot with their vassals that I think I see a petty English exciseman receive more homage and respect than what was paid formerly to their quondam Maccallanmores.' He depicted in turn a degradation of barons and burghs, judges and gentry, soldiers and sailors, tradesmen and farmers, before rising to a plangent climax: 'But above all, my lord, I think I see our ancient mother Caledonia, like Caesar sitting in the midst of our senate, ruefully looking round her, covering herself with the royal garment, attending the fatal blow and breathing out her last with *et tu quoque mi fili*.' Belhaven recalled the ancient Roman loathing of parricide yet declared patricide, murder of a native land, to be an even fouler crime. The Union would benefit England while destroying Scotland, for it would uphold the English constitution just as it bound the Scottish one to 'regulations or annihilations'.

Belhaven then burst out, 'Good God! Is this an entire surrender?' He asked for time to shed a silent tear. After a pause, while the house chatted through his stagey gesture, he resumed in a less emotional tone, arguing that it was folly to agree to the Union before discussing all the articles and moving that the house should begin with the fourth, on free trade.[20]

Impressively as the speech still springs from the page, there must even then have been something about the delivery to provoke ribaldry from certain corners of the chamber: 'it did not quite hold the line', says a modern scholar, 'between the sublime and the ridiculous'. Once Belhaven sat down, it was the sober-sided Marchmont that deflated him with a quip quoting the Book of Samuel: 'Behold, he dreamed, but lo! when he awoke, he found it was a dream.' Seafield dismissed Belhaven's performance too. He reported to Godolphin that it was 'contrived to incense the common people' and 'had no great influence in the house'. But the excitement of the great debate, launched at last, sustained members' stamina and the speeches went on for nine hours: 'It grew at last so late and everybody faint with hunger, for most of us had eat none that day.' There was no hope of bringing the first article to a vote in a single sitting.[21]

A couple of days later, on November 4, debate resumed. Perhaps the government smelled trouble. Anyway, it adopted a stratagem which it was to employ again and again over the next two months, making a tactical concession which ran a risk of compromising a greater issue, just hoping for the best that it would not: by and large the Ministry proved skilful or lucky enough to come through with the treaty unscathed in essentials. At this outset the opposition made a telling point that there was little sense in voting the first article before the rest. The response from the Lord Clerk Register, Sir James Murray of Philiphaugh, man of business to Queensberry, granted that if subsequent articles were rejected, then agreement to the first would be null and void, or rather, that no vote on any article should be of binding effect till all had been approved – which raised a chance that the entire treaty might be defeated if the opposition could somehow gather enough strength to vote down even a single article. At the least, a tactical concession might open doors to concessions of substance. Anne's counsel of intransigence to Queensberry was already coming apart.

The debate continued and at the end of it the first article passed: Mar said of the result, 116 votes to 83, that it was 'a good plurality but fewer than we expected'. The biggest support came from the nobles, 46 for and 21 against. The other estates were more evenly split: counties, 37 for and 33 against; burghs, 33 for and 29 against. The total unionist vote corresponded to the combined strength of the three factions supporting the government, except that a couple of members from the Squadrone dissented. If the whole Squadrone had done the same, the article would have been lost and the treaty would have fallen. The latest and best analysis of this crucial division shows the unionist ranks to have been composed in the first place of 57 consistent supporters of the Court. Another 25 members (most in the Squadrone) had crossed the floor from previous opposition. A further 34 abstaining in earlier sessions now rallied to the government, mainly hangers-on of Queensberry's faction with their various disgruntlements, meanwhile being allayed by fair means or foul. Of 83 votes in opposition, just 43 came from consistent nationalists, so there was consolidation on that side too. The number of abstainers totalled 29.[22]

This last group was more significant than might be supposed. Many appear to have been not mere absentees but abstainers on principle, so to speak – people who were in the chamber on November 4 or who could have been if they had wanted. Such was the Lord Advocate, Sir James Steuart, present but not voting after his pact with ministerial colleagues that this was how to deal with their discord on the Union. The Earl of Aberdeen, a Jacobite coming to the conclusion that only the Union could save Scotland, withdrew to avoid the embarrassment of revealing his position. The Earl of Bute was another Jacobite yet follower of

Queensberry who escaped his own dilemma by not turning up. The philosopher Lord Forbes of Pitsligo had retired to a castle in Aberdeen-shire rather than be tainted by a prospective betrayal of the nation. Sir John Anstruther, member for Anstruther Easter, if of the Squadrone, opposed the Union and refused to budge; so did his Cavalier uncle, Sir Robert Anstruther, member for Anstruther Wester; they truanted together. Two Highlanders, Ludovick Grant, a discreet Jacobite sitting for Inver-ness-shire, and Alexander Gordon, a client in his county of the unionist Earl of Sutherland, cancelled each other out in joint abstention. Others had more personal scruples. Sir Robert Dundas of Arniston, member for Midlothian, a former commissioner for Union, now abstained in the legislation itself, presumably on the grounds he was a judge. Alexander Watson, merchant and member for St Andrews, would vote on the economic interests of his constituency and nothing else. No doubt there were more cautious souls who did not even commit themselves that far.

The point is that in this and in coming divisions the government hardly ever enjoyed an absolute majority of the entire house; a certain propor-tion of it, one in six or seven, abstained but might be mobilised on particular issues – and on a few occasions was so mobilised, if unpre-dictably. Passage of the whole treaty, in other words, could by no means have been a forgone conclusion at the outset, as has been contended by nationalist writers wishing to stress the government's underhand methods of management. Of course it did resort to such methods, but there were also some arguments won or lost on their merits.

Even with that first and most basic article of the treaty approved, the government had no absolute assurance it was home and dry. There could be none so long as it was dubious of the Squadrone, where opportunism ran to obfuscation. One member of it, George Baillie of Jerviswood, wrote to Secretary Johnstone the day after the government carried the first vote, and cannot have left him much the wiser: 'The Union has lost ground, and is fair to be thrown out before the conclusion of the articles, for many of the Old Party [Queensberry's faction] want courage, and I cannot say but some of them are in danger, and the country is stirred up against it partly by the Jacobites and partly by the Presbyterian minis-ters.'[23] If this waffle amounted to anything, it was perhaps that the disaffection out of doors had begun to impinge on members, however much the government sought to seal the Parliament off with displays of armed strength in the High Street of Edinburgh. Mar, too, felt uneasy even after victory in the chamber: 'What with the addresses and the humour that's now in the country against the Union, several members left us, though I'm hopeful many of them will come about again.'[24]

ℰℐ

The 'addresses' on which Mar blamed the defections – in other words, petitions or other written protests against the Union sent in to the Parliament from Scotland at large – represented 'the inclinations and earnest supplications of the people', according to Lockhart. From the counties addresses came signed by 'barons, freeholders, heritors and other gentlemen', that is to say, by landowners; from the burghs by magistrates, councillors, deacons of crafts and burgesses; from the parishes and presbyteries by ministers and laymen alike. Defoe prints the text of one from the burgh of Dunfermline as 'a specimen of the manner how these addresses were usually signed'. Appended to it are signatures of 13 councillors, 29 merchants, 16 wrights, 6 masons, 4 shoemakers, 11 fleshers, 31 weavers, 17 tailors, 7 smiths and 9 baxters, 143 in all. Andrew Symson, notary public, adds a note in Latin, presumably in token of the solemnity of the occasion, certifying that another 36 people had wished to add their names but could not write.[25]

Addresses made an appearance in the parliamentary minutes from November 4, the day the first article of the treaty passed. The earliest arrived from voters of Midlothian, of West Lothian and of Perthshire, 'all against allowing of an incorporated Union with England, and all read and discoursed upon'. Each sitting from now on started with receipt and reading of addresses, in the end 90 or so in all, which were set down in the record without comment. Every one declared against the Union with a single exception, the burgh of Ayr's, which looked at best equivocal; in it Defoe found 'some seeming softness', and David Hume of Crossrigg said it was 'very discreet . . . craving some amendments may be made of the articles of Union, and seems to incline for the Union'.[26] Since Ayr was a pocket burgh of Loudoun's, the surprise is rather that it did not manage a show of greater support. If there was any such show elsewhere, it came in reticence, in not addressing for one reason or another: of 34 counties just 14 addressed; of 66 burghs 19; of 938 parishes 60; of 68 presbyteries 3.

Members of the Parliament for the addressing constituencies voted in almost every instance against the Union. Clusters of addresses arrived from areas under the sway of such nationalist noble houses as Annandale, Atholl, Errol and Hamilton. The whole business may have revealed political pressure exerted on voters by their social superiors rather than any spirit of independence. On the other hand, there was a concentration of addresses from the West of Scotland, where the authors of them clearly looked up what the Covenanters had said in their old remonstrances for religious and civil liberty. Even here, though, addresses appear to have changed hardly any votes inside the Parliament House.[27]

The popular nature of some addresses was, all the same, reason enough for the Earl of Mar to try and discredit them, as signed by the 'commonalty', those whom the opposition's lies had deceived: 'Parliament is the fit judge to consider of the terms of the Union.' The Duke of Argyll was to suggest the addresses should be used for making kites.[28] John Clerk of Penicuik wrote that, though read out to the house, 'they had no impact because the will of Parliament, strengthened by mature deliberation, was considered of more account that the voice of the people led astray by one faction or another'.[29] Daniel Defoe put forward an argument heard for the rest of the eighteenth century and beyond about relations between the British Parliament and the people: the latter 'can have no right to direct those whom they have no part in constituting . . . [they] are meddling with what they have no right to be meddling with, nor are any way concerned in'.[30] This was the sort of thing that made Americans decide they would be better off independent.

Despite self-conscious insouciance at all this in Edinburgh, disquiet arose in London. Sir David Nairne wrote to Mar to ask why the government of Scotland could not answer in kind with unionist addresses: 'I hope there would be as many and as good hands at them as at the other. It would have been of mighty use here, for I find people here, I mean coffee house company, begin to droop or despond to hear of so much doing against the Union without doors and so little for it.' But Mar did not relish this unsolicited advice on addresses: 'It is past time to get very many, and few would look worse than none.' He had in fact tried to organise some, but failed: there was just nobody beyond Parliament House prepared to address in favour of Union. All unionist politicians could do was seek to discourage hostile addresses from places under their influence.[31]

Not till the end of the year did the government feel a need to make any stronger response – and only as plots to launch a more vigorous campaign, even a *coup d'état*, appeared to approach a climax they would never reach. A rattled Seafield warned on December 27 that the government had paid the addresses all the heed they merited but now the subscribers were going too far. To them an inner circle of nationalists had sent out a circular. Clerk of Penicuik gave a lurid summary of it: 'Religion and the state are in peril; your native land lies dying; there is no one in Parliament but ourselves to defend or protect it. You must hasten to help us. Delay will be fatal for us all.'[32]

The circular then urged subscribers to addresses to come to Edinburgh, wait in a body on the Lord High Commissioner and ask him in turn to send a national address to the queen on their behalf. They would be following a solemn Scottish constitutional procedure with precedents dating back to the reign of James V in the sixteenth century. The Duke of Atholl and Andrew Fletcher lurked behind the stratagem, with George Lockhart as draftsman of the circular, this trio backed uncertainly, as ever, by the Duke of Hamilton. They saw it as a potent weapon, one to rob government in Scotland of authority. Lockhart's messages to friends betray his elation about it.[33] The national address he composed spelled out to the queen the 'almost universal aversion to the treaty'. It appealed to her 'to prevent such a chain of miseries as is likely to be the consequence of a forced Union'. She was requested to call a new Parliament and General Assembly of the Church of Scotland.[34]

Before long 500 barons, freeholders or heritors gathered in Edinburgh to demonstrate support for a national address, and more were on the way. Defoe reported that 'at the ferries of Leith and Queens[ferry] unusual numbers of men armed and horses have been seen to come over'.[35] Perhaps they might intimidate the government as the mere mob in the capital could not. Or perhaps, once within its walls, they looked too much like a fifth column awaiting the arrival of insurgent clansmen and Covenanters.

It was about time for Hamilton to get cold feet again, and he did. He told the other sponsors he could not support the national address unless it expressed readiness to accept the Hanoverian succession – anathema to most of them. All attempts to broker a compromise failed. Hamilton and Atholl just bawled at each other. Subscribers to addresses began to drift home again 'highly enraged at being thus balked'.[36] It was then that Seafield proposed a proclamation prohibiting 'all such unwarrantable and seditious convocating'; he got it passed in the Parliament by 112 votes to 62. Lockhart entered a protest that it could not prejudge the rights and privileges of barons, freeholders and heritors.[37] But the opportunity was gone.

എ

By this stage the legislative process proper for the main body of the treaty, once started early in November, was more likely to come to grief on account of the Church of Scotland, not of the addresses. 'If we can but please the ministers in the security of the Church,' wrote Seafield on November 3, 'our greatest difficulty will be over.'[38] Two days before, the motion from Marchmont had already flagged up Presbyterian accommodation to a prospective deal on the Union – that is to say, the work on an Act of Security for the Kirk was nearing its goal. In it William Carstares and his fellows demonstrated their own approach to a dual religious establishment in Great Britain, different from the detailed safeguards demanded by their militant brethren. The clique in charge of the Church would rest content with general guarantees, which amounted all the same to something better than mere verbiage and in fact turned out acceptable to most Presbyterians, as well as of durable value in themselves.

The key, according to Seafield, was that the Act promised 'perpetual security to Presbyterian government'.[39] This was as near to a fundamental law as the British constitution could get – for in theory any Act of Parliament, including the Act into which the Treaty of Union turned, may be amended by any later Act, for a Parliament cannot bind its successors. All the same, no attempt has ever been made to alter Presbyterian government in the Kirk. Parliament has interfered in Scottish religious affairs, notably in the prelude to the Disruption of 1843. Yet that dispute was finally resolved by a new Act of Security in 1921. It did not rescind the Act of 1706. On the contrary, as the Kirk contends to this day, it set out to define the historic constitutional position as precisely as possible, so that not a scintilla of doubt could remain. And in practice it removes the established Church of Scotland from the absolute sovereignty of the British Parliament. Here was the crucial adjustment to Scottish reality of the terms negotiated in London. It would have large and lasting effects.

The work by Carstares and his clique on the Act of Security for the Kirk had reflected their anxiety to keep on the right side of the new British state in prospect; the legislation as introduced remained in the realm of generality. Rather it was the three estates within the Parliament that ventured to show themselves in some particulars more Presbyterian than the Presbyterians in the clerical estate now outside it. During its passage the Act was bolstered. The motives might be mixed: Defoe names the Earl of Erroll, the Earl Marischal, Lords Kilsyth, Kincardine, Oliphant, Stormont and Wigtown as Episcopalian peers who voted for amendments which they hoped would go too far and damage the project of Union.

It is unclear whether Defoe has in mind here, for example, an amendment providing not just 'that the universities and colleges of St Andrews, Glasgow, Aberdeen and Edinburgh, as now established by law, shall continue within this kingdom for ever' – fair enough, indeed commendable – but also that 'professors, principals, regents, masters or others bearing office in any university, college or school within this kingdom' would have to be members of the Church of Scotland. Defoe actually calls this 'a most reasonable demand immediately agreed to by the Parliament'.[40] Yet, while laying the foundation of Scotland's future intellectual greatness, it was not at bottom liberal or permissive. On the contrary, it would prompt witch-hunts hardly conducive to academic freedom. Its eventual most notorious victim would be David Hume the philosopher, turned down for a chair at the University of Edinburgh in 1745 on account of his atheism. The one thing to be said for the clause, by unionists at least, was that without it the treaty might not have gained support from Presbyterians at large. With its amendments the Act would preserve a Calvinist culture for Scotland as far ahead as anyone could imagine. It was a key to survival of the nation.

In essence this Act of Security for the Kirk hauled the treaty, in the form negotiated by the commissioners in London, back from the brink of incorporating Union as espoused by the English towards a position more congenial to the Scots. The crucial clause reads like this:

> Her Majesty, with advice and consent of the said estates of Parliament, doth hereby establish and confirm the said true Protestant religion, and the worship, discipline and government of this Church to continue without any alteration to the people of this land in all succeeding generations; and more especially, Her Majesty, with advice and consent foresaid, ratifies, approves and forever confirms the fifth Act of the first Parliament of King William and Queen Mary, entitled 'Act Ratifying the Confession of Faith, and Settling Presbyterian Church Government'.

The nub of the clause is the word 'true'; the Kirk's worship, discipline and government are guaranteed because they represent the truth; secular legislation to the same effect is ancillary.

By contrast, the crucial clause of the English Act of Security passed later reads like this:

> That after the demise of Her Majesty (whom God long preserve) the sovereign next succeeding to Her Majesty in the royal government of the

Kingdom of Great Britain, and so forever hereafter, every king or queen coming to the royal government of the Kingdom of Great Britain, at his or her coronation, shall in the presence of all persons who shall be attending, assisting or otherwise then and there present, take and subscribe an oath to maintain and preserve inviolably the said settlement of the Church of England, and the doctrine, worship, discipline and government thereof, as by law established within the Kingdoms of England and Ireland, the dominion of Wales and town of Berwick-upon-Tweed, and the territories thereunto belonging.

This argument proceeds not from the truth but from the sovereign, who established the Church of England. It was established not because it represented the truth but because the sovereign said it was. Perhaps the sovereign thought these two things were the same; but while English history might allow of an identity between sovereignty and truth, Scottish history could not.

Certain Englishmen even at the time did see the force of the Scots' logic here. They, according to Defoe, were the ones who 'cry out of the Church [of England] being betrayed, sunk and endangered by the encroachments of the Kirk, and by the growing power of presbytery; that their commons in our House of Commons, and their lords in our House of Lords, will always be ready to vote against the Church'.[41] What else could be deduced from the plain contradiction between the two Acts of Security? They contradict each other not least at Berwick-upon-Tweed (which has resolved the contradiction in practice by opening its fortified gates to ministers of both the Church of Scotland and the Church of England). In any event, all successors to Queen Anne have bound themselves to uphold rival established Churches in different parts of their United Kingdom. So far the politics of the matter has resisted the logic.

What it amounted to was that the commissioners for Union, despite a wish to make it entire, did so on principles which in the first extension to the real world made it less than entire. They wrote a treaty English in character, lacking logic, firm on practice but shaky on principle. Though they had rejected federalism, the Union started to become federal as soon as Scots sought to turn its words into deeds. That happened above all in establishment of two rival Churches. Here lies the best proof, in the eating rather than the pudding, that Union was an accord between parties not indeed equal, yet in the end unable or unwilling to dictate the one to the other.

This is why the Union never produced one nation. On the contrary, it ensured the continuance of two nations under one Parliament. Its evolution in fact vindicated, if untidily, what George Davie identified as the Scottish constitutional theory, entailing 'co-operation of a pair of mutually critical but mutually complementary assemblies, the one concerned with politics and law, the other with the distinguishable, but nevertheless inseparable sphere of ethics and faith'.[42] To be sure, the Scots Parliament would vanish away into the Parliament of Great Britain, which according to the English theory remained sovereign. But the General Assembly of the Church of Scotland would live on, fulfilling its role as constitutional complement and check, only to a different Parliament from the Scots one. Politics and law had been dealt with in the Treaty of Union proper, written in its basic provisions by the English. But for Scotland this was just half the story: the other half lay in the Act of Security for the Kirk, written by Scots more interested in ethics and faith. In that ragged conjunction the true nature of the Union is to be found.

A couple of constitutional authorities of the twentieth century, A.V. Dicey and Richard Rait, entertained no doubt that the treaty was here clinched by a compromise not included in the original terms framed by the commissioners in London, but rendered necessary now to validate them. The old Parliaments passed Acts of Security for the Church of Scotland and the Church of England because 'the Whigs of both countries . . . were fully determined that neither bishop nor presbyter should have power to raise a religious war which might break up the political Union of the two countries'.[43] So in practice the Union forbids any fresh attempt by bishops to establish Anglicanism in Scotland (tried before under Charles I) or any fresh attempt by presbyters to establish Presbyterianism in England (tried before by the Solemn League and Covenant). The two national Churches knew their respective Parliaments were impatient of the religious strife which had caused so much bitterness and bloodshed to so little purpose in the past. It now seemed even less worthwhile under the pressure to forge the Union. The Churches may not have shared the indifference, but there could be no mileage for them in playing the problem up rather than down. The result was moderation – or an end to wars of religion in the British Isles.

This rebounded on politics too. The problem for Scotland was to preserve the existence and liberties of a nation at risk of being destroyed by faction, poverty and the English. Scots' pluck in the face of all their problems had before been nourished by boasts about the antiquity of kingdom and people, their valour and patriotism in defending themselves for 2,000 years and so forth. Now humdrum constitutional reform and promotion of trade seemed rather more useful means to the same end. They were anyway keys to keeping at bay a powerful neighbour that Scots could neither trust nor ignore.

A simple but risky solution might have been to cut away from the Union of Crowns and fight for full national independence if need be, as Jacobites wished. There was also a harder but in the end safer solution, if only it could be formulated – to accept a need for some sort of British outcome, where Scots' relations with their neighbours would be good rather than bad. The problem was then to work out the best deal within that outcome. Even an anglophobe such as Fletcher of Saltoun thought along analogous lines, though widening the terms of reference from British to European level. This rather than his nationalism is what gives his thinking its durable interest.

Later in the century the *Essays* (1753) of David Hume, often castigated as a Tory, and the *Principles of Political Economy* (1767) of the exiled Jacobite, Sir James Steuart, alike saw liberty as an achievement of all modern European civilisation, rather than just of England. To them revolution had come about not overnight in 1688 but by way of a long and tortuous path from feudal towards commercial society which, once at its destination, gave better guarantees of liberty than any overthrow of state or Church could ever offer. Still, a European outlook cut both ways. For others, Fletcher's federalist vision of a modern Scotland in a decentralised British polity recalled nothing so much as the bickering provinces of the Dutch Republic, which had tested to the limit the patience and political skills both of an insider, William of Orange, and of an outsider, Marlborough. Some of those others preferred the radical step of incorporating Scotland into a Great Britain ruled from London. At least sacrifice of the Scots Parliament would spell an end of ruinous faction at home, while free trade might stimulate the economic growth now indispensable for an ancient nation to survive.

The Act of Security for the Kirk finally went further and gained more support in the Scots Parliament than would have been expected. One reason was that the opposition set about loading it with amendments intended to render it less acceptable to the English, yet achieved a different result: they rendered it more acceptable to the Scots. The Act passed by 113 votes to 38, a far wider margin than for the first article of the treaty, suggesting that to many Scots their Church meant more than their state.

The Court kept its following intact while the opposition had its splits exposed, even after contriving to enhance the legislation. The small minority finally voting against the Act did include some, such as Atholl and Hamilton, who were not exactly militant Presbyterians. Others who were, such as Stewart of Pardovan, abstained on grounds that the guarantees won were still not good enough. In fact, more members abstained than voted at all: some were doubtless bigots of one kind and another, yet others perhaps moderates ahead of their time.

The Act passed on November 12, after a week's debate. Now, Lockhart recorded of the clergy, 'most of the brethren's zeal cooled'; he accused them (along with everybody else) of corruption, of worrying about their stipends.[44] If they had united against the Union, rather than been split between insiders and outsiders, Court and Country, the treaty might well have fallen. As things turned out, most of them and their flocks followed the clique in charge of the Kirk to acquiesce in the Union, if not always with enthusiasm. About this Harley, brought up an English Presbyterian, was soon moaning to Carstares: 'We can't but think it highly necessary for the commission of the Church to take some method to show here approbation of it in express terms . . . for it must certainly be most disserviceable to her to be thought averse or indifferent to a treaty, which is to be the lasting foundation of our government'.[45] But enough was enough. The Act of Security for the Kirk would be written as an integral element into the treaty; at their accession all future sovereigns would have to subscribe and swear to it.[46]

Altogether, the month or so from mid-October to mid-November 1706 formed the most crucial period in the whole history of the Union. At the start, three things stood out as necessary if the treaty was to pass. Scots legislators had to be persuaded to vote the principle of a Union of Parliaments. Means had to be found to manage inevitable opposition in the country. Only then could the keystone be set on the arch, the final deal be struck of maintaining an approximation to the old Scottish constitution balanced between Church and state, while reconciling it somehow with the claim to absolute sovereignty the British Parliament would inherit from the English Parliament.

❧

After all that, legislation of the body of the treaty could at last proceed. Debate on it resumed from November 14. The government had scored

vital victories, yet still faced risks that the whole endeavour might come
unstuck. One risk arose over the succession, the subject of the second
article of the treaty which Murray of Philiphaugh now moved. To its
basic provision, that in a future Great Britain the Crown should pass on
the death of Anne to the Electress Sophia of Hanover or heirs of her body,
the opposition did have a viable alternative of sorts.

Hamilton spelled this alternative out. He proposed the house should
address the queen on 'the condition of the nation, and the great aversion
in many persons to an incorporating Union with England, and to
acquaint Her Majesty of the inclinations and willingness to settle the
succession in the Protestant line upon limitations'. His words 'Protestant
line' might have included himself as successor, and some suspected that.
But most members assumed he meant Scotland's acceptance, as an
independent nation, of the Hanoverian succession, which in earlier
sessions they had refused to hear of. Now Fletcher and friends brandished
a fresh list of limitations to make it more congenial. Belhaven again added
colour, in comparing the Union to 'the first and worst treaty that ever was
set on foot for mankind when the serpent did deceive our mother Eve'.
The government of Scotland he likened to Satan, in its saying 'Eat,
swallow down this incorporating Union, though it please neither eye
nor taste, it must go over. You must believe your physicians, and we shall
consider the reasons for it afterwards.'[47]

In the face of all these exertions the government's vote on the second
article fell by just 2 to 114. The opposition's plummeted to 57. This
cannot have been just because of absenteeism, for Clerk of Penicuik says
the house was crowded. It must have been because either Jacobites could
not bring themselves to accept the Hanoverian succession even to save a
free Scotland, and turned up to abstain in person, or else Presbyterians
could not bring themselves to dilute the safeguards available under a
Hanoverian succession to a British Crown, safest of all because both
Protestant and parliamentary and so doubly unlikely to impugn the Act of
Security for the Kirk.[48]

The house meant to proceed straight to the third article, on 'one and the
same Parliament of Great Britain'. Here lay another chance to exploit a
popular cause and push for the Scots Parliament to be preserved somehow, even just as a regional assembly. An impression comes across,
though, that some leaders of the opposition still could not believe they
had lost the second article so badly: like dogs to vomit, they returned to
the succession by entering a protest in advance of debate on the third

article. The Marquis of Annandale proposed a text which called a Union of Parliaments 'subversive of the sovereignty, fundamental constitution and Claim of Right of this kingdom, and threatening ruin to the Church, as by law established' – a clear nod to the Presbyterians. He again urged the house to set aside the articles of Union and proceed straight to settlement of the succession on the House of Hanover subject to limitations.

Belhaven seconded, recalling how much care the house had taken over limitations in previous sessions. It was to him inconceivable that a treaty should now pass without them. But he was still in the Garden of Eden: 'Consult every treaty since the beginning of time, and you will find no precedent for this. I shall instance only the first and worst treaty of all, that which the devil made with mankind, though there was more wit and honesty in it than in this now before us.'

Hamilton intervened too, when it would have been better for him to keep mum. He said: 'Let it never be a reproach to me that in earlier Parliaments I opposed a successor for the sake of a treaty with England, and that now I would reject this treaty on account of the succession.' He was alluding to a triumph of his own in the session of 1704, when he had persuaded the house to make nomination of a successor dependent on a treaty with England: now, as he conceded, he was saying the reverse. He failed to convince. He disgusted the Jacobites, and made sure they would not rally to Annandale's protest. It attracted the feeble total of fifty-three signatures: no advance over the lost vote on the second article. This intransigent minority had yet to see that, since November 14, a new political game was under way.[49]

The government could now press ahead with the third article. Seton of Pitmedden supported it in a speech more notable for a swot's sophism than an orator's passion. He argued in the abstract that the government of Scotland was not a democracy or an aristocracy but a limited monarchy, with the supreme court of Parliament subject to no higher authority. This constitution the Parliament of the United Kingdom would move, as it were, on to a still more ethereal plane, yet preserving, not menacing the rights of the people. As for talk of surrender, nothing could be called surrender which had been subject to a treaty. Seton quoted the Dutch legal philosopher, Hugo Grotius, that 'the rights and privileges of two nations united are consolidated into one by a mutual communication of them'.

In retort, Fletcher cut through the cant with a poignant cry. He said it was hard 'when men are constrained to bring harm on themselves, harder still to give the finishing blow to this Parliament of ours, with whose welfare the lives and fortunes of so many have been intertwined, that we should hack to pieces this body, already grievously wounded, whose unworthy members we are'. But he went on to pose an acute question – just how, after the Scots had reduced themselves to a small minority in a Union of Parliaments, were their interests to be safeguarded? 'Without help or consolation we shall shed tears in vain, the English themselves will laugh at our distress, and the moral will be pointed that we brought it on ourselves.'[50]

Fletcher's telling point gave shape to long debate on the third article. How much trust Scots might place in a British Parliament was a legitimate line of inquiry. A judge and member for Midlothian, Sir John Lauder of Fountainhall, spoke for many when he demanded better guarantees than they had that the terms of the treaty would be respected always. This offered an opening to Hamilton, who proposed Scots MPs at Westminster should retain a veto in 'matters essential and fundamental in the Union'; any breach of the treaty would render it void and the Union would 'be *ipso facto* dissolved'. In other words, Scots MPs should find a way to act as a body in the Commons – perhaps not unlike the Scottish grand committee of the twentieth century – but with a sting available in their collective tail. The Court merely repeated that the English must be trusted, as the Scots had no way of compelling them. It was quite a relief when the unionist coalition held together and the article passed by thirty votes. With that, Mar said, 'the hardest of our work is over'.[51]

The fourth article, on free trade among 'all the subjects of the United Kingdom of Great Britain', came up on November 19. Little dispute was expected here, because it held out the English reward for the Scots' assent to a Union of Parliaments. Fletcher decided the government must get a run for its money all the same. He stood up to argue that, contrary to received wisdom, free trade between Scotland and England would be a bad thing – or at least that different branches of trade operated under different conditions, so what was sauce for the goose might not be sauce for the gander. An illegal trade carried on to the West Indies, for example: what was that good for, even if made legal by the Union? 'Possibly the right to bring in treacle or that American weed called tobacco. But where do we find the money to buy these things and the ships to import them? And even if we do get them here, to whom shall we sell them? Every market in Europe is glutted with such stuff.' Still, Fletcher claimed, it lay within Scotland's grasp to match England's prosperity: 'What we need is not Union but sound legislation here in this house and the sound Scottish virtues of skill and hard work.'[52] He failed to sway the Parliament. The fourth article passed by a huge majority of 156 to 19, only a diehard minority voting against, for many nationalists supported free trade in principle. Had Fletcher meant his arguments seriously? At any rate he was so furious he flounced out of the house.[53]

ల్ఫ

With that the Parliament completed its consideration of the basis of the treaty – the four articles written by the English – with no more than minor modifications of wording. Scotland had accepted in essentials the offer made in London last July: a United Kingdom under one monarch and one Parliament, with internal free trade, colonies included. Yet the treaty contained not just the first four but 25 articles in all – the remainder written, at least in part, by the Scots. The first four articles were short and clear, some of the others detailed and complex, and most technical in nature: yet not to be underrated on that account, for each addressed some particular problem or squared some particular constituency. The fourth article on free trade, for example, fell to be considered not just by itself but along with further articles explaining and modifying it – because, taking one thing with another, the treaty went beyond straight institution of free trade to include measures for protection of vulnerable sectors in the Scottish economy. It was a deal by real men in a real world: it set out not just general principles but also detailed concessions to Scottish interests. That was why the Parliament could continue arguing about them, and to some effect, for a while yet.

It is true that in later divisions the numbers voting tended to sag, no doubt reflecting less assiduous attendance in the chamber; not everyone was fascinated by technicality, while nationalists began to lose heart anyway. However that may have been, there was enough work to keep the house busy for two more months. An obvious ploy for the opposition would be to vote amendments the English Parliament might reject, in hope of reopening the fundamental question of the Union. Defoe waxed quite generous about this tactic of the treaty's foes: 'From article to article they disputed every word, every clause, casting difficulties and doubts in the way of every argument, twisting and turning every question, and continually starting objections to gain time; and, if possible, to throw some insurmountable obstacle in the way.'[54] He might not have meant the comment as praise, yet he brought out their resilience in the situation they now faced. It still did them no good. As Lockhart said, the Court was never 'at the pains to solve the doubts, and answer the objections raised by the Country party, so they continued the same method throughout the whole remaining part of the session, allowing the Country party to argue some little time upon the matter under the house's consideration, and then moving the vote on it'.[55]

Yet it did prove possible to pass amendments. The true task of the Court now was to soothe Scots pride while avoiding any depletion of English goodwill. With a basic deal there, the trick lay in not letting it be diluted by mistakes as the detail was filled in. Still, it is obvious from Mar's letters that he did not expect to carry every single remaining article without changes or clarifications. Members, that is to say, would be able to amend so long as they did not wreck. Mar wrote to his masters in London on November 23: 'We shall endeavour in all the articles to keep as near the treaty as possible. But our people here, even those who have hitherto gone along with us, are so skittish and have advanced so far on amendments to be made that we have little hope of carrying the treaty without alterations.' He and his colleagues sent a memorial asking leave for limited concessions: 'We long for an answer to the memorial, and pray God it may be a satisfying one, else I confess I would be afraid of our success.' The reply was unhelpful. It said Scots should trust the British Parliament to put right any anomalies emerging in due course. 'That is not the language of the place just now,' Mar retorted, 'and one would be stared at if they said so in the house. For the British Parliament is what frights most of our Scottish members that we are forced to manage.'[56]

All the same there was a difference and a distance between what was thought in London and done in Edinburgh. In fact, Scots continued to rewrite the treaty in smaller matters as they had already in a greater one, with the Act of Security for the Kirk. A good example was the fifth article coming up next, on Scottish shipping. Its terms had arrived in the Parliament already set out at length. Now an amendment was passed extending the limit of time for ships purchased by Scots abroad to be registered under the English Navigation Acts. The commissioners for Union had defined that limit to coincide with the end of their own labours on July 22, 1706. They wanted to exclude the distortions liable to follow from any more flexible rule – for example, one which might give Scots a chance to acquire more Dutch ships in advance of the Union, to the detriment (and ire) of the English. On the other hand, the original deadline would have cut across existing contracts freely entered into between Scotsmen and Dutchmen. The Dutch regretted losing the Scots out of their own trading network into the English one, but there was nothing they could do. At least a parting of ways between military allies could be carried out in a civilised manner. After debate, the deadline was shifted to coincide with the date when the Scots Parliament should ratify the treaty, that is, from the summer of 1706 to the spring of 1707. There was still a rush to register foreign bottoms in Scotland, but it occurred once and for all and did not ruin English shipbuilding. This article, as amended, passed on November 23.[57]

The sixth article was by comparison short if just as technical. It provided for England's regime of customs to apply across Great Britain. It was a price Scotland had to pay for free trade over the border and to the colonies: it summed up her economic bargain, entry into a protectionist system for a liberal aim of her own. But there remained a big problem of difference in the structure of trade as between Scotland and England. Scotland exported a narrow range of raw materials in exchange for consumer goods or other necessities of all kinds, while England trafficked in a wider range of superior products. That is to say, the new customs could hardly suit Scotland.

For the government, the Earl of Stair defended the position with legal guile rather than economic expertise. He even argued against Scots' exploitation of their comparative advantage in what goods they did produce: 'Scotland's trade should not be managed differently [from England's] merely because some of our merchants have profits from the import of certain commodities or because landowners have benefited from exporting raw wool. Our poverty can be laid at the door of such people.' He began to sound like Ministers in today's Scottish Executive at their most politically correct: 'Vast fortunes have been made from the import of French wine and the nation has suffered for it. Since we neither make nor grow anything that the French want to buy, we have sent them our money and got wine in exchange! Should not sensible men be ashamed of wasting their substance on drink?'[58] Drouthy Scots were unlikely to agree.

The nationalists in particular were recognising they must mount resistance on this sort of issue because they now had no others. The sixth article was sent into committee, to emerge three-quarters rewritten, with stronger safeguards for Scottish cattle and grain in particular, above all against potential competition from Ireland. Defoe mentions the merchants who turned their hands to this, all provosts of and members for their burghs – John Allardyce of Aberdeen, John Scrymgeour of Dundee, William Sutherland of Elgin, Alexander Watson of St Andrews – together with James Oswald, skipper and member for Kirkcaldy; every one except Scrymgeour a nationalist, Allardyce and Sutherland being Jacobites to boot.[59] The behaviour of the group illustrates the conflicting pressures now coming to bear on the opposition, tending to split rather than bind it: for example, Sutherland of Elgin started off voting against the Union but ended up voting for it. What happened was that nationalism inflated demands for concessions which, if once exacted, served to make the Union more attractive even to its enemies. The sixth article passed after the committee's report was received and approved on December 16.

The seventh article, on the excise, had meanwhile passed on November 28. In theory a principle of equal taxation applied here too, but proved trickier yet. Clerk of Penicuik went so far as to claim that 'a high excise in England and a low excise in Scotland had put the two nations on such an unequal footing with regard to trade that no Union could possibly have subsisted between them'. One example which perturbed Scots was that on beers of superior and inferior quality the English levied two separate rates of tax, both more swingeing than any in Scotland. Thanks to the Union, Scots dreaded, they might have to pay much more for a pint than the wonted twopence a shout. In committee, with expert advice on English tax from the versatile Defoe, the draft was amended to ensure Scots paid only a lower rate; in fact their twopenny ale should never be taxed more than now. Here lurks a provision of the treaty with us yet in everyday life, for while sybaritic Englishmen order up pints by taste (mild or bitter), canny Scotsmen often do so according to the duty the beer pays (60/- or 70/- or 80/-, the numbers having, of course, been inflated in later times). In the seventh article, too, the wording received from London was rewritten in Edinburgh almost entirely. Clerk did not approve: 'If this article had continued to stand as it was at first concerted many of the people of Scotland had given over the idle custom and bad habits they have fallen into, in spending their time and money in tippling the lowest kind of malt liquors called twopenny ale.'[60]

On December 6 debate on the eighth article opened. Yet again it posed a question whether the principle of equal duties might be waived on a special Scottish consideration. Here the commodity was salt, used as preservative for meat and fish. It bore heavy tax when imported into England, but not into Scotland. To poor Scots salt was a staff of life. It kept them alive through long, dark, cold winters in the sense that it preserved the meat of their livestock universally slaughtered in the autumn except for a few breeding beasts. Or else it made palatable the porridge on which they fell back; in his philippic against the Union, Belhaven had mentioned 'saltless pottage' among the oppressions a British Parliament was bound to impose. On this point the ruling class showed something better than its usual callousness towards the hard life of the people – though, of course, nationalists were seeking to exploit any issue they could. They pushed for Scotland to be forever exempt from tax on salt, a demand the English Parliament would then refuse, so the Union 'might split upon that rock'.[61]

The ulterior motives appeared in the debate when Fletcher and Stair got into a spat. Stair was again assuring the house that any worrisome details could be left to a future British Parliament, when Fletcher shouted: 'Don't trust the British Parliament for that! Would the English majority neglect their overtaxed constituents and turn a ready ear to our necessitous begging? Any improvements we want in this treaty should be written into it now.' The argument degenerated till the pair were about to challenge each other to a duel. From the chair Seafield intervened and made them apologise, which Fletcher did with typical ill grace. In the end there was to be in Scotland an exemption from duty on salt for seven years after the Union, and even then Scots would pay less than one-third of what the English paid. During this debate the Court suffered its sole defeat on the treaty, in respect of an amendment demanding drawbacks for export of salted beef or pork, that is, rebates of duty paid on imported salt used in their preparation. On December 26, the article passed as amended, again in a form unrecognisable compared to how it had come up from London.[62]

The ninth article turned from indirect to direct taxation. It limited the money to be raised from Scotland for central government to a fixed proportion of the English total. For every £2 million raised in England, at a standard rate of 4s in the pound, £48,000 was to be raised in Scotland. The ratio of these lump sums to each other, at 42:1, seems to have been regarded as, and perhaps was, a roughly just measure of the relative national incomes of England and Scotland. Next to no argument took place in the chamber over these figures, which had been thrashed out in advance by the commissioners for Union. Some further, minor fiscal articles also passed on the nod.[63]

The fourteenth article drew a line under the tortuous fiscal provisions by specifying that Scotland should not be subjected to any taxes that had been imposed in England before the Union, except as set out in the treaty, while for future taxes Scotland and England would be 'charged equally'. That seemed, on the right level of generality, clear and fair enough. It did not, however, deter a particular demand from the floor of the house that no tax on malt, such as existed in England, should be imposed on Scotland. Malt was in a roundabout way another essential to Scots because it was used for the production and flavouring of beer, in place of the hops used in England; hops do not grow in Scotland. At any rate, Fletcher jumped up to propose Scottish malt should be free of all duty forever, while others proposed different lengths of time. A motion was carried that exemption should be for the duration of the war only. Next day Fletcher widened the argument to move that 'the nation of Scotland be for ever free of all burdens, but what is agreed to by these articles'. In the end the fourteenth article was carried by eighteen votes: the narrowest margin in the whole treaty. Scots would doubtless have been happy to go on discussing for a long while yet the finer points of how they might be exempted from taxation, especially on booze. But it was time to move on.[64]

ↄ৲

On December 7, the house proceeded to the fifteenth article, on the Equivalent. It too was long and complex, offering scope for the objection and obstruction that Fletcher in particular exploited. Still, when the first paragraph giving the amount of the Equivalent – £398,085 10s – went to the vote, it was carried by an overwhelming majority. Even Hamilton and Belhaven supported the government, though Fletcher and Atholl still did not.

A further clause gave compensation for the losses of the Company of Scotland Trading to Africa and the Indies. Under it, the capital stock plus 5 per cent annual interest would be paid off. For this the English Parliament would have to pass an Act raising the money. After that the company could no longer trade; it would 'be dissolved and cease' once the payment was made. In an address to the Parliament the company had protested against this compulsory liquidation of itself, arguing that should be a matter for shareholders. In any event, its survival 'upon the same foot with the East India and other trading companies in England is in no way inconsistent with the trade of the United Kingdom'. But here Scots came up against a reality the English government had to face, the financial power of the City of London – which would not tolerate the Company of Scotland.

The Scottish government for its part fell back on the answer that a company set up by statute could be shut down by statute. A mere sweetener was offered, provision for payments to shareholders out of the Equivalent to have priority even over redemption of Scottish public debt, and to take place within a year. In the event many investors would be kept waiting for their money while arrears of salary and other obligations of the state were paid off; it was not the first time Scots laws had been passed and then ignored. Defoe commented revealingly how people outside the Parliament even at this stage remained so unconvinced the Union could pass that they would still sell the company's stock 'for trifles', at 10 per cent of face value. But inside the Parliament a realisation was dawning that the Union could probably not now be stopped, so creditors of Darien there reckoned they at least ought to get their money back.[65]

The shift of mood could be encouraged by promises of money, especially if it had not yet come in – as out of the rising Equivalent confidently forecast for the more prosperous Scotland of the future with her higher revenue from customs and excise. Members for Aberdeenshire, Stirlingshire, the Borders and Galloway, the chief sheep-rearing regions, had raised the point that after the Union they would be shut out from their foreign markets for fine wool. In England export of wool was prohibited in order to protect domestic manufacture of textiles. And here lay a point on which the English were immovable. In the United Kingdom, Scottish export of wool would have to stop too. The only remedy was to provide an incentive for Scots also to process the raw material themselves, with money earmarked for Scottish purposes out of the rising Equivalent. It might have seemed a fair offer, except there was never in real life to be a rising Equivalent, for the immediate impact of the Union on Scottish trade was to depress rather than boost it. Aid for development in Scotland had in the end to be separately legislated, but that would not happen for twenty years. Meanwhile the fifteenth article passed, as amended, by 112 to 54 votes on December 30.[66]

The fifteenth article had wrapped up the economics of the treaty. The fact this aspect of it comprehended 15 of the 25 articles has been stressed too much by determinist Scottish historians trying to demonstrate an overriding material priority among Scots of the time. Totting up the articles in aid of this is a deceptive procedure. The economics of the treaty can be reduced to three heads: free trade; costs of fusing a heavy and a light regime of customs and excise, offset by temporary aid to Scotland; compensation to Scots for a share of the English national debt. Free trade is enacted in the fourth article, to be read in conjunction with the fifth, sixth, sixteenth and seventeenth articles, these spelling out the consequences in related spheres of shipping, defence, currency, weights and measures. A unified system of customs and excise is dealt with in the sixth to fourteenth articles, containing also concessions to Scottish interests. Provision of the Equivalent to compensate Scots for higher taxes and redemption of the English national debt is found within the fifteenth article, the most elaborate because most disjointed of all. Length and numbering of articles vary according to the disparate nature of the topics they deal with, or legislation behind them; length, not numbers, is the guide to relative importance. It would be absurd, for example, just to equate the eleventh article, which states that Scotland shall be relieved of the English window-tax (and nothing more) with, say, the twenty-second article, many times longer, on Scottish representation at Westminster – or to imply that their consequence in members' minds is to be weighed by their numbers.

છે

Overall and contrary to expectations, the government of Scotland was performing rather well, making small but significant concessions to particular constituencies yet exerting itself to defeat amendments likely to cause problems at Westminster. For example, by Hogmanay the Parliament reached the eighteenth article. It stated that all Scots laws (other than regulatons of trade, customs and excise), would 'remain in the same force as before though alterable by the Parliament of Great Britain'. It recognised a difference 'betwixt the laws concerning public right, policy and civil government and those which concern private right': the former 'may be made the same throughout the whole United Kingdom' while the latter could not be altered 'except for evident utility of the subjects within Scotland'.[67]

This was all fine for Scots as it stood, yet could not deter a last push to even up the score on sacramental tests, so that if Scotsmen had no exemption from an English test then the English would be obliged to take a Scottish test, should they wish to hold a public post in Scotland. The amendment was defeated, if just by a whisker, 68 votes to 62, showing the Presbyterians' resistance to compromise on this. Defoe warned that for members to demand the change 'would be to ask something which they knew would not be granted, and consequently put the treaty to a stop'.[68] Instead the house let a sleeping dog lie, and avoided greater embarrassment: the government had just about attained a degree of control it needed to pick and choose among amendments acceptable or unacceptable to the English.

Even so, it remained an untidy, uncertain business, and the opposite might well be argued about the nineteenth article. This preserved heritable offices in Scotland, declaring them to be 'rights of property'. But into the list of offices the term 'heritable jurisdictions' had been inserted. These were peculiar to Scotland, a result of medieval compromise between Crown and overmighty subjects, by which noblemen assumed judicial powers on their lands if the king could not make his writ run there. The powers took various forms but at their highest were termed regalities – in other words, equivalent to a king's, with the notorious right to 'pit and gallows', to imprison and execute. This did little for Scottish justice but tended to make noblemen absolute masters of the people under them, after a manner by now superseded in England. Defoe said it 'bound down Scotland to the private tyranny and oppression of the heritors and lairds'.[69] Yet not many other Englishmen could even have heard of this blot on national life, and fewer still would have approved; there were many Scots who thought it shameful too. When its beneficiaries wrote a guarantee of it into the treaty they were, as much as anything, trying to hold back a rising tide of domestic demand for reform. They doubtless guessed heritable jurisdictions were a matter so obscure to the English that no notice would be taken at Westminster. The guarantee in the treaty marked a high point of success for collective selfishness in the Scottish ruling class. It would last forty years before repeal after the Jacobite rebellion in 1745, which had exposed its dangers.

Limits to the government's freedom of action appeared also over the twenty-first article, maintaining the equally outdated privileges of royal burghs. Clerk of Penicuik said: ''Tis certain that some of these privileges are hurtful to them, particularly such as restrict the freedom of the citizens within certain bounds and limits in which they can exercise their trades and occupations.'[70] They reveal how far in Scotland concepts of an urban community remained stuck in a medieval mould, rather than pointing the way to modernity: the institution of royal burghs just had no more capacity for useful development. Yet for now the article was needed to sustain the support of members from them – who constituted after all an estate of the Parliament in their own right, though in practice often subservient to the noblemen in the rustic hinterlands of their burghs.

Still, cumulative success for the government's parliamentary management did work a gradual effect on its confidence and morale. Mar had already said on December 24 that he now thought the Union would go through. On the other hand Secretary Johnstone, who was in London, wrote as late as December 31, 1706, to Baillie of Jerviswood of doubts about the progress of the treaty: 'You may, I think, depend on it that the alterations you have hitherto made will not break the Union, but if you go on altering, it's likely your alterations will be altered here, which will make a new session with you necessary, and in that case no man knows what may happen.' Yet by the time he sent another letter on January 4, 1707, his mood had changed, after finding out that the biggest party at Westminster saw nothing offensive, at least nothing it was determined to vote down, in Scots' amendments: 'The Whigs are resolved to pass the Union here, without making any alterations at all, to shun the necessity of a new session with you, provided you have been as reasonable in your alterations as you've been hitherto.' By January 17 he could say: 'Now that the Union is as good as done with you, we have no doubt of its doing here, and that without so much as one alteration.'[71]

Bounds to the government's complaisance had all the same to be reached. They came with the twenty-second article, on the representation of Scotland in the Parliament of Great Britain. The treaty specified 45 MPs in the Commons and 16 peers in the Lords, with English representation left untouched. This was one of the most contentious proposals, concluded in the commission for Union only with difficulty and, ever since published, under fire from Scots. Many still wanted their Parliament preserved in some form; or else, in a British Parliament they at least wanted English representation to be adjusted by criteria, of revenue or population, that had been adopted or might have been adopted for Scotland. All these ideas were to come up in the three days set aside for debate on the article, January 7–9.

Here was also a chance for the discredited Hamilton to stage a comeback, if he had the gumption. He set to with a will. He dreamed up a scheme by which Annandale, as soon as the Parliament reached this article, would move again what he had moved before, settlement of the Crown on the House of Hanover in an independent Scotland. If it was once more rejected, members hostile to the Union should protest and walk out of the house in a body, as they had done in 1702, leaving a rump without effective authority to carry the treaty or anything else. A national address to the queen would then be organised. Hamilton thought a demonstration of how the Union was failing to find a 'secure and legal basis' would impress the English into dropping it.[72]

The Lord Advocate, Sir James Steuart, drafted the text of the protest.[73] It started by challenging the right of the Parliament to overthrow its own constitution without a convention of estates, 'clothed with a more than ordinary power'. It referred to the 'unprecedented number' of addresses against the Union and to the opposition's offer to accept the Hanoverian succession as a better means to understanding between the two countries. The Union, it went on, surrendered power 'to the entire Parliament of another nation'. It would tend 'to ruin the trade and the subjects of this kingdom, by engaging them into insupportable customs and burdens upon foreign trade and home consumption, and by involving the trade of Scotland under the regulations of the trade of England', when conditions in the two economies were quite different. The signatories refused either to 'lessen, dismember or part with our Parliament, or any part of the power thereof', or to accept 'pretended laws and acts of resolve of any pretended Parliament of Great Britain'. It would be lawful for them 'as our ancestors in the like cases have usually done, to vindicate and assert our ancient rights and liberties'[74] – in other words, presumably, by arms.

The English Parliament was meant to take fright, but the Scottish opposition now intended less to threaten revolt than expose the depth of enmity to the Union. Hamilton argued that even if after a walk-out the treaty was still approved by just half a legislature in Scotland, it was bound then to fail in England. He recalled how English commissioners in the abortive talks of 1702 had kept so cool because they knew their opposite numbers, Queensberry and cronies, represented neither the Parliament nor nation of Scotland. Now, by a repetition, nationalists could embarrass the Court in England, encourage Tory enemies of the Union and disconcert its partisans among Whigs.

Hamilton worked to enlist support. Jacobites naturally bridled at any mention of the Hanoverian succession, yet he was able to persuade many that, while necessary as a first step, the protest did not commit them to it in so many words: a still independent nation of the future could not be bound by such a document. It helped that Atholl, if sceptical of the idea, went along with it. Lockhart enthused that it 'caused an universal joy, and great numbers of gentlemen and eminent citizens flocked together that morning about the Parliament House to attend the separating members, and assist them in case they should be maltreated as they came from the house. But all their hopes soon vanished and came to nothing'.[75]

It was Hamilton's fault, yet again. At the last minute he got butterflies in his stomach, though it was toothache he blamed for an inability to leave his apartment at Holyrood, go up to the crucial sitting of the Parliament and stage the protest. Perhaps the government meanwhile had wind of it and managed to intimidate him – a hint of a charge of treason derived from dealings with Colonel Hooke might have done nicely. Yet other members of the opposition refused to take Hamilton's fudge lying down. They frogmarched him into the Parliament House. Here he failed them all over again. He asked who was to present the protest. It had been assumed he would do so himself, as he was author of the whole stunt and anyway leader of the opposition. He refused, saying he would only support a move by somebody else. So much time was spent arguing the toss over this that the business of the house proceeded to a point where the chance was lost.[76]

Lockhart saw this as the end of parliamentary resistance to the Union: 'No other measures were concerted, and everyone did that which was good in his own eyes; and in a few days great numbers of those who had appeared zealously against the Union deserted the house in despair.'[77] While Hamilton enraged his own side, the government heaved a sigh of relief. Seafield later revealed how seriously the risk to it had been taken; if Hamilton had succeeded in his ploy it would have had to 'prorogate the Parliament, and give over the prosecution of the Union'.[78]

With Hamilton a spent force, Atholl led opposition to the twenty-second article. He stressed how 'from the multitudes of addresses and petitions from the several parts of this kingdom that there is a general dislike and aversion to incorporating Union as contained in these articles, and that there is not one address from any part of the kingdom in favour of this Union'.[79] For one thing the treaty gave offence to the peerage of Scotland, hereditary members of the queen's council who were now to become elective, so she would be deprived of her born counsellors and they of their birthright. They numbered 160 against 180 in England yet would be reduced to 16 in the Lords: 'It is plain that the Scots peers' share in the legislative and judication powers in the British Parliament is very unequal with that of the English though the one be representatives of as independent and free a nation as the other, and there is therefore a plain forfeiture of the peerage of this kingdom.' For another thing counties and burghs were to have their representation cut to forty-five MPs so that in the Commons, too, Scotland would be left at the mercy of the English: 'from all of which it is plain and evident that this from a sovereign independent monarchy shall dissolve its constitution and be at the disposal of England whose constitution is not in the least to be altered by this treaty'. The queen should be told of Scots' hostility to the whole project, then be asked to call a new Parliament and seek a 'Union upon honourable and equal terms which may unite them in affection and interest in the surest foundation of peace and tranquillity for both kingdoms'.[80] This was not in itself, then, an anti-unionist case.

But to such hedging of bets Stair, replying for the government, had an answer as stark as it was revelatory: 'You cannot force your will on those stronger than yourself.' It would be to the good of Scotland to have a future share in the honour and dignity of a British Parliament: 'Weigh its authority against that of our Parliament. We might wish to ascribe some slight worth to ourselves, but the world does not know that we exist. Since the Union of Crowns, such prestige and renown as our kingdom once enjoyed have been credited to the English.' So this Union would raise the status of Scotland: it 'means an equal partnership in all things, a sharing of fortunes in good times and bad'.[81] It was about the final contribution to the history of Scotland by Stair, instigator of the Massacre of Glencoe and, for the last two months, the most expert and effective advocate of the Union. A few days later he dropped dead.

It remained to vote on the twenty-second article. Its first clause, giving the numbers of Scots in the British Parliament, passed by 133 to 74, a hefty increase in the government's normal vote. Opposition to the second clause, on a method for Scots peers to elect their representatives, evaporated. The third clause let existing members of the English Parliament continue as members of the British Parliament if the queen so wished. In connection with this clause a sequence of three major divisions took place. The first rejected a wrecking motion 'that the Parliament of Great Britain shall meet and sit once in three years at least in that part of Great Britain now called Scotland', by 102 votes to 59. Then the third clause of the article passed by 106 votes to 54. A final vote, to approve the twenty-second article as a whole, went through by 83 to 65. Diminishing margins of victory doubtless reflected general exhaustion rather than any underlying political shifts.[82]

Not much remained to be dealt with now, just three more articles of lesser import. The twenty-third assured equal status for Scots representative peers, guaranteeing them 'all privileges of Parliament which the peers of England now have, and which they or any peers of Great Britain shall have after the Union, and particularly the right of sitting upon the trials of peers'. Many of the Scots must have rubbed their hands at this for the reason that if they could get to Westminster they would share in the English noble privilege of freedom from arrest for civil process, not least pursuit of debts: Scottish peers spent much time and energy dodging creditors. It was probably Fletcher that here launched a scathing attack against them: 'From now on, noble lords are not to be trusted in matters of business. They can borrow without shame to stuff their tottering palaces, knowing that the law has made them free of their creditors.'[83] But now words were never going to hurt them.

The twenty-fourth article, concerning 'one Great Seal for the United Kingdom of Great Britain different from the Great Seal of either kingdom' and similar matters, passed on January 14. It was amended to guarantee further that 'the Crown, sceptre and sword of state, records of Parliament, and all other records, rolls and registers whatsomever both public and private, general and particular, and warrands thereof, continue to be kept as they are, in that part of the United Kingdom, now called Scotland' – something for which the present author is grateful because it makes books like this possible. The twenty-fifth article, declaring void all laws of either kingdom contrary to the terms of the Union, was approved the same day.[84]

The battle had been lost and won. On January 16, the Treaty of Union and Act of Security for the Kirk were ratified in tandem as the Scottish Act of Union by 110 votes to 67. Since the first major division in November, the government's tally had held steady, while the opposition's had shrunk.[85] It was probably Hamilton that commented: 'And so the darkest day in Scotland's history has finally arrived. The point of no return has been reached, and nothing is left to us of Scotland's sovereignty, nor her honour or dignity or name.'[86] Lockhart could not bring himself even to be there. Queensberry touched the Act with the sceptre straight after the vote.

෴

This did not quite end business in the last session of the Scots Parliament. It still had to find a future mode of electing MPs to the British Parliament, a delicate matter put off during passage of the treaty. The English were happy to leave it to the Scots, who knew the mysteries of their electoral law and practice. They fell to squabbling, needless to say, and only after furious argument allocated, of the 45 MPs, 30 to the counties and 15 to the burghs. These latter, to squeeze into such a small number of constituencies, had to be grouped by districts of four or five, only Edinburgh keeping a member to itself. As for the 16 peers, they were to be chosen by the whole body of the nobility in an open poll rather than by ballotting, though absentees could cast proxy votes. The poll might be held anywhere in Scotland agreed by Her Majesty; a tradition was soon established for it to take place at Holyrood.

Suddenly, while this horse-trading went on, an unsuspected hitch arose. It became known the government in London meant to continue its own Parliament till a General Election due not before 1708. Apart from the light this cast on the English view of the treaty, it posed a problem. How were the first Scots MPs to be returned? The government could not possibly leave that to the voters, because the opposition would win by a landslide. The solution was to have the sitting Parliament name out of its own membership the inaugural delegation to Westminster. Queensberry nominated 13 of the 45, and Argyll 5, while the rest were shared among other bigwigs of the Court; the Squadrone, looking after itself as ever, secured 11. A mere two men got through the process who were anything less than utterly loyal to the government: Lord Provost Montgomerie of Glasgow, whose votes against the treaty at the behest of his town council may by this gesture have been understood and forgiven; and Sir David Ramsay, a member for the Mearns, where it may have been hard to find any unionists. Baillie of Jerviswood explained how all this 'would better answer the ends of the Union than any could be got by ane election in the country which, considering the present ferment, might prove mostly Tory, if not Jacobite'. Indeed, the aim was to get the Union through rather than represent anybody.[87]

In the last throes of the Parliament some other scores could be settled. One gave a measure of official irritation with the priggish Squadrone's extraction of promises in exchange for its support. Revenge came in the allocation of the Equivalent. The Squadrone thought to have taken control of the disbursement of that part of the money set aside for investors in the Company of Scotland, though this would have given it such powers of patronage that the Court could hardly have meant the undertaking seriously. However that may have been, once the treaty got through the deal was off. Instead the British Parliament would set up and supervise a commission for the Equivalent.[88] In vain the Squadrone appealed to friends in London. Neither Godolphin nor the Junto took any notice. They were happy to leave Queensberry's cronies running Scotland.

ↄↄ

In England, meanwhile, the government had played safe and managed the current session of Parliament, convened at the end of 1706, so that it did not at once embark on legislating the Union. Instead, the Commons passed the time on routine business, granting supply and so on, while waiting for the Scots Parliament to finish its work and send down an acceptable version of the treaty. Not till January 22 was this brought before the house.

It met a warm welcome. The sole opposition came from high Tories, who disliked Scots anyway and scorned the whole idea of the Union. They had been pinning their hopes on defeat of the treaty in Edinburgh. Without that, they did not know quite what to do. They might try delaying tactics in their turn. But the system at Westminster could already be manipulated to the executive's ends, and in this case Court and Junto stifled the opposition. It was here, not in Edinburgh, that the treaty was rammed through. Incidentally, it meant agreeing to all the Scots' amendments without demur, yet they were deemed for the purpose acceptable. Secretary Johnstone wrote to Baillie of Jerviswood: 'It's true many of the Commons say this is prescribing to them; why not they make alterations, say they, as well as you, but in all probability this humour will pass.'[89] So it did.

The smoothest path for the treaty lay through a committee of the whole house, where the rules allowed for the subject of debate to be confined to a short enabling clause rather than extended into the details of the treaty; it limited the size of the target offered to the opposition. On February 4, hindered only by vain protests at such an insolent procedure, the treaty was read through in a hurry with no chance of debate. The Ministry justified itself by a claim 'that deliberation always supposes doubts and difficulties, but no material objections being offered against any of the articles, there was no room for delays'.[90] The opposition crumpled. Under ruthless management the bill went through committee in one prolonged sitting. It got its third reading by a vote of 274 to 116 on February 29.

In the Lords the slower pace permitted at least a little deliberation. The Tory peers attacked the treaty for the harm it could wreak on the English constitution in Church and state. The Earl of Nottingham objected to the very name Great Britain on the grounds it would subvert the laws and liberties of England. The judges in the house told him he was talking nonsense. The Earl of Rochester underlined the threat to Anglicanism. But the government pointed out that Thomas Tenison, Archbishop of Canterbury, was even then at work drawing up a bill to offer a guarantee to the Church of England like that already legislated for the Church of Scotland, also to be written into the treaty. Tenison warbled that 'the narrow notions of all Churches have been their ruin; and I believe the Church of Scotland to be as true a Protestant Church as the Church of England, though I cannot say it is so perfect'. Right at the end the maverick Cockney, Lord Haversham, brought up the notion of federalism which, with his usual intuition on the mind of Scotland, he argued would be preferable there. He held that forcing a Union of Parliaments on an unwilling people was asking for trouble and might provoke rebellion; but it was far too late for second thoughts on that scale.[91] Even in the Lords the treaty went through all its stages in three days. Godolphin expressed his relief to Marlborough at 'the best session of Parliament that England ever saw'.

Indeed, one thing all this revealed was how the English no longer feared the Scots. That was the biggest change on the British scene. When Anne had come to the throne the English still disliked and even dreaded their northern neighbours. Yet now it was England's persistence that made the Union possible. The obvious reason lay in the overcoming of deep worries about security. Such was the queen's parting thought to the final sitting of the English Parliament when, on April 24, she urged members to 'omit no opportunity of making my subjects sensible of the security, and the other great and lasting benefits, they may reasonably expect from this happy Union'. Her next message would be to a united Parliament, 'when we shall all join our sincere and hearty endeavours to promote the welfare and prosperity of Great Britain'.[92] The Act of Union, as it must now be called, had passed both houses at Westminster by March 4, received royal assent on March 6, was ratified on March 19 and came into force on May 1.

Meanwhile in Edinburgh, too, ratification of the Act of Union took place on March 19. On March 25 the Parliament, its business completed, was adjourned to April 22. In fact it would never meet again before being dissolved by proclamation on April 28.[93] At that final sitting on March 25, Queensberry, Lord High Commissioner, had already bid farewell to members:

> My lords and gentlemen,
> The public business of this session being now over, it is full time to put an end to it.

> I am persuaded that we and our posterity will reap the benefit of the Union of the two kingdoms, and I doubt not, that as this Parliament has had the honour to conclude it, you will in your several stations recommend to the people of the nation a grateful sense of Her Majesty's goodness and great care for the welfare of her subjects in bringing this important affair to perfection, and that you will promote an universal desire in this kingdom to become one in hearts and affections, as we are inseparably joined in interest with our neighbour nation.

The last word of all was Chancellor Seafield's. 'Now there's ane end of ane auld sang,' he exclaimed as he went through the formal procedure of signing the exemplification of the treaty and returning it to the clerk of the house. It was a great one-liner, a poignant put-down with a punch that made it forever memorable to Scots. But this interpretation may well be deceptive. After all, no man had worked longer and harder than Seafield to still the auld sang: complacency rather than nostalgia might now have been expected of him. Perhaps, like many Scots, he just did not care to reveal his emotions. There was pressing and practical business on hand, to which he and the nation had next to turn.[94]

ɕ

After 1707

*The burgh of Montrose, Jacobite hotbed which could not stop
its parliamentary vote being cast for Union*

'Fair words'

The last battle fought by troops of an independent Scotland had taken place on April 25, 1707, six days before the Union came into force. A fresh campaigning season in the Iberian peninsula was just opening for a unit identified in French sources under the improbable name of Mac Are's regiment, engaged along with Catalan, Dutch, English, Huguenot and Portuguese contingents in the War of the Spanish Succession. Since the allied capture of Barcelona two years before, some of these contingents had been based there. Others were more recently landed in Lisbon before marching east, to the accompaniment of a good deal of rape and pillage, till they reached the shore of the Mediterranean Sea where they meant to winter. The plan was for them all, once spring came, to concentrate at Valencia then advance on Madrid to overthrow the Bourbon, King Philip V, and install in his stead the Habsburg who in Catalonia had already been proclaimed King Charles III of Spain.

But the allied camp was not a happy one. When on the move, Portuguese troops carried with them an image of their nation's patron saint, St Anthony of Padua. It was viewed malevolently, as an idol, by the Scots and their brother Calvinists, the Dutch and then the Camisards of Languedoc, who had recruited and sent a regiment here to fight against the Catholic powers. But the Portuguese were Catholics themselves. They insulted their heretic allies and sometimes this led to fights with knives. When out of sight of their officers, the soldiers indulged in too much drink and violence against one another.

Unfortunately for them they faced a formidable foe in James Stewart, Duke of Berwick, bastard son of the late King James VII and II, now Marshal of France after his capture of Nice from the Duke of Savoy the year before. Berwick was, like his uncle the Duke of Marlborough, on the opposite side, among the first of the modern generals, who moved fast and foxed his enemies while keeping his own troops well supplied by superior logistics. He had arrived in Madrid to take supreme command for the Bourbons in February. A month later he, too, began a march on Valencia, meaning along the way to link up with reinforcements from France under the Duke of Orleans. With superior numbers he could then smash the enemy. By April 25 he had reached Almanza, on a high plain near the border of Castille and Aragon.

The allies were caught out by Berwick's rapid advance. Hastily responding, they hoped to strike at him before his junction with the fresh French force. They set off from the coast on April 16, and on the night of April 24 were in the mountains above Almanza. They decided to mount an immediate assault, despite an outbreak of sickness in the ranks. Next morning the allied regiments were sent on a forced march of 12 miles, so they already felt fatigued by the time they came in sight of Berwick's encampment. When they appeared the French cavalry charged them yet failed to break their formations. Though the allied cavalry counter-attacked and regained some ground, the second French line closed in on the flanks and inflicted heavy losses. The turning point was the collapse and flight of the Portuguese on the right. The rest of the allies could do nothing to retrieve the situation and by sunset the Battle of Almanza was over. Regiments from the British Isles had held their ground but then they retreated back to the mountains, leaving other units on the field to surrender.[1] The Scots lost the last battle they fought as an independent nation. Yet they would win many victories for the Britain of the future.

Almanza was the biggest battle on Spanish soil during this war, and a turning point in the European conflict as a whole. The allies had failed to capitalise fast enough on their own previous victories at Blenheim and Ramillies so as to force the French to the early peace that would have been the most disadvantageous to them. These, from now on, could gradually turn the tables, if never so far as to reverse all their previous losses. When peace finally came at Utrecht six years later, it would confirm that the France which had intimidated Europe for half a century or more was now past her prime, while Britain had embarked on her ascent to global power. All the same, the chance to annihilate the ambitions of Louis XIV was never taken. After a pause for breath under the minority of Louis XV the mortal rivalry of Britain and France would resume.

Lesser peoples were trampled underfoot as these two titans slugged it out. The Dutch Republic had survived again by the skin of its teeth, and the Spanish Netherlands were transferred to no less soporific Austrian rule. But elsewhere France had pushed her frontier permanently to the River Rhine, overrunning old German, Protestant states or imperial cities whose culture and religion she viewed with ill will. Calvinist communities in the Principality of Orange and in the Cevennes were crushed, though not exterminated. The Catalans had struck for freedom under Archduke Charles, but after Almanza they were steadily worn down. In 1711 he left Barcelona on succeeding to the throne of the Holy Roman Empire, from which he at once granted toleration to the Hungarian Calvinists by the Peace of Szatmar, so solving his problems on that front.[2] But for the Catalans the end soon came as the Bourbons' forces closed in.

In the summer of 1713 a ceasefire was called in Catalonia and the allied army, now under the command of the Duke of Argyll, evacuated the province. They retreated to Minorca, which would stay under British occupation for 70 years. Still the Catalans refused to give in. Berwick surrounded Barcelona and stormed the city on September 11: 'Very bloody and obstinate, the besieged disputed every inch of the ground . . . and with their cannon laden with cartridge shot, mowed down their enemies in whole ranks, no quarter being given on either side'.[3] But, forsaken by all their allies, they had to surrender the next day. An exultant Philip V suppressed the liberties of the kingdoms constituting the Spanish monarchy to set up a centralised absolutism, which remained in place under various guises till the death of General Francisco Franco in 1978 and the dawn then of a new era of constitutional monarchy which gave autonomy back to Catalonia.

Rigour was visited not only on the Europe of the Bourbons. In the British Isles, Irish aspirations had been quashed. The end of an independent Scotland can be seen as part of the same process of strategic consolidation by the great powers. The difference was that the Scots had been able to negotiate it. Among small nations they were exceptional, and lucky.

ℰℐ

Still, right up to the Peace of Utrecht, England and France contested each other's spheres of hegemony. While the main theatre of military operations now lay in the Iberian peninsula, Marlborough attacked and captured Lille in 1708; France, for her part, nursed hopes yet of Scotland. In January 1707, Louis XIV had ordered Colonel Nathaniel Hooke to hold himself ready for another mission there. On account of the usual delays, he did not land at Slains in Aberdeenshire till the spring, when the legislation of the Union was almost over. Nothing daunted, he got in touch with those he thought might support a French intervention, in the first place the Dukes of Atholl, Gordon and Hamilton. These contacts proved disappointing. Gordon refused to sign an appeal to Louis XIV for military support on the grounds it would have to bring with it the person of his legitimate sovereign, James VIII and III, who could not possibly be allowed to expose his sacred person to the hazards of war. Then Lord Saltoun, head of a branch of Clan Fraser, visited Slains to warn about Hamilton, who he believed to be in the pay of the English government. This came as a surprise to Hooke after his heart-to-hearts with the duke on a previous visit. But it was confirmed by his host now, the Earl of Erroll.

Few others were willing to deal with Hooke. Several he sought to see said they were ill, presumably with cold feet. As a French spy he had to keep on the move. He rode south to stay at the castle of Powrie, on the braes above Dundee. Here the laird, Thomas Fotheringham, was more positive: he described how 'he durst show himself but very seldom among his vassals, as they pressed him continually to give them leave to arm, reproaching him that the nobility had sold and ruined their country, while the people sought only to take arms in its defence'. Hooke went on to Auchterhouse, seat of Patrick Lyon, member of the Scots Parliament for Angus, a man so eager for the French to invade that he had to be told Louis XIV 'did not pretend to make their cause his principal affair, that he was very willing to assist the Scots to make war, but that he was no way disposed to make war for them, and at his own expense'. Hooke saw letters from Hamilton which had 'sought underhand to break all the measures of the well-affected, and then to excuse himself to them by false pretences, which might lessen their confidence in the king's goodness, and their attachment to France'. He learned that when Lyon and others had offered to take up arms during the crisis last winter, Hamilton told them not to. 'It came into my mind,' wrote Hooke of the duke, 'that he had still an intent of seizing the throne himself.'

Beside the zealots there were the doomsters. Lord Kilsyth, one of Stirlingshire's Jacobites, told Hooke: 'Enough will give you fair words and promises, but that will be all they will do.' Yet Hooke had the boundless optimism of a professional agent. Few of the great men of Scotland were ready to repudiate the exiled Stewarts in so many words. These had come back from exile before. They might do it again. While the intelligence Hooke at length took home to France hardly revealed a Scotland seething with rage at the loss of her independence, Louis XIV and his Ministers still felt taken by the idea of sending over the Pretender, now 19 years old. At the least he could be a nuisance, diverting British men and matériel from Europe.[4]

The French decided to sponsor a landing in Scotland by James in the spring of 1708. He, though suffering from measles, was borne up by boyish enthusiasm and the dream of fulfilling his destiny. The expedition's commander, Claude, Comte de Forbin, felt less keen. Descended from an Aberdonian mercenary who had settled in Provence during the Middle Ages, he had acquired from a few generations of mixed blood a Latin temper: he raged to Louis XIV's face that the whole business was a waste of time, but the king refused to listen. Forbin's subsequent experience did not alter his view. As his thirty ships with 6,000 troops sailed from Dunkirk in March, they were pounded by storms right across the North Sea. Under battened hatches everyone was horribly seasick.

But when they reached the entrance to the Firth of Forth and anchored off Crail and Pittenweem, James's heart lifted. For the first time he gazed on the land of his fathers, the low cliffs of sandstone along the coast of Fife, the picturesque little ports, the queer gables and stairs of the houses, the knobbly hills beyond. Forbin signalled but got no answer. There did not seem to be many Jacobites round here. The nearest ready to declare themselves were some way off, in fact, on the upper reaches of the Forth in Stirlingshire, already raising and drilling recruits in between drinking the Pretender's health, after somehow hearing of his approach. James carried with him a royal proclamation dissolving the Union and promising a free Scots Parliament to decide everthing else. But unless he could go ashore and make the proclamation it was not much use.

Suddenly, a superior English squadron appeared astern of the French, under Admiral George Byng. James begged to be landed, even with just a handful of followers. Forbin ignored the pleas. He knew his own vessels were clean, fast privateers of Dunkirk able to put all necessary distance between himself and the royal navy as long as he weighed anchor at once. So he did, and set sail for the north. Again despite James's entreaties, Forbin refused to go anywhere near Slains, which had an anchorage in Cruden Bay, though he thought of putting into Inverness. But the weather was still foul and he decided to sail for France the long way about, right round Scotland and Ireland. If the voyage hither had been bad, the one thither was ghastly, completed only with great loss of ships and lives.

Thus ended *l'entreprise d'Ecosse*, the second attempt at a Jacobite invasion of the British Isles – and the nearest approach to any armed conflict directly arising from the end of Scottish independence.

The government in London took the threat as seriously as it could. But it faced a problem when nothing had been done to restore the run-down and penniless military establishment in Scotland. Its commander, the Earl of Leven, said that if the French had landed he would have been obliged to retire to Berwick, since there was no way of defending the country. Leven doubled as governor of the Bank of Scotland, at that point crammed with coin and bullion for the change of currency, and he had to face a run on these resources too. About the one initiative the government felt able to take was a rapid and random round-up of people it claimed might collaborate with the French. It was possessed of no hard evidence against any of them. Leven then disgusted the country by sending these prisoners to London.

Some, such as Lord Belhaven, had no time at all for the Jacobites – quite the reverse – and were obviously just being victimised for their opposition to the Union. Others, like the Duke of Hamilton, negotiated their release in a squalid deal. In his case it meant, of all things, alliance with the Junto and Squadrone at the first British General Election then in the offing. Perhaps they needed him more than he needed them, as the voters were about to exact revenge for the outrageous way the initial delegation of Scots MPs to Westminster had been merely nominated. The factions complicit in this would all suffer losses at the polls, though for the representative peers the Court still managed to return a slate of sycophants. Only then could the Scots detained in London return home. All but Belhaven did so: he had died there of 'inflammation of the brain'.

Belhaven's end seems symbolic, like the less harrowing fate of Andrew Fletcher of Saltoun, also taken into custody but not deemed important enough to be hauled off to England. Instead he was held at Stirling Castle. Unlike some of his fellow prisoners he made light of his troubles, knowing there was no evidence against him. Once freed, he felt all the more anxious to get out of Scotland. By September he was back in London, the next year in Holland, whence he made also an excursion to Leipzig. In London once more in 1710, he only returned home during the winter of 1711–1712. In 1715, after the end of the war, he felt delighted to see Paris again. He was over sixty, though, and his health no longer good. By the summer of 1716 his bouts of 'looseness' became more embarrassing. Soon fading fast, he was taken to London by his nephew but could go no further. So he died in England. His last words were: 'Lord have mercy on my poor country that is so barbarously oppressed.'[5]

Fletcher and Belhaven had been left behind by history, but it treated yet more cruelly some others among the last champions of Scottish independence. Hamilton, if he can be counted as such, suffered a horrible death. After being let out of preventive detention in 1708 he never returned to Scotland, but lived in London. He got embroiled in a dispute with his wife's relations over their inheritance and eventually sued her cousin, Charles, Lord Mohun, for £44,000. Meanwhile Hamilton was on his way back into the good graces of Queen Anne, who appointed him ambassador to France in the autumn of 1712 – to his boundless joy but to the alarm of Whigs afraid that, despite the Act of Settlement, he was being sent to negotiate the Pretender's succession to the British throne. While in London waiting to depart, Hamilton bumped into Mohun, who was drunk and challenged him to a duel.

With his 17-year-old illegitimate son, Charles, Hamilton left his house in St James's Square for Hyde Park early in the morning of November 15, 1712. He had fought duels in the past but now he was aged 54, unfit and facing a much younger opponent with the reputation of a brute. All the same the ambidextrous duke, sword in left hand, managed to run his challenger through the chest. Even as Mohun collapsed he slashed at the duke's unprotected right arm, severing an artery. Hamilton staggered away, fell against a tree and died in a few minutes. His furious friends claimed the fatal blow had been struck not by Mohun himself but by his second. In other words, it was murder. Hamilton's widow shed not a tear but raged against her late husband and her relations, while his mother, Duchess Anne, sat in numbed grief at Hamilton Palace, crushed by the tragedy of her son's wasted life.

The readiness, if not eagerness, of gentlemen at that period to risk their all in a duel measures the distance from ours of an age in some respects already recognisably modern. The punctilio about honour might have been understandable in hot-headed youngsters; but for men of years and wisdom and a position in society it is hard to understand what they thought they could gain against everything they could lose. It might at least have struck them that, as time went by, they were in physical terms stacking the odds against themselves. Yet this did not deter them. George Lockhart of Carnwath likewise threw his life away aged barely 50, in a duel in Edinburgh in 1731. The cause was not publicly known and his family kept it so secret that even now historians have no idea whom he fought or why. He seems equally symbolic of a generation in Scotland which had sprung to political life so full of verve and vigour after the turn of the century, yet which soon sputtered out in defeat and disillusion.

෴

To Scots, the Union looked within a distressingly short time to have been a terrible mistake. No economic boom followed, not for now nor indeed for half a century. Businesses closed down rather than opened up in the new British common market. The English dragged their feet in paying the Equivalent; they had promised ready money they did not have. They treated Scots at Westminster with amused contempt. They began to break the terms of the treaty. Soon even architects of it, the Earl of Seafield and the Earl of Mar, regretted what they had done. In the summer of 1711 Mar assured Robert Harley, by now Earl of Oxford, that though he was himself 'not yet weary of the Union' he found the high-handed English attitude 'contrare to all sense, reason and fair dealing'. He added that 'if our trade be no more encouraged than yet it has been, or indeed is like to be, how is it possible that flesh and blood can bear it? And what Scotsman will not be weary of the Union and do all he can to get quit of it?'[6]

By 1713 the Scots at Westminster felt driven to a dramatic demonstration of their discontent. Just as the Treaty of Utrecht was about to be agreed, the British government announced a duty on malt in both Scotland and England, something expressly excluded by the letter of the Union so long as the war had not actually finished. And, contrary to the spirit of the Union, this duty was likely to bear more heavily on the Scots than on the English. It was the last straw to the MPs and peers, who all opposed the tax. They agreed to move for a dissolution of the Union in the House of Lords, to be proposed by Seafield himself. The result of the vote was 54 in favour and 54 against. The deadlock could be resolved only by proxy votes, with a slender majority against, of 17 to 14. The Scots peers had known, of course, that no corresponding motion was ever going to pass the House of Commons. But they made their point, at least partly: the government carried the legislation for the tax yet agreed in secret not to apply it to Scotland. This was in its own terms a successful manoeuvre though it failed to get across that Scottish discontent now amounted to more than another quibble over money.

In fact, within a couple of years armed revolt against the Union would break out. The death in 1714 of Queen Anne, the last Stewart, was the big opportunity for those in England as well as in Scotland who wished to bring back the legitimate regal line and keep Germans off the throne. But such old loyalties would have posed less of a threat to the British Whig establishment if they had not been fired by the utter disillusion of Scots with the Union, extending into the heart of circles which had promoted it in 1707. Mar, indeed, was the leader of the insurrection now (and a grossly inadequate one). Yet at first it succeeded far enough for the Pretender to land in Scotland and get himself crowned James VIII at Scone in 1715, following a tradition of his forefathers. The rebellion found a far firmer base than its more spectacular sequel in 1745, but was hobbled by the military incompetence of Mar and others. In the event the Jacobite risings did nothing to unmake the United Kingdom, rather the reverse. That story must, however, be told in another book.

℃

Not only the noblemen and lairds of Scotland felt unhappy at the consequences of the Union. So, for example, did the merchants who had hoped to do well out of it. And they did do well right at the outset, or rather during the gap between the parliamentary passage of the Union early in 1707 and its entry into force on May 1. During those few months they made a quick killing from a rush of imports – wine, tobacco and other luxuries on which Scottish tariffs were low, all to be re-exported to England once her higher tariffs had been erected right round the new United Kingdom. Politicians at Westminster felt furious but had no remedy. They soon got their own back.

The customs and excise imposed by the full fiscal power of a militarising British state – not only the duties they exacted but also the rigour with which they were enforced – shocked the Scots. They knew nothing of such an authoritarian bureaucracy at local level. Their own customs had been farmed to tacksmen always happy to do a friend a favour, and anyway seldom equipped to lay down the law. Smuggling soon became a national sport in Scotland and remained so till the end of the eighteenth century when one of her own sons, Henry Dundas, made a start on dismantling the prevailing protectionism. Meanwhile the new British state was suddenly everywhere. It set up a presence even in quite small Scottish ports, so long as their foreign trade merited it, in the shape of customs-houses. In times of dearth or rebellion they were often the targets of locals' attacks, who would break in and bear the contents off in triumph. They did so with all the more gusto as the customs was usually manned by Englishmen, Scots being reluctant to work in it.

By lucky chance we can follow one instance of the Union's consequences at this humbler level, far from the world of the aristocracy, through the papers of Adam Smith senior, father of the economist. Born in 1679, he was the younger son of a farmer in Aberdeenshire. After a legal education at King's College, Aberdeen, he had to make his own way in life. He did so as a solicitor, which led to a more promising position as aide to the Earl of Loudoun, one of the last Scottish Secretaries in the independent nation. After Smith then acquired what must have been a sinecure (given the size of the army), clerk to the Court Martial of Scotland, he had more security. He married, first Lilias, daughter of Sir George Drummond, a former Lord Provost and member of the Scots Parliament for Edinburgh, then, on her early death, Margaret, daughter of Robert Douglas of Strathendry, a member for Fife. The young lawyer was moving up in the world.

But for Smith the Union proved a bit of a disaster. The Court Martial of Scotland vanished and he was placed in the 'contingent and dormant list' of civil servants on a salary now 'precarious'. In fact he was not paid for three years. This no doubt explains why he had to seek a job in the customs, even if it made him unpopular with his compatriots. In 1714 he became comptroller at Kirkcaldy. He does not seem to have liked it there, because by 1717 he was appealing to Loudoun for a transfer back to the capital: 'It would be much to my advantage to be at Edinburgh, and put me in a way of being in some things capable to serve your lordship.' That never happened. Smith stayed at Kirkcaldy till his death in January 1723, aged 44, leaving Margaret pregnant with the younger Adam, born in June. Life was hard for her now, with a son to bring up only on such income as, for example, a bond from Loudoun afforded her. She wrote to him in 1730 saying she had so far received none of this money, 'which being very much straitened as I have formerly signified to your lordship, I hope you'll order to be paid me betwixt [now] and Lammas next'. She signed herself 'with all due respect', but the tone of the letter does not give an impression she thought Loudoun due that much respect. She would remain a formidable lady into high old age and lived till 1784, by which time her son had achieved international fame with *The Wealth of Nations*.[7]

How many Scots did the Union render, like the Smiths, worse off? The evidence of rebellion is, surely, that there were many. Yet it is hard to believe that for a majority the Union made much difference. It was actually designed to work that way, with the United Kingdom taking over only fiscal, foreign and military matters, leaving Scots to their own devices across almost the entire range of domestic affairs, notably the law, the Church and the educational system guaranteed in the Act of Union. Because before 1707 Scotland had next to no fiscal, foreign or military policy, this division of labour between new British and native authorities scarcely deprived Scots of any degree of self-government previously enjoyed in practice. The Parliament at Westminster laid claim to absolute sovereignty over Scotland yet did not exercise it except when feeling a need to flex its muscles and show the Scots who was boss – as after the Jacobite rebellions, to make sure these should not recur. What we may term the first phase of the Union, leaving a semi-independent Scotland well alone, lasted more than a century. Since it saw glorious intellectual achievement, the one thing that gives Scottish history any universal significance, it ill behoves us now to complain about it.

A second phase began after 1832, with change right across Scottish society symbolised by the parliamentary reform of that year. It brought a rapid collapse of the settlement of 1707, not only with the overthrow of the political arrangements but also with schism in the Church of Scotland, gradual transfer of the universities into a British system and growing pressure on Scots law to conform to British norms. It is a wonder resistance to all this did not amount to more. Yet if anything the Scottish people welcomed and forwarded the transformation, seeing the United Kingdom as their vehicle to freedom and progress, whereas hoary old Scottish institutions seemed only to be impediments. The nation's intellectual endeavours flagged somewhat (though they could hardly have been expected to sustain the intensity of the eighteenth century). But against that was to be set stupendous material advance, which by the end of the nineteenth century may well have made Scotland the richest country in the world. The essential context was not so much Britain as the Empire, where so many Scots found fortune and fulfilment and the chance to spread a beneficent national influence across the globe. It was the brilliant high noon of Scottish history.

When we look at the Union we have to ask whether, for all the flaws in it which have since emerged, that Scottish glory of the eighteenth and nineteenth centuries could ever have been achieved without it. The glory had its roots in the independent nation. As this book has sought to bring out, the vigour of the Scots' existing traditions and institutions let them shape the Union too, for good or ill. The Union was a genuine choice in 1707, not just a factitious product of English expansionism.

At the opposite extreme of the available range of options was a Scots republic, such as Seafield accused Fletcher of wanting to erect: let us take the point as worth a moment's serious thought. In fact Seafield distorted Fletcher's position, into which it is hard to read a demand for anything more than constitutional monarchy; to call this republican was merely polemical. However that may have been, Scotland remained at too primitive a stage of social and economic development to form a republic. A republic rests on autonomous individuals, whether in an oligarchy, as in Venice, in men of property, as in the early United States, or in the free citizens of modern states. In 1707, Scots were not autonomous; their place in chains of feudal dependence determined their social and political role, if any. The only ones to approach autonomy were landed aristocrats, and in their factional rivalry we see the nearest Scotland might get to republicanism: the sole comparison is with the late Roman Republic, which likewise dissolved into empire. If Scots could not make a kingdom happy or stable, they could not have made a republic so.

In the realm of reality Scotland might have remained an independent monarchy, but only at the price of settling what she would not or could not settle in advance of any other accord with England, the succession. There was, leaving aside the more fanciful Prussian or Savoyard or Hamiltonian options, a choice of two successions: the Hanoverian, or else the restoration of the legitimate line of Stewarts. The arrival of James VIII as King of Scots in Edinburgh on the death of Anne in 1714 would have prompted the arrival of English troops soon afterwards, all the more of them for the fact that peace now reigned in Europe. There can be little doubt that the result of any consequent war would have been no different from the actual outcome of the Jacobite rebellion of 1715: Scotland would have been beaten. She had next to no army, and what she had was commanded by traitors. Union would then have come all the same, probably on worse terms than in 1707.

The final opportunity to avoid the Union of 1707 by peaceful means had really passed with Scotland's spurning the chance to accept the Hanoverian succession as an independent kingdom, an option last presented in the English ultimatum of the Alien Act in 1705. If she had accepted it, the Union of Crowns could have continued and the Scots

Parliament would have survived, as the Irish Parliament did till 1801. There would have been a problem that the Union of Crowns had already proved itself the worst of all forms of government for Scotland, worse than independence before 1603 and worse than the Union of Parliaments after 1707. Perhaps some remedy might have lain in a scheme of limitations. Even so the fiscal power of the English state would surely have been deployed during the eighteenth century to keep a nominally independent but penniless government in Edinburgh under control, just as actually happened with a nominally independent government in Dublin. That Irish government started to exploit its nominal powers from 1781 in an effort to make something real of them. The English would not in the long run stand for it. When the Irish at length revolted, they were crushed. The net result only impelled Ireland in turn towards full Union with Great Britain in 1801. How could an independent Scotland have differed? More likely she would have been driven to the same destination of the Union only by a slower route.

This book has also sought to bring out that the questions facing Scotland in 1707 about how to reconcile her internal problems to the external relationship with England ought to be read in a wider European context too. In those terms, this was an age of imperialism, of expansion by great powers at the expense of lesser peoples. Scotland could not escape it. She would have been exceptional if she had not succumbed and thrown in her lot with one of the empires – as it happened, the most liberal of them. Even the Dutch, always an example to Scots, suffered something of the same fate. The eighteenth century saw them lose the old republican virtues which had fed their heroic struggles for independence, so they faced the choice of becoming satellites to the British or the French. Others did not even have that choice – notably the entire eastern and southern periphery of states from the Baltic region round to the Balkan to the Italian and Iberian peninsulas, some of which vanished altogether, while others submitted to a foreign yoke or at best sank into impotent pettiness.

❧

At length came springtimes of nations, in 1848, in 1918 and in 1989. The great powers of Europe had had their day, declined or collapsed, and the lesser peoples over which they had lorded it emerged once more into the light of history, capable of self-determination again. On all three occasions, Scotland looked on and hardly associated herself with these turning points in the tortuous history of the nation-state. In 1848 and 1918 she just never would have considered herself submerged, let alone oppressed. By 1989 things were a little different, yet not so different as to make Scotland plunge into the surge of national liberation on the death of the last European empire.

All that followed, after a suitably cautious interval, were the electoral shifts – nothing more – leading to the restoration of a Scottish Parliament in 1999. It was not a strong reaction to the end of the worst of the three centuries since the Union. To be sure, material advance had continued, if with interruptions and at a slower rate than in the rest of Great Britain, so that a relative economic decay became evident. Worse than that, the cultural autonomy guaranteed by the Union steadily dissolved. This went hand in hand with a vast increase in the power of the British state at the expense of national institutions preserved in 1707. But though Scotland was in decline, relative or absolute, she could still show just enough vitality to attempt escape from it. Devolution was the outcome.

To me and many others seven years later, it seems a flawed outcome. The government of Scotland probably cannot and certainly will not deviate from the main lines of policy laid down in London. We have inherited a vast apparatus of state from the unionist past. It is all dressed up in tartan with nowhere to go. It wastes its time and money on trivialities, on efforts at micro-management of personal lives. Deeper problems of the nation, of redefining its character and purpose, are hardly even seen, let alone solved. We have done no more than contrive a revised version of the Union of Crowns between 1603 and 1707 – which by any standards counts as the most wretched era of Scottish history. There may indeed be no satisfactory halfway house between the state of the nation as it was before 1603 and the state of the nation as it was after 1707. Now we are travelling back from the destination reached at the Union, if along a less bumpy route. But the question poses itself whether we should not make greater haste to the place where we started, as an independent nation.

Notes

∾

Abbreviations used in the notes to indicate major sources

MANUSCRIPT SOURCES

BL Add MSS – British Library, Additional Manuscripts
Huntington – Loudoun Papers, Huntington Library, San Marino, California
NAS – National Archives of Scotland
NLS – National Library of Scotland

PRINTED SOURCES

APS – *Acts of the Parliament of Scotland*, ed. C. Innes & T. Thomson, 11 vols (London, 1814–75)
Baillie – G. Baillie of Jerviswood, *Correspondence 1702–1708* (Bannatyne Club, 1842)
Burnet – G. Burnet, *History of his Own Time*, ed. M.J. Routh, 6 vols (Oxford, 1833)
Carstares – *State Papers and Letters addressed to William Carstares*, ed. J. McCormick (Edinburgh, 1774)
Clerk History – Sir John Clerk of Penicuik, *History of the Union of Scotland and England, extracts from his MS* De Imperio Britannico, trans. and ed. D. Duncan (Edinburgh, 1993)
Clerk Memoirs – Sir John Clerk of Penicuik, *Memoirs* (London, 1895)
Defoe – D. Defoe, *History of the Union of Great Britain* (Edinburgh, 1709)
HMC – *Historical Manuscripts Commission* (volume specified in note)
Hume – Sir John Hume of Crossrig, *A Diary of the Proceedings in the Parliament and Privy Council of Scotland, May 21, 1700 to March 7, 1707* (Bannatyne Club, 1828)
Hooke – *The Correspondence of Colonel N. Hooke*, ed. W.J. Macray, 2 vols (London, 1871)

Lockhart Letters – *Letters of George Lockhart*, ed. D. Szechi (Edinburgh, 1989)

Lockhart Memoirs – [G.Lockhart of Carnwath], *Memoirs concerning the Affairs of Scotland*, 2 vols (London, 1714).

Marchmont – *Marchmont Papers, a selection from the papers of the Earls of Marchmont*, ed. G.H. Rose (London, 1831)

Ridpath – [G. Ridpath], *An Account of the Proceedings of the Parliament of Scotland which met at Edinburgh, May 6, 1703* (np, 1704)

Seafield – James Ogilvy, Earl of Seafield *et al.*, *Letters Relating to Scotland in the Reign of Queen Anne*, ed. P. Hume Brown (Edinburgh, 1915)

Young – *The Parliaments of Scotland*, ed. M. Young, 2 vols (Edinburgh, 1996)

CHAPTER I

1. All dates in this book are Old Style. Following the Scottish usage, years start on January 1; in England they still started on March 25.
2. Burnet, II, 23; N. Japikse, *Willem III, de Stadhouder-Koning* (Amsterdam, 2 vols, 1933), II, 523; A.M.J. Fabius, *Het Leven van Willem III 1650–1702*) (Alkmaar, nd), 392–3.
3. *Hume*, 79–80.
4. T. Claydon, *William III and the Godly Revolution* (Cambridge, 1996).
5. 'Observations upon precendency', in Sir G. Mackenzie, *Works* (2 vols, Edinburgh 1716–22), II, 517–18.
6. *Letters of John Graham of Claverhouse, Viscount Dundee*, ed. G. Smythe (Bannatyne Club, 1826), 39–49, 64–7, 78–83; *Papers Illustrative of the Political Condition of the Highlands of Scotland 1689–1696*, ed. J. Gordon (Maitland Club, 1845), 106–7, 133–42; H. Mackay, *Memoirs of the War carried on in Scotland and Ireland 1689–1691*, ed. J.M. Hog. P.F. Tytler and A. Urquhart (Bannatyne Club, 1833), 4–7, 17–22, 37–61, 122–32, 223–41, 265–6, 298; *Carstares*, 275.
7. The most dramatic account is J. Prebble, *Glencoe* (London, 1966), the most scholarly P. Hopkins, *Glencoe and the End of the Highland War* (Edinburgh, 1986), which has become still better in subsequent editions.
8. J.R.N. McPhail (ed.), *Highland Papers* (Scottish History Society, 1914), 57–8.
9. Ibid., 65.
10. Ibid., 90.
11. *Andrew Fletcher, Political Works*, ed. J. Robertson (Cambridge, 1997), 56–7; Sir R. Sibbald, *Provision for the Poor in Time of Dearth and Scarcity* (Edinburgh, 1699), 3; P. Walker, *Biographia Presbyteriana*

(Edinburgh, 1827), 25–8; M. Martin, *A Description of the Western Isles of Scotland* (Glasgow, 1844), 14, 76.

12. M. Flinn *et al.*, *Scottish Population History* (Cambridge, 1977), 180–1; I. Whyte, *Agriculture and Society in Seventeenth-Century Scotland* (Edinburgh, 1979), 152–62.

13. Robertson, op. cit., 56.

14. *APS*, IX, 19–40.

15. H.C. Foxcroft (ed.), *A Supplement to Burnet's* 'History of My Own Time' (Oxford, 1902), 415.

16. J. Macky, *Memoirs of the Secret Services* (London, 1733), 125.

17. Burnet, I, 580

18. Ibid., II, 64.

19. T. Maxwell, 'William III and the Scots Presbyterians', *Records of the Scottish Church History Society*, XV (1965), 169–91.

20. *Acts of the General Assembly of the Church of Scotland* (Edinburgh, 1843), 241.

21. P.W.J. Riley, *King William and the Scottish Politicians* (Edinburgh, 1979), 22–46; D.H. Whiteford, 'Jacobitism as a Factor in Presbyterian–Episcopalian Relationships in Scotland 1689–90', *Records of the Scottish Church History Society*, XVI (1967), 129–49; R.B. Knox, 'Establishment and Toleration during the Reigns of William, Mary and Anne', ibid., XXIII (1989), 339–40; L.K.J. Glassey, 'William II and the Settlement of Religion in Scotland 1688–90', ibid., XXIII (1989), 323–9; T. Clarke, 'The Williamite Episcopalians and the Glorious Revolution in Scotland', ibid., XXIV (1990), 436–8.

22. T. Maxwell, 'Presbyterianism and Episcopalianism in 1688', *Records of the Scottish Church History Society*, XIII (1957), 25–37.

23. W. Mackay, 'A Famous Minister of Daviot', *Transactions of the Gaelic Society of Inverness*, XII (1885–6), 244–56.

24. *Lockhart Memoirs*, 9.

25. B.C. Brown (ed.), *The Letters and Diplomatic Instructions of Queen Anne* (London, 1935), 171.

26. D. Greene, *Queen Anne* (1970), 132.

27. Brown, op. cit., 16.

28. *The House of Commons 1690–1715*, ed. E. Cruickshanks, S. Handley and D.W. Hayton, 5 vols (Cambridge, 2002), I, 224.

29. *APS*, X, 59–60.

30. *APS*, XI, 5.

31. *APS*, XI, 26.

32. *Carstares*, 715.

33. *Marchmont*, III, 343, memorial, July 1, 1702; *HMC* Laing, 2 vols (London, 1925), II, 63, memorial, July 10, 1702.

34. *Lockhart Memoirs*, 23.
35. P.W.J. Riley, *The Union of 1707* (Manchester, 1978), 42.
36. *NAS*, GD 248, box 5/2, March 6, 1703; *Lockhart Memoirs*, 42–3; Burnet, V, 97.
37. *APS*, XI, appendix, 148.
38. *Burnet*, II, 72.
39. *Hume*, 91.
40. *APS*, XI, 142.
41. G.P. Insh, *Scottish Colonial Schemes 1620–1686* (Glasgow, 1922), 62–85.
42. Sir W. Alexander, *An Encouragement to Colonies* (London, 1624), 45; W. Paterson, *Proposals and Reasons for Constituting a Council of Trade* (Edinburgh, 1701), 194; M. Buist, *At Spes non Fracta, Hope & Co 1770–1815* (Amsterdam, 1974), 45, 82; B. Lenman, 'The English and Dutch East India Companies and the Birth of Consumerism in the Augustan World', *Eighteenth-Century Life*, XIV, 1990, 100–1; *The Jacobite Clans of the Great Glen* (Aberdeen, 1995), 25; V. Enthoven, 'The Last Straw, trade contacts along the North Sea coast: the Scottish staple at Veere', in J. Heerma van Voss and J. Roding, *The North Sea and Culture* (Hilversum, 1996), 211.
43. *Young*, II, 485–6, 510, 704.
44. R. Saville, *Bank of Scotland, a History 1695–1995* (Edinburgh, 1996), 9.
45. A. Mackenzie, *History of the Camerons* (Inverness, 1884), 214.
46. *Lockhart Letters*, xiii.
47. Notably in Saxe Bannister's edition of *The Writings of William Paterson*, 3 vols (Oxford, 1859).
48. *APS*, XI, appendix, 152–3.

CHAPTER 2

1. Queensberry's report to Queen Anne of what followed is dated September 25; it is not likely he delayed informing her. See W.C. Mackenzie, *Simon Fraser, Lord Lovat, his Life and Times* (London, 1908), 115.
2. Anonymous, *A Collection of Original Papers about the Scots Plot* (London, 1704), 4.
3. B. and M. Cottret, 'La sainteté de Jacques II ou les miracles d'un roi défunt', in E. Corp (ed.), *L'Autre Exil: les Jacobites en France au début du XVIIIe siècle* (Aubenas d'Ardèche, 1993), 94–6.
4. H.K. Fraser (ed.), *Memoirs of the Life of Simon Lord Lovat* (London, 1797), 97.

5. *Hooke*, II, preface.
6. K.J. Holsti, *Peace and War: Armed Conflicts and International Order 1648–1989* (Cambridge, 1989), 47, 68; H.M. Scott, *The Rise of the Great Powers 1642–1815* (London, 1983), 1–66; P. Kennedy, *The Rise and Fall of the Great Powers* (London, 1988), 100–8.
7. J.B. Collins, *The State in Early Modern France* (Cambridge, 1995), 90–1; D. Parker, *The Making of French Absolutism* (London, 1983), 124–5.
8. *Hooke*, II, 16.
9. *HMC* Laing (London, 1925), II, 43.
10. M.J. Braddick, *The Nerves of State, Taxation and the Financing of the English State 1558–1714* (Manchester, 1996), 12–13, 33.
11. Fraser, op. cit., 98.
12. Ibid., 128.
13. *Baillie*, 11.
14. *APS*, XI, appendix, 161; *Ridpath*, 101.
15. C.S. Terry, *The Scottish Parliament, its Constitution and Procedure 1603–1707* (Glasgow, 1905), 37, 48.
16. These figures ignore the handful of members who sat in both Parliaments but for different seats; they do not affect the broad magnitudes noted here.
17. P. Hume Brown (ed.), *Letters relating to Scotland in the Reign of Queen Anne* (Edinburgh, 1915), 2, 5.
18. Ibid., 115.
19. *Young*, I, 227.
20. Ibid., 100.
21. *The House of Commons 1690–1715*, ed. E. Cruickshanks, S. Handley and D.W. Hayton, 5 vols (Cambridge, 2002), II, 833.
22. Ibid., 834.
23. Ibid., 876.
24. Ibid., 835.
25. Ibid., 854.
26. Ibid., 862.
27. *Lockhart Memoirs*, I, 69.
28. Ibid., 95.
29. *Clerk Memoirs*, 49.
30. *Young*, I, x–xii.
31. F.J. Grant, 'State Ceremonials in Edinburgh in the Olden Time', *Book of the Old Edinburgh Club*, XVIII, 1933, 29–30.
32. *APS*, XI, 37.
33. *APS*, XI, appendix, 9.
34. *Ridpath*, 22.

35. Ibid., 6–8.
36. *Early Letters of Robert Wodrow 1698–1709*, ed. L.W. Sharp (Edinburgh, 1937), 256.
37. Ibid., 254; Anonymous, *The Life and Reign of Queen Anne* (London, 1738), 112.
38. The record describes him only as 'a gentleman who represented a northern shire'; *Ridpath*, 20.
39. Ibid.
40. Ibid., 33 et seqq.
41. *Andrew Fletcher, Political Works*, ed. J. Robertson (Cambridge, 1997), 131–6.
42. Ibid., 138–9.
43. Ibid., 161.
44. *HMC* Seafield (London, 1894), rept XIV, appendix III, 199.
45. Lockhart, I, 119.
46. Not named in the record, but I propose Allardyce because of his knowledge of business in the Holy Roman Empire and because of his barely concealed Jacobitism.
47. *Ridpath*, 69.
48. Ibid., 194.
49. *Carstares*, 719.
50. *Ridpath*, 241.
51. Ibid., 250.
52. *Burnet*, II, 738.
53. R.L. Emerson, 'Scottish Cultural Change 1660–1710', in J. Robertson (ed.), *A Union for Empire* (Cambridge, 1995), 128.
54. G. Ridpath, *Historical Account of the Ancient Rights and Powers of the Parliament of Scotland* (Edinburgh, 1703), iv, xiii.
55. *Ridpath*, 46; R. Chambers, *Domestic Annals of Scotland*, 3 vols (Edinburgh, 1858–61), III, 185.
56. *HMC* Seafield, rept XIV, 198.
57. *Ridpath*, 54.
58. Ibid., 269.
59. Ibid., 273.
60. J. Macky, *Memoirs of the Secret Services* (London, 1733), 130.
61. Anonymous, *A Collection of Original Papers about the Scots Plot* (London, 1704), 3.
62. *Burnet*, V, 133.
63. *House of Lords Journals* (London, 1891), XVII, 505–6, 554; *House of Commons Journals* (London, 1891), VI, 222–3.
64. *Lockhart Memoirs*, 1, 87.
65. Robertson, op. cit., 175–215.

CHAPTER 3

1. *The Conditions and Articles of the intended Roup of the Ship Worcester lying in Burntisland Harbour* (np, 1705).
2. G.P. Insh (ed.), *Papers relating to the Ships and Voyages of the Company of Scotland Trading to Africa and the Indies* (Edinburgh, 1924), 252–63.
3. *Hume*, 119.
4. *Marchmont*, III, 263.
5. HMC Laing (London, 1925) II, 63–7; *Burnet*, II, 396.
6. *Lockhart Memoirs*, I, 97.
7. *NLS MS* 7102, f.16.
8. *NLS MS* 7121, June 3, 1704.
9. Ibid., June 10, 1704.
10. HMC Mar and Kellie (London, 1904), I, 228.
11. *Seafield*, 14.
12. SRO GD248, box 2/1, May 1, 25, June 8, 1704; BL Add MSS 34180, 40, May 30, 1704.
13. *Lockhart Memoirs*, I, 112–13; *Burnet*, II, 763.
14. *NLS MS* 7102, f. 26.
15. *APS*, XI, 125–6.
16. *APS*, XI, 125.
17. *APS*, XI, 125–7.
18. *APS*, XI, appendix, 38.
19. [James Hodges], *The Rights and Interests of the Two British Monarchies, inquired into and cleared, with a special respect to an united or separate state* (London, 1703), 2–4.
20. HMC Laing, II, 68–70.
21. Anonymous, *Reflections on a Late Speech by the Lord Haversham* (London, 1704), 8.
22. *NLS MS* 7121, July 14, 1704.
23. Ibid., August 6, 1704.
24. HMC Laing, II, 70–2; *Seafield*, 137; *Lockhart Memoirs*, I, 101.
25. *Lockhart Memoirs*, I, 98; HMC Mar and Kellie, I, 229.
26. *Carstares*, 719, 727.
27. *Seafield*, 150.
28. *Burnet*, V, 171–2.
29. *APS*, XI, 152.
30. *APS*, XI, 128–30; *Hume*, 148.
31. *Clerk Memoirs*, 53–4.
32. *NLS MSS* 7121, ff. 34, 36, 38.
33. *Defoe*, 52–3; *APS*, XI, 133–7.

34. *Lockhart Letters*, 15.
35. *APS*, XI, 205.
36. *Seafield*, 382.
37. Anonymous, *A Present Remedie for Want of Money* (np, 1704), 1–9.
38. *APS*, XI, appendix, 53.
39. *NLS*, MS 17498, ff.70 et seqq; Goldsmiths' Library, MS 81.
40. *Andrew Fletcher, Political Works*, ed. J. Robertson (Cambridge, 1997), 200–1.
41. S. Muramatsu, 'Some Types of National Interest in the Anglo–Scottish Union of 1707', *Journal of Economics*, Kumamoto Gakuen University, III, 1996.
42. Bank of Scotland minutes, March 2, December 15, 18, 1704.
43. *NLS* pamphlets 1,349 (16), *An Essay for Promoting of Trade, and increasing the coin of the nation* (np, 1705).
44. *Lockhart Letters*, 7.
45. *Lockhart Memoirs*, 99.
46. Bank of Scotland minutes, December 19, 1704.
47. H. Chamberlen, *A Few Proposals Humbly Recommending the Establishing of a Land–credit in this Kingdom* (Edinburgh, 1700).
48. J. Law, *Money and Trade Considered* (Edinburgh, 1705); *Proposals and Reasons for Constituting a Council of Trade in Scotland* (Glasgow, 1751).
49. J. Law, *The Circumstances of Scotland Considered with respect to the Present Scarcity of Money* (Edinburgh, 1705).
50. *Lockhart Memoirs*, 169.
51. S. Bannister (ed.), *The Writings of William Paterson* (London, 1859), II, xli–liii.
52. *APS*, XI, 218.
53. *Burnet*, II, 388.
54. E. Simonyi (ed.), *Angol diplomatiai iratok II Rákóczi Ferencz korára* (Budapest, 1871–7), i–iii.
55. A. Crichton (ed.), *The Life and Diary of John Blackadder* (Edinburgh, 1824), 209–10.
56. *Huntington*, LO 8101; HMC Atholl (London, 1891), XII, pt 8, 62.
57. *Defoe*, 84–91; *Burnet*, II, 763–4.
58. BL Add MSS 17667, ff. 497, 515; *Letters Illustrative of the Reign of William III*, ed. G.P.R. James (London, 1841), III, 271; HMC Bath (London, 1897), I, 64.
59. HMC Atholl, XII, pt 8, 63.
60. A. Boyer, *History of the Reign of Queen Anne, digested into annals* (London, 1703–13), III, 157; W. Coxe (ed.), *Private and Original Correspondence of Charles Talbot, Duke of Shrewsbury* (London,

1821), 646–7; *HMC* Portland (London, 1899), IV, 151; T. Harris, *Politics under the Later Stuarts* (Harlow, 1993), 151,

61. R. Sibbald, *The Liberty and Independency of the King and Church of Scotland asserted* (Edinburgh, 1704), I, 11; L.W. Sharp (ed.), *Early Letters of Robert Wodrow 1698–1709* (Edinburgh, 1937), 252.
62. [W. Atwood], *The Superiority and Direct Dominion of the Imperial Crown of England. Asserted* (London, 1704), 541.
63. J. Dalrymple, *Collections concerning the Scottish History preceding the Death of King David the First* (Edinburgh, 1705), 301–6.
64. *APS*, XI, 85, 203, 221–2.
65. *House of Commons Journals* (London, 1891), VI, 368–74; *Letters from James Vernon to the Duke of Shrewsbury 1696–1708* (London, 1980), III, 279–82.
66. *Burnet*, V, 175.
67. *HMC* Portland, IX, 169; G.P.R. James, op. cit., III, 275–9; *Burnet*, V, 182–3; Coxe, op. cit., 647–8.
68. *Baillie*, 18.
69. *Ibid.*, 16.
70. Roxburghe himself subscribed to one of those variations in his famous comment why Scots in the end might agree to Union: 'The motives will be, trade with most, Hanover with some, ease and security with others'; ibid., 20.
71. *Ibid.*, 21.
72. *Ibid.*, 17.
73. [J. Hodges], *War betwixt the Two British Kingdoms Considered* (London, 1705); G. Ridpath, *The Reducing of Scotland by Arms, and Annexing it to England as a Province, Considered* (Edinburgh, 1705).
74. *Ridpath*, 16.
75. *Baillie*, 28.
76. *Ibid.*, 18–22.

CHAPTER 4

1. *NAS*, GD 406/C1/8130.
2. *HMC* Mar and Kellie (London, 1904), I, 275.
3. *Hooke*, I, 203–4, 268–73.
4. *Ibid.*, 387–408.
5. J. Taylor, *A Journey to Edenborough in 1708*, ed. W. Cowan (Edinburgh, 1903), 113.
6. *Lockhart Memoirs*, I, 172.
7. *NAS*, Hamilton MSS, GD 406/1.10344, February 11, 1705.

8. Taylor, op. cit., 117.
9. *Baillie*, 21.
10. Ibid., 35–6.
11. Ibid., 47.
12. Ibid., 114; *Lockhart Memoirs*, 170–7; A. Cunningham, *The History of Great Britain from the Revolution of 1688 to the Accession of George I*, 2 vols (London, 1787), I, 426–7.
13. *Hooke*, I, 335.
14. Ibid., 343.
15. *Lockhart Memoirs*, I, 134–5.
16. Ibid., 20.
17. *Hooke*, 372
18. Ibid., 380.
19. Ibid., 387.
20. Taylor, op. cit., 162.
21. *HMC* Portland (London, 1899), VIII, 177.
22. *HMC* Coke (London, 1889), 53.
23. *HMC* Mar and Kellie, I, 238.
24. *HMC* Seafield (London, 1894), XIV, pt 3, 207; P.H. Scott, 'Why did the Scottish Parliament accept the Treaty of Union?', *Scottish Affairs*, LII, 2005.
25. Taylor, op. cit., 126.
26. Anonymous, *A Dialogue between a Countryman and a Landwart Schoolmaster* (Edinburgh, 1705), 2.
27. F.M. McNeill, *The Scots Kitchen* (London, 1974), 39.
28. Anonymous, *A Copy of a Letter from a Country Farmer to his Laird, a Member of Parliament* (np, 1705). The text is as printed in the tract except that I have reduced the capitalisation. Any resemblance to the vernacular of Irvine Welsh is coincidental.
29. *Baillie*, 60; *Seafield*, 27.
30. *Seafield*, 27.
31. *More Culloden Papers*, ed. D. Warrand (Inverness, 1924), II, 5.
32. *Lockhart Letters*, 19.
33. *Lockhart Memoirs*, I, 114–5.
34. *Baillie*, 55.
35. Sir Iain Moncreiffe of that Ilk, *The Atholl Highlanders* (Derby, nd), 1–4.
36. Sir Walter Scott, *Heart of Midlothian*, ch. 35.
37. John Campbell, 9th Duke of Argyll, *Intimate Society Letters of the Eighteenth Century*, 2 vols (London, 1910), I, 9–31.
38. *Lockhart Memoirs*, I, 133.
39. *Seafield*, 38–45.
40. Ibid., 32, 36, 38; *Baillie*, 79.

41. *Baillie*, 97.
42. G. Davies (ed.), 'Letters from Queen Anne to Godolphin', *Scottish Historical Review*, XIX, 1922, 191–2.
43. Argyll, op. cit., I, 9.
44. *Clerk Memoirs*, 50–1.
45. *Burnet*, V, 221. Paul Henderson Scott has been right to stress in his writings the points made in the paragraph above.
46. *APS*, XI, 213–4.
47. *Seafield*, 49.
48. *APS*, XI, 213–4.
49. *Lockhart Memoirs*, I, 142–3.
50. *Burnet*, V, 221; Argyll, op. cit., 35–9.
51. *Hume*, 162.
52. Anonymous, *An Essay for Promoting of Trade* (np, 1705), 1.
53. Bank of Scotland minutes, June 26, 1705; *APS*, XI, 218.
54. *Seafield*, 58.
55. *HMC Mar and Kellie*, I, 234.
56. Ibid.
57. *APS*, XI, 216.
58. *Hume*, 165.
59. *Seafield*, 60.
60. *Baillie*, 103–8; *Seafield*, 52.
61. *Huntington*, LO 11379.
62. *Lockhart Memoirs*, I, 115.
63. Ibid., 114.
64. Ibid., 116.
65. *APS*, XI, 215, 295.
66. *APS*, XI, 217; *Seafield*, 64.
67. *Seafield*, 62.
68. *Lockhart Memoirs*, I, 120.
69. *Seafield*, 71–2.
70. Ibid., 75; *APS*, XI, 223.
71. *Seafield*, 78.
72. Ibid., 80–1; *APS*, XI, 224.
73. *HMC Mar and Kellie*, I, 235.
74. *APS*, XI, 224; *Seafield*, 85–6.
75. *Seafield*, 85; *Lockhart Memoirs*, I, 130.
76. *Seafield*, 84–5.
77. *APS*, XI, 237.
78. *Burnet*, II, 780, 798–9.
79. *Seafield*, 90.
80. *Clerk Memoirs*, 57.

81. *Lockhart Memoirs*, I, 53–6.
82. *HMC* Laing, II, 119–23.
83. *APS*, XI, 243.
84. J. Slezer, *Theatrum Scotiae* (London, 1693), a.
85. *APS*, XI, 299.
86. *Baillie*, 125.
87. Cited in D.W. Hayton, *The House of Commons 1690–1715* (Cambridge, 2002), 225–6.
88. *Burnet*, II, 329, 356.
89. H. Bosc, *La Guerre des Cévennes 1702–1710* (Presses du Languedoc, 1990), V, 99; James, Duke of Berwick, *Mémoires du Maréchal de Berwick* (Paris, 1778), I, 196–7.
90. Bosc, op. cit., V, 256.
91. Anonymous, *The Deplorable History of the Catalans* (London, 1714), 5–23.
92. *House of Commons Journals* (London, 1891), VI, 476; *Burnet*, II, 786.
93. *Burnet*, V, 240.
94. ibid., 240–1.
95. *HMC* Mar and Kellie, I, 239–51.
96. *Baillie*, 142.
97. Ibid., 144.
98. *Lockhart Memoirs*, I, 95.

CHAPTER 5

1. J. Macky, *Memoirs of the Secret Services* (Roxburghe Club, 1895), 84.
2. J. Swift, *Journal to Stella* (Oxford, 1948), I, 355.
3. *The Letters of Daniel Defoe*, ed. G. Healey (Oxford, 1955), 132.
4. R. Rowan, *Thirty-Three Centuries of Espionage* (New York, 1967), 102.
5. *BL Add MSS* 6420, July 31, 1706.
6. Healey, op. cit., 133.
7. *Lockhart Memoirs*, I, 142.
8. Ibid., 134, 140.
9. *The Review*, October 10, 1706.
10. *Carstares*, 692.
11. *HMC* Mar and Kellie (London, 1904), I, 270.
12. Ibid., 279.
13. *Marchmont*, 299.
14. *Clerk Memoirs*, 58.
15. *Burnet*, II, 792.
16. *Lockhart Memoirs*, I, 142–3.

17. *The Marlborough–Godolphin Correspondence*, ed. H. Snyder, 3 vols (Oxford, 1975), II, 756; *Lockhart Memoirs*, I, 191.
18. *HMC* Mar and Kellie, I, 271.
19. *Lockhart Memoirs*, I, 156–6; *Carstares*, 751.
20. *HMC* Mar and Kellie, I, 143–51.
21. *Carstares*, 743–4; *HMC* Marchmont (London, 1894), appendix 3, 158.
22. *APS*, appendix, 165–6; *Clerk*, 60.
23. *Carstares*, 742–9.
24. *HMC* Portland (London, 1899), IV, 309–10.
25. *Lockhart Letters*, I, 25.
26. *NAS*, GD 45/14/336/32; *APS*, XI, appendix, 166.
27. *APS*, XI, 165–6.
28. *Lockhart Letters*, I, 157; *NAS* GD 18, box 119, 3131.
29. *Clerk Memoirs*, 62.
30. *Minutes of the Commissioners for the Treaty of Union* (np, nd), 54.
31. *APS*, XI, appendix, 184.
32. *Clerk History*, 86–9.
33. *Defoe*, 84.
34. *APS*, XI, 406–13, and appendix, 201–5.
35. *HMC* Mar and Kellie, I, 271; *Clerk Memoirs*, 63.
36. *Clerk Memoirs*, 64; *Lockhart Letters*, 36.
37. Macky, op. cit., 135; *Seafield*, 385.
38. *Clerk Memoirs*, 123.
39. J. Macky, *Memoirs of the Secret Services* (London, 1733), 135; *Seafield*, 385.
40. *HMC* Mar and Kellie, I, 291.
41. *Lockhart Memoirs*, I, 216; *HMC* Mar and Kellie, I, 288–304; *Seafield*, 96.
42. *Huntington*, LO 8307, 8310, 8313, 8452, 8476.
43. *Lockhart Memoirs*, I, 272.
44. A. Legrelle, *La Diplomatie Française et la Succession d'Espagne* (Paris, 1887), IV, 299; J. Macpherson, *Original papers, or the secret history of Great Britain* (London, 1776), I, 666.
45. *Huntington*, LO 8776, 9114.
46. *Lockhart Memoirs*, appendix, 405–20.
47. Ibid., I, 264–6.
48. *HMC* Portland, V, 114.
49. Ibid., 115.
50. *Lockhart Memoirs*, I, 262–72.
51. *BL Add MSS*, 34180, f.1.
52. *HMC* Mar and Kellie, I, 255, 286, 312–4; John Drummond, seventh

Duke of Atholl, *Chronicles of the Atholl and Tullibardine Families* (Edinburgh, 1908), II, 57–8, 73.

53. *Huntington*, LO 7269, 8479.
54. *NAS*, GD/124/15/43 and 462.
55. *Defoe*, 33, 64, 229, 264.
56. *Lockhart Memoirs*, I, 250.
57. J. Clerk, *A Letter to a Friend* (Edinburgh, 1706), 7.
58. *APS*, XI, 325.
59. T.C. Smout, 'The Burgh of Montrose and the Union of 1707 – a Document', *Scottish Historical Review*, LXVI, 1987.
60. *Lockhart Memoirs*, I, 171–2.
61. S. Macdonald Lockhart, *Seven Centuries* (Dunsyre, 1977), 88 et seqq; HMC Mar and Kellie, I, 255.
62. G. Mackenzie, Earl of Cromartie, *Parainesis Pacifica, or a persuasive to the Union of Britain* (London, 1702) passim; *Trialogus* (Edinburgh, 1706) passim.
63. *Clerk Memoirs*, 36.
64. Ibid., 45.
65. *Huntington*, LO 9347.
66. C. Kidd, 'Religious Realignment between the Restoration and Union', in J. Robertson (ed.), *A Union for Empire* (Cambridge, 1995), 145–68.
67. R. Wodrow, *Analecta* (Edinburgh, 1842–3), 344.
68. *Hume*, 188, 191; *Defoe*, 387, 627–31.
69. G.E. Davie, *The Scottish Enlightenment* (London, 1981), 5.
70. [J. Hepburn], *Humble Address of a Considerable Number of People of the South and Western Shires* (np, 1706).
71. *Clerk History*, 231n.
72. *Clerk Memoirs*, 54.
73. *The Humble Address of the Presbytery of Dunblane* (np, 1706); *The Humble Address of the Presbytery of Hamilton* (np, 1706).
74. J. Webster, *Lawful Prejudices against an Incorporating Union with England* (Edinburgh, 1707), 4–5.
75. *Early Letters of Robert Wodrow*, ed. L.W. Sharp (Edinburgh, 1937), 285.
76. Ibid., 291.
77. J. Hodges, *The Rights and Interests of the Two British Monarchies* (London, 1706), III, 49.
78. Ibid., III, 8.
79. *Seafield*, 101; HMC Mar and Kellie, I, 315.
80. National Register of Archives (Scotland), report 800, Fraser MSS, 14.
81. *NLS*, MS 7104, f.60.
82. Letters to Principal Stirling, Glasgow University Library, MS Murray 652/5, I, 75; *Huntington*, LO 7819.

83. *Seafield*, 102.
84. Healey, op. cit., 140.
85. *Seafield*, 110.
86. *Hume*, 178.
87. Webster, op. cit., 11.
88. *Clerk History*, 98–9.
89. A. Aufrere (ed.), *The Lockhart Papers* (London, 1817), 162–3.
90. NAS, RH14/559; H. Armet (ed.), *Extracts from the Burgh Records of Edinburgh* (Edinburgh, 1967), 128–9.
91. *Clerk History*, 105.
92. *Defoe*, 236.
93. *BL Add MSS* 33049, f.21.
94. G.E. Todd, *History of Glasgow* (Glasgow, 1934), III, 66–71.
95. Letters to Principal Stirling, Glasgow University Library, MS Murray 652/5, I, 84.
96. *Lockhart Memoirs*, 273.
97. NAS, PC 1/53, 507–8; R. Renwick (ed.), *Extracts from the Records of the Burgh of Glasgow* (Glasgow, 1908), 399–401.
98. *APS*, XI, 341; *Lockhart Memoirs*, 281.
99. *NAS*, PC 1/53, 492.
100. W.McDowall, *History of the Burgh of Dumfries* (Dumfries, 1986), 508–12.
101. Perth Burgh Records, B 59/34/17/3.
102. Atholl MSS, Blair Atholl, box 2, bundle II, 223, 248.
103. *HMC* Mar and Kellie, I, 347.
104. Healey, op. cit., 146–7.
105. *Orain Iain Luim*, ed. A.A. Mackenzie (Edinburgh, 1942), 225–6; *Lockhart Memoirs*, 281.
106. *HMC* Mar and Kellie, I, 302–7.
107. *Lockhart Memoirs*, 283; *Marchmont*, 422 et seqq; *Seafield*, 94.
108. *Baillie*, 170.
109. John Campbell, 9th Duke of Argyll, *Intimate Society Letters of the Eighteenth Century*, 2 vols (London, 1910) I, 49–52; *Lockhart Memoirs*, 285.
110. *HMC* Mar and Kellie, I, 336.
111. Ibid., 353.

CHAPTER 6

1. *HMC* Portland (London, 1899), IV, 398.
2. Letters to Principal Stirling, Glasgow University Library, MS Murray 652/5, III, 32.

3. *Clerk Memoirs*, 67–8; *The Marlborough–Godolphin Correspondence*, ed. H.L. Snyder, 3 vols (Oxford, 1975), II, 765.
4. *HMC* Mar and Kellie (London, 1904), I, 389.
5. *Orain Iain Luim*, ed. A.A. Mackenzie (Edinburgh, 1942), 225–9.
6. *Hume*, 197; *APS*, XI, 418.
7. G.W.T. Omond, *Fletcher of Saltoun* (London, 1897), 138–9.
8. *NLS MS* 16502, ff. 208–9.
9. *Clerk History*, 95.
10. B.C. Brown (ed.), *Letters and Diplomatic Instructions of Queen Anne* (London, 1968), 190–1.
11. Letters to Principal Stirling, Glasgow University Library, MS Murray 652/5.
12. *HMC* Mar and Kellie, I, 280; *BL Add MSS* 6420, July 31, 1706; *Seafield*, 170.
13. *APS*, XI, 305; appendix, 98.
14. *Lockhart Memoirs*, 250.
15. *Seafield*, 80.
16. *APS*, XI, 343.
17. *APS*, XI, 312.
18. *Lockhart Memoirs*, 272.
19. *Defoe*, 312–16.
20. *The Lord Belhaven's Speech in the Parliament, Saturday, the second of November* (Edinburgh, 1706), *passim*.
21. J. Robertson (ed.), *A Union for Empire* (Cambridge, 1995), 219.
22. I. McLean and A. McMillan, *State of the Union* (Oxford, 2005), 28–9.
23. *Baillie*, 166–7.
24. *HMC* Mar and Kellie, I, 312.
25. *Defoe*, 632–6.
26. Ibid., 387; *Hume*, 188.
27. K. Bowie, 'Public Opinion, Popular Politics and the Union of 1707', *Scottish Historical Review*, LXXXII, 2003, 242–3; McLean and McMillan, op. cit., 32.
28. *HMC* Mar and Kellie, I, 321–3; *Lockhart Memoirs*, I, 170–1.
29. *Clerk History*, 107.
30. D. Defoe, *A Fifth Essay at Removing National Prejudices* (London, 1707), 7.
31. *HMC* Mar and Kellie, I, 320, 328; Bowie, op. cit., 249.
32. *Clerk History*, 97.
33. *Lockhart Letters*, 37.
34. *Lockhart Memoirs*, I, 201–3.
35. *The Letters of Daniel Defoe*, ed. G. Healey (Oxford, 1955), 182.
36. *Lockhart Memoirs*, I, 203–5.

37. *APS*, XI, 369–71; *Lockhart Letters*, 37.
38. *Seafield*, 99.
39. Ibid., 102.
40. *HMC* Mar, I, 318; *APS*, XI, 319; *Defoe*, 55 and note, 251.
41. *Defoe*, 109.
42. G.E. Davie, *The Scottish Enlightenment* (London, 1981), 5.
43. A.V. Dicey and R.S. Rait, *Thoughts on the Union between England and Scotland* (London, 1920), 220.
44. [G. Lockhart], *A Dialogue betwixt a Burgess of Edinburgh and a Gentleman Lately Arrived in Scotland* (Edinburgh, 1712), 11.
45. *Carstares*, 756.
46. *APS*, XI, 320; *Hume*, 182.
47. *APS*, XI, 365; *The Lord Belhaven's Second Speech in Parliament* (Edinburgh, 1706).
48. *Clerk History*, 126; *The Lord Belhaven's Second Speech*, op. cit.
49. *APS*, XI, 370; *Clerk History*, 122–5.
50. *Clerk History*, 127.
51. *APS*, XI, 328; *Hume*, 183; *HMC* Mar and Kellie, I, 325–9.
52. *Clerk History*, 134.
53. *APS*, XI, 331–2; *Hume*, 184; *HMC* Mar and Kellie, I, 328–30.
54. *Defoe*, 254.
55. *Lockhart Memoirs*, I, 177–8.
56. *HMC* Mar and Kellie, I, 328–30.
57. *APS*, XI, 341.
58. *Clerk History*, 140.
59. *Defoe*, 88.
60. Ibid., 93–4; *Clerk History*, 191–2; P.N. Furbank and W.R. Owens, 'Daniel Defoe and the *Tipponyale*', *Scottish Historical Review*, LXII, 1993, 86–9.
61. *Defoe*, 161.
62. Ibid., 140–1.
63. *APS*, XI, 350–60.
64. *APS*, XI, 361.
65. *APS*, XI, 369–72; *Lockhart Memoirs*, I, 177.
66. *Defoe*, 156, 441.
67. *APS*, XI, 370.
68. *Defoe*, 445.
69. Ibid., 458; *APS*, XI, 383.
70. *Clerk History*, 196.
71. *Baillie*, 178.
72. *Defoe*, 462.
73. *Lockhart Memoirs*, I, 206–14.

74. Ibid., 207–10.
75. Ibid., 190.
76. Ibid., 214.
77. Ibid., 214.
78. Ibid., 325.
79. Ibid., 386–7, 402–14.
80. *APS*, XI, 386–7.
81. *Clerk History*, 164–5.
82. *APS*, XI, 395.
83. *Clerk History*, 167.
84. *APS*, XI, 398.
85. *APS*, XI, 402–14.
86. *Clerk History*, 170.
87. *The House of Commons 1690–1715*, ed. E. Cruickshanks, S. Handley and D.W. Hayton, 5 vols (Cambridge, 2002), I, 510: *HMC* Mar and Kellie, I, 367–72; *Baillie*, 181–9.
88. *HMC* Mar and Kellie, I, 379; *Clerk Memoirs*, 67–9.
89. *Baillie*, 179.
90. A. Boyer, *History of the Reign of Queen Anne* (London, 1707), 439–40.
91. *House of Commons Journals* (London, 1891), VI, 563–5.
92. *Burnet*, 802; *House of Commons Journals*, VI, 555–6.
93. *HMC* Mar and Kellie, I, 389.
94. *Lockhart Memoirs*, I, 223.

CHAPTER 7

1. H. Bosc, *La Guerre des Cévennes 1702–1710* (Presses du Languedoc, 1990), 583–601.
2. M. Bucsay, *Der Protestantismus in Ungarn 1521–1978* (Graz, 1978), I, 201.
3. Anonymous, *The Deplorable History of the Catalans* (London, 1714), 68–97.
4. N. Hooke, *Secret History of Colonel Hooke's Negotiations in Scotland in 1707* (Edinburgh, 1760), 5–39.
5. Saltoun Papers, NLS MS 16503, ff.173–4.
6. *HMC* Mar and Kellie (London, 1904), I, 490.
7. *Huntington*, LO 8612, 9411, 12620.

Index

BIRLINN LTD (incorporating John Donald and Polygon) is one of Scotland's leading publishers with over four hundred titles in print. Should you wish to be put on our catalogue mailing list **contact**:

Catalogue Request
Birlinn Ltd
West Newington House
10 Newington Road
Edinburgh EH9 1QS
Scotland, UK

Tel: + 44 (0) 131 668 4371
Fax: + 44 (0) 131 668 4466
e-mail: info@birlinn.co.uk

Postage and packing is free within the UK. For overseas orders, postage and packing (airmail) will be charged at 30% of the total order value.

For more information, or to order online, visit our website at **www.birlinn.co.uk**

Birlinn *Limited*
Other Imprints – JOHN DONALD · POLYGON

Tel: (0)131 668 4371
info@birlinn.co.uk
www.birlinn.co.uk